DR. KINSEY

AND THE INSTITUTE FOR SEX RESEARCH

DR. KINSEY

AND THE INSTITUTE FOR SEX RESEARCH

WARDELL B. POMEROY

1982 EDITION

YALE UNIVERSITY PRESS

NEW HAVEN AND LONDON

This book is dedicated to the
scientific spirit and method
in research that Alfred C.
Kinsey epitomized and to which
he gave his life.

Portions of this book appeared in the March 1972 issue of *Psychology Today*.
Copyright © 1972 by Wardell B. Pomeroy.

Foreword copyright © 1982 by Yale University.

Printed in the United States of America.

Library of Congress Cataloging in Publication Data

Pomeroy, Wardell Baxter.
   Dr. Kinsey and the Institute of Sex Research.
   Originally published: 1st ed. New York: Harper & Row, 1972.
   Includes index.
   1. Kinsey, Alfred Charles, 1894–1956.   2. Institute
for Sex Research.   I. Title.
HQ60.P65 1982   155.3′092′4 [B]   82–4924
ISBN 0–300–02801–6 (paper)   AACR2
        0–300–02916–0 (cloth)

10 9 8 7 6 5 4 3 2 1

CONTENTS

v

FOREWORD

Twenty-five years after his death, Alfred C. Kinsey stands as the most important pioneer in research on human sexual behavior. His work is far-reaching in its importance and will undoubtedly remain so for some time to come. Without Alfred Kinsey, sex research as we know it would not exist.

Kinsey asked thousands of men and women of all classes, races, and religions about their sex lives. This approach was a major breakthrough. His studies legitimized sex research and pointed the way for sex researchers who followed.

The fact that Kinsey was primarily a classifier, a taxonomist, allowed him to bring to the assessment of human sexual behavior the same approach he brought to his previous studies on insects. That he began his work without a particular theoretical model distinguished him from many of his colleagues in the field of sexuality during his time, particularly from those who were wedded to the psychoanalytic model of sexual development. He displayed an unbiased openness in the descriptions and classifications of the information which emerged from the sexual histories he solicited. This proved to be of critical importance for his scientific advances in the field of sexuality.

Kinsey's work corrected many widely held misconceptions and changed many basic concepts. In the area of women's sexual behavior, for example, his work set the stage for the development of a separate concept of female sexuality—up to then seen only as an addendum to male sexuality. Kinsey's data on women's sexual responses and his own knowledge of the biology of the sex organs revealed that the vagina was not the ultimate and most frequent site of orgasm. His observations were subsequently confirmed by Masters and Johnson's laboratory studies demonstrating that clitoral orgasm is far more prevalent than vaginal orgasm. Thus, it finally became clear that clinicians, most of them men, could not tell women how they *should* have an orgasm in the face of evidence on how they *did* experience it. Kinsey did not support the theory that women were less sexual than men, and he confronted the double standard, which prevailed at his time, that postulated vast sex differences between women and men—in premarital sex, extramarital sex, and sexual enjoyment in general. No wonder the outrage was greater in response to his volume on female sexual behavior than to his book on male sexual behavior!

Subsequent sex research has emphasized and confirmed the correctness of his observations. The differences between men and women have diminished even further. For instance, consider the data on premarital sex. Kinsey's studies showed that by age 16 three percent of women and 39 percent of men had engaged in premarital intercourse. For age 19 this figure increased to about 20 percent for women and 72 percent for men. In 1973, Robert Sorenson assessed sexual behavior and attitudes in a nationally representative sample of adolescents and found that 30 percent of girls and 44 percent of boys had had sexual intercourse before age 16. These figures went up to 57 percent for girls and 72 percent for boys by age 19. More recent studies show a further overall increase in premarital sexual activity at an earlier age and even fewer differences between young women and men in this respect. The major change has obviously taken place for young women, and Kinsey's statement that the sex differences in respect to sexual behavioral patterns were much less than had been assumed has proved to be increasingly correct.

A marked sex difference still exists in regard to masturbation in adolescents. While the figures are around 90 percent and above for adolescent boys, they are only approximately 30 percent for young women. This difference may be due to sociological factors of persistent inhibition among women or to a combination of sex education and physiological factors having to do with the different anatomy of the male and female body.

Consider how far we have come since Kinsey in regard to female sexuality, however. It was controversial for Kinsey and his co-workers to state that masturbation was a normal sexual outlet for many men and women, and his statement that women who had masturbated to orgasm before marriage often reported greater enjoyment in marital intercourse was scandalous. Today, feminist writings advocate that women masturbate in various ways, including the use of vibrators, in order to become more comfortable with their own bodies. Masturbation training for adult women is part of many sex therapists' treatment courses and integral to sex manuals.

Another major breakthrough of the original Kinsey studies affected popular thinking regarding homosexuality and bisexuality. The revelation that many "normal" men and women have bisexual experiences in various degrees was essential in seeing homosexuality as something different from a mental illness afflicting only a small portion of the population. Furthermore, the concept of a spectrum ranging from heterosexuality to homosexuality on which all people can be classified was crucial for the acceptance of homosexual behavior as a variant of normal adult sexuality. Kinsey's concept of sexual orientation in this respect is still not uniformly accepted. The prejudice that people who engage in homosexual behavior are mentally ill persists in spite of numerous investigations that fail to show any consistent differences in psychological adjustment between homosexuals and heterosexuals.

The Kinsey method of using a semistructured interview to assess sexual arousal and behavior in a face-to-face situation became a model for many subsequent sex research studies. The chapter on interviewing in *Sexual Behavior of the Human Male* by Kinsey and his co-workers remains a classic and is standard reading for students of sexology.

From the few examples cited it is evident how much Kinsey's thought and work have influenced our thinking, whether we are actively involved in sex research or interested participants in times of changing sexual mores. This book familiarizes the reader in a very entertaining way with Kinsey the man, the pioneer who dared to ask questions about people's intimate sex lives, the scientist who passionately embarked on his self-selected mission of accurately assessing and describing human sexual behavior unfiltered and uncensored by a priori theoretical assumptions or religious taboos. Pomeroy's account of his years of work with Kinsey, the development of the Institute, the friendships with other co-workers, especially Paul Gebhard and Clyde Martin, the determination to complete their mission, and the obstacles which ultimately became overwhelming make this an absolutely fascinating account for anyone. The book has the qualities of a novel that one cannot put aside until finished. More importantly, it makes some of the scientific advances more comprehensible, more memorable, and provides us with a perspective in which to place present-day work on sexual behavior.

Alfred C. Kinsey emerges as a man whose life plan was decided once he had stumbled on the enormous gap in our knowledge of a universal aspect of behavior. He discovered this dearth of information when asked by Indiana University to teach a marriage course to students in 1938. He set out to collect 100,000 sexual histories, but lack of funds and his untimely death in 1956 left this goal unreached. Still, he collected the largest sample of in-depth sexual interviews ever reported in history.

Kinsey was highly selective in choosing his close colleagues, and he demanded of them almost total devotion to his life work. One gets the impression that, because of his single-minded commitment to sex research, he must have been difficult to live with at times, but one also senses the excitement of breaking new ground that pervaded those years of hard work. Pomeroy's picture of Kinsey includes kindness and warmth, an uncanny ability to ask anybody about her or his sexual history, and unconditional integrity in guarding the confidentiality of all those he interviewed.

In November 1981, the twenty-fifth anniversary of Alfred C. Kinsey's death, his former colleagues and students, family, friends, and representatives of the generation of sex researchers who followed him gathered for a two-day commemorative meeting at the Institute for Sex Research in Bloomington, Indiana. The formal

presentations and the informal conversations revivified the importance of Kinsey's work and life. There was much to celebrate in
Bloomington. Appropriately, the meeting ended with the official
renaming of the Institute as the Alfred C. Kinsey Institute for Sex
Research. Those of us who were present took away from it great
hope for the future of sex research.

The new edition of this book is highly relevant and will be fascinating reading to anyone who is interested in human sexual
behavior.

—ANKE A. EHRHARDT, PH.D.

New York
1982

PREFACE

The writing of this book, I suppose, really began as early as 1943, although it was years later before I began to think of it consciously. Two decades had gone by, the Kinsey years were behind me and I was practicing in New York as a therapist and marriage counselor when the idea of writing a biography of Kinsey began to take hold. By that time I was able to arrive at some kind of perspective on my life with Kinsey and the Institute, and I could see that there was a great deal to be told that the world did not know and which a man and a project of such historic significance well deserved to have disclosed.

Even as I worked with Kinsey in the early days of the project, when it was only beginning, I was aware of this significance and wondered whether I shouldn't be keeping a journal. I made the mistake of mentioning this idea to Kinsey. He was adamantly opposed, for reasons I have made clear in the book, and if I had persisted, it would have been necessary to keep such a journal surreptitiously. That fact plus Kinsey's stern opposition, my own inertia and our staggering work schedule all combined to preclude any attempt at journal-keeping.

As I began to develop my practice in New York after 1963, I

began to realize the tremendous debt I owed to Kinsey and to my
Institute experiences. It occurred to me often that if Kinsey had been
motivated in that direction, he would have been one of the greatest
therapists in history. His empathy toward all kinds of people, his
sharp insights, his direct approach to problems and his understanding of them were evident, over and over, in his history-taking. It was
also clear to me, as time went on, that the greatest figure in sex
research since Freud was on his way to being forgotten by the general public. Young people, particularly, often could not even identify
a man who had been one of the best-known people in the world only
two decades or so earlier. Kinsey the man had been virtually unknown at the height of his fame, and now, it seemed to me, there was
real danger that both the man and his work would be forgotten by
the people he hoped to help, even though he had left his stamp
indelibly on the scientific community.

If anyone was going to preserve his memory, it appeared, I would
have to do it if only because I was the logical one, having been his
closest associate for thirteen years, and with access to the materials
that would be necessary to reconstruct his life and work. Even with
these advantages, however, I would not have been able to put the
pieces together without my close collaborator of the past five years,
John Tebbel, who had worked with me on two earlier books, *Boys
and Sex* and *Girls and Sex*. In doing those two books, we had developed a unique relationship far beyond the usual collaboration arrangement; sometimes, in our work, it seemed that *he* was the
analyst and *I* was figuratively on the couch.

To his work with me on a book about Kinsey and the Institute,
John brought other qualifications which were unique and indispens-
able to the task. For one thing, he had known me since my early days
at the Institute. Perhaps even more important, he had known Kinsey
and been his good friend from those first days. In fact, Kinsey in 1950
had tried hard to persuade him to join our staff, believing that he
would be a help not only in interviewing, but because his long media
experience would be able to assist us in our growing problems with
the press. But John, who had just embarked on his own book-writing
career, which went on to encompass more than thirty books of his

own, declined as gracefully as one could decline a man of Kinsey's extraordinary persistence.

Fortunately, John's decision unwittingly prepared him for this volume, because his subsequent career led him not only to a comprehensive knowledge of writers and the press, but to a wide acquaintance, and some collaboration, with many noted figures in sex research, through which he also became thoroughly acquainted with the literature. Consequently, his coming to work with me on a book about Kinsey and the Institute was one of those arrangements which could only have been made, as they say, in heaven. We have worked together closely and smoothly on every aspect of this volume, and he has done the actual writing.

Our first task was to go through some 45,000 letters in the files of the Institute, and we are much indebted not only for the access to them the Institute provided but for permission to use them. We have expressed our gratitude in a more concrete way by making a joint contribution of $25,000 to the Institute.

Before we went to Bloomington for this formidable task, we had spent long hours together while I plumbed my memory, under John's prodding and questioning, for every last piece of recollection I could get down on the tape. Later we did a series of taped interviews with key figures in Kinsey's life, those we thought knew him best. We also had access to fifty-odd statements and reminiscences about him which were solicited by the Institute after his death.

There are so many people who have helped in the gathering of material for this book that it is not possible to mention them all by name. Specifically, however, we want to express our gratitude to the following people for their help in making the book possible: Mrs. Clara Kinsey, Dr. Paul Gebhard, Cornelia V. Christenson, Dr. Glen Ramsey, Glenway Wescott, Dr. Robert Winters, Dr. Vincent Nowlis, Mrs. Eleanor Roehr, Dr. Clyde E. Martin, Ralph Mills, Dr. Frank Edmonson, Mrs. Dorothy Collins, Dr. Martin Weinberg, Dr. Alan Bell, Mrs. Rebecca Dixon and the staff of the Institute Library and Archives, William Dellenback, Dr. Clarence Tripp and

Morris Ernst. We want also to thank our wives, Martha Pomeroy and Kathryn Tebbel, not only for the customary forbearance which authors must have when they are working, but for their painstaking and critical readings of the manuscript, with resulting valuable suggestions.

—WARDELL B. POMEROY

New York
August 27, 1971

PART ONE

THE MAKING OF
A SCIENTIST

CHAPTER

I

THE MAN NOBODY KNEW

WHEN ALFRED CHARLES KINSEY DIED in August 1956 at the age
of sixty-two, he was one of the most widely known scientists of this
century, a household name in the United States and a familiar figure
in the remainder of the civilized world. Many of his peers believed
then, as they do now, that he ranked with Freud. Kinsey's two landmark volumes, *Sexual Behavior in the Human Male* (1948) and *Sexual Behavior in the Human Female* (1953), raised one of the most
violent and widespread storms since Darwin, not only in the scientific community but among the public at large. It is fair to say that
Kinsey brought sex out of the bedroom and into the world's parlor.
If he did not succeed in making it completely respectable, he laid the
foundation for the greater freedom of sexual behavior and the far
better understanding of it that we have today.

Yet it was the supreme paradox of this complicated man whom
everyone knew about, and about whom millions of words were written, that he remained virtually unknown to the public as a human
being. People saw his face so often in their newspapers and magazines (and eventually enshrined on the cover of *Time* magazine) that
they recognized him easily in public places. Columnists told endless
and usually fanciful stories about him. Clergymen from thousands of
pulpits pronounced him morally unfit for human consumption, while
other thousands extolled him. His scientific work, filtered through
hundreds of lay articles, often inaccurately, was discussed by millions

3

of people who would never read his books, although they were best sellers. He may have been the most talked about and least read author of our time; the majority of people got their opinions about his work at second hand.

Kinsey could not help his fame, but he clung fiercely to his privacy and never deviated for a moment from the work that was his life. He was seldom interviewed, except about his research, rarely lectured except to professional groups and others from whom he hoped to obtain sexual histories; and he refused every television interviewer except one, Arlene Francis. Once he had begun it, he confined his writing strictly to his project, about which his whole life revolved.

It was natural, then, that the public's knowledge of Kinsey the man was as secondhand as their conception of his work. "What was he *really* like?" so many people have asked me, and sometimes I have tried to give an offhand answer, until realization came that it would take a whole book to tell myself, as well as others, what kind of protean figure I worked beside nearly every day of my life for thirteen years.

Officially we were called Kinsey's associates, but "family" would have been a better word. We were working for a genius who maddened us, delighted us, drove us to the point of exhaustion, but most of all inspired us to share something of his total dedication. Our grand design, in simplest terms, was to try to find out—by means of face-to-face interviewing followed by statistical analysis of the facts we had collected—what people did sexually. Many were repelled by that image of us—a group of humorless, cold clinicians extracting the most personal kind of information from people whom indignant critics often called "depraved." Our subjects were in fact individuals of every variety. Kinsey dreamed of getting 100,000 sexual histories. He had to settle for 18,000, of which I took about 8,000 and Kinsey another 8,000. The remainder were taken by other staff members.

Clinical our staff certainly was, but humorless and cold we were not. We were all on the faculty of Indiana University as well as the staff of the Institute for Sex Research, as the project came to be known after its incorporation. Aside from this common identification, however, the people behind the names signed to the famous Reports—Kinsey, myself, Paul Gebhard and Clyde Martin—were quite unlike as human beings.

To begin with, we differed physically. Kinsey dominated us in that respect, as he did in every other. When I close my eyes I can see him now in dozens of imaginary brief newsreel clips—walking toward me, a tall and bulky figure, slightly rounded about the shoulders (although not quite humped) as the result of the rickets that made him a frail child until he was ten. His arms were longer than the average and he swung them a little, palms outward, when he walked. His hair was crew cut in the Middle Western style—like a shock of Kansas wheat, as one observer wrote. His eyes were extraordinarily penetrating and intelligent, and there was an intensity in his face and manner that reflected the inner tension which propelled him. Kinsey was forever intent and curious, not only about people's sex lives, but about the natural world around him, on which he was also an international authority.

It was his warmth that I think first impressed everyone who met him. It rose out of a genuine deep concern for humanity, and people could feel almost tangibly his empathy and understanding. Where human beings in general were concerned, he was never cynical, backbiting, or faultfinding, although he could be severe and angry enough with the staff on occasion. But with the interviewees, no matter who they were, he radiated a bright aura of warm understanding to which they responded. Sometimes he even wept when one of them had told him a particularly harrowing story.

Kinsey was "a human investigator," as one of his old friends put it, "more human than most investigators so zealous for data." Perhaps that explains why the evidences of common humanity he produced in his research provoked people, both physicians and laymen, to giggle, smirk, criticize and make jokes when his work was mentioned, as some still do. His name came to symbolize sexual curiosity, but not everyone realized that it was a good, constructive and creative curiosity.

Kinsey's attitudes permeated the staff and we were all strongly affected by them. That was fortunate, because occasionally it would have been easy to be hypercritical, or even disdainful, of some of the people we interviewed.

The impression he made on others was often profound. For instance, a New York photographer named Clarence Tripp, who later became a psychotherapist as a direct result of Kinsey's inspiration, visited Kinsey in Bloomington, where the University and Institute are situated, shortly after the *Male* volume was published, in 1948, and wrote to him afterward:

It is almost impossible for me to tell you how much I learned from you during my visit last week, and what an impressive experience it was. Little wonder you win cooperation from everyone. I feel it in myself . . . an urgency to contribute anything you could possibly use. When I look back over it, at first I think it is your drive that makes everything such a success, then the honesty and personality stand out. For me, the greatest thing seemed to be the way you meet objections and the unspoken generosity you give at those moments when you meet something in another person which is contrary to what you know to be the case, or the kind way you have of rejecting what you consider worthless. Anyway, I'm with you for life and everything I can do is not enough.

That, I think, is how the staff felt too, for varying lengths of time and in different degrees. We were with him, if not for life, at least as far ahead as we could see. At staff meetings he regarded us, benevolently or accusingly as the case might be, as his family. Besides myself, as I have said, there were Gebhard and Martin, as senior members; the others were specialists who came and went.

Paul Gebhard was a tall man, about six feet, thin, with reddish hair and a mustache, which he refused to shave even though Kinsey was frankly disturbed by it. He hated beards. (I often think with what distaste he would have viewed this hirsute generation, some of whose full-beavered members are on the Institute staff which Gebhard now directs.) Only a senior member such as Paul could have survived Kinsey's displeasure over mustaches. In history taking, Gebhard was dogged, persistent and low-keyed. He held a Ph.D. in anthropology from Harvard, awarded to him about four months after he joined the staff.

Clyde Martin was about Gebhard's height, a soft-spoken, dark-haired, attractive young man, with a B.A. in economics from Indiana. He was a man capable of first-rate insights, whose approaches and reactions were likely to be artistic and aesthetic. Martin looked even younger than he was—a misfortune I shared with him—and he was always a little deferential, possibly out of a feeling of inferiority because he did not have an advanced degree. Eventually he became much more involved in the statistical side of our work, making the numerous charts and graphs we used. That took him virtually out of interviewing, which pleased him.

As for me, I was of medium height, five feet nine inches, and consequently the shortest of the four. I had dark, wavy hair and looked about five years younger than I was. Looking back, I think I was more intense temperamentally and more extroverted than the others. I was less scholarly than Paul, and less esthetic than Clyde, but more interested in human contacts and interreactions than either.

By and large, we worked well together. There was a considerable rapport among us, so that we could occasionally produce a united front against Kinsey when we disagreed with him. It seldom worked, however; Kinsey was a master at defending himself. I must add that the front was not a permanent fixture, by any means. We worked together, and Kinsey had lines out directly to each of us, in different ways.

As time went on, the cohesion among us increased. We traveled thousands of miles together, worked long hours in Bloomington together and shared such things as the unwritten interviewing code, not known to anyone else. It gave us a private language we used when we were talking about sexual subjects in a place where other people could overhear.

I was aware, as we all were, that Kinsey exercised a kind of benevolent repression over us—or, if not benevolent, at least without malice. If I went on a trip with him and it fell to me to take the history of someone important, in the division of our labor, when we came home again Kinsey always wrote a personal letter to the subject I had interviewed, thanking him and regretting that they hadn't had the opportunity to meet and talk. He simply took over, not permitting us to develop such relationships.

This strong-minded control had other aspects. Kinsey would not tolerate any public disagreement among those who worked for him. If we failed to agree on something, the rule was that we would thresh it out privately and preserve the public image of the project that Kinsey strove so zealously to maintain. There were few serious disagreements, however, and they were usually resolved quickly—always in Kinsey's favor. Paul and I might find ourselves opposing him on some point, and privately we would build up what we thought was an unbeatable case, with which we would confront him. In thirty seconds he would have us on the defensive, arguing on some other ground than the one we had chosen. I never saw anyone get the better of him in an argument, and I doubt if anyone could.

Yet he could be sensitive to the rasping of his aggressive personality on other people, and quick to correct himself if he thought some little idiosyncrasy was irritating us—as long as it was not directly related to the conduct of the research. For a time it was his custom to say at the end of every long working day, "Well, thanks for the day's work." Innocent though it was, the remark annoyed us. It seemed unnecessary and, worse, condescending.

After talking it over, we replied one night, "And thank *you* for the day's work." It was said jokingly, because we had no wish to hurt him, but he understood and took it seriously. He never thanked us in that way again.

He controlled, or attempted to control, our lives as far as they related to the work, and sometimes went about it with the same scientific zeal he applied to the research. In 1951, when I was about to return to Bloomington after a semester of graduate work at Columbia University, I wrote to Kinsey and advised him that I was bringing some rather large models, designed by Dr. Robert L. Dickinson (we inherited them when he died), which showed the reproductive and coital processes. Kinsey wrote back with explicit instructions for my trip home:

I hear through Martha [my wife] that you hope to get back by Friday afternoon. This is impossible by a car which is carrying our fragile models and impossible if you intend to get the history in Pittsburgh. I have talked the matter over carefully with Bill [Dellenback, our photographer] and there must be at least 24 hours allowed for the drive. This means an average of 35 miles per hour and in order to do that it means driving at 50 m.p.h. where the roads are clear. Anything faster than that is not safe for such a heavy load. You cannot stop in a hurry and you dare not bounce on roads that have been damaged by winter freezes. If you do, the models will be severely damaged.

Neither do I want you to attempt to take the history in Pittsburgh unless you have had a night's sleep. You cannot take a history that is special enough to go to Pittsburgh for unless you have had rest. This means stopping for at least one night's sleep, even if you do piece out the second night by sleeping in the car. This adds up to a minimum of 40 hours from New York to Bloomington. If you want to make it faster than that, you will have to come home some other way on your own. In that case, forget the Pittsburgh assignment and I will go after it myself in the next week or so. It would be very advantageous for Bill to have someone else with him to handle the load and if you are not coming with him I may consider some other arrangement for someone to drive with him.

That was Kinsey, the mother superior, keeping us within the strict boundaries of his schedule, yet we did not often resent it. He simply did not want anything to interfere with carrying out the project; that was his overriding concern. One of the things he repeated most often, so often that it became an Institute joke, was his quick, explosive outburst whenever something threatened to impede the project's operation, even in the smallest way. "You're setting back the research countless thousands of hours!" he would roar at us accusingly—and, a few minutes later, might tell us how pleased he was by something.

This kind of perfectionism met another kind in the personality of our photographer, Bill Dellenback, a superb technician whose schedules could be as rigid as Kinsey's. Occasionally they came into conflict. Once when Bill appeared likely to stay in San Francisco on an assignment longer than planned, Kinsey wrote him indignantly:

You put us in a fix by extending your stay a week longer than we had originally planned. We discussed the matter before we left Bloomington and on the way out there and I told you then that if you were back by the 15th it would take care of the situation. I have gone ahead and planned several visitors with this in mind and it completely gums up things if you get back here later than that. It would have been sensible for you to have arranged your whole vacation for the Pacific Coast, but since it was not scheduled ahead of time, it was not part of our planning here. There is work to do with several of the people here and material that you need to get ready for them to use. It is unfortunate to have Dr. Shadle's porcupine material here and for it to be utterly unusable when some of the country's top experts in the field are coming . . . I could have fitted all this if you had planned your schedule ahead of time, but the only agreement we had ahead of time was that you were to be back here by the 15th.

Kinsey was in fact an aggressive individual, and I think it was because of his hidden fear of failure. One of the things he dreaded most was to be turned down if he asked someone for a history, or requested an opportunity to lecture to a group and get their histories, which was one of the methods he used. He wanted to be quite certain in advance that he would get a positive answer, and consequently he usually got it. When he was able to get a 100-percent sample, always the goal, it became a personal conquest for him. He wanted everyone in any group he encountered to give a history, and he went to considerable lengths sometimes to see that he got it—100 percent.

He was aggressive, too, when someone attempted to "get something" on him. Sometimes I might feel hurt by a remark he had made to me, and after licking my wounds for two or three weeks I would make an attempt at revenge by trying to trap him in some inconsistency. Kinsey would have none of it. Just as he did when Paul and I attempted to beat him in an argument, he would have me completely on the defensive again, arguing myself out of an untenable position. He often did the same thing with whole audiences who opposed him. His mastery backfired only when, a few days later, after there had been an opportunity to think over one of these individual encounters, someone might resent what had been done to him.

Nevertheless, Kinsey usually avoided any kind of confrontation if it was possible. "Do your best," he always seemed to be saying in the conduct of his own life. "Do your best, and let other people react as they will."

As I have suggested, however, he was far from passive under fire. He complained bitterly about people who attacked sex investigators, particularly when it became clear in 1954 that the Rockefeller Foundation, whose president was then Dean Rusk, was about to withdraw its financial support under pressure from within and without, even though Rusk had proclaimed the Foundation's responsibility to protect scientific research. Tripp, who was visiting in Bloomington during this period, remembers that Kinsey could be heard muttering, "Damn that Rusk," from time to time as he walked about the Institute.

Yet he could be extremely gentle with others, if the issue was important. It was only among people he really trusted, such as the staff members, that he permitted himself to let go with sharp words, exaggerations and harsh language. To Tripp this was merely a front, but I am convinced he meant every word he said. He was a stubborn man, so determined to win arguments that occasionally he found himself defending positions and opinions he had previously attacked. During one argument I had with him, I was busy assaulting Freudian psychoanalytic theory, in much the same terms I had often heard Kinsey use, when he turned on me.

"The trouble with you, Pomeroy," he said severely, "is that you don't appreciate the value of Freud. He was a great man."

I was too astonished to think of an answer.

Always, and particularly, Kinsey was a teacher. Sometimes when I walk across the Indiana campus today, I can hear him beside me saying amiably, instructively, "Pomeroy, look at that bird over there. It's a most unusual specimen," and then launching into a brief ornithological lecture. Again, driving between Indianapolis and Bloomington, I hear his eager, intense voice in my ear expounding on the geological details of the terrain. He could not help himself, and he was forever teaching us as we traveled around the country on our interviewing. After listening to Professor Kinsey for years, I learned how to identify oak trees, and how to have good table manners, among other things. There were hundreds of other short courses in nearly as many fields. At first I sat at the feet of the great man and absorbed it all, but I confess that after a few years I began to find it boring. As he grew older, of course, he often forgot what lectures we had heard from him, and we had to remind him. He didn't mind; we laughed together over his faulty memory. In trying to understand Kinsey, however, it would be a mistake to underestimate his intense urge to teach people about what he had learned. It was a vital part of his motivation.

Sometimes it seemed to me there was no end to the paradoxes Kinsey presented. About money, for example, he had the most ambivalent ideas. He could be extremely generous, but because he had come from a poor family he could not accustom himself to spending money, even when he had it. True, he had little enough himself, but he was reluctant to spend Institute funds at first, even when they were available. As long as he was on the Indiana faculty, a matter of some thirty-six years, he never asked for a raise in salary for himself, and in fact often said, with a kind of curious pride, that until 1948, when the *Male* volume was published, he never made more than $5,000 a year from the University. Where the staff was concerned, however, he was generous with salaries, and at Christmas and Easter he gave elaborate gifts to their children. He bought these gifts himself and delivered them personally. Often he spent as much as $400 on them, a good deal of money in those days, especially for one on his salary.

Though cautious in money matters, he was a bold explorer when it came to his work. That was as true with his history taking as it had been with his study of the gall wasp, the career he had established before the project began. As soon as he found something different or striking in a history, he began to explore and probe toward other possibilities.

We called him "Prok," affectionately, a nickname originating in the summer camps he had worked in, where the young campers had simply abbreviated the name by which they called him, "Professor K." To his childhood and college friends he was Al, but few who knew him as an adult would have thought of calling him that. He was too formidable, too impressive. Publicly he liked to be identified with the discipline in which he had started out, and always signed his letters, "Alfred C. Kinsey, Professor of Zoology."

Because we were ourselves such different people, everyone on the staff viewed Prok differently. Martin remembers a multitude of small characteristics: How a slight Scottish burr crept into his voice when he would begin a lecture, the result of uneasiness. How he always seemed to operate best when he felt challenged. How his cheeks turned pink under stress. He seldom got angry, although Tripp recalls that Kinsey was once so furious at him (in an argument over instinct) that he turned and walked out of the room. Those who knew him best could read the signals of inner irritation: pursed lips, eyes kindling, red cheeks. Nothing made him any angrier than hypocrisy. He hated it.

Another of Kinsey's primary dislikes was sloppiness, personal or otherwise. He insisted that the staff wear neckties in the office—a far cry from the extremely informal attire at the Institute today. He himself always had on a bow tie. Clothes were never a concern with him; he wore them casually, but neatly. He used a hat only when it rained, but even so, I don't remember seeing him wear one more than five times. (So eager were publicists of every description to take advantage of the *Male* volume's popularity that a public relations man for the hat industry managed to plant a story in the newspapers citing Kinsey as one of the ten best-hatted men in America. I have seldom seen Prok laugh so hard.) Except in the coldest weather, he never wore an overcoat, and often went to New York in March without one. No one would ever, in fact, have accused Kinsey of being a well-dressed man. His trousers were often baggy and his jacket wrinkled, but while unpressed, he was never sloppy. The impression he gave was one of tweedy, academic, Middle Western casualness.

In spite of the driving intensity with which he pursued his work, his day-by-day demeanor was as casual as his clothes. He was not the kind of genius who swings between moods of blazing enthusiasm and black despair. We rarely saw him in a real depression. Customarily he was a buoyant, happy, interested and curious individual—and that was natural, because he spent every day doing what he wanted to do most in the world. Nevertheless, his work ethic drove him on, often beyond what could be characterized as normal enjoyment of living. Frequently he worked eighteen hours a day, late into the night. He was much more of a night than a day person, and had to force himself to get under way in the morning.

One of Kinsey's most remarkable talents was his ability to organize speeches in his head. He never drafted a speech on paper but when he began to speak the sentences rolled out fluently, logically, the paragraphs connecting, the points developed precisely, with never the slightest hesitation. He could hold the absolute attention of any group whether they were prison inmates, eminent business executives, or professionals like himself.

I can see him now, sprawled casually in the back seat of a taxi, riding with me to some place where he was booked to make a speech, and remarking thoughtfully, "Well, what will we tell 'em this time?" Then he fished about in his pocket until he found an odd piece of paper and on it jotted down two or three items. That would have been scanty enough preparation at best, but he put the paper in his pocket and never looked at it again. No matter how many times I witnessed this performance, I could not help marveling when I saw him on the platform a little later, delivering a speech that was a model of organization and clarity, speaking impeccably without hesitating, stumbling, or groping for words.

I suppose I must have spent more time with Kinsey than anyone in the world except his wife. We traveled together constantly when we were interviewing and spent a great many hours alone—driving in a car, on trains, or after work, when we leaned back and talked. What would an ideal society be, from a sexual point of view? What were the best ways to identify homosexuals? What were the real differences between male and female sexuality? Those and a thousand other questions we discussed. Because there were no secrets between us, we could draw on our own experiences in these talks.

For one whose major interest was exploring the private lives of other people, Kinsey had a highly developed sense of privacy. Perhaps that was why he was so careful to protect the privacy of the lives he had invaded with his research. Someone might say in a letter, "I am a homosexual," or "I am a transvestite," or offer us some pornography or sex literature. When he replied, Kinsey was careful never to refer directly to sex, using such circumlocutions as "thank you for your interesting history," or "your interesting material," without being specific, just in case the letter fell into someone else's hands. If people asked him about his own sex life, he would always say, "I've contributed my history to the project, and I will protect it just as I will protect yours when you give it to me."

He hated to be lionized socially. His friend Robert Winters, a Princeton economist, and his wife often entertained him. One night when Winters met Kinsey at the station, he thought to make a small joke by informing Prok as he got in the car that twenty people had been invited for dinner to meet him. Kinsey's utter dismay was almost comic, and his great relief obvious when he found that no one but the family was at home.

Since he was with people so constantly, it was difficult for him to find any time alone, but rather than confess that this was what he wanted, he would undertake any dodge. Thus, in a letter to Dr. Charles M. McLane in which he agreed to come to a conference on abortion at Arden House, in Tuxedo, New York, Kinsey wrote:

I am in difficulty when it comes to sharing a room with anyone. I sleep badly, intermittently, and consequently I am often up for an hour or two in the middle of the night doing other things. It is, therefore, impossible for anyone to get sleep in the same room with me. We should be glad to cover the extra expense of the room used singly.

Kinsey may possibly have been sleeping badly at the time, but certainly he shared rooms with Gebhard or me countless times on our field trips, and always slept the sleep of exhaustion except when his occasional leg cramps woke him. At Arden House, he simply did not want to share a room with a stranger.

He refused to answer any personal questions about himself, which scarcely deterred some would-be interviewers, who supplied their own answers. Especially he would not answer questions about his politics or his religion. I have no idea to this day what he thought about politics; we never discussed it.

Kinsey could, however, discuss almost anything else. His ability to master knowledge in fields outside his own, about which I shall have more to say, was the result of a mind deserving of that outworn and misused word "brilliant." Kinsey never thought of himself in such terms; if he prided himself on anything, it was his perseverance. But brilliant he was, by any measurement. Academically, he had achieved the Phi Beta Kappa key and excelled in everything he studied. Beyond that, he possessed a clear, logical mind of extraordinary power and comprehension.

It was not without flaws. New theoretical concepts were not his forte. What distinguished him most intellectually was his doggedness, his incredible persistence. Making no claims himself to high intellectual distinction, he found himself uncomfortable in the presence of men who were extemporaneous theoreticians, as though he felt himself inferior.

In his work there were failings, too. He made some choices which could charitably be called unhappy. But it must be remembered that there were few precedents to guide him when he began. Later, in the light of new knowledge, Kinsey was inclined to be defensive about what he had done, and felt some people had not given him enough credit. So many critical reviews of his books, he believed, centered on method instead of content.

Kinsey was intensely aware of other people's reactions to him, and he made them feel that he cared about everything. He might not care in a positive way, but he noticed the smallest things. If the pictures on the wall in Dellenback's photographic laboratory had been changed, he noticed it.

He had, too, a special way of putting other people at ease—part of his superb power of persuasion. Tripp recalls riding with him in a taxi in New York, about two weeks after he had made his first trip to Bloomington, and feeling somewhat star-struck and uncomfortable. Sensing Tripp's discomfort, Kinsey remarked casually, "It's always pleasant to see someone the second time. Then you don't have to be on your best behavior."

2

If it were possible to bring all the facets of Kinsey's many-sided personality together and put a single label on them, I believe there is only one word that would suffice. Kinsey was a *collector*, and perhaps the most unusual one this nation of collectors has ever seen. As a boy he collected stamps, in the classic style, but it was the only collection he ever made that was not designed to be useful. Serious collecting began for him when he was a graduate student at Harvard, and for the first time began to explore the life of the gall wasp. By the time he came to Indiana as a young assistant professor, this master collection, ranking with his sexual histories in relative importance, had become a preoccupation. Far more than scientific sampling done to supplement his scientific study of the insect, it was a full-fledged collection, as other men might collect books or art forms. His search for the galls led him all over the United States and into Mexico, and in the end he acquired not only all the known species but possessed a good representation of each kind. Ultimately he presented his collection to the American Museum of Natural History, in New York; it was the largest collection of any kind ever given to that institution, numbering more than four million different specimens.

His next collection was, of course, his most important one—sexual histories—and he pursued it with the same zeal that had led him to exhaust the possibilities of the gall wasp. Again, it was not only a necessary scientific instrument for his work, as the wasps had been an adjunct to his labors as a taxonomist, but a collection in the true sense. He was always conscious of how many histories he had in his files, and he was so anxious to get more that his estimates of what he had were always ahead of the actual records by about a hundred or so, representing the ones he expected to obtain soon.

This idiosyncrasy partially accounts for the mistake in the dedication of *Sexual Behavior in the Human Male* to "the 12,000 persons who have contributed to these data, and to the 88,000 more who, some day, will help complete this study." The goal of 100,000 histories always lay temptingly ahead of him.

Somewhere between gall wasps and sex histories, chronologically, was Kinsey's collection of day lilies and irises. He had acquired two and a half acres surrounding his house in Bloomington, and after turning over a half acre of it to vegetables, he devoted the remainder to shrubs, trees and flowers. It was the flowers he loved particularly, and characteristically he began to specialize. He searched for all the varieties of day lilies and irises he especially liked. Naturally, in time he possessed all or nearly all of them, and the garden became a showplace to which people drove for hundreds of miles when the flowers were in bloom. Only another collection could displace this one. When he became completely involved in sex research, Kinsey had to let the garden go because he no longer had the time to devote to it.

A collection he never gave up was classical recordings. Every Sunday evening he invited a group of friends to his house for a recorded concert, which he had carefully planned in advance. I went to three or four of them, but since I am totally uninterested in music I found them boring, much to Kinsey's disappointment. Martin, however, and Gebhard to a lesser extent attended rather faithfully.

This interest was inspired by Kinsey's boyhood piano study. Having had to choose at one point between a career in music or science, he chose science, but he could never quite forget the other. As long as he lived, he continued to build up his record collection, and enjoyed it whenever possible.

Still another interest was Kinsey's library. When I came to Bloomington, in 1943, it was only a small working assemblage of previous studies in sex research. Soon after my arrival he began to buy books in this field, not simply for their content but because he could not resist the urge to collect. He spent hours in secondhand bookstores, purchasing anything he could find about sex, from the outright erotic to the scientific. In time this collection, as the Institute's library, became the largest of its kind in the world, exceeding those of the Vatican and the British Museum; I shall have much more to say about it in the last chapter. As with most collectors of books, Kinsey had time to read only a fraction of what he owned. He was not a prodigious reader in any case, although he read in many fields.

Out of book collecting grew still another interest—erotica, of which the Institute archives now has the largest assemblage anywhere. Sometimes Kinsey was asked, about this and his other collections, what drove him to do it. He always answered that if an individual collected anything widely enough, in time it would have some value. He did not refer to monetary value, but to usefulness. In the case of the erotica collection, and the library itself, he was right. Their value to science has only been tapped, and their uses in literature and art are just beginning to be explored. The presence of scholars and scientists from all over the world in the Institute's library and archives is living proof that Kinsey was right about his collecting.

While it may seem frivolous, I can scarcely overlook Kinsey as a collector of drinks, that is, of recipes for them. I doubt if there is a larger collection of recipes for rum drinks, even in Jamaica. It was a practical pastime, true, but it was also a collection, like the others, and Kinsey was proud of it.

To most of the people who wrote asking him for various things after he became a world figure, Kinsey had to say a polite no. But one request he never refused. To anyone who wanted Kinsey's signature for an autograph collection Prok invariably complied and added a note of commendation. He had a deep fellow feeling for other collectors. A characteristic reply was this one to a boy in England: "I believe in people who make collections, and consequently, I am glad to add my autograph to your collection." Sometimes his enthusiasm carried him away. Sending an autograph to a man in Waukegan, Kinsey ended his letter: "I approve of people collecting hobbies."

I have tried to suggest in this portrait what a complicated personality Kinsey was, how many aspects there were to this man about whom the public knew so much and so little. What I have not done is provide any comprehensive idea of how many areas of human life his mind and research penetrated. He did, as I have said, become an expert in a great many fields related to his own, and in others that were not directly related. To me, one of the most fascinating aspects of Kinsey's life and work was the way in which his inquiring brain reached out, probing, analyzing, challenging old ideas, introducing new concepts. A simple listing of the incredibly wide range of his interests would be long and impressive.

Reading his correspondence, and remembering my own experiences, there seems no end to his versatility. He could discuss with a noted Chicago physiologist the encephalograms he had made of sleeping persons and the possibility of obtaining records of sexual arousals, citing the work of an obscure experimenter in Argentina who had obtained electroencephalograms of human subjects in orgasm during sleep. One of these was published in the *Female* volume and, as Kinsey pointed out, threw considerable light on the nature of orgasm and particularly on its similarity to certain aspects of epileptic responses.

He contributed to a medical book on hormones, pointing out that the periodic fluctuation in female responsiveness was generally believed to depend on hormonal factors, and that this might be one of the reasons why it was more difficult to condition women sexually. He added that he had already observed the same phenomenon of less frequent conditioning in female cats, rats, cattle and other laboratory and field animals. He also made an attempt to get histories of castrates in order to study the effect of hormones on behavior.

Nothing was too obscure for him. Asked about a possible connection between acne and homosexuality, he could cite a number of cases where severe cases of acne so interfered with a boy's social adjustment that he found it difficult to make approaches to girls and so was thrown back on his own sex. There was no physiologic connection, of course, as he was careful to note, but he could point to several cases in which acne, along with obesity, crippling, or other physical handicaps, were factors in the development of homosexual patterns.

His work was so highly regarded by specialists in other fields that he was asked by the Brain Research Project at the New York Psychiatric Institute to study the effects of prefrontal lobe brain operations on sexual behavior.

No aspect of sex, however seemingly frivolous, was a matter for disdain as far as Kinsey was concerned. He was genuinely pleased when a New Jersey psychotherapist contributed to the research a splendid collection of graffiti copied from the walls of ladies' rooms in such exotic spots as The Meat Ball and Tony's Restaurant in New York; Jack's Tavern and Barrel's Inn in Perth Amboy, New Jersey; and similar watering places.

I know of only one instance in which Kinsey showed no particular enthusiasm for further research. In 1952 State Senator Thomas C.

Desmond, of New York, asked him to speak at a public hearing on the subject of "Sex in the Later Years." Declining, Kinsey wrote:

I am not sure that you need me at the meeting anyway, because the problem of sexual adjustment for the aged is much less pressing than the problem of sexual adjustment for any other part of the population. Both the females and the males are beginning to pass out of the sexual picture when real old age approaches.

It is clear, I think, from everything I have said that Kinsey bristled with paradoxes. For a man whose whole life was based on order and organization, it was preposterous that he never balanced his bank account, claiming that he always knew how much he was spending. For a long time his own account and the Institute's were the same until his secretary, Eleanor Roehr, discovered the situation, with horror, and ended it. Miss Roehr was the last and one of the best of his secretaries, working with him through the most difficult years, until the end. She learned to imitate his correspondence style so well that he once said, "Sometimes I can't remember whether I wrote these or you did." But when she tried to persuade him to abandon such colloquialisms as "get ahold of," he refused, and asserted it was perfectly good English.

Many people thought him humorless, and so he may appear in some aspects of his story as I tell it, but his wry, professorial humor keeps cropping up. At a meeting in Boston, Kinsey was addressing a group convened by Lester Dearborn, the marriage counselor. A member of the audience questioned a statement about the peak of sexual drive and response on the part of the male. The inquirer, saying he had just read a book by a doctor who asserted that a man was at his peak sexually about the age of forty-eight, asked, "What do you think of that, Dr. Kinsey?"

"I think the age of the author was about forty-eight," Kinsey answered.

Again, Prok was entering the Institute parking lot one day with a visiting friend from Chicago. He pointed to a new convertible, then to my car, and finally to his own, which was of ancient vintage.

"With us," he explained, smiling, "rank and model are inversely related. Our librarian has the fanciest and newest model while I, the top man, have the shabbiest one."

He never joked about politics, no doubt because he was completely apolitical. He had, for instance, read translations of the work of Max Hodann, of Germany, a pioneer in the field of sex research, and was extremely enthusiastic about his work. When a friend reminded him that Hodann was an avowed communist who had died in exile, Kinsey answered, "What has that to do with the excellence of his work?"

Though he could not joke about others, Kinsey was capable of laughing uproariously when the joke involved him. Dr. Robert Winters had a friend from Texas who, convinced that Kinsey was pulling the public's leg, asked Winters if he could persuade Prok to take his history, so he could prove his thesis by telling the biggest lies he could think of. The request was put as a personal favor and Winters, thinking no harm could come of it, made the arrangement. When the Texan returned from his interview, Winters asked him how he had done. "I simply couldn't lie to that man," he reported ruefully. Kinsey roared when Winters told him the story.

It was the idiosyncrasies, the little human things, as well as the obvious fact of his dedication and absorption with the project, that his friends remembered Kinsey for when he was gone. Six years after he died, one of his old friends, Dr. Frances Shields, wrote:

So many pictures come clearly to mind—his bow ties (always a little askew), his gathering together the crumbs on table or tablecloth and then picking them up a few at a time and dropping them on a plate; his broad grin and the infectious laughter which accompanied it; his running his fingers through his hair when amused or annoyed, thus more than ever resembling the "truck driver," as he was originally described by the press. . . . I remember one sparkling day when I drove him from San Francisco to Big Basin to sit among the giant Sequoias. We ate lunch at the cafeteria in the park and he was *so* pleased when the cashier recognized him.

Having viewed Kinsey whole in the preceding pages, it is obvious that some large questions remain. Foremost among them, I think, is the one central to my story: How was it possible for a sickly, religious boy who grew up to be a serious college student with an obvious talent for biology and an abysmal ignorance of sex—how did this young man evolve into a world authority on sexual behavior who could be mentioned in the same breath with Freud? And a corollary:

How was it possible to organize, maintain and carry out a scientific project so huge and of such a nature that it was certain to arouse the fiercest emotions of prejudice and bigotry in large sections of the population? And finally: What did Kinsey really find out about sex? What, in the end, did it all mean for humanity?

It is these questions I intend to answer in the pages that follow.

CHAPTER

II

EARLY DAYS

No one could have predicted that the young Al Kinsey would ever become the world's foremost sex researcher, but in retrospect the circumstances of his early years shaped him in every particular.

It was part of Kinsey's unique personality that he knew little about his relatives or his family antecedents, and apparently cared less. Where most people are much aware of uncles, aunts, cousins and other family members, he was not even sure about his grandfather's name. When a professor in the State College of Agriculture and Engineering at the University of North Carolina wrote to him and suggested that they might be related, Kinsey agreed that they probably were, but in response to his distant relative's request, he was able to tell everything he knew about family history in a half-dozen sentences:

As I understand it, we are descended from three brothers who were connected with the Quakers who settled under William Penn in Philadelphia. One of the brothers became superior court justice in the state of New Jersey. I know very little of the early family history back of my grandfather (whose name, I think, was Charles) who settled in Mendham, near Morristown, New Jersey. His youngest son was Benjamin Kinsey, who married into the Seguine family. Their eldest son was Alfred Seguine Kinsey, my father. My father's boyhood was spent in Mendham, but they moved then to Hoboken, where my father was married when he was 21 years old, and I am the oldest child.

Hoboken was Kinsey's birthplace. He was born there on June 23, 1894, but his family moved to South Orange when he was only ten years old. The father was a forceful, energetic, single-minded man who had only an eighth-grade education and had begun his working life as a shop technician at Stevens Tech, in Hoboken, and in time worked his way up to become a full professor of engineering, a fact of which he was justifiably proud. The mother had only a fourth-grade education, but appeared to be better educated. She seemed to be so ill at ease socially that she made few friends. Although Stevens was not a large college, the Kinseys seldom entertained or carried on the usual kind of campus social life; friendships with other faculty members were not encouraged.

I often heard Kinsey tell a story about his mother that appeared to stir anger in him whenever he thought of it. She was a collector of one of the early equivalents of Green Stamps, and made her son go all the way across town to a particular store that issued them, even though he could have bought anything she wanted in a store nearby. That, he told me, was characteristic of her. The anger burned so deeply in him that, as an adult, he refused to accept trading stamps or even to charge anything.

Kinsey was not particularly close to either of his parents, nor was he much closer to his brother, Robert, who was fourteen years younger. The brothers saw each other only occasionally as adults. Robert remained in New Jersey, and for some time was in charge of the park system of Essex County. He now has his own business. There was also a sister, Mildred, two years younger, who suffered from thyroid disorders and has since died. Of them all, Kinsey was perhaps closest to his mother, in spite of their disagreements. She died in 1938, and his father died soon after, in the spring of 1943.

For the first ten years of his life Kinsey was ill much of the time with rheumatic fever and rickets, but after this first troubled decade his health rapidly became better. The aftereffects of the disease, however, prevented him from getting life insurance at one period, and exempted him from the draft in the First World War.

There was a more important, more lasting effect from his child-hood diseases. Never robust as a schoolboy, he was consequently not active in sports and felt himself physically inferior to other boys. By way of compensation he became verbally adept, and from the first demonstrated an extraordinary ability to persuade people to do what he wanted. It was this facility that meant so much to him at the inception of the great project, when he began to induce people to give their sexual histories. Kinsey told me that he believed his early illness had given him a skill which proved to be of the greatest value to him in his lifework.

As he entered adolescence, stronger now, Kinsey discovered the out-of-doors; it was an instant love affair that was never to diminish. Hiking and camping were his chief pleasures, and quite naturally he became a Boy Scout, traversing the merit badge tests until he became an Eagle Scout, one of the first in America. He organized a Scout troop himself, and was its acting scoutmaster; at seventeen he was still too young to qualify for full rank. He took the neighborhood boys on hikes, and with them he began to exhibit the characteristics of the strong leader he was to become.

About this time, in his early adolescence, Kinsey published his first work, although no copy of it is extant and diligent research has failed to disclose where it appeared. Called "What Do Birds Do When It Rains?" it was based on hours of observation in the field and marked the authentic start of his career. He was already a trained student of nature. As an adult researcher, he often remarked that he found most irksome the fact that social mores made it so difficult to witness human sexual behavior. Nonetheless, he saw a great deal and before he died had probably observed more human sexual behavior than any scientist in the country at that time—or since, excluding Masters and Johnson.

In these adolescent years, Kinsey had found another compelling interest, the piano. He mastered the instrument by means of zealous practice and, as I have said, at one point seriously considered a concert career. For the first time, he had a talent that gained him some degree of popularity. He was always in demand to play the piano at various functions. Young Al Kinsey was also known in South Orange High School as the boy who never had a girl.

There were those who were genuinely fond of him, however, as he discovered, or rediscovered, after the *Male* volume was published and he became a celebrity. Letters from former classmates and teachers, recalling the old days, came to him from every quarter, and they were revealing. Here, for example, is his former science teacher, writing from Lake Worth, Florida, to her "Dear Alfred":

"Have tried to visualize you from recent photographs but the one in Time . . . seems more like my 'boy.' Have wanted to write to you so often."

She talks about her garden, and how much pleasure she gets from it, and says, "Remember the iris you gave me, way back? I still have plants in the Stamford garden which, alas, has suffered from severe winters and neglect. . . . How I'd love to see you all and especially *my* renowned boy and his wife."

When Kinsey replied to this letter, he fell easily into the high school pattern and addressed her as "My dear Miss Roeth." He went on:

I have thought of you several times since the book came out, and hoped that you were where you would have a chance to see it. Have you seen the book? If not, you are one of the select few to whom I would send a copy.

I shall always consider that you did more than anyone else at the very crucial age to turn me into science. That is saying a good deal. . . . I hope things have gone well for you. You did an exceedingly good job in giving individual attention to science students at South Orange High School, and you must know that a good many more than I are indebted to you for it.

Later that year, Kinsey had a happy reunion in New York with his former teacher.

Another correspondent who recalled the old days was Dudley W. Rice. He had been a member of Kinsey's Scout troop, and remembered that he had studied for merit badges under him, particularly bird study. "I recall your home," he wrote, "and the room in which you had set up, more or less, your den, with a great deal of scouting projects in evidence."

It was enough to stir a vague nostalgia. Kinsey replied:

It seems a long time since I have had contact with any of the group that was in the Scout troop at South Orange. I have thought sometimes of taking the days and weeks that might be necessary to hunt up as many as could be located.

We did have good times together, and you must understand that from that Scout troop I began to learn some of the things that made it possible for me to do some of the research that we are now engaged in.

After seeing a story and picture in *Time* magazine about Kinsey, another old schoolmate, J. A. Wolf, of Kirkwood, Missouri, wrote a letter to the publication, a copy of which he sent to Kinsey, complaining that the article gave the impression Kinsey was a "detached recluse," shying away from life in the pursuit of hard facts, a dogmatic man, impatient with others, withdrawn and hard. None of this, said Wolf, tallied with his memories of the Al Kinsey with whom he had spent a summer at Kamp Kiamesha in northern New Jersey, when Kinsey was only sixteen. Describing those days, Wolf wrote:

His tent, with his nature "library" of a dozen volumes, was a rendezvous for dozens of campers during the day and well into the night, even after taps had sounded and we were supposedly tucked in. Al not only had the facts but the rare ability to create enthusiasm in the youngsters, and make them thirst for more information. Almost any morning, well before daybreak, our "bugologist" might be seen going from tent to tent with an oil lantern and a list of those who wanted to be wakened for the bird, or flower, or snake hunt. The boys loved "Al" and couldn't get enough of him. He had a merry eye, a wide smile and a hearty laugh and his quiet humor was never missing. Always ready for the latest camp prank, he was just as ready to pitch in and help any kid in trouble.

When St. Clair McKelway was preparing a profile of Kinsey in 1948, he encountered another resident of Kamp Kiamesha, Joseph K. Folsom, later a noted sociology professor at Vassar, who was a fellow counselor with Kinsey for three summers. Folsom's letter to McKelway, which the writer passed on to Kinsey, recalled more of the days in this boys' camp for the Newark YMCA:

He was in charge of nature study and I assisted him and often carried on the work when he was not there. . . . Unlike most of us, Kinsey had had experience at several other camps also; was an active leader in Boy Scout work, often wore his Scout uniform. A camp history refers to war games in 1914 with "a victory for the German forces under———against the allies under Generalissimo———and Field Marshal Alfred Kinsey." Youthful, unassuming, still a college undergraduate [by this time Kinsey was a student at Bowdoin], he was by far the greatest specialist in that group of young men. He had many of the earmarks of what we called a "genius." But he also participated in almost everything and was thoroughly enjoyed as a companion by everyone. The only important skill he was still learning is indicated by one of my notes, "Tried teaching Kinsey to swim."

On August 13, 1912, Kinsey and I led a party of 12 on a four-day hike with blanket rolls across the Delaware into Pennsylvania. We walked up to the house of the Hon. Chief Forester of the United States, Gifford Pinchot, and asked for him. Mr. Pinchot came out of the house and held out his hand. . . .

Kinsey gave many of the evening talks at the camp, on animal and plant life. He became so expert in this field that his services were in demand by many other camps, including many of the private camps in Maine. He would spend summers going from camp to camp, spending a week or so in each, in this way earning his way through college. Later I paid him a visit at Bowdoin College, where he was studying biology, and the genial President of the college, William DeWitt Hyde, took us both as his guests to a college baseball game. Every time I cross the Androscoggin at Brunswick, riding into Maine, I look down at the great pool of water below the falls and think of the canoe trip I had with Al Kinsey on that occasion.

I do not recall that Kinsey at that time was interested in sex as a distinctive problem as we know it today. He was intensely interested in the whole wide world of nature, he had a tremendous capacity to observe and to convey to others his love of nature, his enthusiasm for the very process of living.

He was always soft-spoken and informal; what he had to say was listened to eagerly because it came as from someone who had no axe to grind, no personal vanity or desire to show off his knowledge, but whose eyes and ears and mind were so keen that anything he had to say seemed to make the world a more interesting place to live in.

If that was how Kinsey appeared to his friends circa 1914, it was also the way he appeared to me as an adult. In the basics of his personality he did not change.

Not all of those who graduated with him from South Orange High School in 1912 viewed his subsequent career with pride and approval. In his class was a girl who later became a missionary in Asia. They had not known each other well, because he had attended the Methodist church and she was a Presbyterian. When she heard the news that he had written a best seller, she wrote him from Thailand that she was "rather proud that our little class of twenty-five had produced you." She had not read either of his books, but had read reviews of them in church publications, and one of them had "stirred me to the point of writing you, urging you to look at your findings with God in view and His provision in Jesus Christ to deal with sin as a remedy. . . . As a missionary, I urge you to read this article [the review she had sent him] and put God into your thinking."

Kinsey, who received frequent letters of this type, sent her the same reply he gave the others. He used it also to answer crank letters and those that gave him some outlandish argument or theory about sex. It was a response that covered adequately all the letters he wanted to acknowledge but did not want to answer:

Thanks for your interest in our research in Human Sex Behavior. It is very good of you to write, and I am glad to have your thinking on this matter. We shall be glad to take it into account as we continue our research.

Brought up in a strict religious atmosphere, Kinsey began to lose his beliefs as a college student, when his study of science disclosed to him what he saw as a basic incongruity between it and religion. Having so decided for himself, he could not understand why every other scientist did not think as he did.

After his first year at Indiana he stopped going to church and never went again. No doubt that was when he also stopped talking about religion to other people, and in fact it was rather late in our association before I heard him speak at any length about theological matters. We were riding in the car on a trip one day, and as usual Kinsey was lecturing, this time on large matters of philosophy. I began to get the idea from what he was saying that he still entertained religious feelings. Surprised, I said, "Prok, I've known you a long time and I've never heard you talk this way. Do you really believe in God?"

"Don't be ridiculous. Of course not," he replied, equally surprised that I should have drawn any such inference.

He had no theories about life after death. If anyone asked him such a question, he would shrug and reply, "Who knows?" If pressed, he would respond bluntly: "I believe that when you're dead, you're dead, and that's all there is."

When his son Bruce was about four or five years old, they were in the garden one day and Bruce said, "Look at the pretty flower, Daddy. God made it."

"Now, Bruce," Kinsey said gently, "where did that flower really come from?"

"From a seed," Bruce admitted. He had learned his father's lessons well. Yet Bruce and the other Kinsey children went to church and Sunday school. Both parents felt that it was a cultural experience they should have, and besides, the children wanted to do what their peers were doing.

(People often wondered, incidentally, about the sex education of Kinsey's children, and they would write him nasty or sarcastic letters about it, which he never answered. In fact he did not neglect the subject. The Kinsey children learned from frank and open discussions at the dinner table and elsewhere. They knew about the work their father was doing, and they grew up treating sex as a natural part of ordinary communication. All the children gave him their histories, and said later they were not in the least embarrassed by it because they had grown up to accept sex naturally. They grew up, in short, with the same attitudes toward sex as their father, and in spite of the worst prophecies of the more indignant and outraged letter writers, all of the children are happily married and have children of their own.)

If Kinsey ignored organized religion as a participant, he was far from dismissing it as a powerful factor in human affairs. Two of his four favorite books concerned religion. They were *Man and His Gods*, by Homer Smith (1952), and *Sex Laws and Customs in Judaism*, by L. M. Epstein (1948). (The other favorites were *Pastorals of Longus*, in what he considered the most accurate and complete edition, published in Athens in 1896 by the Athenian Society; and the Earl of Rochester's *Collected Works*, in a 1926 edition published by the Nonesuch Press, London.)

Kinsey knew a great deal about the Judaeo-Christian tradition, and he was indignant about what it had done to our culture. He often cited the inaccuracies and paranoia in which he asserted it abounded. He was quite blunt in talking about this tradition and its effect on the sexual lives of people in our own time, and he backed up his opinions with a sound background of knowledge acquired not only from extensive reading but from numerous discussions with historians who were expert in the subject. He could, in fact, hold his own with scholars. The knowledge was useful to him in a variety of ways. Talking about sex offenders, for example, to the officers at San Quentin prison, his entire lecture was an effort to show them the relation of religious tradition to sexual behavior, an aspect most of them had probably never considered.

Except for his love of nature, Kinsey carried into his adult years little of the baggage he had accumulated as the hero of Kamp Kiamesha, the Eagle Scout admired by his peers in the organization. Nature never failed to move him as long as he lived, not only in the specific areas he studied, but in its broad, grand, majestic sense. He told me once, with the nearest approach to reverence I ever heard him make, how moved he had been by a walk in Muir Woods, the red-wood stand north of San Francisco, where he had gone one day to relax while we were on a history-taking trip to the Coast.

Kinsey retained no interest in Scouting as such once his college days were behind him. About the only aspect of it that remained was his love of camping; his honeymoon was a camping trip. As for the simplistic values of Scouting, Kinsey began to lose his belief in them during his scientific training in college. He lost it entirely when his sex research began, and he could see the obvious gap between pro-fessed values and behavior.

One could say, I suppose, that his garden was a carry-over from Scouting days. When I went with him to Kansas, on the first inter-viewing trip I ever made, the wild flowers for which the state is noted were blooming in glorious profusion. Kinsey took time to collect some and bring them home carefully to be transplanted in his gar-den. As a biologist he had a wide knowledge of plants. He was forever giving us little lectures on flowers, their names, origins and charac-teristics, sometimes to the point of exhaustion for those of us who did not share his interest in growing things.

The Boy Scout organization did not forget Kinsey, however, as he forgot them, although they might well have wished they had. In 1947, the Scouts asked their most famous Eagle to give them his advice about modification of what they called their "conservation section" in the Scout Handbook, in which sex is discussed. Replying to the New York executive who sought his help, Kinsey carefully made the distinction he always drew in these cases, namely, that he was making no moral or social judgments.

But he did have five complaints. One was the "erroneous intima-tion" in the Handbook that the testes were the source of the ejaculate and that ejaculation "wasted" sex hormones. Then he attacked the Handbook's condemnation of masturbation as "the source of very considerable personality disturbance for a high proportion of the boys." On the contrary, he said, "it is impossible to condemn mastur-bation without causing disturbance in a high proportion of the teen-age population. . . . Our years of research have failed to disclose any clear-cut cases of harm resulting from masturbation, although we have thousands of cases of boys who have had years of their lives ruined by worry over masturbation."

Then Kinsey annihilated another of the Handbook's implications, that sexual activity has a deleterious effect on athletics. Citing his histories of hundreds of athletes, he told the Scout executive:

We find athletes with every type of sexual history and those with the most active sexual histories are successful fully as often as those with restrained or apathetic histories. We have many histories of athletes whose perfor-mances were definitely improved by regular sexual outlet. We have specific records on athletic performances that were lost because the men had worked themselves into a nervous disturbance through sexual restraint. In our histories of athletes who do abstain for considerable periods of time from any sexual activity, they are very clearly the histories of persons who would have been apathetic in sexual performance under any conditions. Because of the custom among many coaches to forbid sexual activity, the athletes who are sexually active rarely admit it to the coaches, but we have the precise records on hundreds of such individuals now.

He might have added that we had the history of one track star who broke a national record within an hour after masturbating.

There was a touch of sarcasm in his polite closing: "We should be glad to serve wherever the Boy Scouts can use factual material. You and others interested in social and moral problems will have to make the interpretations of our data."

Kinsey began to leave Scouting and the sexually sterile world of his boyhood behind him when he graduated from high school. At once there occurred a stormy confrontation with his father, who wanted him to attend Stevens Tech and study engineering. It was a contest of stubborn people, but Kinsey was still sufficiently under the influence of his father to give in. For two years he pursued his engi-neering studies, hating every day of it. Even so, his remarkable mind would not permit him to do bad work.

At the end of his sophomore year, he had concluded that he could never be an engineer. Biology was his real interest, and for reasons not entirely clear, he wanted to go to Bowdoin to study it. Again he confronted his father, who was outraged by the idea and told his son bluntly that he could expect no further financial help if he carried out his plan. But Kinsey wrote to President Kenneth Sills at Bowdoin, explaining that he wanted to attend and asking for scholarship help, which he got, and at the beginning of his junior year he transferred. His father bought him a twenty-five-dollar suit and, carrying out his threat, never helped him financially again. Afterward, a kind of armed truce existed between them; they saw each other occasionally in subsequent years, but when Kinsey left home for Bowdoin, he left his family behind him for good.

With the help of the scholarship money, and by dint of spending his vacations as a biology instructor in summer camps, Kinsey was able to complete two happy, productive years at Bowdoin, where his biology professor, Dr. Alfred Gross, with whom he did his major work, considered him the brightest student he had ever known in his long teaching career at the college.

His life at Bowdoin was curiously like his high school years in some respects. He continued to play the piano for the entertainment of his fellow students, and never had a date with a girl. As one of those bright boys who try to take everything, Kinsey, a biology major, also had a major in psychology, as he liked to point out in later years. In both fields he excelled and was not surprised to learn that he had made Phi Beta Kappa.

Austin MacCormick, later professor of criminology at the University of California, Berkeley, recalls that he sometimes saw Kinsey, from the vantage point of his dormitory window, slipping through the side door into the Music Department, which was in the rear section of the chapel. Kinsey had a key to this door and permission to use the grand piano in the department, which he did late in the afternoon when there were no classes. Through his open window, MacCormick could hear his friend playing, sometimes for an hour or more, and often tempestuously. MacCormick theorized that he was releasing the tensions built up by the long hours he spent in the laboratory. No one thought of him as a tense person, however.

As he had at home, he continued to go to church and Sunday school with some regularity, although these ties were beginning to weaken. He was still unbelievably innocent, an innocence that amused Kinsey when he recalled it years later. He was fond of telling about how a classmate came to him one day and confessed that he was masturbating excessively, as he thought, and had to tell someone. Kinsey took his friend to his dormitory room, knelt with him beside the bed and prayed that God would help the boy to stop.

Aside from his studies, Kinsey's major activity at Bowdoin was the debating team, where his natural talent for verbal communication made him a valuable member. After Kinsey became famous, a fellow debater, Arthur B. Chapman, who had become superintendent of schools in Pulaski, New York, wrote congratulating him on finding "pleasure and fame in the pursuit of logical conclusions." Another member of the debating team had been elected to Congress; the fourth man was a restaurant owner in Maine.

Kinsey was also a fraternity man, a member of the Lambda chapter of Zeta Psi, but after college he left this kind of life behind as thoroughly as he had Scouting. When the fraternity tried to involve him in its alumni activities after he became a celebrity, he resisted firmly.

Graduating from Bowdoin with a Bachelor of Science degree in 1916, he took the next logical step and went to Harvard, where he was fortunate enough to get an appointment as instructor in biology and zoology while he studied for his doctorate at the university's noted Bussey Institute, which was equally divided between botany and zoology. Kinsey's major was in taxonomy, including animals as well as plants.

Early in his work at Bussey, Kinsey became intrigued by the life of the gall wasp, an insect found mostly on oak trees and rosebushes. The burgeoning collecting urge grew within him and he began to pursue the gall wasp with the fervor he later devoted to sex histories. In time he became the leading authority in the world not only on these insects, but on oak trees as well. At Bussey, too, he made field trips into the woods to collect plants; in addition to describing and classifying these, he compiled recipes for dishes that could be made from them. Gathering all his information, he wrote in collaboration with Dr. Merritt L. Fernald, *Edible Wild Plants of Eastern North America*. It was not published until 1943, but it sold well and even won an award.

Whenever he could, Kinsey was avidly on the trail of gall wasps. He ranged over the country in every direction, carrying a pack on his back and traveling as cheaply as possible. He camped out, slept in the back country and carried on the expedition as though it were a long Scout hike.

On his travels he encountered a lower social level of people than he had ever known before—uneducated back-country people. At first he was a little timid about meeting them, as he inevitably did when he had to ask them for permission to hunt gall wasps on their land, and there were a few who intimidated him, but as he talked to them more and more he discovered that his talent for persuasion was making it relatively easy to get their confidence. Soon he was having no difficulty in convincing all kinds of people to show him where oak trees were, and he was beginning to develop a genuine liking for unsophisticated country people. Obviously it was splendid preparation for his sex research. Small wonder that he became a master interviewer of people at lower social levels, the most difficult part of any sample to interview on such a subject as sex.

Kinsey did a prodigious amount of work with the gall wasps, at Harvard and later. By present standards his sampling was not rigorous, but it was as good as or better than other such studies of the time.

There were also curious anticipations of his great project. Since it was impossible to tell where oak trees with wasps were located, Kinsey might travel for days until he found some, and then he gathered as many galls as he could. In the early days of the sex research, Kinsey had to be equally opportunistic in securing histories whenever and wherever he could get them, without much concern for a sampling design. At Harvard also, he often sampled every gall in a given tree, or in a given grove of trees, and from this developed his system of 100 percent sampling of human material.

When he got the galls back to the laboratory, Kinsey found that it took meticulous study of about twenty-eight different measurements to record the evolution of these insects. It was laborious work; he spent hours over the microscope. After that came the equally laborious work of recording his findings, and for this purpose he began to develop a shorthand system he had invented, using small symbols. Out of his experience came a coding device which is equal to any such system I know about. Translated to the uses of sex research, it enabled us to gather the equivalent of as many as twenty to twenty-five typewritten pages of interview data on a single sheet. I use the same system, in a modified form, in my own marriage counseling work now, and Martin also employs it in his research work at Johns Hopkins.

With this kind of valuable preparation behind him at Harvard, Kinsey emerged as a freshly minted D.Sc. in 1920, and looked about for his first teaching job. There were a good many openings for graduates with his qualifications, and from several offers Kinsey chose Indiana University. He arrived in 1920 as a young assistant professor. His real lifework awaited him there.

CHAPTER

III

INDIANA PROFESSOR

KINSEY WAS NOT long in the rural fastnesses of southern Indiana before he got married. This shy and lonely young man who had avidly pursued gall wasps instead of girls found someone as reserved as he was, a chemistry major named Clara Bracken McMillen. She met him fortuitously in May of her junior year. Prok, on a traveling fellowship from Harvard, had stopped off at Ohio State when a telegram from Indiana caught up with him, inviting him to be interviewed for a job.

They met in Bloomington at a gathering of Sigma Xi, the national honorary scier.tific fraternity, into which Clara had just been inducted. Prok had been invited to attend the meeting. He was still undecided about coming to Indiana; two weeks of summer work at Culver Military Institute, which he hated, had given him a bad impression of the state. He was assured southern Indiana was nothing like the north, and soon accepted the assistant professorship that had been offered him, at $2,200 a year.

Clara did not forget Prok over the summer, but she couldn't remember his name when they met again in the fall. They renewed their acquaintance at a Zoology Department picnic, to which Clara had been invited by a friend in the department whom she had told she wanted to revisit the forest preserve where the affair was to be held. At the picnic, Prok demonstrated the cooking skills he had learned with the Scouts, and his chief assistant in the outdoor kitchen turned out to be Clara.

After that the romance developed rapidly—another meeting at a dinner with mutual friends, and still another at a Phi Beta Kappa meeting, when he asked if he might walk her home. She had come with another young man, but to her relief he forgot his coat after they left the building and had to go back for it; she went on alone with Prok.

Then, following a script which now seems hopelessly old-fashioned, they went for a walk one night and Prok proposed. He appeared profoundly disappointed and surprised when she did not say yes immediately. The fact was that Clara was entertaining another proposal, and promised herself some time in which to make up her mind—"to be sure." On Saint Valentine's Day he took her to a basketball game—"we never went to another one after that," she said later—and after the game they became engaged. The following June, Kinsey married the first girl he had ever dated. The year was 1921. Clara didn't take her trunk home or even attend her own commencement. With her new husband she went off on a two-week camping hike through the White Mountains.

It was a mating of two people who were peculiarly suited to each other, by background, temperament and interests. She, too, was a dedicated naturalist, as she is today, and shared his every interest with sympathy and understanding. He called her Mac (her college nickname) as we all did later.

After ignoring, or being ignored by, girls all his life, Kinsey had found the one in a million who was as fascinated by insects as he was. When she was a child in Brookville, Indiana, Mac had collected butterflies in her grandparents' phlox garden. She kept a killing jar at the corner drugstore, in case a cecropia moth happened along. At night she waited for moths by street lights, and even advertised for caterpillars in a weekly paper.

It was not surprising that she joined enthusiastically in the hunt for gall wasps. Even the coming of children was no impediment. After their arrival—Don in 1922, Anne in 1924, Joan in 1925 and Bruce in 1928—other members of the family went on Kinsey's field trips with him. One Christmas their friends received cards adorned with a photograph of Bruce holding bags of galls. (Don, the Kinseys' first son, had died of diabetes after an operation for exophthalmic goiter, just three months before his fourth birthday.)

His search took Kinsey to the western United States, Mexico and Guatemala. He climbed the academic ladder—by 1929 he was a full professor—and his companions were his graduate students in zoology.

Kinsey's Mexican adventures were a far cry from Cambridge, or from Bloomington for that matter. On one expedition he wanted to go into a wild, mountainous region, but the Mexican government refused him permission to enter because, as the officials told him, the natives were considered extremely dangerous. Kinsey resorted to his persuasive powers and eventually the officials gave in, taking the precaution of having the crazy American sign a document releasing the government from any responsibility in case he was killed.

With this dubious blessing, Kinsey went off happily into the mountains. On the first night he set up his tent and went to sleep quickly, exhausted by a long day of collecting specimens. Next morning he emerged to find himself virtually surrounded by a circle of impassive Indians, who sat on the ground and studied him solemnly, with what purpose he did not know. Casually he set up his camp stove, then drew a chocolate bar from his pocket. He bit off a piece and ate it, to show that it was not poisoned, and offered a piece to the man nearest him. Then he divided the bar, giving a small piece to each man. When they had eaten it, he invited one of the Indians to examine his galls. The offer was accepted. After a few minutes of peering at them, the Indian called on the others to join him, and they took turns looking, equally interested. A few hours later, the hills were covered with natives searching for galls to bring to the American professor.

The technique he had used with the Indians was quite characteristic. Through the whole episode he never smiled, never moved backward or forward, never exhibited any positive emotion one way or the other. Kinsey believed one should never show weakness, but simply let people know what you want and allow them to come to you. Later, in Chapter Two of the *Male* volume, he wrote eloquently about the altruism of people as he had come to know it in obtaining their histories. "For each group," he wrote, "the mode of the appeal is different, but in each case it is based on the measure of altruism that is to be found—if one knows how to find it—in nearly all men."

Kinsey employed the same technique he had used with the Mexicans in such matters as debating with professionals in his field. He did not push; there was no hostility. In sum, he never gave out report cards to other people, and they almost never failed to cooperate with him.

Recognizing this ability in himself, Kinsey often told about an episode from his youth when he was still weak, not yet over his rickets, and found himself besieged on the street by a bullying group of other boys. Thinking quickly, he threw pennies into the crowd, and while the boys who had been threatening him broke off to dive for the money, he escaped.

Not all Kinsey's adventures in Latin America were as dramatic as the encounter in the mountains, but some of them were full of portents for the future. In Mexico City, for instance, he saw his first movie that could be described as erotic. It was not actually "blue" but rather an extremely low-grade Hollywood product. Kinsey was amazed to hear the audience booing and hissing the romantic scenes —a far different reaction than anything he had expected.

The incident started Kinsey thinking about the different attitudes at varying social levels toward sexual behavior, something his research later confirmed. I believe Kinsey's lack of sophistication made him more aware of differences among groups of people, and more impressed by these differences. Certainly he was acutely aware of them.

On another trip, this one to Guatemala, his Mexico City experience was confirmed in another way. Accompanied by two graduate students, he went to a village official to get some information about routes. It was the middle of the day and very hot; consequently all three were wearing short-sleeved shirts. As they walked in, the perspiring official stopped them before they could make their inquiry and delivered a brief reprimand for the way they were dressed, pointing out that they should be wearing long-sleeved shirts, as he was doing. Then he gave the required information and Kinsey asked him if there was any place in the vicinity where they might swim. Yes, the official said, there was a swimming place, a river on the edge of town.

Late in the afternoon, Kinsey and his students went down to the river. Most of the townspeople were already in the water, splashing about—all of them completely nude. The Americans were astonished and a little embarrassed. They went a short way upstream to swim, but a few minutes later the same official who had reprimanded them for impropriety earlier in the day spotted them and swam up with his wife and his fifteen-year-old daughter, all nude, and amiably engaged them in conversation. Obviously, clothing and nudity depended on the time of day and the place.

Kinsey learned a variety of things on these trips over the border in pursuit of the galls. He learned, for example, that if you locked your trunk in a foreign country, it was an invitation, a challenge to someone in the hotel to break the lock and steal from you. If you did not lock it, on the other hand, the help considered you a fool for being so careless and robbed you anyway. In Mexico, Kinsey discovered how to escape the dilemma. He pasted thin paper tapes over all his unlocked luggage, as though he were saying, "Please don't. See, even a child could break in." He was never robbed after that.

As he settled into the life of a professor at Indiana University, Kinsey experienced no such culture shock as he had south of the border. The transition from East to Middle West was so smooth that people often found it hard to believe he had ever lived anywhere else. Of course, in several ways he stood out from the natives. He may have been the first man in Bloomington to work on Sunday in his front yard clad only in shorts, wearing heavy, thick shoes and carrying a spade with which he tended his favorite irises. Because the shorts were nearly flesh-colored, nearsighted neighbors and passersby soon spread the rumor that Kinsey was working naked in his yard. Even when this was proved false, there was a certain uneasiness about him for a time in some quarters.

At the University, one of his early students was Ralph Mills, now a retired insurance and real estate man in Bloomington. Mills had taken Kinsey's biology course not because he needed the credit, but because he had heard that taking a course from Kinsey was an experience. Already the young zoology professor was marked as an unusual man. Attending his class for the first time, Mills was conscious that Kinsey was not at all like the usual instructor. For one thing, he was far ahead of his time pedagogically, teaching in his own informal way and not even demanding that he be addressed with the usual academic respect. It was not surprising that his students responded with real affection. One of the things they liked best about him was that he always seemed to have time for them, and this, once more, was a reflection of Kinsey's ability to establish relationships with people. He did it equally well with taxi drivers, farmers, janitors, or other professors. Calm and unassuming in the classroom, he gave students such as Mills the sense that they could always feel at home with him.

Mills went on field trips with the biology class, and recalls that Kinsey used to talk about sex to his students even then; the students came to him often with their sex problems, which he was not yet equipped to answer.

After he was out of school, Mills handled the deal by which Kinsey bought the land in Bloomington where his house now stands. In those days it was considered out in the country, but now the property blends in with the sprawling, confortable university town which looks so like hundreds of others in the Midwest. Mills remembers that when he brought the mortgage papers to the house where Kinsey was then living, Bruce, about four or five years old, opened the door —in a primitive state of nakedness. Mills held Kinsey's $3,500 mortgage on his house and land; the land alone would be worth $50,000 today.

Kinsey took considerable pride in building his home. He prized especially the new type of rough, dark-red brick that was used in the construction. Mac helped in the planning and wanted so many windows that, as her husband complained, he couldn't show off his brick properly. There was a magnificent persimmon tree on the property which Kinsey could not bring himself to tear down, so the house was designed in an L shape around it. The Kinseys furnished it with the hickory chairs, painted black, and the braided rugs that later became so familiar to all of us who visited there. Prok was very fond of these things.

In his celebrated garden, which he now began, he experimented endlessly. The iris garden, which was to be his pride and joy, was planted on a slope of grass directly behind the house; a small stream ran through the plot. Kinsey's principle in landscaping, as he said, was the old maxim "Straight is the line of duty but curved the line of beauty." Certainly Bloomington could boast no more beautiful sight than his garden.

In these early days, Kinsey also laid the foundations for his survival when sex and sex research became an issue on the campus. As it proved, one of his best investments of time was his membership in a faculty discussion group which he joined soon after he came to the University, long before there was any controversy about him. The group met regularly on an informal basis. There were about a dozen scholars who took turns presenting papers in their disciplines, and then discussed them with the others.

It was a valuable association for Kinsey. He was able to try out some of his early data on them, and because of his long association with the group and their friendship with him, they could discuss the work freely without prejudice. It was also a way of letting a limited number of influential faculty members know about what he was up to in a project filled with potential academic dangers. One of his other friends was Professor Herman Wells, who later became president of the University and Kinsey's most powerful defender when Prok was assaulted from both without and within, when his resignation was demanded and the more conservative members of the legislature began to bay at the heels of the whole University.

But all this occurred after he became a national figure. In the twenties he was a model Indiana professor. A graphic portrait of him at that time is provided by Professor Louise Rosenzweig, of Washington University, in Saint Louis, who was a student at Indiana from January 1926 through the summer of 1929, majoring in biology. She was Kinsey's laboratory assistant for three years.

Mrs. Rosenzweig saw Kinsey for the first time when

on the dot of the hour, he entered the classroom to lecture in general biology at the beginning of the fall term in 1926. He came in . . . with a long, measured, rather brisk step. He was a tall man; his blond hair was closely cut in pompadour, his shoulders somewhat stooped. He had large eyes with lids that drooped slightly over them and wore horn-rimmed spectacles. His suit was dark, his shirt white, and he wore a black bow tie. He walked to the front of the room, looking neither to right nor to left, went immediately to the blackboard where he wrote, in print-like letters, an outline of the important topics, with subheadings, to be covered in the day's lecture. When he turned and began speaking he had a precise manner of enunciation, richly modulated, as though he enjoyed using the English language. For most of the hour he stood in one spot, except when he occasionally referred to the outline on the blackboard. His restrained manner seemed both aloof and shy. As he lectured, his enthusiasm for the subject matter warmed the rather awesome atmosphere of the room.

Dr. Kinsey felt that the beginning student should not be burdened with the more complicated aspects of biology. He wanted to inspire the student with the wonders of nature—with the marvel of just being alive. His whole emphasis was, as the motto of his biology text for high-school students states: "Look at the World! Be glad that you are alive in it!" The beginning student should be taught ecology in nature and, above all, the careful observation and reasoning of the scientific method; taxonomy, for instance, was to be reserved for the more advanced student.

On field trips with the class, Mrs. Rosenzweig notes, "not only the clothing he wore but his demeanor as well assumed the protective coloration of the field. He was never obtrusive or flamboyant. He expected his students to pick out and comment on the things they observed. Then he would add his experience and knowledge, and he was always eager to have us ask further questions. Sometimes he would say: 'I was wondering if anyone would see that!' "

Kinsey, as this former student observes, was impatient with mediocrity, and he took what would be a highly unpopular attitude in these egalitarian days toward those Midwestern farm boys and girls who, he thought, did not have the capacity or the interest to be college students. He believed these youngsters should stay on the farm, where they could make a practical contribution, instead of pretending to be students of topics they did not have the ability or the background to grasp. He was equally intolerant of faculty behavior at committee and other administrative meetings. Mrs. Rosenzweig remembers that he sometimes came back to the lab after one of these sessions muttering, "What nonsense!"

Kinsey's laboratory and office was a corner room on the second floor of Biology Hall, which was entered through a windowless vestibule. Most of the floor space was taken up with rows of insect cases, stacked five feet high, leaving just enough room to walk comfortably in between. Visitors were impressed by the amount of research data Kinsey had managed to compress into these quarters. It was the gall wasps Kinsey was inordinately proud of. If a visitor happened to express an interest in the insects, beetles or butterflies left over from earlier collecting, Kinsey would say, "Oh, they're pretty enough," and dismiss them.

He had amateurs collecting for him in the United States and in foreign countries, his assistant recalls, and a box arriving from some other land always produced a wave of excitement in the lab. Kinsey showed the utmost respect for these dedicated amateur collectors. Some of them were high school students. He admired such figures as the French naturalist Henri Fabre, who, as Kinsey often remarked, had no formal training in biology but saw and exploited the natural possibilities of a vacant lot.

To his assistant and his students Kinsey was an informal figure, never wearing a jacket unless he was going to a meeting or a lecture. When he appeared for work on Saturday, he dressed in a khaki shirt without a tie, and with his sleeves rolled up. Already, long before sex research consumed his time, he ate lunch at his desk and went on working.

"Dr. K. often used a green eyeshade while working at his microscope under the desk lamp," Mrs. Rosenzweig remembers. "The ceiling light was usually off. He worked quietly for long periods, then suddenly might remark: 'Astounding!' or 'Remarkable!' 'This *is* something!' or simply 'Wow!' These interjections were not directed at me (the only other person in the room) but were merely expressions of his exhilaration at his discoveries. Sometimes he would smile at me, rise from his chair for a moment and then quietly continue his work again. He did not discuss his work with me; I had too little background to appreciate its intricacies."

A frequenter of the lab was Kinsey's field assistant, Brandt Steele, a tall, handsome boy, now a Denver psychoanalyst, whom Prok chose not only for his interest in nature but because he had known Booth Tarkington and once accompanied the author on a canoe trip down the Tippecanoe. Prok considered this relationship an evidence of Steele's cultural breadth.

When he was preparing to go with Steele or someone else on a collecting expedition, Kinsey was as excited as an adolescent. Being in the field meant so much to him that if he came back with fewer specimens than he had hoped to get, he was never frustrated or dejected.

Mrs. Rosenzweig sometimes saw Prok reading at his desk and chuckling over a book he appeared to reread often. It was by his former professor, the Harvard entomologist William Morton Wheeler, and was a satire on termite society with human implications. Kinsey had reprints of it and occasionally lent one to a graduate student, always admonishing him, "Please don't forget to return it."

On his desk also, among current periodicals, was the professional magazine *Endocrinology*, and since it was the only journal except the American Association of University Professors' *Bulletin* which was not directly related to his research, Mrs. Rosenzweig once asked him why he read it. It was because he was interested in the thyroid gland, he told her. His sister's and son's thyroid problems impelled him to keep abreast of new research.

Until he became a controversial figure, Kinsey lived this kind of quiet life, making field trips in search of gall wasps, publishing monographs and books, raising his family and carrying on his classroom teaching as a zoology professor. Yet there was one event that made these years far from ordinary for him. It was his friendship for a student, Ralph Voris, who studied with him through his graduate work, made many of the field trips with him and eventually went to teach biologic sciences at Southwest Missouri State College, in Springfield. Voris became the closest friend Kinsey ever had; their relationship probably meant more to him than any other. The letters written to Voris after Ralph left the University to teach show Kinsey at his most human, and unlike the thousands of other letters he wrote in his lifetime, many of these are in his own handwriting.

What drew them together? Aside from the psychological factors which make close friendships between people, it was probably the personality traits they shared, and their kindred scientific purposes. Like Kinsey, Voris was a small-town boy (he was born in Newkirk, Oklahoma, June 23, 1902) who had become imbued with scientific zeal early in his life and found a bug to pursue. His specialty was the staphylinid beetle. Under Kinsey's direction at Indiana, he studied this insect with something of his professor's dedication to the gall wasp.

As a student, Voris was easily the star among Kinsey's earnest toilers toward the Ph.D. He had much to talk about with his professor because he, too, wanted to be a taxonomist and a zoologist. Voris loved the outdoors, as Kinsey did, and he had something of his mentor's ability to deal with people, showing the same adeptness in meeting back-country natives on the field trips they shared. His work with the beetles took him from Ohio to Florida to California, and many of these trips coincided with Kinsey's search for the gall wasps.

As soon as Voris took his doctorate, in 1928, and moved to Springfield for his first teaching job, the long correspondence began. The following summer, 1929, Kinsey described to Voris the 7,000-mile "bug collecting" trip he was planning to take in August, through the Colorado Rockies, the length of Utah, Zion National Park, Bryce Canyon, down across the Kaibab Plateau and the Grand Canyon into northern Arizona, back through New Mexico and the Texas Panhandle—"as varied country biologically as there is, I think, in the whole world," Kinsey truly remarked. He wanted very much for Voris to go along, but there was the troublesome question of money. The University funds on which Kinsey was financing the trip did not permit him to pay the living expenses of an assistant. All he could supply was three dollars a day for about thirty days. Kinsey knew this was not much to offer and he feared that Voris' wife would not be happy if her new husband went on a month's bug chase. Kinsey suspected she would be "ready to murder me." Nevertheless, he concluded, "if you can go, there is no man I would rather have along." Voris made the trip.

Though such good friends, and men who were master persuaders of other people, Voris and Kinsey demonstrate in their letters how difficult it is for inhibited people to come close to each other. Six years after Voris was out of college, and after a voluminous interchange of correspondence, field trips together and social meetings between the two families, Kinsey in 1934 was still addressing his ex-student as "Dear Ralph Voris" and signing himself "Alfred Kinsey." It was more than a year later before he could bring himself to begin, "Dear Ralph." As late as 1936, although he could now salute Voris as "My dear Ralph," he still signed his letters "Alfred C. Kinsey," and even though the two families had spent much time together, he always referred to "Mrs. Kinsey," although he called Voris' wife Geraldine.

These rambling, handwritten letters of the mid-thirties perfectly reflect Kinsey's relatively placid professorial life, when it seemed that this was what he might go on doing forever. He traded scientific shoptalk about beetles and gall wasps, discussed the state of his garden and passed on such homely details as these:

Following your lead, I have adopted shorts and nothing more as the garden costume, and have the best tan ever, more than I ever thought a bleached blond could have, and the most glorious live feeling that my skin has ever known. Incidentally, I weigh just 20 pounds less than I did in February, from 162 to 142, and practically all that came off the waistline. Had all my trousers let out last February and now every pair is in folds at the waist. . . . And would you believe it, when hot weather came on, I went to the city swimming pool (which my family patronizes every day) and finding it hot as soup, I turned to the University pool and swam at the end of every day until school closed. The first time I have been in University pool since you deserted me here. . . . All three of the children are good in the water. [Bruce was so good that he became a champion swimmer at Oberlin.]

In the same letter Kinsey revealed that he was not altogether happy at Indiana. It was a time of ferment in the administration and faculty, leading to the shift of power that brought Wells to the presidency, and Kinsey could sympathize with Voris, who appeared to be unhappy for much the same reason at Southwest State. "I know your environment isn't the best," Kinsey wrote "but remember that out of 200 on our I.U. faculty, we haven't a half-dozen who are really getting anywhere on research, and my best friends on the Harvard faculty are forever cursing their 'poor benighted institution' (not in public)." And he closes on the note that runs through all these letters: "If there is any chance of our getting into the field together, I would very much like to. It was a glorious day we spent together last fall."

One of the reasons for Kinsey's disturbance with his academic life was what he considered the relatively lower quality of his graduate students, although it is not impossible that they seemed inferior to him because they were not like Voris. As often as he could, he persuaded his friend to join the field trips he took with the students, even if only for a short time. Once, after Voris had traveled with him for four days, Kinsey reported:

I had two of the slowest, least biologic of any I have ever gone in the field with. Two of our brightest and most likeable grads in the department now, but having such a good time in the world that they had no notion of keeping up the pace we set in the field. Ready to throw away everything that wasn't sorted by 9:30 P.M., loving the morning cup of coffee and the pipe of tobacco so they just couldn't be primed to a decent start in the A.M. God, how I needed you that week, to show them that someone besides myself considered our field technic worth working for! Rainwater and Breland [two other students on the trip] spoke of you many times after you left. Rainwater was astonished at your ability to sit beside an uninhabited pile of dung until it came to life with bugs—and that example did more for him than all my say-so. . . . Mrs. Kinsey, approving all of the four days you were with us, immediately recommended you as the doctor for the second two. They discussed infinity, and the possibility that matter was not real but all an illusion—for two whole days, without seeing a thing of the biology in that intensely interesting Louisiana and Mississippi country. Then I told them to butt their heads against a stone wall, and bring me the answer concerning the reality of matter.

A little more than a year later, after a second trip to Mexico, Kinsey reported better luck with his graduates. It had been a long, grueling expedition, covering 9,000 miles in that country and Guatemala, handicapped by unseasonable rains for the first month and a half, and by tortuous roads, particularly the mountain grades in Guatemala, where the average speed was well under ten miles an hour. An unexpected shortage of oaks in the territory they traversed had also cut the harvest of gall wasps; Kinsey reported bringing back "only about fifty thousand insects." As for the students, he wrote to Voris:

The two boys on this trip were splendid. Breland is a remarkably good field man with a great flair for bug hunting. I want you to know him better. We both agreed many times on the trip it was a shame that you were not along, but we also agreed that the chance of your getting Staphylinids would not have repaid you for coming. In actuality, none of us saw a single one of the beetles on the trip, and it was hard to imagine how the Staphylinids would have lived in these relatively barren, ordinarily dust-dry, high mountain altitudes. It will always be one of my regrets that your bugs and mine do not always live in exactly the same places.

If "publish or perish" had been faculty policy at Indiana, Kinsey would certainly have been in no danger of perishing as he worked industriously in the field he had chosen. By mid-1936 he had finished his new book on methods in teaching biology, which Lippincott published the following year, and also completed one of his books on the gall wasps, published by Indiana University Publications. It had taken him five years to produce these volumes, but they had been accompanied by numerous monographs drawn from the material. At this point he saw his authority in the field as nearly established, and wrote to Voris: "At long last I may be able to convince somebody that

I have been laying a foundation in all these eighteen years on which the finished structure may now rise rapidly."

In this same letter, written on a train en route to Ames, Iowa, where Kinsey was to make a speech, he gave Voris some financial advice, on the strict conservative lines by which he shaped the part of his life that lay outside what would soon be considered radical work. He wrote:

Years ago my banker . . . gave me this advice about investments and savings. Diversify. Buy life insurance and annuities. Pay for your home. Have a thousand dollars in cash or instantly convertible securities on which you can draw for emergencies. After each and every one of these items has been achieved (in order), put the next few thousand in sound 3% investments (do not look for bigger returns; if buying stocks or bonds, put it all in investment trust shares which give the small investor the same diversification that the big investor enjoys). For you and Geraldine I should hesitate to advise any serious inroads on your savings until you are well along on the above program.

There was a distinctly paternal note in that letter, confirmed by a remark Kinsey made a few months later, when, discussing Voris' work, he wrote: "Were you flesh and blood of my own, I could get no more satisfaction out of the research you turn out."

Yet in this same letter there were contradictory overtones which make Kinsey's attitude toward his good friend appear somewhat ambivalent. One is no more than assured, after reading the above, that Kinsey's feeling about Voris was that of a father toward an older son who qualified as a chip off the old block, when another paragraph casts a different light—Kinsey talking to an ex-student who has now been away long enough to be treated as an equal, as well as a dear friend. He wants Voris to come to Bloomington for a visit, for a

long enough time to really do something! There are worlds to talk about, scientific problems to discuss, more gossip than we can hope to cover short of days. Added over 300 volumes to my own library in the last six months —surely there ought to be enough to do to keep you here a while. Our home is yours as long as you will stay. Mrs. Kinsey will be delighted to have as much time with Geraldine as I want with you—and the four of us should find enough in common to make it a delight.

Somehow, in spite of all his inconsistencies—or perhaps partly because of them—Kinsey moved slowly toward the close of his career as an insect taxonomist, having for eighteen years laid the foundations for an entirely different kind of structure than the one he visualized. There was something climactic in the freshet of publication that came from him in 1936 and 1937—the books mentioned earlier, six monographs in scholarly journals, scientific summaries of his Mexican work, a short note on a small collection of cynipids from the Marquesas Islands, two generic monographs, and a general paper on the nature of species, designed for the benefit of geneticists who had not yet come around to Kinsey's views.

Meanwhile, change was in the air at Indiana. A political upheaval had occurred, and Wells had come in as president. Kinsey was not at all certain he would like the new climate at the University, and for the only time in his life seriously considered leaving, as he wrote to Voris early in 1938:

If it comes out right in this shuffle, I.U. will be a good place to stay; if it is screwed up as some things threaten to be, I shall be in the market for another job. Someplace where there is active genetic work, and a graduate program that allows a better grounding for taxonomic-cytologic-genetic studies.

Already, however, he was moving rapidly into the real work of his lifetime by a route he would never have dreamed of—a marriage course.

CHAPTER

IV

THE MARRIAGE COURSE

I N THE SUMMER of 1938, Indiana University took a bold step, in the context of the times, and began a marriage course. Since no professor on the faculty was considered qualified to teach it singlehanded, and in truth no one was, it was decided to draw on men from the law, economics, sociology, ethics, medical and biology faculties to talk about marriage from the viewpoint of their specialties. For reasons which are still not entirely clear, Kinsey was chosen to be coordinator for the course.

It was quite a problem, as Kinsey told Voris, "to whip the faculty into some sort of coordinative program," but he did it successfully. Immediately it became a personal challenge as well, because he discovered almost at once that there was little adequate research material in the field, and it was quickly obvious that he would have to do his own.

Kinsey had been faced with this problem at the University before. Not long after his arrival, in 1920, he had been asked to teach a course for high school biology instructors. He accepted the assignment, but soon after he began, he realized he did not know much about high school teaching. Characteristically he set about to learn. Out of the learning came first his high school biology textbook, *An Introduction to Biology*, published by Lippincott in 1926, which eventually sold 440,000 copies, and then, in 1934, his *Workbook in*

Biology and, in 1937, *Methods in Biology,* a text for teachers, both of these also from Lippincott's presses.

This sequence was quite typical of Kinsey. Once he started on something, he tried to do it the best possible way. It had been like that with the gall wasps, then with the biology class, and now he began to apply the same principle to the Marriage Course.

The course, however, was still rivaled in his interest by the bugs, and there are indications that it was a while before he became really involved with it. As late as November 1938 he mentions the new course only casually in a letter to Voris, and in July 1939 the first order of business is the galls; he tells his friend that in the past six months, the busiest he has ever known, he has measured thousands of bugs and "gotten a series of variation curves and correlation maps that are startling." But then he describes the remarkable growth of the Marriage Course. It has "prospered and multiplied." He goes on:

In the first four semesters, we have had 100, 200, 230, 260–290 students. A few flurries with unfavorable criticisms from older faculty who had no first-hand knowledge—but even that is gone. The students would do anything to defend us, their appreciation is so great. We have their written comments at the end of each semester. Several have written personal letters to express their appreciation for their personal benefit. . . . The Gridiron banquet brought only one reference to it—a reprimand to a couple of the boys for having engaged in biologic activities "without benefit of Kinsey's course in connubial calisthenics." The personal conferences totaled 280 for me alone during the single semester Feb.–June. It has given us a wealth of material by which, Mr. Man, I hope to prove to the world someday that any subject may be a profitable field for scientific research if zealously pursued and handled with objective scholarship. We have over 350 histories now—I will have my 1000 within another year and a half. Gosh, I wish I could discuss with you these data, the summaries, etc. I have presented a progress report to our faculty discussion club, nearly bowled some of them over, but they were game and objective, and most encouraging in their approval of further investigation. Wish you were here to see this material.

Here one sees the mixture of careers Kinsey was trying to carry on at this point, before sex research won out. The Marriage Course had produced the inevitable questions about personal problems from students, and they had come to him for advice. Many of their questions he could not answer with any certainty, and he went to the literature for enlightenment, the procedure any scientist would have

followed. But the literature was a severe disappointment. He discovered comparatively little in it about sexual behavior, and it was clear
to him after reviewing it that there was no reliable body of statistics
extant on what people did sexually which might serve as a guide
when people asked for the kind of advice he was expected to give.

What had worked for gall wasps and the biology course must now
be applied to the Marriage Course, Kinsey decided, and in July 1938
he began to learn what he could about sexual behavior at first hand
by taking the histories of his students. They were not quite the
detailed histories we eventually took in our interviewing, but they
were substantially the same, needing only expansion and refinement.

For example, these early interviews covered age at first premarital intercourse, the frequency of this activity and the number of
partners. Later, in the refining process, we amplified that line of
questioning, adding such details as the number of prostitutes and
nonprostitutes involved, the age of the oldest woman with whom the
subject had had premarital intercourse, age of the youngest, age of
the youngest after the subject was past eighteen, the percentage of
partners who were married, the subject's age preference in partners
and the nearest relative with whom he had ever had intercourse. In
brief, these early interviews covered the basic material, which I will
describe later, but they were amplified after the project was under
way, when Kinsey had a better idea of what information he wanted
to obtain.

A year after he began, as he told Voris, Kinsey had 350 histories
and was looking forward hopefully, as he always did, to more—in this
case, his first thousand. Yet, along with the history taking, he was
doing counseling, 280 sessions in a single semester, as he noted;
making his first field trip to Chicago to take histories; and carrying
on his work with the galls. That summer, he told Voris, he planned
a field trip to Colorado, Utah and Arizona, and that was only a part
of his program.

I am teaching entomology and evolution this summer (10 hours credit)
plus the Marriage Course. A total of 27 hours scheduled classroom work per
week, plus more than that in individual conferences. But I thrive, nonetheless—what with a half-day Saturday and the whole day Sunday in the garden.
. . . We have acquired the lot to the west of us—a holdup financially, but we
at least know that no one can build close to us. Planted 250 shrubs and trees
on the new place this year.

By this time, Kinsey had refined the Marriage Course to a point where it had become a model for other institutions. Inquiries began to come in about what he was doing, and he was ready to describe how all lectures were delivered to the staff before being given to the students, and how the entire staff attended all the lectures in class at least once. Students gave their anonymous comments on each lecture for guidance in revamping the course as it went along. Kinsey exercised "considerable pressure" as director to modify lectures he believed were not as scholarly and as well integrated with the program as others.

Questions were raised about whether there was too much biological material in the program, but the students themselves voted at the end of each year for an increase in the biological material and a reduction in the sociological discussion. They were quite free about giving their histories.

Like a young social worker who has not yet learned he must not become involved with his cases, Kinsey found himself helping former students of the Marriage Course with their personal problems, even after they had left the University. He was similarly drawn into becoming a voluntary social worker with the inmates at the Indiana State Penal Farm, and their families, and soon began to take histories there. It was three or four years before he learned that he had to stop this kind of case work if the research was to survive.

The business of taking histories had not been in progress more than six months when the general shape of the grand project had begun to take form in his mind, and its ground rules laid down. The Indiana University trustees had already ruled that the histories would be completely confidential, and Kinsey was telling prospective history givers that "we have seen so much of the personal lives of our students that we are surprised at nothing, make no moral evaluations, and are interested primarily in the scientifically objective fact."

At this point, Kinsey was still trying to provide the kind of help for those who sought it that he would later have to deny on the ground that the Institute was not composed of clinicians. A woman in Tennessee who had taken the Marriage Course wrote to him that she was now married but was having trouble reaching orgasm. Kinsey reassured her that this was "a very common" problem among newly married people who had not had previous intercourse, and went on to explain the climax and the possible physical causes for interference. If the foreskin of the clitoris was adhering, he said, a not uncommon problem, she might "have difficulty in finding a doctor who knows this, though a clever surgeon could perform the operation with a minimum of time and expense. We have gotten the cooperation of one of the best physicians in this town, and he performs the operation for something like $3.00 for our girls, and it has been a material factor in correcting difficulties of several of our married women."

Kinsey, whose own knowledge of sex was rather recent, was already able to give expert advice. In the same letter, he advised the Tennessee lady that perhaps she could not obtain orgasm in the usual position and might try reversing—a novel idea but still valid today —or perhaps the contraceptive was the difficulty, and he remarked that a condom was sometimes too slick to bring adequate response in certain cases. A diaphragm might be better, he went on, and told her how it was used and fitted, reminding her that it must be done by a doctor and recommending one in Bloomington who would do it for two dollars, a quarter of the charge other physicians were making, he pointed out thriftily. Many would not do such work at all, he said.

Students and ex-students were grateful for his help. In these early days, there was a continuing relationship with many of those who had given their histories while they were at Indiana. They wrote to Kinsey later and told him of their marriages and the arrival of their children. Nor was Kinsey himself ungrateful. "You two were among the first who ever contributed to our records," he wrote to one couple, "and I deeply appreciate the help which came from those who risked things at the start."

Again, he writes to a former student in the course who has asked his advice about marrying his first cousin, and says: "I feel honored in having your inquiry. It is encouraging to find that those who have taken the Marriage Course feel that they got enough out of it to warrant their return for further help." Then, answering the question, he points out that "the traditional social reaction and legal reactions to cousin marriages have no scientific basis, but Indiana considers such a marriage incestuous and illegal."

In the midst of this case working and the development of the Marriage Course, Kinsey could not bring himself to give up his work with the gall wasps. To a friend in Ann Arbor he wrote as late as December 1939:

The work with the gall wasps continues; I have been making a variation study on that variable winged Utah species which you may remember. Last summer I went back to the identical localities and made a second collection series just ten years after the first collection was made. That material is now emerging from our breeding bags and will give us a good comparison. I wonder if we will discover evolution errors in our sampling methods or something else.

But a combination of factors was pulling Kinsey more and more into total involvement with sex research. For one thing, a growing controversy was disturbing his relationship with the Marriage Course, despite his earlier optimism about it. The course had been frank because that, Kinsey concluded, was what was needed and wanted by the students. In a letter to a publisher's editor who had asked his opinion about an idea for a book on modern marriage, he had set down his position bluntly:

As for the frank treatment of the biological aspects of marriage, I of course feel anything else than that is not honest. Moreover, the experience over the country has indicated that the students seriously object to Marriage Courses that are not frank. On this subject we are undoubtedly franker in our treatment here at Indiana University than in a majority of the institutions. Certainly the students do not object to that, and the written statements which we have from all of them at the end of each semester show their approval of this policy and their commendation of the biological material much more often than their approval of the sociologic and economic material. As they so often put it, they have heard various talks in these fields, but are not able to obtain the desired information in the biological field elsewhere.

Nevertheless, it was a frankness that some people could not stomach. People in the community who had never heard the lectures began to complain about them to President Wells.

One of Kinsey's early critics, who in the end proved to be perhaps the severest, was a bacteriology professor named Thurman Rice, who taught in the University's medical school, in Indianapolis. It is clear now, I think, that his opposition stemmed largely from simple jealousy. Dr. Rice considered himself an expert on sex. He gave the "sex lecture" in the hygiene class, a required course at the University. I remember that course well. As a sophomore, I took it along with other bored boys (no girls were admitted) and we heard the usual slightly blue jokes at which no one laughed, along with the customary bumbling array of misinformation that was so typical of such lectures in 1932.

Later, Rice went to President Wells and asked for Kinsey's resignation, professing himself to be morally outraged because the coordinator of the Marriage Course had talked to coeds about their sex lives behind closed doors. Rice charged that Kinsey had even asked them about the length of their clitorises, which indeed he had. Rice also asserted that because no disapproval of premarital intercourse had been declared, by implication such conduct was approved. He demanded the names and addresses of people whose histories had been taken so that he could go to them and ask questions to find out if they were telling the truth.

After I came to the Institute, Kinsey and I met Rice one day on a street in Indianapolis, where we had come to take the histories of lower-level blacks. An argument ensued, but suddenly Rice said, "I guess the only way I'll ever have of knowing what you ask in a history is to give my own." Kinsey took him up on it at once.

Dr. Rice did not, however, become a supporter of the project after he had given his history, as so many of our other critics did. He remained a particularly virulent enemy of Kinsey and the research until the end, and it was his original opposition to the Marriage Course that helped to crystallize the opposition.

Masking his hostility behind protestations of friendship, he began to attack Kinsey early in 1939. His objections to the course were, first, that it was too long, which would have the dual effect of making the students think they knew all about the subject while, in some cases, providing too much stimulation. Then he objected to the slides shown in the course; one, he said, was "even stimulating to me." Third, he was afraid that some little "rosebud" of a girl from the country would be stimulated into having a baby, and her parents would blame Kinsey and the University. If the legislature ever found out about the course, he said, raising a fourth objection, they would turn Wells out of office and cut off appropriations until it was ended.

The course was also bad (fifth) because there was little emotional and subjective content, the substance of the marriage experience; and (sixth) sex, especially coitus, was beginning to get undue emphasis in the minds of young people.

Kinsey tried manfully to be polite and responsive to the letters Rice sent him, marshaling his arguments and facts carefully, but Rice would have none of it. He told Kinsey that Bloomington High School students were excited by what they had heard about the course, and he declared that Kinsey had set up a chain of circumstances over which he had no control. Rice was convinced, too, that the data Kinsey had already compiled would not persuade him even if he looked at it, as Kinsey had invited him to do, because he believed that sexual behavior could not be analyzed by scientific methods.

The controversy simmered on in letters, and Rice attacked Kinsey publicly whenever he could find a platform, meanwhile carrying on in the faculty a fight against both the course and the history taking.

In the end, however, it appears that the combined ministerial weight of the Bloomington clergy was more effective in ending the Marriage Course, or at least Kinsey's part in it, despite the fact that students and former students were vociferous in his behalf. Two girls, former members of the class, and their mother sent a joint letter to President Wells declaring that Kinsey's biological lectures had been unembarrassingly objective, dignified and not in the least destructive of any sound idealism.

Without this factual biologic basis the marriage course would be a vague, emasculated travesty of its original self. Together the staff present a useful, inspiring concept of marriage, but without Dr. Kinsey's contribution the course would lose all force of appeal, all pertinence of service. College students have a right to sexual information. How can they better get it than from a dependable, socially approved marriage course? . . . For some students with complex and insistent problems, the course and conferences offer not only vital information but also a very real safety valve for psychological stresses.

Nevertheless, the aroused clergy, representing the silent majority of the community, continued their pressure until in late summer of 1940 Kinsey reported to a friend in the Athletic Department at DePauw:

The ministerial opposition to our own Marriage Course here has reached proportions that leads the administration to consider restrictions or abandonment of the course. The students are so aroused over this that I think we may save the course, but it shows that a great many of these people who talk about sex education really don't want any information passed on.

Kinsey did what he could to save his course. He reviewed what he had accomplished in a short time—a growth from 100 to 400 in enrollment during the first two years, with a total of 1,432 students, faculty members and wives listening to the lectures.

The record indicates [he wrote to President Wells] that there is a great body of students who are biologically and legally adults, who are legally entitled to marry even without parental consent, who are interested in the course and want its continuation as it is now organized.

We have the written judgments of nearly 400 of these students. They give almost unanimous approval of the course. These more than 100 pages of first-hand judgments should be studied before too much importance is attached to resolutions drawn up by a small group of men who, with only two or three exceptions, have had no first-hand contact with the course. . . .

The marriage counseling service which we have provided follows the best practice of other institutions. It has been used by over 1,000 persons in the last two years. About a third of these represent older alumni of our institution and others in the state who look to the University for such leadership. . . .

Reactions to the course from outside the University have included a few adverse criticisms, but we have a much larger body of approval from parents, from leaders in other institutions, from civic and parent groups, etc. There are increasing requests for lectures and programs from high schools, from other colleges, from groups of parents, from Y.M.C.A.'s, Y.W.C.A.'s and from church groups. . . .

Objection to a scholarly analysis of the problems of marriage is a challenge to the University's right to engage in research, and to transmit the results of such research to our students. Obviously it arises in a fear that some of the problems which have hitherto been considered theological may become matters for legal criticism, for sociologic study, and for biologic investigation.

It is no new thing to have these rights challenged by clerical authorities. The right to investigate the shape and the rotation of the earth, the nature of organic evolution, the forces which are basic in our social and economic organization, have been challenged by one or another group ever since the founding of universities. But in the long run matters that are legal, economic, or physiologic will be submitted to students of law, economics, or biology for study.

We have arrived at a day when these aspects of marriage are being subjected to that very sort of investigation. It is best that the ethical aspects of marriage should be presented, as they are, by clergymen in our Marriage Course; but interference from clergymen with studies by students in these other fields is a challenge to the University's right to provide the scholarly leadership which the people of this state have a right to expect.

It was no use. President Wells was personally sympathetic to Kinsey and the course, and in later years proved himself an unflinching defender of the Institute, but at the moment he felt he had to concede to the pressure. Perhaps, like Dr. Rice, he feared the wrath of the conservative legislature, descending upon the head of a new president as well as on Kinsey.

He offered Kinsey a choice between the Marriage Course and his case history studies in human sex behavior. As a research scientist, Kinsey had no real choice. He resigned from the course in September 1940. "No scholar," he pointed out to Wells, "will voluntarily waive his right to disseminate information in the field in which he is especially qualified."

There was no doubt that Kinsey's resignation had been forced, or that his departure sharply diminished the course's usefulness. In a year the enrollment dwindled by 50 percent. As for his conferences with the students, which as Kinsey suspected were feared more by the ministers than the course itself, they were as popular as ever. If the suppressors had hoped to eliminate them by having Kinsey removed as coordinator of the course, they were disappointed, and if they had further hoped to have his burgeoning sex research stopped, they found President Wells ready to draw the line there. Those who did not know Kinsey well had erroneously supposed that he would choose the lectures and quit the research.

If they could have read his correspondence, they would have known better. In a few personal letters he wrote, his growing excitement about sex research glows from every paragraph. Loss of the Marriage Course was a blow, but in reality it would have been only a matter of time, and no doubt a short time, before he would have had to relinquish it anyway, just as he did his beloved gall wasps. The search for histories was beginning to absorb him completely, and as he came to realize that he was working in a research field virtually unexplored, the scientist, the collector and the teacher came together in Kinsey the researcher in human sexual behavior.

Nothing could have expressed his growing excitement and dedication better than a letter he wrote to Voris from Chicago, a few months before the climax of the Marriage Course controversy. Talking about the 570 histories he had already compiled, he exulted:

It is the most complete, exhaustive record ever had on single individuals, and already 2½ times as much in quantity as the best published study has. While agreeing with previous studies as far as they go, our data go much further. Since we are getting entirely new types of histories and still new slants on interpretations, as we get additional histories, it becomes clear that we need many more before we have begun to tap the true study of human sexual behavior. Will get my first thousand men in another year or so, when I will publish the first findings. The thousand women will be accumulated a bit more slowly. Our records are on much better and fuller forms than the cards you saw, and the whole thing in a form that has convinced the several psychologists, psychiatrists, sociologists, etc. who have looked over the set-up. We will *prove* to these social scientists that a biological background can help in interpreting social phenomena. Wish so much that you could go over this material with me. You are among the very very few individuals to whom I can ever tell *all* of the story and the part that has too much dynamite to get into even the most objective, scientific print. Your reactions would mean much to me—as your common sense advice has so often before.

At this point a singular thing happens. The letter concludes with the usual signature, but then it is followed by four more pages, on which Kinsey has printed in block letters "PERSONAL" at the top of each page. Here he explodes some of the "dynamite" he has just talked about, and apparently he has concealed it in this way because he thinks it may offend Voris' wife, Geraldine, or else believes it would be discreet not to let anyone but Voris read it. Voris will be able to show the first part of the letter to his wife, and read the last four pages privately.

As one examines these pages, it becomes clear why Kinsey thought they were "dynamite." His mission in Chicago was to collect homosexual histories, because he had the perception to realize how much could be learned about heterosexual behavior by studying its opposite. There was another motive too. This aspect had scarcely been explored by anyone at all in previous studies, and Kinsey was highly excited, as any scientist would have been, to plunge into unknown territory.

He well knew the dangers to which he had now opened himself. Even in this private letter to Voris he could not bring himself to write the word "homosexual," in case someone should accidentally read these "personal" pages. He wrote it "H——histories." The wrath of the clergy over his conduct of the Marriage Course would have been dwarfed by their outrage if they knew what direction his sex research had taken. In trying to keep secret, as long as possible, the details of his research, he seemed to be anticipating the later storms of controversy that the moralists would unleash. Fortunately, by the time secrecy was no longer possible, the Institute was well enough established to be defended successfully.

Kinsey had begun to take these histories on his first trip to Chicago, in June 1939, when he spent five days persuading three people to contribute. After a few more trips he could pick them up at a rate of five to seven per day, as rapidly as he could find time to make the records. Each case led to other introductions, and soon he had a half-dozen centers in the city from which he could make contacts. When he wrote the "dynamite" letter to Voris, he was on his sixth trip, this one for eight days. He describes his progress:

Am trying to get cases in all classes, from the most cultured and socially-economically [sic] to the poorest type of professional street solicitor. Am waiting right now the arrival of a taxi driver whose amazing experience of seventeen years here is already half in my history—all the rest of it promised. He learned through a friend that I was collecting data, came around to volunteer (gratis) all he knew. If there is anything anyone knows about variety and organized erotics, he is the one who knows it. Have the histories of a number of women, and men all the way from beginners to those with thirty years active experience—a total now of about forty histories out of Chicago who have had first-hand experience with a total of about 12,000. You can figure the average. Several with 2000 and 3000 each.

The most marvelous *evolutionary* series—disclosing as prime factors such economic and social problems as have never been suggested before, and a simple biologic basis that is so simple that it sounds impossible that everyone hasn't seen it before.

Have been to Hallowe'en parties, taverns, clubs, etc., which would be unbelievable if realized by the rest of the world. Always they have been most considerate and cooperative, decent, understanding, and cordial in their reception. Why has no one cracked this before? There are at least 300,000 involved in Chicago alone.

What I would have done without your earlier help, I do not know. For instance, I have had to do more drinking in single weekends than I thought I would ever do in a lifetime, and I still think it bitter. I have diaries from long years—I have whole albums of photographs of their friends, or from commercial sources—fine art to putrid. Some of the art model material is gorgeous. I want you to see it. . . .

These Chicago histories are merely extensions of what I am getting on the I.U. campus. The campus gives me a better series of incipient cases, with all of their evolutionary significance. Several extreme cases also from the campus, with small town and sophisticated variations that Chicago does not give so well. Now have a total, from all sources, of 120 H——histories. Also getting some other types of histories here in Chicago—some interesting divorce histories. One of the men in our sociology department is working on divorce cases for a governor's committee—and turning the sexual end of the investigation over to me. Our special clinic head . . . intends having all his cases turned over to me as routine on sexual history.

More than anything else, in this ferment of discovery, Kinsey yearned to discuss with Voris what he was doing. He was full of the project, and had no one who was both fellow scientist and close friend to discuss it with. His letters are full of hopeful suggestions about possible meetings. But it was not to be. Only a few weeks after Kinsey had written him from Chicago, Voris contracted pneumonia, fought the disease for four months in the hospital, and died at last, in his thirty-eighth year, on May 9, 1940.

A week later, heartbroken, Kinsey wrote to O. P. Breland, who as a graduate student had shared many field trips with him, and was now teaching in the Zoology Department at the University of Texas:

Last Saturday night I started to Springfield, Missouri, for Ralph Voris's funeral, which came Sunday afternoon. It is a very great loss to me. I had traveled more miles with him than anyone else. I so regret the fact that there were not more contacts in the last ten years. It has greatly broken me up. Now I have the responsibility of his entire Staphylinid collection on my hands, together with the superb library on those bugs which he had accumulated. It is a magnificent opportunity for somebody to carry on, and I don't immediately know who this can be. The collection and the library are mine, and I shall want to see, of course, that it is handled as a continuation of Ralph's work.

. . . Man, keep yourself in physical trim, for we must carry on with the things we have started. I never had a chance to discuss with Ralph the endless things that this new study of mine has developed. He would have understood so much better than almost anyone else.

Sadly Kinsey turned back to his work. It was only beginning, and soon there would be room for very little else in his life.

CHAPTER

V

THE PROJECT BEGINS

KINSEY WAS FOND of remarking that when he began his research, we knew more about the sex lives of farm animals and laboratory animals than we did about the human animal. That was true, but he might have added that we also knew precious little about nonhuman animals. Before he was through, Kinsey had contributed much to our knowledge of both.

An objective, nonmoralistic approach to understanding human sexual behavior began about the same time as the emergence of psychology as a separate science—that is, at the turn of the twentieth century. There is, however, no connection between the two beyond the coincidence of time.

Freud and Havelock Ellis were the founding fathers of sex research, although their approaches were quite different. Freud developed his ideas mostly from the case histories of a few neurotic upper-middle-class Viennese patients; the remainder was supplied by his intuitive genius. Ellis developed his from the more naturalistic medium of upper-middle-class Englishmen who were willing to correspond with him. Neither of these pioneers was American, of course, nor were the other writers and clinicians who led the way in the late 1800s and early 1900s—men such as Krafft-Ebing, Moll, Bloch, Rohleder, Stekel and Hirschfeld.

Although Kinsey was in general somewhat disdainful of the work of Freud and Ellis, I am sure he never underestimated their fortitude, which he compared with that of Galileo and Copernicus. One must remember that our Judaeo-Christian culture was, and is, as inhibited and restrained about sex as any known culture in the world. The proscriptions that Jews placed on sexual behavior after their return from the Babylonian exile were not only formidable, but bordered on the paranoid. The Christians, whose early advocates were to a large extent Jewish, inherited these ideas and added to them asceticism, emphasizing the philosophy of the procreative purposiveness of sex.

Thus was added to the antiscientific posture of the Christian church a special denial of the body and a belief in the worthlessness of sex except as an unpleasant act in order to beget offspring. No wonder that as science began to come into its own with the Reformation, the utilization of its approach to the study of human sexual behavior lagged behind for several centuries. It took unusual courage for Freud and Ellis to attack the problem in the face of universal social condemnation.

It was 1915 before an American physician, Dr. M. J. Exner, was courageous enough to ask nearly 1,000 male college students, through mailed questionnaires, eight questions about their sex lives. With this survey began, slowly and falteringly, a series of studies on human sexual behavior; there were only nineteen of them by 1938, when Kinsey started. Most of these studies employed the questionnaire method, a notoriously poor way of getting people to expose the socially taboo items in their histories, and almost all of them used college people as subjects. The questions covered amounted to somewhere between 1 and 20 percent of the number needed to understand total sexual life in an individual. Such were the inadequacies Kinsey faced in the summer of 1938 when he began his work.

The piece of research before his own that impressed him more than any other was G. V. Hamilton's work of 1929 titled *A Research in Marriage*. (It later emerged in a popularization called *What's Wrong with Marriage?*)

What impressed Kinsey most about Hamilton's work was the technique employed—face-to-face interviews rather than the questionnaire, although it was done in a primitive way, with the questions written on cards, so that it was in reality half questionnaire. Still, it was an improvement over previous methods. Hamilton interviewed

100 married males and an equal number of married females, half of them representing pairs of spouses. The sampling was mostly of upper-level people, and 21 percent (an excessive number) had been psychoanalytic patients. All were from New York City. Nevertheless, Hamilton's research had been forthright, direct, objective and unafraid—all qualities that Kinsey admired. Our own research later upheld much of his findings, within variable percentages. Hamilton's questions covered nearly 20 percent of the items we used in our own study, and included more areas than anyone had explored before. Researchers call his kind of work a "directed interview."

Before Kinsey could arrange to meet him, Hamilton died, a missed connection Prok always regretted. In a sense, the background of his approach had been somewhat like Kinsey's, since he had begun with nonhuman studies—chimpanzees, in his case. By profession he was a psychiatrist.

As for the earlier pioneers in sex research, Kinsey's attitudes toward them varied. He had no use for Krafft-Ebing's unscientific cataloguing of sexual behavior, but on the other hand, he approved of Moll's *Sexual Life of the Child*. If he did not always agree with Moll's specifics, Kinsey admired him, at least, for his insistence that children do have sex lives, a radical idea for his time and still considered so by the uninformed today.

Kinsey could not agree with the work of the noted psychologist G. Stanley Hall because of Hall's moralistic attitudes, and about Freud and his followers he was even more biased. He was profoundly against the psychoanalytic approach to sex research, and of course that outraged the analysts when the results of his work were published. It is not too much to say that Kinsey was downright contemptuous of Freud in some respects. He was shocked by the moral judgments Freud constantly made, especially in the case of masturbation. Freud considered it infantile at best and inappropriate in adults; Kinsey simply accepted it as a common form of sexual behavior at every age, which is the prevailing view today.

We acquired for our archives reports of some of the early conferences at which Freud and his followers lectured in Vienna, and Kinsey was appalled (as he himself would have put it) to read how these early analysts treated masturbation as though it were a sickness and a sign of immaturity. Kinsey pointed out, too, that much of

Freud's work was not subject to verification, but relied only on his subjective impressions. One major difference between Freud and Kinsey as sex researchers was that Freud never divorced himself from his middle-class background, while Kinsey's removal from it was complete, as far as his work was concerned. What he felt for Freud Kinsey extended to such prominent followers as Stekel, whose psychoanalytic approach to "aberrations" he considered little more than absurd.

Kinsey did not admire Havelock Ellis any more than he did Freud, but for quite different reasons. He respected Ellis as a pioneer —as he did, in fact, all the others, even Freud—for his courage in doing sex research at all, but his esteem for Ellis dwindled when he learned that the British researcher was a timid man who could not talk to his subjects face to face, and whose work depended almost entirely on letters written to him. Nevertheless, Kinsey thought more of Ellis than he did of Freud, if only because Ellis was not psychoanalytically oriented.

Great names, Freud's or anyone else's, did not abash Kinsey when it came to evaluating the kind of research to which he had devoted his life. He was, for example, offended by Magnus Hirschfeld's open proclamation of his own homosexuality—not because of the behavior, but because he thought Hirschfeld was a special pleader in his work and not an objective scientist. Hirschfeld's famous questionnaire on homosexuality, however, had produced an estimate of 27 percent of such behavior in the population, not far from Kinsey's figure.

Prok was also disdainful of Bronislaw Malinowski, the Polish anthropologist who made pioneer studies of the sex lives of the Trobriand Islanders. He believed Malinowski was actually afraid of sex and had been taken in by the Islanders, and cited as an example Malinowski's acceptance of the Islanders' magical explanation of pregnancy. Kinsey argued that the Trobrianders could not really have believed in any such mythology because they had seen intercourse and pregnancy in the animals they owned and were capable of relating it to their own behavior. Malinowski, said Kinsey, was essentially a prude.

Since he held no better opinion of the anthropological approach to sex research than he did of the psychoanalytic, it is not surprising that the anthropologists were mightily stirred up when Kinsey's Reports were published, and attacked him full force. Oddly, however, there were several noted anthropologists who not only assisted us in the research but came to our defense when the books were assailed. As a final irony, Gebhard was an anthropologist when he came to the Institute.

Nevertheless, Kinsey was often in conflict with contemporary anthropologists, particularly Margaret Mead. They once had a heated argument during a symposium at the American Museum of Natural History, during which Mead accused him of talking only about sex per se, and not about such things as maternal behavior. Kinsey, who considered her one of the worst examples of feminism —I suppose he would be called a sexist today—replied that if she wanted to study maternal behavior that was her prerogative, but it was not the aim of his project. This was the same reply he gave to Karl Menninger, who complained that Kinsey had studied sexual behavior and not love. Menninger believed you could not separate the two; Kinsey thought the opposite.

It is true that Kinsey was intolerant of every other approach to sex research than his own—just as, in fact, other researchers were intolerant of him or any deviation from their particular beliefs. Like them, he was a true believer, and on the whole he did not suffer gladly those who did not believe as he did. Yet, as I have said, in a large sense Kinsey was not without respect for the pioneers in sex research. He admired them because they broke new ground, as he had done, and he never failed to give them credit for that. "They made our job possible," he always said.

In the *Male* volume, we surveyed nineteen previous studies in sex research and Kinsey set down there his criticisms and appraisals of each one. He did not know most of these researchers, but among those he did know and admire was Dr. Robert L. Dickinson. He did not let his friendship interfere with his conviction that Dickinson was a clinician, whose studies of sex were not therefore as relevant to sexual behavior as his own.

One of the contemporary researchers was interviewed as a possible addition to our staff. As usual when we considered anyone we might hire, we took his history first. Kinsey and I did this one together. When we were finished, Kinsey put down his pen and said, "I don't think you want to work for us."

"But I do," the researcher insisted.

"Well," Kinsey observed, "you have just said that premarital intercourse might lead to later difficulties in marriage, that extramarital relations would break up a marriage, that homosexuality is abnormal and intercourse with animals ludicrous. Apparently you already have all the answers. Why do you want to do research?"

I have rehearsed these attitudes of Kinsey toward earlier research not only because of the light they throw on his personality, but because they emphasize the radical departure Kinsey made from everyone who had preceded him.

When he first talked to his colleagues and friends at Indiana University about getting human sex histories, most of them were enthusiastic, but there were some who were horrified by the idea, which foreshadowed the divided reactions of those who ultimately read our books. No grand design ever began in a more humble, unobtrusive way. On his own time, and asking no one's permission, he began to take histories of students in the circumstances I have described earlier. In six months he had 60, by the end of the first year 300.

During that first year he began to take the histories of noncollege young people and found to his surprise that they were usually quite different from those of the students, both in content and in attitudes toward sex. Kinsey liked to tell the story of a campus policeman, a man with an eighth-grade education, who came to him one day in agitation and declared he thought the students must be a bunch of perverts. They would lie under the trees on the campus, he said, and pet and pet without having intercourse, and that must be some sort of perversion.

Branching out from the campus, Kinsey began to go into the small towns and larger communities around Bloomington, taking histories from a wide assortment of people. Writing to Breland in the autumn of 1940, he describes his prison work:

I have been going to the State Penal Farm at Putnamville two or three times every week for the last two months and shall continue to through most of the winter. I have 110 histories from inmates there and can get as many hundreds more as I want. The prison authorities are dumbfounded that I have been able to win the confidence of the men. I have the complete confidence of the five men who are the inner circle of inmates who are in the institution, and their tips to the other men result in their willingness to tell me everything without fear of exposure to the prison authorities. This will give us the first real study on sexual adjustments in prison. I find the actuality is considerably different from the guesses in the current criminology literature. More important than that, these histories are giving me a look-in on a lower social level, and the patterns of sexual behavior are totally different from those of college students. After all, our college students constitute less than one per cent [actually, it was about 5 percent] of the population and it is the great mass of the population which is reported in the group that I am now working.

Even before his departure from the Marriage Course, Kinsey was deep in sex research. At first it was a problem to get histories, but by the spring of 1940 it was difficult for him to find time to record all that were offered. Students were volunteering in increasing numbers. Two entire fraternities offered a 100-percent sampling, which Kinsey had already set as his goal for taking histories from groups.

His fame, still local, was spreading. Every day's mail brought requests for conferences whenever he might be traveling in the correspondents' vicinity. In April 1940, following up some of these requests and hoping to get histories, he lectured in a small town at the request of a clergyman, and was rewarded with ten histories the next day. Then he gave a series of three lectures to a group of 180 parents at Anderson, Indiana, which yielded histories of every variety, from the parents themselves to their high school children. The high school administration, in fact, was so enthusiastic that Kinsey was promised a thousand histories there if he wanted to take time for them.

Connections at the YMCA in Indianapolis started him on a new series of histories there, and his Chicago and Saint Louis contacts began to spread, as he put it, "like the branches of a tree." With 700 histories recorded at this point (1940), his tabulations, curves and correlation charts began to be impressive. Already it was proving to be hard, exhausting work, but as Kinsey told Voris, in what may have been the last letter before his friend's death: "By scheduling things closely to the hour, I manage to keep things going without any physical disturbance."

Plainly Kinsey had found his mission in life, and this fact was perceptively noted by an old friend, Edgar Anderson, who had become director of the Missouri Botanical Garden, in Saint Louis, and had stopped off in Bloomington to visit him. After he was home again, Anderson wrote to Kinsey:

It was heart warming to see you settling down into what I suppose will be your real life work. One would never have believed that all sides of you could have found a project big enough to need them all. I was amused to see how the Scotch Presbyterian reformer in you had finally got together with the scientific fanatic with his zeal for masses of neat data in orderly boxes and drawers. The monographer Kinsey, the naturalist Kinsey, the camp counsellor Kinsey all rolling into one at last and going full steam ahead. Well, I am glad to have a seat for the performance. It is great to have it done and great to know that you are doing it.

Busy though he was, Kinsey could not resist his social-work urge to help some of the people whose histories he took, just as he had done for his Marriage Course graduates. Out of dozens of incidents one could cite, here are a few examples:

A lawyer in Wabash is preparing an appeal case for a boy Kinsey met at the Penal Farm and seeks Kinsey's help. Prok replies that he believes this is not the kind of boy society should keep in prison, and offers to help on a retrial, if the court will accept him as an expert witness. But he is cautious about it. He wants to be free to go as far as possible in exploring the facts in the case, and to refuse to testify if the record is not entirely clear. He will take no fee, not even expenses.

Another inmate of the Penal Farm, about to be released, writes to Kinsey and asks for a small loan to help him "keep out of trouble." Kinsey declines, but leaves the door open. He reminds the man that he has rewarded those who helped him with gifts, a dinner, or even a small fee paid for a history, but has had to draw the line at personal loans. However, since he needs the kind of histories the would-be borrower can give him when he is released, he suggests that it may be possible to pay him for them.

At the request of an inmate's wife, Kinsey talks to him about the divorce she wants, which he agrees to with conditions. Whether he will live up to his agreement Kinsey will not guarantee because, as he tells the wife, "Sam's opinions as to what he will do and will not do change from moment to moment."

Kinsey writes to a man in the Cook County jail in Chicago, saying he understands from the inmate's wife that he is in trouble again.

This time the social work is in the form of supportive therapy:

You helped a lot in our scientific studies when I was last in Chicago, and I shall always appreciate that. You are a very distinctive individual; your energy and independence, and your ability to get along in the world are considerably above the average. The stuff of which you are made is so unusual that I shall always consider that you have contributed to our studies in a fashion that very few other people could.

He promises to find the man the next time he comes to Chicago and talk to him about his difficulties, and concludes with a homely personal note:

I have a garden with about two and a half acres in it, made up chiefly of flower beds. When I am not studying humans, I am studying bugs, and for recreation I dig in the garden when the weather allows. It is an interesting old world, even if it does have troubles in it on occasion—isn't it?

Breaking a rule, Kinsey sends money to a man in Indianapolis who has asked him for help, but in doing so he discloses some facts about the problems that paying for histories and his subsequent social work have raised:

My trip to Indianapolis this last weekend netted me four histories at a cost of $17.00. I contributed my spare change, which was 75¢, toward a supper for———. In fact, I took him to the restaurant for supper but he was still so much under the influence of gin that he was unable to eat. So I gave him the cash instead. I have never paid anyone except . . . prostitutes for histories, and obviously we can not undertake such a thing if the study is to remain objectively scientific instead of undesirably commercial. It has been a pleasure to develop the personal relationships with you and with all the others in my histories, and I consider such entertaining as I have done as an expression of my appreciation rather than pay. All of it comes out of my pocket personally and not from any University or other funds.

Since I esteem you I will tell you frankly that I can not be a party to such drinking as jeopardizes one's economic status or contributes to delinquency. I like you and therefore will do nothing more to contribute to your heavy drinking. Will you understand that I still am making no judgments as to what you should or should not do, but I want to make it perfectly clear that I, myself, do not want to contribute to your drinking. I hope we can still be friends on these terms.

A woman in Arkansas who, with her husband, has given him her history, at which time he gave some advice about their marital problems, writes in despair. She is not responsive to her husband, and he

has a physical attraction for a girl at the office. Her already strong
sense of inadequacy is now worse than ever, and she feels hopeless.
But remembering how much confidence Kinsey gave her before, she
appeals to him again. Replying, Kinsey talks to her about the domi-
nating influence of a mental set, an idea, over the mechanics of
behavior. For eighteen years she has been building up attitudes
toward sexual contact which she now wants to abandon, and he urges
her not to be discouraged if it takes time. "I should say that in the
average case it would take many months—a half year or more—to
learn to make responses which have been inhibited over such a
period of years. If it can be done more quickly, then count it fortune."

Many of the problems people wrote to Kinsey about, in these
early days and later, had to do with homosexuality. From their interviews with Kinsey, and later from his *Male* volume, people with
problems of homosexual behavior learned quickly that this researcher would not make moral judgments about them, that he understood their anxieties and was honestly anxious to learn more
about them and their lives. Their response was grateful, and sometimes overwhelming. A young homosexual student in Evanston, for
example, who helped Kinsey get histories at Northwestern University, wrote later: "In some ways I think you can understand me better
than my adviser-friend here. You have a strange, poetic and warmly
human (rather than *humane*) quality that enables you to cross all
sorts of barriers and talk directly to another's heart and soul. I know
that you will not regard me as No.XXXX case study."

Kinsey had some specific advice to give to the homosexuals who
wrote to him, and it flew in the face both of accepted psychologic
theory and of psychoanalytic and psychiatric practice. But as he liked
to point out, no published study had a quarter as much material as
he already had on the subject. By the end of 1940 he had recorded
more than 450 homosexual histories, enough to convince him that
the psychologists were making matters worse by starting with the
assumption that homosexuality was an inherited abnormality which
could not be cured simply because it was inherent. Kinsey was convinced that there was absolutely no evidence of inheritance.

The physical basis, he believed, of both homosexual and heterosexual behavior was a touch response. When an individual had a

pleasurable first experience, of either kind, he looked forward to a repetition of the experience, often with such anticipation that he could be aroused by the sight or mere thought of another person with whom he might make contact. Unsatisfactory experience, on the other hand, built up a prejudice against repetition. Whether one built a heterosexual or a homosexual pattern depended, therefore, partially on the satisfactory or unsatisfactory nature of one's first experience.

There were social factors, too, which forced an individual into a totally heterosexual or homosexual pattern, he observed. Most social forces encourage the heterosexual, but society's ostracism of the homosexual forces him into the exclusive company of other homosexuals and into an exclusively homosexual pattern. Without such social forces, Kinsey was convinced, many people would carry on both heterosexual and homosexual activities coincidentally.

For homosexuals who wanted to change their pattern of behavior Kinsey had a program. To begin with, he said, the only way to change was to develop satisfactory heterosexual relations that might become acceptable as a substitute, rather than to try to persuade oneself that one did not enjoy homosexual behavior. Psychiatrists accomplished nothing, he thought, by discrediting the homosexual.

In Kinsey's files were the records (as early as 1940) of more than eighty cases of men who had made a satisfactory heterosexual adjustment which either accompanied or largely replaced earlier homosexual experience. Males continued to arouse them, but they found it increasingly simple to avoid male contacts if they built up satisfactory female relations. Kinsey warned these men not to try to acquire heterosexual experience by means of prostitutes, whom he considered to be rarely satisfying, even to the most heterosexual males.

The course of training Kinsey recommended to those who wanted to change began by associating with heterosexual men, then taking opportunities to make social contacts with girls, and finally starting physical contacts of the simplest kind, working up slowly to intercourse only after definite arousal in petting. Sex relations with males had to be avoided as far as convenient. (Later, Kinsey changed his mind on this point.) To one homosexual boy who wanted to change, Kinsey gave a final piece of advice:

Do not be discouraged if you find the male still arousing you more than the female; it may take time and abundant heterosexual experience to bring you satisfaction equal to what you have known in the homosexual. Sometimes, however, I have known the homosexual pattern to change almost overnight, as the result of a fortunately satisfactory heterosexual experience.

In prescribing this course for those who wanted to take it, Kinsey always warned that it might not work. He had known it to be successful in many cases, but he had also seen it fail. And he reminded those who were unsuccessful, or who decided to stay homosexual, that they should associate with heterosexual groups, because, as he said, "Friends should be chosen for all of their qualities, not merely for their sexual patterns, else you cut yourself off from many worthwhile folk in this world."

Later, many of Kinsey's critics were highly critical of his preoccupation with "outlets" for sex, asserting that this had nothing to do with love and reduced sexuality to a mechanistic series of statistics. But even in this beginning phase of his research, Kinsey understood how important outlets were to sexual health, and the advice he gave to a boy struggling with his homosexual problem could just as well have been given to any person who was troubled sexually:

The thing that is most immediately necessary is some sort of outlet for your aroused states. As a biologist, that seems as necessary to me as the tying off of an artery that has been cut, the provision of air for a suffocating man, or food for a starving man. On that point I am very certain. Whether the outlet, the food, comes from one source or another may ultimately be of some social significance, but it is not the thing that is most immediate in the treatment of the starvation. Until you get something like sufficient and regular outlet, you are never going to think straight on things, not going to find the grip on yourself, the confidence which will carry you through to the things of which you are capable.

Biologically there is no form of outlet which I will admit as abnormal. There is no right or wrong biologically. There are situations which may cause terrific psychologic disturbance, and that is the wrong of the state you are in now. As to the desirability, socially, of one outlet or another it is also possible to secure objective data. You can decide that after you get your head cleared by sufficient sexual outlet.

Of this I am certain on the basis of the many hundreds of specific cases I have watched: No outlet is ever abandoned for a program of complete abstinence. It takes another outlet, equally available and equally attractive, to replace another one. To attempt abstinence is nothing more than the thing that has brought your disaster. I doubt if there are more than 2% who ever accomplish such a regime, and the effort is the source of the worst sexual difficulties for endless folk. If you are to substitute with any other outlet, it will take time to learn, effort, and friendly guidance. That is the sort of thing I wish I could give you.

In the last line was the essence of Kinsey's success in these early days of the project—his earnest reaching out to people, his obvious desire to help them as well as to get their histories. It rapidly became impossible for him to give help, but for a time what he was able to do, his plain intentions and his natural persuasive powers enabled him to establish his contacts and begin to fill his files with histories.

He used his persuasive powers skillfully, adapting them to each of the contacts he made, at whatever level they happened to live. Sometimes, as he said, he had to pay as well, usually about one to three dollars, to people whose livelihood depended on sex and to the very poor. But that was only at the beginning. Soon there were so many volunteers, and so many groups ready to give him 100 percent samples after Kinsey spoke to them, that he no longer had to buy his way to get any history.

Mostly he relied on persuasion, of the kind so well displayed in this letter to a homosexual, a graduate student at the University of Chicago, who was making a study of the subject:

I am of the opinion that you are not particularly interested in meeting me, and whatever your reasons, they are definitely wrong. If you have heard correctly, concerning my study in Chicago, you must have learned that I am absolutely tolerant of everything in human sex behavior. It would be impossible to make an objective study if I passed any evaluation pro or con on any sort of behavior or on the behavior of any person. Moreover, you must have learned that I have absolutely preserved the confidence of all individual records, and that I would go to the limit to defend a record. Whatever personal conversation you and I may have would be as confidential as anything in the 4500 histories, which we have; and no one has ever had any reason to suggest that anything in these histories has been betrayed.

It is desperately [one of his favorite words] strategic that our civilization realize something of the diversity in human sex behavior, and acquire some sympathetic understanding of that which is different from one's own. The subject which you and I have been studying [he is careful not to say homosexuality] is one in which all possible information needs to be pooled, if we are ever going to affect public understanding of these things. If you have any real interest in improving scientific and public understanding . . . you should find time to help me by talking to me when I come to Chicago next time.

With the project established and in motion, Kinsey began to feel the strength and meaning of his commitment. The gall wasps and the Marriage Course were slipping away and his whole life turned in from the many paths it had followed before to the long and hazardous road which lay ahead. It was a challenge of the first magnitude, and Kinsey responded to it as only a scientist of his superb attainments could. He wrote to his friend Dr. Dickinson:

For more than twenty years I have worked on individual variations in the population of insects. This work brought me a star in the last edition of the American Manual of Science. In the course of that work, I have explored throughout the length of the continent in the most remote desert and mountain areas. This unearthing of the facts in Human Sexual Behavior proves a much more difficult and much more dangerous undertaking; but the very difficulty is one of the things that leads me on. . . . We shall . . . need all the help we can get.

That help was forthcoming.

CHAPTER

VI

EARLY LANDMARKS

Early in 1941, Kinsey realized that the project could not continue to grow and become what he visualized unless he was able to get financial aid of some kind. He was paying incidental expenses out of his own pocket, and his pocket was limited by the meager salaries the University paid its professors in those days. When he got his annual appointment letter from President Wells in May 1941, he was informed that the trustees had fixed his salary for the coming academic year, on a ten months' basis, at $4,950—scarcely enough for his own needs, let alone the research.

Turning to the most obvious source, he applied directly to the National Research Council Committee for Research in Problems of Sex, an arm of the Council's Medical Division, which was getting its funds from the Medical Division of the Rockefeller Foundation. After interviews and correspondence, a small one-year grant was made to aid in collecting and analyzing histories. It was only $1,600, however, and Kinsey immediately applied for a second grant.

Before it was made, a delegation from the Council came to Bloomington on an inspection tour. It was headed by Dr. Robert Yerkes, a psychologist noted for his studies of primates, and included Dr. George Corner, an equally noted endocrinologist, and Dr. Lowell Reed, of the Department of Biostatistics at Johns Hopkins, a statistician experienced in population studies.

These were gentlemen of the old school. Yerkes, dignified and white-haired, hoped that Kinsey would not get into studying "perversions," but on that score Kinsey stood his ground, grant or no grant. He argued that there was no way of forecasting what kind of sex behavior might be produced when a history began. In the end, the visitors were satisfied with Kinsey's explanations, because they were scientists themselves and they respected him as one. Besides, their visit had convinced them that Kinsey was up to something remarkable.

There was also some discussion about the interview as opposed to the questionnaire, a controversy still alive today. Kinsey held out solidly for the interview. It gave people an opportunity to explain as they went along, he said, instead of being confined to the cold alternatives of the questionnaire, and it made them much more responsive. It also made it easier to assign answers to their proper categories.

Making a report later, Reed wrote to Yerkes:

I was very much impressed with his undertaking and the spirit in which it is being done. From the point of view of quantitative science, I think he is doing an excellent job. His methods of taking the observations are objective to an astonishing degree when one realizes the complexity of the problem he is undertaking. His very method of recording not only assists in keeping the information confidential, but also yields observed material that is capable of quantitative analysis, which very often is not the case in studies of this type. I found his statistical approaches sound in general. . . . My impression of the project in general was very favorable indeed, and I certainly hope that nothing will come up to interfere with the continuation of a study as valuable as this one.

Kinsey did not see that letter until January 1950, when a copy was sent to him by Corner, who had asked Reed's permission to do so. This came about because of an odd controversy over whether Reed had actually endorsed the project, arising from a reference to Reed in the *Male* volume which implied that he had. In the heat of the subsequent public debate over the book, Reed was apparently embarrassed, since by this time he had found some objections to Kinsey's statistical methodology which reinforced the critics. The controversial reference was a simple statement of fact, as Kinsey pointed out, recording that "the statistical setup of the research was originally checked by Dr. Lowell Reed of the School of Hygiene and Public Health at the Johns Hopkins University."

What annoyed Kinsey in this argument were statements made by Reed which were used in the critical attack on the book, particularly that Reed had made suggestions about the methodology which were not followed. Kinsey denied it categorically, and wrote to Corner: "The important question is, of course, what is there about our procedure that Dr. Reed would like to see modified now? I should be glad to listen to any such suggestions from him or anyone else who will take time to examine exactly what we have done."

In any case, the report of the visiting delegation in 1942 was so favorable that a second grant of $7,500, was made, followed the next year by one for $23,000. Thereafter, the grants were raised each year: $25,000, $28,000, $35,000, and, beginning in 1947, $40,000, a figure which remained constant until the Rockefeller Foundation cut off its support in mid-1954. The devotion of the Committee to the project can be measured by the fact that, as of 1947, Kinsey was getting about half of its entire annual resources.

In the official history of the Committee's work, it is noted that support was not

a matter of course or always unanimously voted. All the objections that have been raised against the propriety of the research, against its isolation of sexual from other aspects of life experience, and against its techniques of sampling and calculation, have been discussed at Committee meetings where indeed some of them were first expressed.

The Committee, however, has constantly been impressed by the importance of this study and by the competency and honesty of Kinsey and his associates. Well aware of the difficulties imposed upon its sponsored investigators and upon the Committee itself by emotional and moralistic attitudes with regard to this delicate topic, it has staked its reputation for wisdom in judging research programs and research workers on uninterrupted and increasing support and encouragement of the Kinsey program. The administration of Indiana University has shown equal confidence and has strongly supported the work.

Certainly the Committee's original grant was a turning point in Kinsey's career. Now he not only had money enough to meet his immediate needs, which were acute, but he had won national recognition for his project, with the promise that he could expect more of both. With the research firmly established and beginning to be financed, he could go forward with confidence.

Confidence was needed at once. Not long after the initial grant,

Kinsey was projected into the first public controversy of his life, if one considers the quarrel over the Marriage Course an intramural, private battle. The center of the dispute was Glenn Ramsey, a schoolteacher from Peoria, Illinois, who did his graduate work in educational psychology at Indiana, after which he returned to Peoria to teach general science in a junior high school. Later, in 1941, he became director of health education at Woodruff Senior High School.

Ramsey finished his residence requirements at Indiana in 1939, and planned to do his dissertation while he was teaching. The investigation he had chosen was potentially dangerous, as Kinsey no doubt warned him from his experience with the Marriage Course. Ramsey's plan was to interview seventh and eighth graders to find out how they got their sex information, and the nature of their sexual behavior. The histories Ramsey was taking were designed to be similar to the adult records Kinsey was compiling, and subsequently 350 of them were incorporated into the files. The results of the study were useful in checking the recall of adults about their childhood.

As soon as he began teaching, in September 1939, Ramsey began his research study. He enrolled about 150 boys, divided into five classes, who met with him an hour every week during regular school time. The parents were given a general notification of the project, but were not specifically asked for permission. This was a calculated risk. As soon as the classes were organized, Ramsey began taking personal interviews—two hours during school time and an hour after school, netting him about three interviews a day.

It was a well-constructed plan. In his first interview with the boys, Ramsey got his basic data and the age at which they had first been given information about thirteen items of sex knowledge, where the information came from and what it was. In the second interview he took their sex behavior histories. The first interview helped the second, and the classroom work helped both. Ramsey found the boys extremely cooperative, and he had faith in his findings.

Kinsey was in touch with Ramsey frequently as the work went on, questioning whether the young researcher had been right not to inform the parents fully, but fascinated by the results and beseeching Ramsey to keep checking his figures, some of which he found startling. "How any boy in seventh or eighth grade could be as ignorant as 90% of your boys are is mighty difficult to understand," he wrote.

"On the other hand, I have a sneaking suspicion that it is true rather generally, and that certainly shows the necessity for such an educational program as you have in hand."

Ramsey's research went forward without any discernible difficulties. He even had occasional letters from parents who were pleased with what he was doing. As the research broadened, it became more and more an out-of-school project. Ramsey took his histories in places like the YMCA and settlement houses, all of them now after school hours. He was able to secure the cooperation of some of the leading clergymen in Peoria, as well as a judge of the county court, who referred many cases of sex delinquency to him for help. Parents and some community organizations supported him. Ramsey's principal knew about what he was doing and approved.

But as the small, determined group of Bloomington ministers had demonstrated with the Marriage Course, it took only a minimum of opposition where the subject of sex was concerned to create an uproar. A year after Ramsey had collected his data, published his dissertation and received his degree, a local doctor who was president of the school board began to move against him, and on a January night in 1942 the board of education suspended him until March 25, after which he was to be fired. It was the kind of weasel-worded attack with which Kinsey was familiar, and which he would encounter often in the course of his own work. The board did not attack the research itself, but the implication was that there were serious moral objections to Ramsey himself. The real difficulty, which Kinsey had no trouble diagnosing, having been through the same kind of argument with Thurman Rice, was the president's belief that no one who did not have an M.D. should undertake such research. At a full meeting of the board, in fact, the doctor admitted that there were no specific charges against Ramsey on moral grounds; the issue was the propriety of the investigation.

Kinsey came to Ramsey's defense by every means possible. He shared with his friend the expense of obtaining a lawyer, and gave his time to preparing a case, which included making a trip to Peoria and attempting to explain to the school board the nature of his own program, since they knew that Ramsey had contributed to it. To Kinsey it was not simply a matter of supporting a friend and collaborator, but the defense of a principle as well. He explained his feeling in a letter to Dr. Arthur W. Clevenger, an official of the North Central Association, an accrediting body, which Kinsey urged should conduct an investigation.

It looks to us as if a fundamental principle was involved. If School Boards are allowed to determine what is acceptable science in this case, they will determine what is acceptable science in any other case which interests them, they will determine what is acceptable science in any other field in which teaching is conducted, and they will decide what a teacher can or cannot do in preparing himself in his own field.

He was even more explicit in a letter to Ramsey's lawyer, Joe Johnson:

If we let them get away with this in Peoria now, the Board will repeat this same throttling control in every other field in which teachers are teaching in your city; . . . this precedent will encourage Boards elsewhere to do similar things; and . . . this precedent will encourage Catholics elsewhere, perhaps here in Bloomington or anywhere else, to try the same tactics against us here and against the entire research program.

Nevertheless, nothing was done. Ramsey was fired. The damage suit Kinsey recommended was never filed, the principle never tested in court (no doubt it would have lost if it had been). School boards everywhere still exercise the kind of control over curriculum that the Peoria board employed. They still fight sex education in the schools in many places, still try to keep "controversial" books out of the school library. If he had been more familiar with secondary education in the United States, Kinsey might not have wasted his time tilting at this particular windmill, but it is to his credit that he made a conscientious effort to defend the principle.

As for Ramsey, he soon went into the Army, after a brief period of working for Kinsey, and during the war kept up an informative correspondence with his friend. When the war ended, he went to work for the Counseling Service at Princeton. Kinsey tried his best for some time afterward to persuade him to come to Bloomington and join the staff. For personal reasons Ramsey declined, and finally joined the Department of Psychology at the University of Texas, from which point their correspondence continued in the most friendly way.

Meanwhile, the grand design in Bloomington, to which the Peoria affair was only a sideshow, continued in an ever expanding fashion. I am sure Clyde Martin will be surprised to find himself considered a "landmark" of these early years, but so he must be counted, since he became the first full-time member of the staff.

When the project began, Martin was a student at Indiana, working his way through school. One of his jobs was part-time librarian in the Zoology Department. On his way to work one day, he was walking outside Biology Hall in a downpour, and saw Kinsey approaching him, wearing the whaler's hat he often donned when it rained. Struck by this unusual headgear, and having no idea who Kinsey was, Martin blurted out, "*Where* did you get that hat?" Kinsey smiled, stopped and exchanged a few brief words with him before he went on.

Later, the two met again in the library. Kinsey remembered their encounter, and they talked for a few minutes. Prok identified himself and remarked that he was occupied with taking sex histories. When they parted, he invited Martin to come and talk with him further, no doubt in the expectation of getting another history, which of course he did.

During the autumn of 1939, while these events were taking place, Martin was seriously considering dropping out of school. Even with three jobs he had barely enough money to live. Discussing his problem with Kinsey, he learned that the professor had acquired two lots beside his house for a large garden, which was now under cultivation. Prok asked him if he would like to spend his spare time working in the garden for money to help him stay in school. Other students had been working for Kinsey, but they did not stay long, disdaining the gardener's job as an occupation of dismally low status. As soon as they could find another job they quit.

Martin was a different kind of person. He found Kinsey likable, and he enjoyed gardening. For him it was a pleasant change from inside work and study, and he had always liked the outdoors, which particularly endeared him to Kinsey. He knew nothing about gardening, but Prok, who knew everything, taught him, yet not with any air of authority, Martin remembers; instead Kinsey made him feel that he was not working for him, but with him. Martin became a good gardener, and gardening is still one of his hobbies.

As gardener, Martin was virtually a member of the family. Kinsey valued what he was doing, especially when he built a tool rack which Prok admired, lacking mechanical ability himself. Occasionally Kinsey talked about the research he was doing, and appeared pleased by Martin's response. "He told me he thought I was educable because I hadn't made up my mind about things," Martin said later. As a consequence of these conversations Kinsey asked him if he would like to work in the research laboratory a few hours a week, as well as in the garden.

The "laboratory" at this stage was Kinsey's old office in Biology Hall, a large room filled with cabinets, the gall wasp collection overflowing everything from the paper cartons atop the cabinets to the floor. It was a cluttered, busy place. Sometimes Martin would be working on a table in the back of the office, among the cabinets, while Kinsey was giving an oral examination at his desk in the front, or preparing a biology lecture.

As time went on, Martin found himself in Kinsey's position—involved partly with gall wasps and partly with sex research. The research was taking more and more of Kinsey's time and was gradually getting priority. He was reluctant to give up the galls, and had Martin making color drawings of them when he wasn't helping to correlate the sex research data. It was a transition period for Kinsey; he found it hard to leave biology, which had absorbed him so deeply. He had taken an active part in the controversies that had swirled around his discipline in the late twenties and early thirties. The Scopes trial was still fresh in his mind, and he was much interested in the continuing arguments over genetics.

Until 1941, Kinsey paid Martin out of his own pocket. When the first grant from the Council came through, there was money enough not only for the first research assistant but for the purchase of a calculator and rental of IBM tabulating equipment, which made it possible to switch the sex research entries from handwritten records to punchcards. Since neither had any experience in this kind of work, both Martin and Kinsey made the mistakes beginners usually make, and it took some time to effect the transfer properly.

What these mechanical helps meant to Kinsey he described in a letter to Ramsey:

I immediately see that it will save us endless hours of work in analyzing our data. It will be possible for us to run correlations of an indefinite number of factors, at least eighty in any one problem—a thing which is utterly impossible by any hand calculation. Wherever we have a tabulation of more than perhaps five hundred cases, wherever we have a problem of figuring frequencies, and wherever we are interested in correlations, it pays to transfer our data to our punch cards and get the answers by machine. We have just completed our first set of punched cards which covers the heterosexual-homosexual formulae for the entire lifetime of the individual, and such correlative items as age of adolescence to frequency of outlet per week, etc. I had despaired of ever analyzing these formulae by hand techniques. The machine will do it for us at the rate of 400 cards per minute. This new equipment is a godsend to our particular problem.

Martin went with Kinsey to a meeting of the American Association for the Advancement of Science, in Dallas, where Prok gave his first paper on the research. It was a long trip, and Martin went along mostly to help with the driving. They came back on a swing through the South, and during the hours in the car Kinsey talked to his assistant for the first time in a personal way—about his father's determination to make him an engineer, and how angry and disappointed the elder Kinsey was when young Alfred decided to transfer to Bowdoin.

It is worth noting that this was a subject Kinsey came back to in such isolated situations. He said much the same thing, in the same circumstances, to Bill Dellenback and to me. Apparently the break with his father had been a deep hurt, even though Kinsey had so little feeling for his family, and seldom talked about them at all in later years.

Martin came on the staff full time in 1941. It had been a gradual process, from gardener to lab assistant to researcher. He was still a student, and in 1942 took the Marriage Course that Kinsey had begun. By this time it had been reconstituted in the Medical School, as Kinsey had feared. Martin, with the new knowledge he had gained working in the laboratory, was dismayed to see how the course had become dehumanized; it was now nearly entirely about the reproductive process.

At last, as a result of the money he was making from Kinsey, Martin could do something more positive about marriage on his own account. In a sculpture class he met a girl named Alice who attracted his attention because she had chosen to do the hands of a nude female model. "What a waste!" Martin thought, and introduced himself. The romance developed rapidly, and soon Martin told Kinsey he and Alice had decided to get married. "Fine," Prok said, "but it will have to be done in our garden." That settled it. He even fixed the time. When Martin told him they planned an August wedding, Kinsey said it would have to be put ahead to May because that was when the day lilies would be in bloom, and they were the glory of the garden. The willing couple assented and the wedding came off splendidly. Kinsey, as always, was an excellent host.

Now Martin was truly a member of the family, and was invited to attend the Sunday evening recorded musicales which, with the garden, were Kinsey's only relaxation, his only link to the world outside the project that consumed his life. Martin had no background in serious music, but he had a considerable interest in it, and he and Alice came regularly.

The programs were carefully planned and varied, Martin recalls. They might include some of Kinsey's favorites: William Walton's First Symphony, and the Seventh of Sibelius, along with selections from the Dvorák repertory. Kinsey was catholic about music. He loved the pure classicism of Wanda Landowska as much as the ebullient romanticism of a conductor like Sir Thomas Beecham. He was not committed to any school, turning easily from the baroque to the romantic with equal pleasure. In music, as in all the arts, however, his tastes were on the whole conservative.

Only once did Martin hear him play the piano. It stood in the living room, silent most of the time, as these instruments do in so many other Midwestern houses, survivors of a time when someone in the family "took lessons." Coming in one day from the garden with Martin, Kinsey sat down abruptly and, remarking that he hadn't played for years, performed briefly. Martin did not know enough about music to know whether he played well or badly, but it was clear that Kinsey was impatient with the imperfections of what he was doing. It was in his nature to excel, and long ago he had realized that, proficient as he was, he would never be a virtuoso, and if that could not be he would quit music.

Kinsey was particular about whom he invited to his concerts. He wanted people who interrelated, whether they knew much about music or not. He believed strongly that listening should be shared, and that the sharing should be almost devotional. Consequently he was highly annoyed by guests who obviously were not paying attention while they listened; often they were not invited again. It was his conviction that men reacted more strongly to music than women— a conclusion he would certainly have rejected as a scientist.

Among the regular visitors to the musicales was Professor Frank Edmondson, of the Astronomy Department, and his wife, Margaret. Kinsey and Edmondson had become friends soon after the astronomer had joined the faculty, in 1937. Kinsey had come to him to discuss the statistical problems he was having with his gall wasp research (some of them were the same problems that plagued him in the sex study) and Edmondson helped him with his statistics. Prok had approached him because he knew his own limitations; he had no false vanity. Finding that they could talk comfortably about many other things, the two became good friends.

Like the others, the Edmondsons were invited to the musicales for a time or two on a kind of tentative, trial basis, while Prok decided whether they were the kind of people who would truly appreciate his programs. Having passed, they were asked to come every Sunday. One condition of membership was that a regular member, if he could not attend, was to call Kinsey and tell him, so that someone else could be invited. Not only the programs, but the seating arrangements, were planned carefully.

There was always an intermission for refreshments and general conversation, followed by more music. Occasionally Kinsey even talked about his research. Sometimes the Edmondsons were asked to stay after the others left, and the research conversation went on.

In this select group Kinsey was the arbiter. People who were too dogmatic and argued with him unduly were not invited back because they had spoiled the "tone" of the evening, in Kinsey's opinion. "Tone" was important to him at the musicales.

The evenings continued, with interruptions for research trips, until Kinsey began to have his periods of illness during the last two years, when they tapered off. After his death, Mac made no attempt to carry them on; they had been Prok's show completely.

Among the faculty members, Edmondson was an important factor in Kinsey's life, then and later. The astronomer thinks Prok used him as a sounding board, always deferring to his expertise, "even when I didn't have it." It was Edmondson who advised Kinsey that he should get in touch with some expert statisticians as he developed his research, and it was this good friend, too, who frequently acted as a buffer between Prok and his critics, both at the University and in town. Edmondson often found himself explaining Kinsey to people, telling them that the tales they had heard about the "sex doctor," which were so prevalent, were wrong. At any given time there were always several rumors floating about concerning Kinsey and the Institute, and invariably they were without any foundation.

By the end of 1942 the work was well under way. Kinsey had 3,400 histories, and Martin's help in correlating the data from them. One of the significant results that had emerged from his work was the 0 to 6 scale measuring homosexual behavior, one of Kinsey's major contributions to sex research. It placed such behavior on a scale ranging from completely heterosexual at the 0 end to completely homosexual at the other end, with the incidence of homosexuality in a subject's history determined by his or her position on the scale. Kinsey explained why he developed it in a letter to the noted Stanford psychologist Dr. Lewis Terman, with whom he later had a bitter quarrel over Terman's review of the *Male* volume.

We had spent some time trying to classify our cases on the basis of single items such as technics involved, usual experience, frequency of contact, total number of contacts, psychic reactions, etc. etc. Any classification based on a single item alone proves very inadequate in regard to many particular cases. This 0–6 scale which we have used tries to take into account all of these things. It is, admittedly, a subjective evaluation, but one which we find can be applied with remarkable uniformity. There are four of us involved in the study of this material and we are repeatedly comparing the ratings made by each one of the group. The ratings that we are finally using on each case have in every instance been worked out independently by two or more persons.

Kinsey did not mention this development in the annual report he filed with the University on June 30, 1942, but his accomplishments were impressive enough without it. For example, although it was wartime, he was still able to hold his staff together. Martin's draft board had deferred him because of the national significance of the research. (Kinsey was called in by the Army several times as a consultant on sexual problems in the armed services.) Glenn Ramsey had come to work briefly, taking histories, preparing material for laboratory analysis and studying bibliographic materials in the field, but his draft board in Peoria would not defer him and he had enlisted in the Army the week the report was filed. He was subsequently given a direct commission in the psychologic services of the Air Force.

All in all, 1942 had been a critical year, a turning point. Two other encouraging things had happened. Kinsey had been relieved of most of his teaching duties; he expected to have six months for full-time research in the coming academic year. Then, in the spring, just before it was time to compile the annual report, he had been notified of the National Research Council grant, which elicited a letter from him to everyone at home—"Dear Mac, Martin, Ramsey, Bruce, Joan (be sure to show this to Martin)"—written on the road, and beginning exuberantly:

And what do you think of the research council grant? Wow! That means increased support from every quarter. Just because the NRC Committee has approved to this extent! . . . The doubting Thomases may sit up and think again. . . . It is the largest single grant ever made for a year of research at IU. For a job they all predicted would be stomped on by the Trustees, by any and everybody. We'll prove to them yet that this is the most important piece of research ever undertaken at IU. I felt so four years ago when there were damn few of them who were not ready to knife it. I am sure of it now—and this is only the beginning of the recognition it will bring. Without you, Mac, Martin, Ramsey—Kroc [Robert Kroc, a colleague in the zoology department] and a few others—it would have been impossible. It is recognition of the faith and loyalty you all have put in it—the queerest and most human the most taboo and the most important job we could have tackled.

Discussing, in the annual report, the populations he had under investigation, Kinsey provides a fascinating summary of what he has already learned:

The isolated, relatively inactive prison population has given us the best insight into the nature of erotic stimulation in populations outside of prison. Comparisons of age groups offer the best developmental data. The homosexual is illuminated by comparison with the heterosexual; but, more astounding, the development of exclusively heterosexual patterns appears in an entirely new light after we have analyzed the homosexual histories. Comparison of racial groups (white, Negro, Mexican) offer an opportunity to untangle biologic, psychologic, and sociologic factors. Upper and lower social levels in our own society prove to differ as much as their patterns of sexual behavior as some distinct anthropologic groups; and the psychologic and sociologic significance of this will prove great. The nearly unresponsive drug addict, or chronic alcoholic, helps our understanding of eroticism in other groups. The prostitute's personal history provides the best illustration of the relative importance of physical and psychic factors in sexual activities of the normal population.

About the future Kinsey is optimistic and enthusiastic. He observes that in the first three years he has surmounted most of the preliminary obstacles and has gone a long way toward sampling a number of the populations involved. In 1942 he alone took nearly a thousand histories. "If we can find the right collaborators to help," he concludes, "the major objectives can be reached in a reasonable period of years."

In more informal communications Kinsey expressed this need in a sentence that appears over and over again: "We need more hands." They were particularly needed as 1943 began, to push the project into high gear, and in a few months he had two more willing hands. They were mine.

PART TWO

THE MAKING OF

THE BOOKS

CHAPTER

VII

INTERVIEWING

As a student at Indiana, I had seen Kinsey briefly from time to time, but these encounters had been so casual they meant nothing to me. We came together in the meeting that was to change my life early in 1941. At that moment I was working in South Bend, Indiana, as a psychologist in the Department of Public Welfare. Learning that a professor from my university was to give a talk to a social work organization on the subject of sex in prisons, I determined to hear it. Before coming to South Bend, I had been a psychologist at the Indiana Reformatory, in Pendleton, and consequently thought I knew something about the subject of prison sex.

After I heard Kinsey's lecture it was clear to me that I didn't know as much as I had imagined. His speech was brilliant as always, and it had the ring of authenticity. Obviously this man had been in the field and knew what he was talking about—as indeed he did, after his experiences at the State Penal Farm. I was deeply impressed by his knowledge of both prisons and sex.

After the lecture I went up to talk to him, and he said to me, as he was to say to so many thousands of others he met, "I'd like to get your sex history." A day or two later I came to his hotel room in South Bend, where he was taking histories of the social workers who had heard his lecture, his usual follow-up practice after an appearance. It was an early-morning appointment, 9 A.M., and when I knocked on the door Kinsey's distant voice called, "Come in." He was still shaving, standing before the mirror. He apologized for not being ready. Martin was with him, but soon left the room. After Kinsey dressed we sat down and he began to take my history.

I found myself telling him things I had never dreamed of telling anyone else. Occasionally, as he deftly and persistently questioned me, I hesitated a moment, but then I said to myself, "Of course. I must."

When we were finished, Kinsey told me he was impressed by my attitudes about sex. I appeared to be relaxed, he said, and without fear or unwarranted modesty. He said he would like to keep in touch with me, and went on to talk about how he wanted to get more histories, especially from professional people. This was his habitual practice—getting people whose histories he had taken to help him enlist the people *they* knew. The method worked as well with me as with others. I went back to the Welfare Department and succeeded in getting a dozen or more colleagues to contribute their histories to him.

I had no way of knowing it at the time, but my attitudes disclosed by the interview must have been a sharp, and no doubt refreshing, contrast to some of the histories he had taken on that trip. Writing to Ramsey about it the following week, he said of the welfare workers:

They are responsible for much of the advice given the courts handling sex cases up there, and they are making an awful mess of it. The histories of some of those that I got are the most prudish and most restricted in their understanding of sex that you could find. Fortunately, the two top men are bright and understand their need of my material so that I think I am in for some additional lectures to them. . . . It was probably one of the most important groups to whom I have ever talked.

As time went on, I had occasional lunches with Kinsey when he came to South Bend on field trips, Our conversations convinced him of my growing interest in his project and reinforced our personal friendship, which we carried on through correspondence. I could have sensed from Kinsey's first letter to me that he had more than a casual interest. After our initial meeting, he wrote to thank me and added: "It was unusually good of you to contribute a history, but it was more significant that you gave me the several hours for discussion of our common problems. The discussion helped me very much and I should be glad if it contributed in your work."

As the year went on, he was quite specific about how the group of social workers in South Bend could help him. He wrote:

I have the story of sex offenders from the sex offenders themselves. Now I want to get the viewpoint from the law enforcement and other social workers. Whatever my final conclusions as to the meaning of the data, what I want to do is to get the viewpoint of the law enforcement and social workers without any attempt on my part to influence them in their opinions or to direct their further activities.

As I see it now, it would involve the examination of such records as may be on file, on sex offenders, who have been handled by your local courts or by your public welfare people. If in addition to that I could get the law enforcement agents and other social workers to give me their further information concerning some of these cases or to explain to me why they reacted as they did to these cases, that would be valuable data for me. You will understand and all the others should understand that I am first of all interested in securing the facts as to the way sex offenders are handled by social agencies in the gathering of data. A scientist must not allow his own personal reactions or any anticipation of his final conclusions to affect the data in any way; and in consequence I should want it understood that I will offer no criticisms of anybody or any procedure while I am gathering data. If in the publication of my material the generalizations offer any suggestions for the modifications of procedure, that is another question which would not be involved in the gathering of data.

I found this kind of conversation with Kinsey, by letter and in person, the most stimulating thing that had ever happened to me, and since he had mentioned how much he needed "more hands" in his work, I wrote to him in February 1942 and told him that I felt I was getting into a rut in South Bend, and wondered if there was any possibility for me in Bloomington. Kinsey replied promptly but rather cautiously. He would like to talk about it, he said, but he would rather do it personally. We did talk, through a weekend spent partly in Indianapolis and partly in Bloomington. Kinsey offered me a job, but when he mentioned the salary I had to say no. It was not much more than I was making working full time in the personnel department of the United States Rubber Company at $200 a month and moonlighting in the Welfare Department for another $75. Kinsey had offered me $300, which was hardly a significant increase.

There was another deterrent, a professional one. As a freshly graduated psychologist with a career ahead of me, I could not visualize myself tied to sex research, and to a single project at that. It was well enough for Kinsey, I thought; it was his project and he was dedicated. But it might conceivably hurt my standing in the profession. Reluctantly I wrote to Prok and told him I thought I would give personnel work more of a trial, but I tried to leave the door open by telling him that if it turned out to be the wrong decision, I would be in touch with him again.

Kinsey was clearly disappointed, but he approved of the decision to stay with my new job in personnel at least long enough to find out more about it. "We should very much like to keep you as a tentative possibility for collaboration at some future time," he wrote, "for I think we have many things in common in our thinking." He added that he was particularly glad to meet Mrs. Pomeroy and the children, and noted rather cryptically, I thought, that he was "much pleased to see the realness of your home."

We continued to work together, and only a month later he complimented me as an "efficient individual, and I am amazed at the way in which you have handled your diverse jobs. Without your help, it would have been a much slower business for us." He asked me to keep in mind "the possibility of collaborating with us at some time in the future."

I was keeping it in my mind more than I realized, as my wife seemed to know. "Wardell," she said one day, "I think you want that job." She was right; I did. She had said exactly what I wanted to hear. I wrote to Kinsey and told him I would like to reconsider.

On the day before Christmas, 1942, Kinsey still hadn't quite made up *his* mind. He wrote to Yerkes, with whom he was now in more or less constant contact, asking his advice, describing me in flattering terms and finding nothing really to object to but my age. I was twenty-nine. "I wish we could find someone past forty," Kinsey wrote to Yerkes, "but under the present circumstances I wonder if it would not be wise to accept Pomeroy's help even though he would be limited for a few years in contacts with certain older groups." (Nothing could have been further from the truth, as it proved.)

Apparently Yerkes agreed that it was safe to take a chance on my youthfulness, because Kinsey wrote to me on January 19, 1943, offering me a staff job. Oddly, the salary figure was left blank, so I wrote accepting the offer and telling Kinsey I assumed he had omitted the salary when he was dictating, so his secretary would not know (this was, in fact, true; he always did so), and had forgotten to insert it before mailing. Apologizing, Kinsey told me the figure was $3,000 a year, or $250 a month—$50 less than his first offer. But I accepted, and also promised to carry out Kinsey's suggestion that I work on my Ph.D. at Indiana. Prok was delighted. He offered to put me up in his own home for "a week or two or three" until I could find a house.

There was less backing and filling over my joining the staff than was the case with other Kinsey negotiations. My job was to be chiefly interviewing, and he was extremely careful about whom he chose for that work. There were not more than nine interviewers altogether, and three stayed only a short time. Kinsey and I between us took about 85 percent of the ultimate 18,000 histories, dividing them almost equally between us, as I have mentioned. This was of course a vital part of the project, and Kinsey was never more arbitrary than when he was considering hiring interviewers.

His hiring difficulty arose because he was looking for people who embodied three paradoxes: they must be happily married, but be able to travel about half the time; they should have an M.D. or a Ph.D. in some related science, yet they must be able to like and get along with people from lower social levels; and they must have been born and raised in this country and exposed to our mores and customs, yet never evaluate what others did sexually. That third point was the largest stumbling block, but Kinsey was ruthless about it.

He had sound reasons for his paradoxical demands. He wanted interviewers who were happily married because people who had never married were suspect to a good many Americans. It was necessary for them, obviously, to be able to work with lower socioeconomic groups, and he wanted to avoid ivory tower academic types who could not do so. Karl Lashley, of the National Research Council, once remarked that very few psychologists really like people, and I feel there is a certain amount of truth in this observation. Finally, it was important for an interviewer to be familiar with our culture but not be prone to moral evaluations, as far as humanly possible, because there were few areas of research where the investigator's own system of morals was so challenged and so crucial as in the study of human sexual behavior.

There were other considerations as well. One applicant fulfilled all the qualifications, but his wife was an alcoholic and completely untrustworthy. Another would have been hired except that he had been so active in anti-religious, anti-integrationist and pro-union activities that his presence on our staff would have been a constant source of difficulty in securing cooperation in many quarters. We had to avoid hiring anyone who was identified with either ultraradical or ultraconservative movements or institutions. Of course, we had our opinions and attitudes about social issues, but we learned not to expound them in public.

It was suggested to us that we ought to have women interviewers to interview women, and Negro interviewers for blacks. By that logic, Kinsey pointed out, we would have to have prostitutes for prostitutes, drug addicts for drug addicts and so on. The qualities of the interviewer, not his sex, race or personal history, were the important variables.

Kinsey made his viewpoint on this matter clear in a letter he wrote to the noted sociologist David Riesman, who was then in the Department of Sociology at the University of Chicago:

We do not feel that the sex of the interviewer in relation to the sex of the interviewee is of particular importance if you get the right interviewer, properly trained. We know several women who would have made excellent interviewers on our staff, two of whom we did attempt to train. . . . We failed only because our interviewing has called for considerable travel and our demand that interviewers be happily married. It is much more difficult for a woman to stay happily married and travel away from home a good deal. The women on our staff, therefore, had to be assigned to tasks which kept them here for the most part, or entirely here. I know several women clinicians who are fully as successful in getting the most confidential sexual material from their subjects as any man I know.

As proof positive of the fact that we, as male interviewers, have not failed in securing our data from females, you should look at the comparisons of the data which we have secured from males and from females. These comparisons are to be found at several points in our female volume. A striking case, showing how closely the reports we got from females matched those from males, is to be found, for instance, on page 77 of our volume on the Female. It does not look like the women covered up very much because we were male interviewers.

Kinsey had one rather strange idiosyncrasy about hiring. He believed that names were important. An odd or offbeat name, he thought, might be harmful in establishing rapport with a subject. A man named Tatin-Pottberg was told he could not be hired unless he dropped one or the other side of the hyphen. Kinsey was distressed by the names of two other applicants and raised serious objections to hiring them, although they were otherwise well qualified. Kinsey was also concerned about using anyone with a Jewish name because he thought some WASP interviewees might object. That was a curious blind spot in him. There was nothing bigoted about it, however; he was simply opposed, for purposes of research efficiency, to the idea of matching individuals to groups. When people argued that he should hire blacks and Jews, he always returned to the women-for-women argument. Only WASPs, he felt, could interview everybody. Apparently it did not occur to him that they were identifiable, too —or else he thought it unimportant.

His requirements for interviewers, in fact, were so narrowly defined that only a few people could hope to qualify. Even for the less highly skilled jobs on the staff he took particular pains to secure people who were completely trustworthy, mature and stable, and especially would not be offended by the kind of material with which we dealt. Such people were hard to find, and they had to be paid more than the ordinary person filling such jobs as secretary, statistical calculator, translator, or librarian. Even janitorial service was a problem because of security restrictions. In twenty-three years we had a change of janitors only twice. When one man had to retire because of age, failing vision and general decrepitude, we spent a considerable amount of time and energy with security checks before we felt we were ready to entrust the night key to his successor. For the same reason, we were not able to use the ordinary student help that lightens the load in other university projects.

In hiring me, the objections were my lack of a doctorate, which Kinsey insisted I remedy as soon as possible, and my age, about which nothing could be done. For a while, considerable attention was given to ways of "making Pomeroy look older," until Kinsey saw that it did not help. In any case, he was overjoyed to get a qualified full-time staff member, now that he could afford one. He turned to me in one of his infrequent outpourings of feeling and said, like a boy, "Gee, I'm glad you're going to be on the staff."

For my part, when I walked into Kinsey's office on the first day,

I had a somewhat let-down feeling. I had seen it before, but not as a place where my life would be centered. It was a typically drab office in a typical gray stone Middle Western university building, left over from the last century. The office was large, but it was designed for utility, not comfort, about which Kinsey cared little. It had a musty, institutional air, and it was still cluttered with the remains of the gall wasp collection, which gave it the air of a biologist's workroom or laboratory instead of the psychologist's ambience with which I was familiar.

I had that odd feeling of academic strangeness a professor often has when he happens to visit a part of the university remote from his own field—an English professor lost in the chemistry lab. The thing that impressed me most about Kinsey's office was his growing library of books on sex research. At once I resolved to read them all.

Aside from the office atmosphere, I could not help being impressed from the beginning with Prok's supreme dedication. He was a fired-up human being, full of a driving resolution which he communicated to me and the other staff members. He spent most of the first day talking to me about plans for future research, and outlined how he intended to train me for the work in two-hour sessions every day.

In academic terms, there was not quite the usual relationship between us. As one so young and only recently the possessor of an M.A., I could have expected to be treated as an extremely junior member of the club by a full professor. Kinsey, however, always treated me as a colleague, never making me feel inferior or that I ought to be subservient and show him a proper respect.

More and more as I began to work with him, I came to esteem his total dedication. We rarely talked about anything but sex research in general and the project in particular. Like many scientists, he was hardly capable of dealing with the commonplace preoccupations and amusements of other people. I could never forget how one day, as we lunched together at the Oliver Hotel in South Bend just before I joined the staff, he announced he had heard a sexy joke he wanted to tell me. I waited with some anticipation, wondering what kind of smoking-car story the authority on sex would produce. He told it straightforwardly, without a hint of humor. It was a terrible joke, badly related. I tried to laugh, but my polite appreciation was as grim as the joke. Kinsey didn't appear to notice, and laughed at his own humor with the heartiness which always sounded so convincingly Midwestern, even though it came from a former New Jersey boy.

It was the only time that I heard him try to tell such a story—mercifully, I might add. He had a particular horror of any interview that threatened to degenerate into joke telling, because for him every interview was a sober inquiry and he discouraged levity. When someone told him a blue joke he would respond by dissecting it psychologically, and the story died an agonizing death before the narrator's eyes. He never used four-letter words in his conversation, but he did employ them freely in interviews when he knew that these were the only terms the subject understood. It was Kinsey's opinion that people who told off-color jokes frequently were not comfortable about sex, and in time all of us on the staff fell into his opinion about these and other matters.

Kinsey found an office across the hall from his own and promptly divided it into three parts, for me, Martin and a secretary who would work for both of us. Our offices, like his, were soundproofed so we could take histories in them, and that had not been as easy as it might seem. The Office of Buildings and Grounds had no experience in soundproofing, since such privacy did not exist anywhere else in the University, and their first effort resulted in a test which showed, dismayingly, that anything above forty decibels could be heard plainly. Kinsey said that would not do; the figure had to be eighty. Buildings and Grounds protested. They would have to tear down the whole thing and do it over, they said. Kinsey was adamant. If that was what had to be done, so be it. His insistence was characteristic; he was a perfectionist. Time and again we were to see and marvel at his unflagging attention to every detail, his dogged insistence on coming as close to perfection as a human being could.

2

My wife, Martha, came down to Bloomington about two weeks after I went to work. Not long after that, she gave her history to Kinsey. She had been quite anxious about doing it, even though she had met him in South Bend and entertained him in our house when he came late one evening. She had given him ice cream and cookies, knowing that he loved ice cream, and she had been a little in awe of him, as might be expected of the young wife of a young psychologist. On that occasion Kinsey had been at his most charming, and for once the conversation was purely social, though for Kinsey it had a purpose. He wanted to meet and know the wives of those who worked with him.

Nevertheless, it was another thing to give him her history, and Martha had qualms about it. But Kinsey made the experience so easy that she could not help having a warm feeling toward him. Her anxiety, she thought, had been caused chiefly by the fear that she could not remember things honestly. The night before she was to see him, it suddenly occurred to me that after her history was in the files, I would know everything that was in it, so I suggested that we trade histories. We told each other everything we could remember, and this honesty was at once refreshing, amusing and strengthening to both of us.

I may have had a little anxiety myself about doing interviews. As an undergraduate I had been warned by my professors that there were two areas of study fraught with danger. One was the study of hypnosis, the other the study of human sexual behavior. If anyone asked why these areas were dangerous, the response was either a cold stare or considerable harumphing and evasion. At least two psychology departments had dismissed researchers in the early 1930s because the administrators were not yet ready to look at sex objectively. Before 1940, only five psychologists had published anything approaching good statistical data on sexual behavior, and consequently, in spite of my tremendous confidence in Kinsey, I ventured into the deep water with some initial, and concealed, reservations. It was only momentary.

Kinsey was concerned that I be drawn into the project very gradually. The first history I took was that of a male college student. Prok called these "baby histories," because the young men were like lambs jumping after each other and their histories were innocuous by comparison with, say, those of inmates he had interviewed in prisons. Consequently this first history made little impression on me.

Before I could begin, of course, he had had to teach me the code. I was so anxious to get started that I learned it in a little less than two months—a phenomenal time, and possible only because I worked at it night and day. This was the code used in taking the histories. There was another code, involving a rearrangement of the symbols, which was the key to identifying histories in the files. I was so wrapped up in my work that I cracked this second code by myself, and soon, examining the files, to which of course I had access, I was able to identify Kinsey's own history, his wife's, his daughter's and those of about six other people.

I told him at once what I had done, and at first he appeared irritated, but then was quickly pleased because I had shown myself so anxious to absorb everything as quickly as possible. Nevertheless, he prudently changed the coding of the names so that no new person coming to the project could do it as easily. He took every conceivable precaution to protect the identity of the people who had given histories. The codes themselves did not exist on paper; they were taught by rote, verbally, to those few who had to know them.

Since so many of the interviews at first had come from the campus itself, a primary consideration from the beginning was the necessity to keep the identity of the people and the facts related to them absolutely secret. No one was more insistent on this point than Kinsey himself, who recognized that it was his guarantee of absolute confidence to those who gave histories that made the research possible. Not only did he protect the histories themselves by every conceivable means, but he persuaded the trustees to demand of him that he not reveal any confidences, so that this became an official affirmation on his part. He was acutely conscious of his responsibilities in this respect, and he drilled it into everyone who came to work for him. Everyone had to understand the supreme importance of respecting confidences.

I believe there was something more to this than Kinsey's basic rocklike integrity. I think he liked secrets, that their possession gave him a sense of power. And there was no question that the histories did give him a unique potential power. They included political, social and business leaders of the first rank, and with his intimate knowledge of their lives Kinsey could have figuratively blown up the United States socially and politically. On the Indiana campus alone, as would be true of any campus, there were at least twenty professors with homosexual histories unknown to anyone else, not to mention the numerous extramarital experiences recorded. Kinsey had no psychological need for the power he possessed, but perhaps he liked to feel sometimes that he was putting something over on the world.

Martin thought Kinsey never ceased to be amazed that people, especially in high places, would tell him the things they did. At the beginning he himself was so naïve that everything was a revelation to him. He came to believe, however, that people would tell him anything about themselves if the circumstances were right, and the way the research was conducted gave them the proper circumstances. Nevertheless, at the start, he was constantly astonished by the difference between public behavior and private acts.

I wondered how Prok could have taken his own history, but he told me that he had given it to himself just as Freud had analyzed himself. After I joined the project, I took his history about every two years, and he took mine. This was not only good practice at the beginning, to perfect techniques and discover possible inadequacies, but it helped to measure the percentage of error in recall.

The staff discovered that we could converse with each other in the same shorthand we used in taking histories. We did it in ordinary conversation in private, and of course it permitted us to speak much more openly in public. I might say to Kinsey while we were going up in a public elevator, "My last history liked Z better than Cm, although Go in Cx made him very er." Translated: "My last history liked intercourse with animals better than with his wife, but mouth-genital contact with an extramarital partner was very arousing."

A man wrote in one day to inquire: "I wonder how many of your interviewees walk in feeling gay and confident, and walk out feeling like a sack of wet feathers?" There was, I am sure, a tremendous amount of public curiosity about exactly what it was we asked in taking a history. People viewed the idea sometimes with horror, sometimes with fear or distaste, often with anticipation of various kinds, but in reality there was nothing mysterious or frightening about the interview, as nearly all of our 18,000 subjects discovered. In that number we found only six people who were visibly upset in the course of history taking. Some of these were nauseated, others nearly fainted or displayed visible sweating and palpitations. Three of them were psychiatrists, one of whom was asked to rate himself on the 0 to 6 homosexual scale. On the basis of the history he had given, he was obviously a 4, and when he was compelled to face this fact, he rushed to the bathroom to vomit.

But time after time people would say, "This has been one of the most therapeutic experiences I've ever had," or, "We should be *paying* you," or commonly, "I've told you things I never thought I'd tell anybody." One psychiatrist told us, "I've been in therapy for three years, and this is the first time I've ever put it all together."

The interview was, of course, at the core of the project and Kinsey's success must be attributed in large part to his complete mastery of the interviewing art, applied to this most difficult of topics. For the *Male* volume he wrote a truly extraordinary chapter describing the techniques we used. It remains, in my opinion, one of the best accounts in the literature of how to interview, and has been cited innumerable times in other works.

In the chapter Kinsey told about how contacts were made, and enumerated some of the questions his subjects had asked *him*—such as the ubiquitous "Am I normal?", whether there was any harm in "excessive" sexual activity, the usual fearful queries about masturbation's supposedly harmful effects, and the individual's anxiety to know how he "rated" in comparison with other people. Kinsey listed, by occupation, the range of the people who had given us histories. The list began with bootleggers and ended with women's-club leaders. Thieves and holdup men were cheek by jowl with YMCA secretaries; lawyers and male prostitutes were joined snugly in alphabetical sequence.

Kinsey described how he established rapport with his subjects, employing his two key principles: making it clear that as a scientist he would have no objection to any kind of sexual behavior in which the subject might have been involved; and assuring the interviewee that whatever he said would be kept in strictest confidence, no matter what happened.

Graphically Kinsey indicated how the interviews usually went— how the subject often began by admitting only a small part of what he had been doing sexually, and then added more details gradually as he became more confident that the interviewer would not disapprove. "Yes, I have been approached for such relations, but I did not pay attention," the subject might say. Or, "Yes, there were physical contacts, but they did not interest me." Or again, "Yes, there were complete contacts—but I was asleep." The admissions often became less grudging, more freely given: "Yes, I liked it well enough, but I don't think I wanted any more of it." Or, "Well, yes, I did try it again." And finally, "Yes, since then I have become interested, and I have had a good deal of it lately."

Writing about interviewing, Kinsey recorded his own answer to the question asked so often: "How do you know you got an honest response, when people weren't boasting, covering up or otherwise distorting their record?"

"As well ask a horse trader how he knows when to close a bargain!" Kinsey figuratively snorted, in one of his rare departures from strictly scientific prose.

The experienced interviewer knows when he has established a sufficient rapport to obtain an honest record, in the same way that the subject knows that he can give that honest record to the interviewer. Learning to recognize these indicators, intangible as they may be, is the most important thing in controlling the accuracy of an interview. Beyond that there are cross-checks among the questions, inconsistencies to watch for, questions which demand proof, and other devices for testing the validity of the data.

Kinsey was at pains to describe how carefully the histories were guarded, observing, for example, that individual histories were never discussed outside the staff, not even with professional friends, nor were they ever used as illustrative material in public lectures or even in group conversation. People were always trying to get information from us about those who they knew had contributed histories. Husbands and wives wanted to know about each other. Parents asked about children. All kinds of requests were made, but the answer was invariably a firm "No."

Further on in his discussion of interviewing, Kinsey talked about the technical devices we used. He described how we put our subjects at ease, how we insisted on holding the interview in a private place, and he summarized the sequence of topics. In doing so, he noted that the order varied in accordance with the subjects' social background, age and educational level. For example, the sequence for unmarried college males went from nocturnal emissions to masturbation, premarital petting, premarital intercourse with companions, intercourse with prostitutes, animal contacts and homosexuality. For males who had not gone beyond tenth grade, however, the sequence placed premarital intercourse earlier because it was accepted at that level, while masturbation had to be approached more carefully, and later in the interview. Kinsey also noted that it was easier to get a record of homosexual activity from females than to record their masturbatory activity. Older males, too, were more ready to talk about their premarital intercourse than their masturbation. Paradoxically, it was easier to get a female prostitute's professional record than to obtain the details of her sex life with her boyfriend or husband. Understandably, a timid older woman from a remote farm would not require nearly as much questioning. Knowing when to drop a line of inquiry if it was proving to be painful or embarrassing, coming back to it later when the subject was ready for it, was, Kinsey believed, the key factor in his ability to get 12,000 histories completed (at that point) with only three or four incompletions.

In each history, there was systematic coverage of a basic minimum of about 350 items. A maximum history covered 521 items. However, whenever there was any indication of sexual activity beyond what the questions covered, we would go as far beyond the basic interview as we thought necessary to get the additional material. In that way we obtained histories of people who were blind, deaf, crippled or otherwise handicapped; people who had lived abroad; those with experience in military groups; and others who could give us special information. It was also helpful to find a highly intelligent person who had had wide experience with socially taboo behavior, because he would be able to analyze it for us. "As scientific explorers," Kinsey wrote, "we . . . have been unlimited in our search to find out what people do sexually."

While our questions were not standardized in form, we defined them strictly according to the points they covered. For example, when we asked about a subject's relationships with his parents, a specific period of time was used. If we asked a subject about his petting experience, we defined the word as we understood it, so there would be no confusion. Similarly, in asking about relationships with prostitutes, we made a clear distinction between "cash on the barrelhead" and girls who were only "promiscuous." If we asked about an individual's health, it was to pinpoint the illnesses which might have interfered with his social adjustment.

We were careful to avoid bias in the interview. That is, if a subject found it hard to estimate the frequency with which he had been engaged in some activity, we were careful not to provide him with any idea of what the frequencies in the general population might be, or what he himself could be expected to have. Instead we suggested that his activity might average once a week, or three or four times a week, three times a day, or once a year—indicating the widest possible range. We were also on our guard against people who were obviously highly suggestible, being careful to avoid implying an answer and to check the answers for consistency.

We asked our questions directly without hesitancy or apology. Kinsey correctly pointed out that if we were uncertain or embarrassed in our questioning we could not expect to get anything but a corresponding response. Unlike previous researchers, we did not say "touching yourself" when we meant masturbation, or "relations with other persons" when "sexual intercourse" was intended. "Evasive terms invite dishonest answers," was Kinsey's dictum. We also never asked *whether* a subject had ever engaged in a particular activity; we assumed that everyone had engaged in everything, and so we began by asking *when* he had first done it. Thus the subject who might want to deny an experience had a heavier burden placed on him, and since he knew from the way the question was asked that it would not surprise us if he had done it, there seemed little reason to deny it.

It was important not to ask multiple questions—as every teacher knows. If we asked a subject if he was ever erotically aroused by seeing nude males or females, he might answer that he was always aroused by seeing females, thus avoiding having to say that he was also aroused in some degree by seeing males.

Since there were so many questions to be asked, the questioning went as rapidly as the subject could comprehend, but there was a better reason for doing this. Under the rapid fire, the subject was much more likely to answer spontaneously without thinking too much, and so it would be virtually impossible for him to fabricate answers. We looked our subjects squarely in the eye and fired the questions at them as fast as we could. These were two of our best guarantees against falsifying.

In making cross-checks on accuracy, we used the device of interlocking questions. Before we ever asked direct questions about homosexuality, for instance, there were twelve preliminary inquiries, whose significance only a psychiatrist would have recognized; and it would have been hard for anyone with more than incidental homosexual experience to deny it after he had answered them. We also used argot as a cross-check. Asking a female subject how many years she had been "in the life" would only cause confusion and inability to understand in anyone who had not been a prostitute, unless she had been professionally knowledgeable about prostitution in her job, perhaps as a social worker or in some agency dealing with prostitutes.

If we thought a subject's answer was wrong or incomplete, we tried to rephrase the question so that he would have to prove his answer or expose its falsity. If a subject was of low mentality we might pretend that we had misunderstood his negative reply, and ask another question as though he had answered affirmatively; for instance, "Yes, I know you have never done that, but how old were you the *first* time that you did it?" To make it as easy as possible for subjects to correct their answers, we ignored contradictions, accepting the correction as though it were a first reply. On a few occasions, as Kinsey recalled in the *Male* volume, we took a complete history even though we were convinced from the outset that it was going to be a fraud, then put it aside and told the subject, "Now give it to us straight." Naturally, we had to be sure of our ground in such cases. Kinsey pointed out that the false record, viewed against the corrected record, gave us valuable insights into an individual's public admissions compared with his actual behavior.

If we thought a subject was offering to contribute his history only to satisfy his curiosity and had no intention of giving us an honest account, we were severe with him and would refuse to proceed with the interview. It was a technique we came to use reluctantly, but more and more as we went along it seemed necessary in a few cases, especially some older teen-age males and some women in underworld groups. By not taking a firm stand, we would expose ourselves to the possibility that the investigator's standing would be lowered in the groups to which the subjects belonged, and we would be unlikely to get honest histories from them. There were times, too, when we did not recognize the falsity of an interview until after it had been given, and in those cases we went back to the subject and demanded that he correct the record. These cases included feebleminded subjects, prison inmates and even clergymen. We did not lose a single history by taking such action. It was Kinsey's firm belief that giving a history was voluntary, but once the commitment was made, the subject assumed responsibility for its accuracy.

In most cases we were careful not to let the interviews run longer than an hour and a half, or two hours at the most, because we found that if it did the subject became fatigued and the quality of his response dropped. Extending it by even a few minutes might have that effect. This put a definite limit on what could be included, and reinforced Kinsey's argument that it was impossible to include any of the numerous suggestions for further questions, that came from people with special interests.

Another way of reassuring our subjects was to make it clear that we had no desire to have the names of people with whom they had been involved sexually. If names were given anyway, we let the subject know that they were not being recorded. Even so, it was obviously impossible to avoid identifications in many instances, and that was why we found it hard to get histories from some married people, or from those who had had sexual relations with relatives or people prominent in their communities. It was also difficult in the case of those who were involved in deeply emotional love affairs, and might find it hard to avoid identifications.

As I have noted before, we made no moral evaluations of anything we heard in the interview, since we were scientists, but we also avoided any discussion of racial, religious, political or economic issues, especially when we were dealing with lower-level, rural, or minority groups. To make a scientific study of a human population, Kinsey believed, there was no alternative to absolute abstention from all discussion of controversial social issues.

In the case of children, we had to abandon our sequence of questions, obviously, and take a different approach. With at least one of the parents always present, the procedure went as follows, as Kinsey described it in the *Male* volume:

The technique is one in which the interviewer looks at dolls, at toys of other sorts, joins in games, builds picture puzzles, romps and does acrobatics with the vigorous small boy, tells stories, reads stories, gets the child to tell stories, draws pictures, gets the child to draw pictures, shares candies and cookies, and withal makes himself an agreeable guest. Tucked into these activities are questions that give information on the child's sexual background. If the picture book shows kittens putting on nightgowns for bed, the child may be asked whether she wears nightgowns when she goes to bed. When the interviewer tussles with the four-year-old boy, he may ask him whether he similarly tussles with the other boys in the neighborhood, and rapidly follows up with questions concerning tussling with the girls, whether he plays with any girls, whether he likes girls, whether he kisses girls.

It would be difficult to imagine anyone who could practice these techniques better than Kinsey did. He was adroit at using play activity as a lead into particular questions, and he was also able to find considerable significance in the children's drawings, as any psychologist would understand. Kinsey thought of the interviews with children as an information test, not an examination of overt sexual activity, and he considered the reaction of the child to the questions more important than whatever specific information he supplied. If a four-year-old boy, for example, calmly admitted that he played with girls in his neighborhood, his response could be evaluated in a different way than if he had been hesitant about it, or giggled, or seemed to be embarrassed by the question. As Kinsey observed, it was possible to discern adult attitudes toward some items of sexual behavior in the responses of three- and four-year-old children, and to see the difference in attitudes among social levels.

The kind of understanding of his subjects that Kinsey demonstrated in his dealings with children was a prime element in all our interviewing, and he considered it of the greatest importance that we have the necessary background knowledge in order to establish rapport. We had to let the subjects know that there was nothing they could tell us that we did not know about, or would fail to understand. It was particularly important that we know the sexual viewpoint of the cultures from which our subjects came. Kinsey illustrated this point with the case of an older Negro male who at first had been wary and evasive in his answers. From the fact that he listed a number of minor jobs when asked about his occupation and seemed reluctant to go into any of them, Prok deduced that he might have been active in the underworld, so he began to follow up by asking the man whether he had ever been married. He denied it, at which Kinsey resorted to the vernacular and inquired if he had ever "lived common law." The man admitted he had, and that it had first happened when he was fourteen.

"How old was the woman?" Prok asked.

"Thirty-five," he admitted, smiling.

Kinsey showed no surprise. "She was a hustler, wasn't she?" he said flatly.

At this the subject's eyes opened wide, he smiled in a friendly way for the first time, and said, "Well, sir, since you appear to know something about these things, I'll tell you straight."

After that, Prok got an extraordinary record of this man's history as a pimp, which would not have been possible without his understanding that Kinsey knew all about his world.

Again, we would ask a prostitute when she "turned her first trick," not "how old were you when you were first paid as a prostitute." Then we might ask her how many of her tricks returned after their first contact, and much later in the interview we would inquire how often she "rolled her tricks," that is, robbed them. If she had reported that few of the men ever returned, and then later said that she never robbed any of the men, we would tell her that we knew it didn't work that way. If she didn't roll them, why didn't they return? Very often that question would produce a smile and the admission that, since we seemed to know how the business operated, she would tell us the whole story—and it was usually that she robbed every time she thought she could get away with it.

If, at this point, there is any further curiosity about the questions we actually asked, let me give you a guided tour through the interview, which has been so much debated and discussed.

Before a subject arrived, we would record certain data in advance —the date, the number of the interview (to be rerecorded for our files later), whether the subject was male or female, and the source of the history, meaning how the subject had come to us. When he arrived, we began with some general conversation, thanking him for coming, perhaps explaining the value of the contribution he was making, if we had not discussed that before. There would even be desultory chat about the weather. I always made these preliminaries brief. Kinsey tended to spend more time than the rest of us, mostly reaffirming the confidential nature of the research and reassuring the subject.

Then we asked, "Do you have any questions?" Usually the subject did not, but occasionally there were casual inquiries, and sometimes he would ask a question about his sexual problems. We had a standard answer ready for that contingency: "Well, we need to get your history first. When I have more information about you, we'll come back to that."

The first question was "How old are you?" We also asked for birth dates, which people always gave readily, almost automatically, thus providing a check on what they had told us about their age. Routine questions followed: "Where were you born?" "Where have you lived for at least a year?" These answers were placed in chronological sequence. Obviously we were establishing bench marks with the early questions. For example, a subject might say he had lived in Connecticut until he was fourteen, then moved to California. This made it possible to ask such questions later on as "How old were you when you first masturbated?" If the subject said, "Fourteen," we could say, "Oh, that was after you went to California?" To which he might respond, "No, it was before," and thus we could tell whether he was older or younger than fourteen when this behavior first occurred. With the aid of further questions we could then pin it down more precisely.

Next we took a religious history, both the subject's present status and his relationships with religion from his early days onward. That would give us some idea of what his particular frustrations might be and where blocks might occur. Then came his health and marital histories. We asked about his hobbies, his interests, and obviously all of this was nonthreatening material. People concentrated so much on answering these questions that they began to forget they were giving a sex history at all.

We moved on to the subject's nonsexual activities in high school, if he had attended, or in college, and went on from that point chronologically to his marriage: how long the marriage had lasted, how long he had known his wife, and so on. From that series we went to family background—relationships with brothers and sisters, occupations of father and mother, and similar questions.

It took about fifteen or twenty minutes to answer all these, and not one of them had been about sex. Consequently it was usually easy at that juncture to go on to early sex education. Again the subjects did not feel threatened, because these things had happened when they were little children and they did not feel responsible for them. Here, too, we began using sexual terms for the first time, asking questions about how the subject got his first knowledge of sexual matters, and where. We asked, for instance, how old he (or she) was when he first learned that babies grew inside mothers, how old he was when he first learned there was such a thing as intercourse, how he acquired a knowledge of such things as condoms and how he found out about homosexuality. Males were asked how they first ejaculated, females when they first menstruated. That led naturally to questions about when pubic hair developed, when the voice changed in males, how quickly or how slowly growth occurred. When this series had been answered, our bench marks were firmly established.

Now we could go directly to early sex experiences. It was still fairly easy going for the subject, because again it had all happened when he was small and he was not responsible.

From this point, the order of the questions varied. For example, with upper-level males we could go next to masturbation, a natural consequence of the question about first ejaculation, and then we got a history of the subject's masturbation, the fantasies accompanying it and his reaction to it. Naturally, this would be followed by questions about nocturnal emissions, details of the subject's petting experience and his premarital intercourse, if any, his extramarital intercourse and his use of contraceptives. In the questions about masturbation, we would ask about their use of the basic techniques. If we found a man who had used all or most of them, this would open the way to pursue with other questions what further techniques he might have used, and the frequency as well.

Specifically, we asked male subjects about five techniques, including manual masturbation, making coital movements against a bed or some other object, self-fellation (possible for only a few men, but attempted by most), insertions of various objects in the urethra and anus. As for other techniques, we inquired about the use of such things as melons or similar objects to masturbate in. We asked about any unusual position that the subject might have employed, the use of ropes to tie up the penis, or the use of toilet paper tubes, bottles and condoms as an aid to masturbation. We were quick to explore any lead the subject gave us into any rare or unusual activity, because the purpose was to record the whole range of human sexual behavior.

If it was a female who was giving us a history, the masturbation questions were naturally a little different. Routinely we asked about the subject's use of clitoral friction, about her bed masturbation (that is, lying on her stomach and making coital movements), crossing the legs and using thigh pressure, stimulation of her own breasts and insertion of objects into the vagina. If it became obvious that she was using a wide variety of techniques, that would open the way to such questions as whether she used a vibrator, or whether she practiced anal stimulation.

With both men and women, we routinely asked about the content of their erotic fantasies during masturbation, and if these were elaborate we might spend several minutes eliciting further details. In this as in other types of behavior, answers to questions about one kind of activity would tell us whether nothing more was to be learned, or whether we could explore a subject with additional questioning.

We asked about erotic response—that is, how people responded sexually to reading about sex, or seeing it, or hearing music which might excite them, or whether they were excited sexually by traveling in vehicles. From such questions we could get clues to the homosexual content of a subject's history. His erotic response to dreams, for example, might be greater, he would say, if he dreamed about masculine figures, and that might be supplemented with similar images when he masturbated. It was possible, then, to build up a picture of the relative components of the individual's sex life. Another clue to homosexuality might be a subject's desire to look at his penis while masturbating.

Now we were at the core of perhaps the deepest and strongest of the taboos—that against homosexuality—in people who had no idea they had such feelings, or who were aware of it and had tried to suppress it. If there was any resistance to be encountered, this was where we would find it.

There followed the details, if any, of the subject's sadomasochistic feelings. Did he bite when he was having intercourse? Did he enjoy being bitten? Similar questions completed this aspect, if it existed. We asked if the subject was aroused by seeing animals copulating, and this would lead to queries relating to his own sexual activity with animals, if any. Questions were asked about the individual's anatomy, that is, the size of his penis, whether he was circumcised and the angle of the penis in erection.

With lower-level males, we could go directly from here to intercourse, then back to masturbation, petting, wet dreams and homosexuality. It was the same with lower-level females. If an individual had an extensive homosexual history, from the point where we discovered he had one we could go into 250 more questions. If he did not, of course, these questions would never be asked. The two major extensions from the questions were in the areas of homosexuality and prostitution.

Some people remained tense through the whole interview, but that was because of the taboos the questions touched upon. Sometimes things went along quietly enough until we got to one of these areas, and then, sensing the subject's rising tensions, we would move to something else momentarily and come back in a few minutes to the disturbing place, hoping it would be easier.

Though the average time of an interview ranged from an hour and a half to two hours, college students did it usually in an hour, partly because they were so quick and precise in their answers, having less to remember and more rapid mental reflexes. Older people might take as much as three hours while they worked their way along slowly. Those with multiple marriages quite naturally took more time. The order of the 350 questions was different for females than for males, and there were other variations. One must remember, too, that the questions, all 350 of them, had to be memorized.

To the millions of people who read about the interview, I am sure the one question in the minds of most was "How do you know people are telling you the truth?" I am equally confident that those who hated the whole idea of the research, or were skeptical of it for other reasons, would never believe anything Kinsey or I or anyone else might say in answer to that question. Yet the answer is a simple one. There are only three possible ways of not telling the truth: by denying or covering up, by exaggerating, or by remembering incorrectly. Exaggeration was almost impossible with the system we used for asking questions rapidly and in detail. People who later told us they had tried deliberately to exaggerate reported little success. Not remembering accurately could be dealt with statistically; the errors one person might make were offset by errors another one made in the opposite direction.

Covering up, however, was the most serious problem, since there were so many taboo items in most people's histories. But there were numerous cross-checks, so an answer at one point actually gave us a clue to an answer elsewhere. We took histories of husbands and wives and could cross-check certain parts of their backgrounds. We made some retakes after a minimum interval of two years, and an average interval of four years, to see how well people could reproduce the same material. In most cases, the cover-up factor was very slight, although some leeway had to be made for it.

We did not get everything in a subject's history, but the omissions were more qualitative than quantitative. Questions were added as the project developed. For example, it was not until 1948 that we started asking about extramarital petting. We were late in getting to this primarily because Kinsey was still a little naïve on the subject and because he resisted changing the interview questions. The later histories, then, were better and more productive. Yet there were few changes. Of the 350 questions in the basic interview, only about ten or so were changed.

It was possible to get the equivalent of twenty-five typewritten pages on one page by using our code. This was a position code, devised in the conventional way by first figuring out what kind of data were needed, then what kind of questions would secure that kind of data, and finally grouping the questions to provide a sequential sense in going through them. The groups of questions were organized in blocks, each block as small as possible. The code signs had to be of a kind that could be inserted quickly, and the system Kinsey worked out was extremely practical. A check mark appeared on the sheet in different places, with a different meaning in each place. One check mark, for instance, would mean "yes" in answer to a question, and might appear in several different positions.

The recording of a history was a sensitive process because we were taking down not only the answer but also the tonal inflection. The answer might be "YES " "Yes!" or simply "Yes," or perhaps a very hesitant "Ye-e-e-s." These answers would be recorded four different ways. In order for the various interviewers to be sure they were setting down the inflections in the same way, it was necessary sometimes for Kinsey and me (or any other combination) to record simultaneously, which also gave us an opportunity to criticize each other's techniques.

Understandably, it was an anxiety-producing situation the first time "the master" sat in while I took a history, but I got used to this, as did the others. When we observed Kinsey taking a history, we tended to be a little deferential, partly for the obvious reason and partly because he was quite defensive; he had an explanation for everything he did. We found we were able to record a history simultaneously with about 98 percent accuracy.

The longest history we ever took was done thus, conjointly, by Kinsey and me. We had heard through Dr. Dickinson of a man who had kept an accurate record of a lifetime's sexual behavior. When we got the record after a long drive to take his history, it astounded even us, who had heard everything. This man had had homosexual relations with 600 preadolescent males, heterosexual relations with 200 preadolescent females, intercourse with countless adults of both sexes, with animals of many species, and besides had employed elaborate techniques of masturbation. He had set down a family tree going back to his grandparents, and of thirty-three family members he had had sexual contacts with seventeen. His grandmother introduced him to heterosexual intercourse, and his first homosexual experience was with his father. If that sounds like *Tobacco Road* or *God's Little Acre,* I will add that he was a college graduate who held a responsible government job. We had traveled from Indiana to the Southwest to get this single extraordinary history, and felt that it had been worth every mile.

At the time we saw him, this man was sixty-three years old, quiet, soft-spoken, self-effacing—a rather unobtrusive fellow. It took us seventeen hours to get his history, which was the basis for a fair part of Chapter Five in the *Male* volume, concerning child sexuality. Because of these elaborate records, we were able to get data on the behavior of many children, as well as of our subject.

At one point in his history taking he said he was able to masturbate to ejaculation in ten seconds from a flaccid start. Kinsey and I, knowing how much longer it took everyone else, expressed our disbelief, whereupon our subject calmly demonstrated it to us. I might add, in case this story confirms the worst fears of any surviving critics, it was the only sexual demonstration among the 18,000 subjects who gave their histories.

Few interviews were anything more than routine—or seemed so, after the first few thousand—but some responses were memorable. Early in the interviewing we learned that the most embarrassing question we asked, particularly for women, was "How much do you weigh?" I remember, too, the female psychiatrist, quick and sharp in her answers, who answered when I asked how she found out about masturbation: "I invented it, and if I could have patented it, I'd have made a million dollars." Memorable, too, was the female gynecologist, an inhibited old maid, who observed, "There are two questions I never ask my patients—their age or anything about their sex lives." She told us she thought masturbation was normal unless it was excessive. When we asked her what "excessive" meant, she said, "Anything over once a month." Not surprisingly, her own masturbation occurred once a month.

3

Always, in the interviewing, we had the example of Kinsey before us, and it was inspiring, to say the least. He was never the rigid, academic college professor, but a scientist whose pragmatism and willingness, even urge, to experiment at any time gave him the flexibility to handle any kind of problem. Abandoning the early questionnaire method after he was well under way with it was a splendid early example of his flexibility, as was his invention of a new recording system.

He was inflexible about one thing, though. He was determined to get sex information from people, and he intended to get it no matter what obstacle might intervene. If he went into a house and found every room occupied, so that it seemed impossible to find a place for confidential interviewing, Kinsey would nevertheless find one. Sometimes it was a bathroom, more than once an attic. If there was no room inside, he would take a history sitting out on a lawn under a tree. Often he used his car, if nothing else was available.

Kinsey (and I, too) took histories in every room a house could boast. We interviewed in cellars, on trains, and once took a history from a waitress during the lunch hour, sitting at a table near the kitchen door and getting our information in snatches as she paused to sit with us between orders. I took the history of a leading psychiatrist in the library at Bellevue Hospital, in New York, where the doctor worked. As people came close to us in the stacks, we had to lower our voices, and when the intruders moved away we raised them again.

One of the things we most admired about Kinsey's interviewing was his master salesman's ability to persuade people to give their histories. He was acutely attuned to the verbal and facial reactions of the prospective history givers, and if he saw that he was getting a negative reaction, he was careful not to confront them. If the reaction was positive, he did not ask them to cooperate but simply assumed they were going to give their history and went on to discuss when and where it could be done.

In taking histories, he went on the broad assumption that everybody had done everything and it was only a question of remembering the details. The burden of denial was then on the subject. This is a common enough technique in salesmanship, but Kinsey's development of it was another example of his resourcefulness and ability to innovate. He had the complete self-confidence of the man who is utterly sure of himself and of what he is doing.

Martin and I, who were trained for the interviewing together, began with considerably less confidence, but we learned rapidly. For Martin, as he recalled later, interviewing meant shedding some cherished preconceptions. He found, for example, that there was no relationship between the sexy appearance of a girl and her actual sex life. I had to learn such elemental facts, too, and in time I could differentiate between the authentic and the spurious almost at a glance.

As soon as Martin had learned the code and was ready to interview, he was able to read the earlier histories that Kinsey had taken, including those of students who had been in classes with him, and whom he had heard boasting about their sexual exploits in dormitory bull sessions. Their records disclosed the truth, and Martin was astonished by the discrepancies.

I broke the identification code while we were learning, as I mentioned earlier, and the new one Kinsey devised to replace it was far more difficult. Still he was constantly watchful to see that no accidents occurred. Those outside the Institute seemed to understand that every conceivable precaution was taken, and there was no feeling on the campus that Kinsey was engaged in some kind of exposé. His personal integrity was never questioned. People trusted and believed in him, and this confidence was extended to the rest of us. His integrity was part of a total personality that can only be characterized by a phrase that is descriptive if not particularly grammatical —a scientific gentleman. He was a man who always observed the little amenities. In going through doors he deferred to people and held them open. Those who visited him—and they included everyone from celebrities to ex-prisoners—were charmed by his hospitality.

Certainly he was most considerate and understanding in getting me started on the interviewing. About two months after I came to work in Bloomington we made our first field trip together, to Purdue University. He lectured to a sociology class, and following practice, asked his audience to give him their histories. We set up appointment schedules for each of us; Kinsey was to take the females while I took the males. This distinction was made because the females required a different procedure, which I did not yet know. It never occurred to us that at any given hour we might have two males or two females scheduled, and I would be compelled to take female histories as well. When we realized it, at the last moment, we sat up almost all night before the interviews began, while Kinsey taught me how to take female histories.

Fortunately for me, the first girl whose history I took proved to be a gentle married graduate student who was not frightened or ill at ease and seemed to me an understanding person. Consequently I felt justified in explaining to her that she was to be the first female I had interviewed. She assured me that she would do her best to help, and almost patted me on the head. I have always been grateful to that girl, whose name I have long since forgotten, because she quickly gave me the confidence I needed on that nervous morning.

In April 1943 we went with Kinsey to Nicodemus, a tiny hamlet in the northwest corner of Kansas, near Hill City. It had been an exclusively black community since its founding, in 1877, and we went there to take histories of lower-level Negroes. Nicodemus could boast only two stores and three houses, so it was not difficult to get the histories of three-quarters of the township's people over fifteen.

"Not difficult," that is, given Kinsey's powerful ability to knock on a door and persuade people whom others would surely have thought unpersuadable.

We were in Nicodemus over Easter Sunday, and hoping to prove ourselves impartial, I went to services at the church of the Methodist minister who had been our contact in the community, while Kinsey and Martin attended the Baptist church. Kinsey told me later that the pastor had built the service around the theme "And wise men came from afar."

At the church I attended, the minister related the story of Jesus wrestling with the Angel of Death after his entombment, graphically describing Death in the form of the Devil, with horns and a tail ending in an arrow-shaped deadly stinger. After conquering Death, the minister told his congregation, Jesus reached down and pulled the stinger from the Devil's tail, saying, "Oh Death, where is thy sting?" Somehow, in that quiet, tiny church, among these earnest, devout people, it seemed reasonable.

It was in Nicodemus that I encountered my first real interviewing problem. He was a thirty-five-year-old man who lived in nearby Hill City, whom I met one night at a farm where he was visiting. When I had taken the histories I had come to obtain, I asked him if he would mind giving me his. He consented readily enough, but there was nowhere in the crowded little farmhouse where we could get any privacy, so I suggested we get into my car and do the job there.

We drove out a little way into the country, I stopped and turned on the dome light, then began to take his history. By this time it was near midnight, but I gave no thought to any possible difficulty until I discovered that my subject was a homosexual—the first one I had encountered since I began interviewing. We had switched seats so that he sat behind the steering wheel, leaving me free to write. Fortunately that gave me freedom in both directions, since I found myself able to fend him off with my left hand and write with the other.

In the course of taking so many sexual histories over the years, it was hardly surprising that we encountered a few sexual approaches, both male and female. The men were usually more direct about it than the women, although not always. Kinsey taught us that the best way to handle this situation was to remain completely impassive, neither making any motion forward in an interested way, nor backing off in obvious disinterest; it was the same technique that had worked so well with the Indians in Mexico. Nothing cools sexual ardor more than impassivity, he told us, and he was right. As time went on, we got fewer and fewer of these approaches as we learned to anticipate them and deftly turn them away.

At Nicodemus I had my first experience interviewing people who lived on a different level than the students with whom I had begun, and I was thankful that I had behind me the work with welfare cases in South Bend. I could see that the problems of communicating with a wide variety of people—who used widely differing sexual and non-sexual vocabularies—was much greater here than in most areas of research. Later I found that the drug addicts had their own argot, too, and we learned it along with the special languages of the prostitute, the criminal, certain homosexuals, the lower-level black man and the beatnik.

Perhaps the most difficult part of the technique for me to learn was how to control the interview. In the limited amount of training I had been given as a clinical psychologist, I was taught that "the customer is always right." This might have been good practice in therapy, I discovered, but it could be disastrous when one was attempting to extract accurate information from a subject. There were many cross-checks in the history itself that gave us information about his truthfulness, and hesitations, blushing, uneasiness and changes of topic gave us further clues to possible falsifications.

For example, we asked about a dozen questions indirectly related to a person's homosexual history before we came to the direct question: "How old were you the first time you had sexual contact with another person of your own sex?" By this time we would be fairly certain whether or not he had extensive homosexual experience. If at this point he denied an overt history of homosexuality but there were enough indicators in a positive direction to make us reasonably certain he was covering up, we learned to challenge his denials.

Then it became necessary to say, with firmness, even vehemence, and yet always with kindness, "Look, I don't give a damn what you've done, but if you don't tell me the straight of it, it's better that we stop this history right here. Now, how old were you the first time this or that happened?"

Surprisingly, in not a single case did a person refuse to continue. In all the histories we took, fewer than ten persons refused to complete one once they started. Of the few who did, most were among those interviewed in the early years of the research, when our techniques were less developed and we were less perceptive about some of the sensitive areas in the interview.

Working in the field, especially at the beginning, we had to deal not only with those whose histories we took, or hoped to take, but with the police and public authorities, who did not always understand what we were doing. Late in 1941, for example, Kinsey went to Gary, Indiana, where he secured seventy-one histories of blacks, nearly all of them females, and in the process had his first brush with the police, who were highly alarmed when they heard rumors of what he was up to in the black neighborhoods. Unable to make the patrolmen understand, Kinsey was taken to the station house, where he made his explanation to the night captain, who called the University. As soon as Kinsey's identity was established, there were no further objections.

After this encounter with uncomprehending authority, Kinsey armed himself with a letter from H. T. Briscoe, dean of the faculties at Indiana, which identified him and his work, and closed with the understatement that the letter was to be used "in the event that the nature of his research takes him into localities where the purpose of what he is doing might not be clearly understood."

Nevertheless, when he was interviewing in places where he might have trouble, Kinsey took the further precaution of getting identification from local authorities, as he did in Indianapolis soon after I joined him, when we began to take histories in the black community. In time the staff was fully supplied with credentials, including a letter from the National Research Council, signed by Detlev W. Bronk, its chairman; one from President Wells; one from William H. Remy, president of the Indianapolis Board of Public Safety; the one from Briscoe already mentioned; and one from Ross G. Harrison, also of the National Research Council.

Once I had plunged into the interviewing, I found it endlessly fascinating, as people themselves are fascinating. A thousand incidents return easily whenever I recall those days. I remember, for instance, taking the history of an Armenian scientist who spoke broken English, so that I had some trouble understanding him.

"How old were you the first time you ever ejaculated?" I asked him at one point.

"Fourteen," he answered.

"How?" I asked.

"With a horse," I thought I heard him say.

My mind went into high gear. This subject was telling me voluntarily about animal intercourse, and my instinct was to jump far ahead in the questioning and pursue the subject.

"How often were you having intercourse with animals at fourteen?" I inquired.

He appeared confused and taken aback, regarding me amazedly.

"Well, yes," he said, "it is true I had intercourse with a pony at fourteen."

Later in the interview it developed that what he had said was "whores," not "horse." He thought I was a genius to have known somehow that he had had intercourse with animals.

Interviewing women at the executive level, we found them to be extremely matter-of-fact about sex, treating it more or less as just another commodity. They were easy to interview, and there was a little less emotional content in their response than with a comparable group of housewives.

As types, those who took the most romantic view of sex were, understandably, people who were most religious—clergymen and their wives especially. Those who were bubbling over to tell us everything they could were usually homosexuals, particularly when they discovered by our use of homosexual argot that we knew all about the kind of lives they led. They would almost visibly expand with relief and eagerness to talk.

Since female prostitutes were reticent when we touched on their private lives, we began at once with questions about their business, and although it has long been the conventional wisdom that prostitutes are inveterate liars, they did not lie to us when they understood we knew all about them and could use their language. They trusted us from that point on. College students were also very open, the men slightly more so. Perhaps the most common thing people told us in interviews was, "I've never told anyone this before."

When we took a history we would record, at the end, our own

description of the subject—fat or lean, introverted or outgoing, difficult or easy to talk to, poorly dressed, or whatever. Only infrequently
was it derogatory. Martin always remarked about skin, which seemed
to fascinate him. Though we included an assessment of intelligence,
we never used any of this material in our final work because it was
not standardized. I tried to get Kinsey to do so, without success.
Apparently he considered it no more than a catharsis for the interviewer, who had to control his reactions so completely during the
interview itself. It is regrettable that Kinsey was so stubborn on this
point because the material could have been correlated with the
interview scientifically and possibly proved valuable.

At least these descriptions and evaluations demonstrated that the
long succession of people who passed before us were not faceless, by
any means. They were individuals, and Kinsey wanted to record that
much, even though he refused to standardize the data. It was, however, difficult to remember people unless they were outstanding in
some way. Early in the research I went to a cocktail party in New
York with Kinsey, and a dozen or so psychiatrists were among the
guests, accompanied by their wives or mistresses, as the case might
be. We resolved to obtain the sexual histories of everyone there. I was
only thirty years old at the time, and viewed the prospect with some
anxiety, since I was a little overawed by the company.

Spotting a pretty young girl in her twenties, I concluded that it
would be easier for me to ask for her history than to confront one of
the older and more formidable psychiatrists. Employing everything
Kinsey had taught me, I appealed for her cooperation, citing the
scientific approach, the anonymity and the need for the information
we were collecting. Everyone at the party was going to help us, I told
her.

She listened attentively to everything I said, and when I paused
she smiled sweetly and remarked, "But, Mr. Pomeroy, it's been less
than two weeks since you took my history."

Making a rapid recovery, I assured her, "Well, you see, there's the
proof—we not only forget the histories after we record them, but we
forget the people, too." I hoped she found this reassuring, if not
flattering.

Since we never knew what we would get in an interview, it was
necessary to ask all the questions, even when some of them did not

seem applicable to the subject. Interviewing an upper-upper-level woman with an advanced degree, for example, we would nevertheless ask her, "Have you ever been paid for intercourse?" and sometimes the answers to this question were surprising. A Chicago social worker of whom I asked this question answered, "Yes," and gave me a long history of prostitution before she got her job. She had had no intention of giving us this information until we asked the question. Through the questioning, people often stumbled into things they did not mean to tell us.

The interviews were numbered at the time they were taken, and then renumbered in Bloomington when they were filed. Gebhard was once taking histories in a famous music school where we knew there were a great many homosexuals. As one subject sat down, he saw Paul write "69" on the sheet, and looked up at him in amazement, thinking his sexual behavior had been categorized before he had even begun to talk.

While we encountered relatively few difficulties with the interviewing itself, there were endless problems on the road, as one might imagine from the constant traveling we did from one end of the country to the other. It tried our constitutions as much as it did our endurance. Still vivid in my mind is a trip to Miami with Kinsey and Gebhard, during which Prok went through one of his periodic obsessions with a certain kind of food. This time his passion was tropical fruits, and as he did when he was in this frame of mind, he saturated himself with it. We joined him on this fruit binge, and as a result I got a severe case of diarrhea.

Our suite at the hotel consisted of two bedrooms with a connecting bath. One morning I was taking histories in one of these rooms, while Paul worked in the other. About noon, having finished with his morning appointments, Paul speculated whether I was through or not, and whether he should wait for me to go to lunch. To see how far along I was, he tiptoed into the connecting hall and put his ear to the keyhole of my room; he would be able to tell from the questions I was asking how near I was to the end of the interview.

I was taking the history of a married woman who had been living a difficult, painful sex life which she was trying to tell me about as best she could. Suddenly I felt a wave of diarrhea sweeping over me. Much as I hated to interrupt, I knew I must reach the bathroom with the greatest possible speed, and, with a muttered excuse, I rose and almost ran to the door, pulling it open and exposing Paul in the process of straightening up. When I returned, I tried to explain to the lady what had happened, but I'm sure she must have thought he was listening to her answers, not my questions.

In Miami we started work at 9 A.M. and did not finish until 11 or 11:30 at night. Then, for relaxation, Paul and I hurried over to a nearby miniature golf course and got in a round before it closed at midnight, while Kinsey watched gloomily. Philip Wylie, the writer, whom we had met earlier, had another plan to help us relax. He invited us to come deep-sea fishing with him, to the very spots he had written about in his memorable Des and Crunch stories in the *Saturday Evening Post*. But Prok turned him down, to our disappointment. He had no interest in fishing, for one thing, and more important, as far as he was concerned, fishing had nothing to do with the project and he grudged the hours that would be spent on the ocean away from it.

Kinsey improved his own time in Miami by giving a Sunday morning sermon at the Unitarian Church, with the understanding that afterward the minister would make an appeal for histories. This clergyman gave Kinsey one of the most unusual introductions he was ever fortunate enough to have. "This morning we are going to hear a scientist who will speak about an important subject we don't talk much about," he said. "We *should* talk about it. I don't talk much about it myself, but I should. And I will. The subject is sex, sex, sex. Dr. Kinsey." We got histories from more than two hundred churchgoers.

The interviewing trips were a grand tour through America. From conventional Miami or Philadelphia, we might be plunged into the life of minuscule communities like Nicodemus, Kansas. Suburban matrons would be followed by prostitutes in prisons, highly placed executives by underworld characters. Often, in our explorations, we would plunge into a subculture that was unknown to people not only in the city where it existed, but to 90 percent of the public in general. I am thinking especially of the world of homosexual prostitution in the Times Square area of New York.

As early as 1942 Kinsey had heard something of this world from inmates of the Indiana State Penal Farm, and decided to explore it.

He came to Times Square with no contacts whatever, and hung around the bars on Eighth Avenue that he recognized as gay. Observing for hours at a time on different occasions, he noticed a man who also seemed to be constantly hanging around. Going over to him, he said, "I am Dr. Kinsey, from Indiana University, and I'm making a study of sex behavior. Can I buy you a drink?"

That the man accepted is a testimonial to Kinsey's personality and the persuasion he could put into the simplest statement. I suppose, too, that such an invitation coming from someone who looked like the squarest of the square to a Times Square denizen had the ring of authenticity. No one would be likely to make it up. Still, the man was skeptical until he was having his drink and listening to Kinsey, who had turned on the full power of his persuasion. It was impossible, one must believe, to doubt this clear-eyed, earnest, friendly man from the Midwest. In the end, the pickup agreed to give his history, which proved to be filled with drugs, prostitution and prison terms. From then on, he became a valued contact and persuaded other male prostitutes to cooperate.

This man's rooming house, which was full of others engaged in the same kind of work, was a gold mine for Kinsey, who had no such histories up to that point. The word got around in the Times Square underground and soon Kinsey was as well known in the area as its habitués. Later, taking histories at the Astor Hotel on a trip during which I accompanied him, we finished one day's work just before midnight and walked out on Broadway looking for a place to have a snack before we went to bed. Not far from the hotel, a towering Negro male prostitute came running after us, having recognized Kinsey.

"Hey, ain't you the sex doctor?" he demanded to know. Kinsey admitted it. "Then why ain't you come around to get my history?" Prok made some kind of affable excuse and told him to call for an appointment, but the man was adamant. He wanted to give his history, and he wanted to give it that night. There was nothing for it. We took him back to the Astor for the history taking, and when the hotel people in the lobby—particularly the house detectives, who had watched us walk out a little before—saw us return they looked skeptical, although the entire staff had been briefed about what we were doing.

We had come to the Astor in the first place because we had been ejected from our previous interviewing place, the Lincoln Hotel. There, too, the manager and his staff had known what we were doing, but apparently the parade of prostitutes, drug addicts and other members of the Times Square underworld through the lobby and in the elevators unsettled them. They told us we would have to leave. We remonstrated that we were doing nothing illegal or immoral. The manager was adamant. "Nobody's going to undress in our hotel rooms," he said. We protested that this was not what we were doing. "Yes, but you're undressing their minds," he insisted. We had to go.

This incident occurred during the war, when hotel space in the Times Square area or anywhere else was hard to find. Evicted from the Lincoln and unable to find another place, we went to the Salvation Army and explained our predicament. They let us use their quarters on West Forty-eighth Street, and when we told them there would be some rough characters coming and going, they reminded us gently, "The Army rejects no one." Nor did they reject us, while we were between hotels. We had contacts with the Army in many different cities, and our respect for this organization increased after every encounter.

On subsequent New York trips we spent many hours in gay bars, watching the customers, observing how they made contacts. We never pretended we were anything we were not. We told them who we were and what our interests were. Some assumed we were there to make homosexual contacts, but persistent refusals, coupled with our obvious interest in other people's lives, produced a good many histories.

Everywhere we went there were friends in increasing numbers to help us. Dr. Carney Landis, chief psychologist at the New York State Psychiatric Institute, who had published widely in the field of sex behavior, became interested in our research and was helpful in securing histories from his staff. We set about getting them, but following our usual procedure of beginning with the lecture, we were handicapped in this instance because several of the staff could not be present to hear Kinsey talk. Consequently there were several prospective subjects who did not know who we were or what we were doing.

In these cases Landis was a great help. He would call up one of them and say, "Hello, Joe, this is Carney. I have in my office a Dr. Kinsey [or Pomeroy] who is doing some research. Would you have a couple of hours to give him?" Then we could walk into Joe's office and tell him what the research was about. The reaction was usually surprise at first, and occasionally some reluctance, but since they had already agreed to see us we lost no subjects.

While we had much professional help of this kind, there was often a problem, understandably, with other professional people, particularly psychiatrists, some of whom found it hard to accept what we were doing. The outstanding example of this was the Menninger Clinic. In 1943 Kinsey was invited to speak there, and the letter indicated that they had heard of our research and wanted to know more about it. Prok was quite willing to lecture to this or any other professional audience, because close behind Kinsey the researcher came Kinsey the teacher. At the time we had decided that we needed a good many more histories of psychiatrists, so we resolved to combine the lecture with history taking, as we usually did, but Kinsey accepted without telling his hosts about his plan, fearing that they might put him off.

The lecture was held in the large board room of the Clinic. To our surprise, there were more than thirty psychiatrists sitting around the large board room table. Plainly this was not intended on their part to be a simple lecture about the research. Later we learned that at least some members of the Clinic were opposed to everything they had heard about the research, and they had set a trap for Kinsey, confronting him with an entire board of professional inquisitors whose intention was to show him up. The questions were biting, snide and hypercritical, and there was little warmth in the room.

But that was exactly the kind of arena where Kinsey excelled. He fielded every question deftly, often even counterattacking. By the end of the session, respect if nothing else had been achieved. As the meeting came to an end, Kinsey said, "Just a moment, gentlemen. We are here to get your histories, and of course I expect all of you to contribute." They were set back a little by this announcement, but they had no rebuttal. As scientists they felt compelled to cooperate. We spent ten days there collecting histories, and went away with a 100-percent sample.

Although I shall have considerably more to say later about sampling techniques, I might note right here that in the early stages of the research Kinsey was really quite lax about them. Such a wide world of people with sex histories stretched before him that he was like a boy in a candy store. It was only gradually that he developed more rigid criteria, particularly his 100-percent sampling. All of us on the staff attempted to increase the pressure to make his sampling more rigid, and we had some effect on him, but the techniques were still a long way from being completely satisfactory in those early years. If the President of the United States had offered to give his history, Kinsey would not have hesitated to take it, even though it might be completely unrepresentative of a total group.

After an appearance in the University of California field house, we did what I consider our outstanding piece of sampling. Kinsey had asked for people in the audience who could provide him with total groups, and he was so besieged by offers that he was finally able to select as many as seventeen different groups on the campus—fraternities, sororities, classrooms, Sunday school classes, dormitories. He got 100 percent from each one.

What I remember most, I think, from thousands of hours of interviewing, is the driving, driving, driving under the lash of Kinsey's determination to get more and more histories. On one field trip to Chicago we were taking histories of schoolchildren and faculty in a private school during the day, and in the evening we took homosexual histories from the Near North Side. Because of the hours the homosexuals kept, we often worked late into the night, but the next morning we had to start in early with the school histories. Kinsey always wanted to take "just one more," although I was ready to quit by midnight.

In this homosexual community one evening, Kinsey encountered a sailor from the Great Lakes Naval Training Station, and after a brief conversation, decided it was imperative to get his history. We took him back to our hotel room, which we shared. There was no place for me to stay while Kinsey took the history, so we decided to do it conjointly. Kinsey did the interviewing, while I recorded simultaneously.

It was a long and complicated history. At 4 A.M. we were still at it, and by this time Kinsey for once was completely exhausted. There was a long pause in the questioning and I looked up to see that he had fallen asleep in the middle of a query. I went on with the questioning until Kinsey could rouse himself and take over once more. The sailor was startled at first, but he smiled and indicated he understood.

Kinsey, in fact, once fell asleep while he was lecturing at the University after a strenuous night of interviewing. I was often just as exhausted, but like Kinsey I kept going through sheer willpower. Like him, too, I could see the goal shining clearly before us in the distance—not so much the remote figure of 100,000 histories, but the opportunity to correlate everything we were taking down and produce a book which would make a truly significant contribution to sex research. By the time I had been with Kinsey a year or two, we were well along the road toward that goal.

CHAPTER

VIII

ABOUT HISTORIES

Writing to a man in Chicago who had given him a history, Kinsey once philosophized: "I wonder why folk talk to us sometimes, and then I conclude that it is because they all realize that the world can be a more comfortable place for everybody if we get at the bottom of these things."

The realization was Kinsey's, not the "folk" who gave us interviews, but he somehow managed to convey this idea to nearly everyone he asked for a history. Moreover, he gave them a sense that what they were doing was important, and that all histories were equally valuable to him. He would take time to explain carefully to an old-maid biology teacher in a small Indiana town that the importance of a history could not be measured by the amount of experience in it. He had so few histories of older unmarried persons, he went on, that she would be doing something of real value by talking to him.

He was not in the least disturbed by doubters, secure in his confidence that he could convince anyone if he was only given the opportunity. The key to his argument was the objectivity of his approach, of the history itself, and the uses to which it would be put.

But there were those who attacked him on that score, and one of the chief complaints was that he compiled too large a proportion of homosexual histories. There was some truth in this, and I shall discuss it later, but there was also truth in Kinsey's defense—and he was inclined to be quite defensive on the point. Certainly it was true, as

138

he argued, that a great deal could be learned about heterosexual behavior from studying homosexuals, and it was equally true that the literature on homosexuality was nearly nonexistent when he began his work. He was speaking the truth, too, when he told a doubting doctor in New Wilmington, Pennsylvania, whom he was trying to persuade to give a history:

We are not particularly interested in any sexual aspect of human sex behavior. We are interested in the entire story. The homosexual is a very much larger portion of human sexual behavior than most people realize, and consequently, we have an abundance of data on it, but a proportionately large or larger amount of material on other aspects of human behavior.

Kinsey was aware of the difficulty of unearthing homosexual experience from a history and he considered it probable that what he recorded was not the whole story—"the reality," as he was fond of saying. But that was equally true of many kinds of sexual behavior considered socially taboo, and while the problem was a fact of life to be accepted, he did not consider it an invalidation of his data, by any means.

Critics often speculated about how much cover-up took place when people gave their histories. Kinsey, aware of this danger, not only made retakes, but employed other statistical means to measure what he called "inadequacies," and the results were incorporated in the final presentation.

The danger of inadequacies was not so great in the case of the homosexual histories. These people usually poured out their lives to us with a minimum of cover-up, and because society had made them feel like such special cases, they often took a greater interest in remembering or recording their experiences. They came from every part of the country, and from every social level.

In a city like New York or Chicago, where these histories were more available, Kinsey employed every means possible to get them. He did not like to pay anyone for a history because he thought it put the whole transaction on too mercenary a basis, but he was more than willing to show appreciation by entertaining, with dinner, drinks, or tickets to a concert, someone who had been especially helpful. Those who went out of their way and took considerable time to introduce him to groups where he could get histories, and then helped him make the appointments, Kinsey paid generously. In his practical way, he was not above reminding a male homosexual prostitute contact that he could earn more by working for the project for a few weeks than he could at his regular job.

It was part of Kinsey's persuasive technique to point out that he had no prejudices about behavior and was not interested in changing anyone's way of life. He wrote to his most valuable New York homosexual contact:

You should understand that we are concerned with a scientific survey and are in no way concerned with modifying human behavior. Others may use our data in their own peculiar ways, as it may serve their religious, social, or romantic theories; but we cannot in any way be concerned with these ends. To do so would disqualify us as scientists and involve us in all of the conflicting arguments of priests and libertines, individualists and busybodying reformers. . . . If you think that objective exploration, an accumulation of scientific data on human sex behavior, is a worthwhile project, you can help a lot in introducing us to sources of data. If you know what the world should be told and persuaded to do about the homosexual, or any other sort of sex behavior, before the scientific data are collected and objectively analyzed, you cannot have much use for our project.

One of the most convincing arguments Kinsey had to offer potential subjects, besides the objective nature of the project, was the protection he guaranteed. Not only would the individual histories be safeguarded, but he promised never to publish a summary of one for a particular college, penal institution, or social group.

Actually, the legal premises on which our history taking rested still remain in doubt because they were never tested in court. The legal status of the study and of the researcher were alike doubtful, and in a country where more than 90 percent of the men and 80 percent of the women could theoretically be sent to prison for what they had done sexually, none of us felt completely confident about his own status. Legally, we considered the interview as in the nature of a privileged communication, and so in the same category as communication between lawyers and clients, doctors and patients, clergymen and parishioners. (The extension of this doctrine to media reporters is even now a matter undecided in most states, and awaits further clarification from the courts.) We were assured by several lawyers that our position could be upheld in court, and there is no question that Kinsey would have gone to any lengths to prevent disclosure, as he vowed. We were prepared to destroy the records and throw ourselves on the mercy of the court.

The only kind of legal testing we were confronted with was the attempt by the United States Customs Bureau to prevent us from receiving several shipments of erotic books, pictures and objects sent to us from abroad. Customs seized these materials and it took us seven years and many thousands of dollars in legal fees to win the battle. But the decision in this case was unequivocally in favor of the right of scientists to have access to such material for study and analysis. Our struggle with the government underlines the fact that there are few, if any, other areas in the behavioral sciences where greater risks and greater care are necessary in scientific exploration than that of research into human sexual behavior.

The legal doubts, however, were our concern. I suppose they rarely occurred to potential interviewees, whose histories continued to proliferate in a bewildering number of places as the project moved forward. To provide only one example of their infinite variety, consider the number of opportunities Kinsey had waiting for him in early 1947, a year before the *Male* volume was published.

He was getting a good many histories from prisons and hoped to expand his work in that area, having been offered cooperation from every kind of institution in the country. Available for interviews was a colony of one hundred castrates, whose histories he considered of fundamental importance to science and social thinking. He had eighteen large manufacturing plants in Chicago willing to provide access on company time to their employees. Exploration of the Times Square underworld had begun. Colleges of such distinction as Sarah Lawrence and Vassar were prepared to open their doors to him. The Divinity School at Yale had agreed to his coming. The Salvation Army Settlement House in the stockyards area of Chicago was ready to help with a thousand histories.

"And so it goes without end," Kinsey wrote plaintively to Glenn Ramsey, trying to persuade him to come on the staff and provide the "hands" he so badly needed to follow up these opportunities. "Nine years of our time is gone," he lamented, "and if we are going to complete this in another twenty years, we will have to get more hands into it soon."

I remember going with Kinsey to New York at the end of August 1943 for a conference on patterns and problems of primate sex behavior, sponsored by our own sponsor, the Committee for Research in Problems of Sex. Yerkes had arranged it, and we found our old friends there—men like Corner, Lashley, Frank Beach, Carl Hartman and Carney Landis—along with some new ones. Kinsey believed later that it was one of the most profitable trips he had ever made, with material influence on his research. Afterward, Kinsey stayed on with Martin and me and took histories from scientists nearby, often through leads supplied by people at the conference. He was welcomed by the psychiatrists at the New York State Psychiatric Institute, for example, and by the staff of the Psychiatric Hospital at Bellevue. He got histories from a large part of the State Institute staff and was promised the remainder when he returned. A similar harvest was reaped at Bellevue, where the chief psychiatrist also promised him histories from any of the patients, including a number of special groups which would provide experimental material to help in the solution of more general problems.

On another trip to New York, Kinsey got the histories of thirty women members of the International Ladies' Garment Workers' Union, with the help of its educational director, Mark Starr. Conscious, as he had been for some time, of how useful his history taking could be, beyond the published results, Kinsey observed to Starr:

We very much need to understand more about the people who are in your group. Our brief sampling suggests that we may have something to contribute to your thinking if we can get an adequate sample. Many of your women have had desperately hard lives with worthless husbands and disrupted marriages, as you probably know. Any further insight into such situations should probably help.

Earlier, Kinsey had perceived how useful his studies would be to the burgeoning specialty of marriage counseling. In 1944, after exploring the work of Dr. Emily Mudd in Philadelphia, Kinsey saw how his research could be made available to the general population by the writers of marriage manuals, by the marriage counselors themselves and through the abundance of less formal advice available from a variety of other sources. While he correctly foresaw a great development in marriage counseling within the next few years, Kinsey warned Dr. Mudd that it might "very well miss the mark unless someone takes time to evaluate the extent to which this advice actually affects the lives of the individuals who are advised."

Kinsey was particularly hopeful that what he was doing would be useful to the institutions he visited. He had been singularly adept from the beginning at getting histories from inmates, and what he had learned from them profoundly impressed him with a sense of injustice. Many people in prison should not be there, he was convinced, and he was stirred often by the pitifully inadequate attempts at rehabilitation, and even worse, by the lack of understanding on the part of some institution officials.

An insight into these activities and his feelings about them is conveyed by a letter he wrote to Miss Emily F. Morrison, head of the Sleighton Farm School for Girls, in Darling, Pennsylvania, trying to persuade her to let him come and take histories there. Near the end of a long description of his work, he says:

Our institutional experience is extensive. The institutional cases are of interest, both because they give us insight into the sort of person who gets into an institution, and because of the special problems raised by institutionalization. The most valuable part of our institutional study is the many thousands of histories we have of persons who never got into an institution. This makes it possible to analyze the particular factors which are involved in the institutional cases. This comparison has even more abundantly emphasized the fact that the institutional cases are not fundamentally different from the norms from their portion of the population.

I worked for four years in one of our penal institutions for men in the state. I have nearly one hundred per cent of the histories of the women who have gone through our Women's Prison at Indianapolis during the past three years. . . . In no case is the history of the individual inmate disclosed to the administration or to any other person, but it is possible for us to provide summaries of the population as a whole, and to provide information on particular aspects of the sexual picture which has helped them at the Women's Prison and at several of the other places we have worked. We have been in the Feeble Minded Institution at Coldwater, Michigan. We have the histories of one hundred per cent of the boys and girls who go through the Bureau of Juvenile Research at Columbus, Ohio. The committee studying the Court for Wayward Minors in New York City has asked us to take charge of the portion of the study dealing with sex cases.

The uses of the institutional histories in improving the practices of penology were limited while Kinsey was alive, but after his death, in the publication by the Institute of the book on sex offenders, it bore more fruit.

While it was not difficult in most cases for Kinsey to get histories from prisons, other kinds of institutions occasionally gave him trouble, especially colleges and universities, where the religious and scientific biases of administrators or faculty could operate more freely against him than they did at his Indiana base. One of the few outright rebuffs he ever experienced in getting histories came from McGill University, in Montreal, where he had been invited by Dr. E. Ewen Cameron, head of the Department of Psychiatry, to come and lecture on "Sexual Customs." Kinsey agreed, with his usual stipulation that he have an opportunity to get histories from his audience.

In the negotiations over his appearance, it was suggested delicately to him that the Montreal community was probably "much more conservative" (i.e., Catholic) than many of the other places where he had taken histories after a lecture, and so matters would have to be arranged more carefully. The department hoped he would want histories only from married people who were not undergraduates, and that recruitment would be on a voluntary basis.

But then a new difficulty arose. Following his practice, Kinsey told Dr. Cameron that he would not read from a prepared paper and so could not provide anything for publication, and he insisted that the press be excluded, which had also been his policy. It was August 1947, not long before the publication of his first report, the *Male* volume (January 1948), and Kinsey was anxious that his research not be misrepresented by premature or unbalanced accounts. He volunteered, however, to meet the press after the lecture and give them something without reporting any of his specific findings.

Whether or not it was a matter of the history taking, as one suspects, Kinsey's stand on the question of publication and publicity gave Dr. Cameron a way out. He told Kinsey that the chief purpose of the department's lecture series was public education, and it was essential to disseminate the information through radio and a considerable range of discussion groups. The invitation was gracefully rescinded. No doubt Prok regretted not getting a collection of Montreal histories, but he could not feel badly about avoiding another invitation to speak.

At a dinner one night, someone asked Kinsey, "Are there some histories that are harder to take than others?"

"No, there's no difference," he told the inquirer.

I was astonished to hear him say so, knowing it was not true.

"I think I agree with you, Prok," I said, trying to be diplomatic, "but wouldn't you agree with me that some are easier?"

And he did agree when I put the proposition that way, because for him nothing was hard, or harder, to do. Everything could be overcome. It was only that some things were easier.

How easy it was for him he demonstrated one evening when the wife of a friend he was visiting told him her housekeeper didn't approve of his work and could not understand why anyone would give him a history. Kinsey's eyes sparkled; he regarded it as a challenge.

The housekeeper was called in—a sweet, distinguished-looking, gray-haired old lady—and Kinsey was introduced. He began to talk with her easily, in his familiar manner, and soon was asking her what she loved best in the world. That was easy, she said. It was the young people around her—the family's children, her own relatives, her young friends. "Well, then," Kinsey said, "now that you know the real purpose of my work is to help young people, so that they feel more comfortable and are able to lead happier lives, would you deny me a history?"

The old lady capitulated gracefully. Kinsey's charm, warmth, logic and keen insight into her, even in so brief a time, had won her over.

As for myself, I found it less difficult to take histories of people in my own peer group, particularly at the beginning when I interviewed a good many students who were not much younger than I. Kinsey agreed with me that students were the easiest. Without being patronizing in the least, he regarded them as highly conformist. I often wonder what he would think about today's generation of students, so unlike those of the thirties and forties. My guess is that he would be appalled (to use one of his favorite words) by some of their practices and attitudes—although not the sexual ones—but he would conclude that more information about them was *"desperately"* needed.

I have every confidence that he would get their histories as easily, as persuasively if need be, as he got their fathers'.

CHAPTER

IX

TRAVELING WITH KINSEY

Our search for histories led us in every direction. Kinsey was adroit not only at the business of getting them but at spreading the gospel of the project in places where it would do the most good. Everywhere he was helped immeasurably by his extraordinary ability to speak to any kind of group, large or small, on short notice and under all kinds of conditions.

Once in Chicago he was invited by a social worker to come to her organization and talk about "Sex and Young Children," a subject Kinsey had never spoken on before. He agreed, thinking he would be sitting around a table, talking informally to the lady and her staff colleagues. Instead his hostess led him through a door and he found himself in a small auditorium, where two hundred people were waiting expectantly to hear him. Prok was not in the least dismayed. After the brief introduction, he rose and delivered his usual perfectly organized speech.

Aside from his natural talent, he could perform such feats, first, because he was so saturated with his subject and, second, because long years of teaching had given him the ability instantly to organize subject matter and develop points.

I think the most impressive exhibition of his speechmaking ability I ever saw, one that was memorable to everyone present as well, occurred at the University of California, on the Berkeley campus.

The announcement that he was coming generated tremendous interest, and when the university realized it, the meeting was switched from the auditorium to the field house. There gathered to hear him a crowd that was larger than any the building had ever held, even at the height of the basketball season.

Before Kinsey began the lecture, there was some uneasiness in the huge audience, no doubt inspired by the subject. There was much shuffling of feet and nervous laughter. But then Kinsey began to speak in his usual direct way, not beginning with a joke or an informal remark, as nearly all speakers do, but plunging right into his subject. When he began to talk about sexual outlets, citing cases of people who had them only once a week or once a month, but remarking that there were also those who had seven or more a week, some student in the audience emitted a long, low whistle, and for a moment it seemed that the spell he had put on them would be broken. Kinsey never paused.

"And then there are some," he went on smoothly, "whose outlet is as low as that of the man who just whistled." The audience reaction was tumultuous. There was no further trouble. Kinsey continued for more than an hour and the students sat in rapt silence, not missing a word.

A somewhat similar incident occurred at Rutgers in 1952, with sinister overtones and a display of considerable courage on Kinsey's part. The students had invited him to lecture there, but a university official had written to him beforehand, warning that Catholic students had been encouraged to break up the lecture by causing some kind of disruption.

Kinsey accepted the challenge. Before he appeared that night the gymnasium was filled to capacity, and part of the audience appeared to be strangely restless, stomping their feet and talking loudly. Then Kinsey came on the stage, and as he began to speak there was an audible swelling of the disturbance.

"The Institute staff and I have found out some things about sexual relations which I think will help you," Kinsey told them, loudly and firmly. "If there is anyone who doesn't want to hear it, let him walk out now."

He paused, and a ripple of laughter spread through the auditorium, changing to admiring applause. His courage and forthrightness had been recognized. Needless to say, he gave his usual splendid speech, and no one left the hall.

Occasionally, as we drove across the face of America in search of histories, Kinsey would give me one of his lectures about the inadequate idea Easterners had of the nation's geography. Although he was an Easterner himself by birth and education, he had lived long enough in Bloomington to acquire the Middle Western disdain for anything east of the Appalachians. He often proclaimed the truism that New Yorkers were not aware there was anything west of the Hudson River, and this conviction was frequently reinforced by events.

Once the noted Philadelphia psychiatrist O. Spurgeon English flew to Indianapolis for a visit at the Institute. As we drove him from the airport to Bloomington, he remarked that since he had come this far west he might as well visit his friends at the Menninger Clinic.

Kinsey regarded him suspiciously. "That's quite a way," he said.

"But isn't Kansas the next state over?" Dr. English inquired in some surprise.

With considerable enjoyment, Kinsey told him that he was as far from Topeka as he was from Philadelphia.

On another day, Prok and I went to the ticket counter in Pennsylvania Station, New York, to buy rail tickets back to Indiana. The girl behind the counter remarked brightly, "I have a girl friend out in that part of the country. Maybe you know her."

Kinsey sighed. He seemed to know what was coming. "Where does she live?" he asked.

"Idaho," she said.

In the early days of our traveling the going was often primitive, partly because we had so little money in the budget, but even more because Kinsey was so reluctant to spend it. I remember a cold, wintry night in New York, when Kinsey and I emerged from a late meeting to find ourselves shivering at Park Avenue and Sixty-second Street. "We'll walk two blocks over to Fifth, catch a bus to Thirty-third Street and from there we can walk to the Pennsylvania Hotel," he announced. I shivered in anticipation, but Prok stepped off briskly toward Fifth, while I watched longingly as empty taxis passed us. At Fifth, there were no buses in sight, and I had had enough.

"Look, Prok," I said, "let's take a taxi and I'll pay the difference out of my own pocket."

The difference (in those happy days of lower fares) was exactly thirty-five cents, as it turned out.

I also have a vivid memory of carrying my heavy bags on a hot day all the way from Broad Street Station in Philadelphia to the Ritz-Carlton Hotel because Kinsey refused to take a cab.

Just before the *Male* volume came out, he changed in his attitude toward spending, but only when he realized at last that penuriousness was detrimental to the research because it took time. If he could save ten minutes for research by taking a cab, he would take one. At that, he was not really convinced until we were interviewing in all five Philadelphia medical schools at the same time, jumping from one to the other, and that obviously could be accomplished only by using taxis.

Kinsey was a constant check grabber in spite of his caution about money—not out of excessive generosity (although he was generous in other ways), but rather because he thought it was a good way to establish rapport with people.

As we walked the streets of cities and ate in countless restaurants, the anonymity with which we began was ended by the publication of the *Male* volume, and Kinsey was recognized everywhere, even without benefit of television. He pretended to be irritated by this sudden attention, and complained that he was no longer free to observe people without being observed, but he would have been less than the very human man he was if he had not been pleased and proud to be recognized. I knew that he was, but I would never have heard it from him.

We traveled together amicably, not an easy accomplishment for such different people. However, one had to deal with him on his terms, such as his irritating insistence on total cleanliness at prescribed times. He demanded, for example, that on trips everyone must take a shower every morning. I grumbled about it for a while, because my routine was to take a shower in the evening, but I gave up and fell in with the morning habit, and retain it to this day. Gebhard was not so easy to conquer, however. He pretended compliance, but he was not above going into the bathroom, turning on the shower and letting it run for the proper time while he did something else.

This particular obsession had its roots in the time when Kinsey was traversing a good part of the United States and the Mexican wilderness in search of gall wasps, and had set up his own rigid standards for the conduct of these field trips, perhaps derived from Boy Scout training. As early as 1931 I find him writing to Ralph Voris, describing his troubles with enforcing cleanliness on field trips—not simply the morning shower, but the idea of daily ablutions itself:

You helped me establish certain traditions in our field work which I have had to fight to maintain. For instance—the daily bath, conditions permitting. You may know of the scrap I had with———and———[other graduate students] one day in West Virginia. When I discovered they had sidestepped the bath, I sent them back to their room, and like good boys they disrobed and took to the water. Well, I had a scrap with———on this Alabama trip. I reckon he missed 3 baths out of 5 days. Discipline, man! —What with our difficulties in keeping decent in field work anyway. We kept sweet enough in the subsequent argument, but he calmly insisted that he wouldn't bathe. After all due warnings, I left him in Southern Tennessee—at Columbia, in fact— the place where we gathered tiny pegoriachoides on a freezing wet day— where the old colored woman came out with a big stick for us, some years ago. He beat his way back, of course, O.K. He hasn't come around yet to promise any reformed behavior, so I'm not quite certain he goes to Mexico with us. But perhaps we can teach him some hygiene and discipline before we are done trying to make a taxonomist of him.

As a psychologist, I suppose I should be able to say with assurance why Kinsey was so insistent about morning showers, but I can only guess. Perhaps it was just his love of routine.

Showering, of course, was merely one of his idiosyncrasies. I had been on the staff only a short time before he involved me in another. He came to me one day and said he had a personal problem. Naturally I was flattered, but when he confided in me I took a different view of it. He neither smoked nor drank, he said, and had come to think this might be a handicap in relating to people whom he wanted to put at ease. He asked me to teach him how to acquire these habits, so that he would give the appearance of being an accomplished drinker and smoker. I saw that he was perfectly serious. It was simply his practice to get an expert to teach him anything he didn't know and wanted to learn. I was the elected expert.

We sat down with a pack of cigarettes, but after a few fumbling lessons I could see that it was going to be impossible. He was hopelessly inept and obviously hated the whole idea. (I had yet to learn how much he really despised tobacco.) I had to tell him he would be well advised to forget about smoking cigarettes, but to soften the blow I also told him—and it was the truth—that I thought his smoking would not materially improve his ability to relate to people, inasmuch as he already did that extraordinarily well.

I would have been better off if I had persisted, at least enough to make Kinsey a mild addict, if that had been possible. As it happens, I am an inveterate pipe smoker, and before long it was plain that my habit offended Kinsey. Whenever we were driving in the car and I felt the smoker's urge to light up, I had to roll down one of the windows, even on the coldest winter day. In the hotel rooms we shared I was obliged to open the window and keep the air clear of smoke, no matter what the temperature outside might be. Even then, Kinsey was obviously unhappy about my pipe. In those days, only cigarette smoking was allowed on aircraft, and Kinsey was fond of pointing out that this was proof that pipe smoking must be offensive to the general population. He even went so far as to suggest that I might be offending many of my interviewees by smoking.

Kinsey's feelings about pipe and cigar smoke were intense. Gebhard and I were sitting with him one day in the waiting room of the Thirtieth Street railroad station in Philadelphia, a vast, cavernous place with a ceiling several stories high. As we sat there Kinsey sniffed the air suspiciously and declared, "Someone's been smoking in here." We howled, but Kinsey only looked puzzled. He failed to see the joke.

Drinking turned out to be another matter. In the kind of work we were doing, it was extremely important to be able to drink. We were often in bars, or at cocktail parties, dinners and other social events where to refuse a drink would not only be rude, but might discourage potential history givers.

I sat down with Kinsey one day with the idea of having him sample various kinds of drinks, including my own favorite, Scotch whisky. I enjoyed this lesson more than the smoking instruction, but Prok did not share my enthusiasm. After dutifully sampling everything, he declared that he liked rum best, and as he did with everything else, he directed his scientific zeal and passion for collecting toward the potent drink. Planter's Punch was one of his favorites, but he was also partial to the Charleston Cup and the Zombie. Although he cared nothing about drinking for its own sake, or for the effects of alcohol, he became a collector of drink recipes, had an excellent bar built into his home and was able to make from it an almost professional selection. It pleased him greatly to be complimented on what he concocted there. The Charleston Cups he served at the reception following his daughter's wedding were considered by serious drinkers present to be unexcelled.

Kinsey did not drink often. If drinking was not demanded by his work, in fact, he would go for days without thinking of it, and I never saw him drunk in any circumstances, although on two or three occasions he had the traditional rosy glow. But that was all—and he was scrupulous about not drinking when he took histories.

These smoking and drinking lessons produced one more Kinsey paradox. Hating tobacco smoke, he nevertheless made sure that we always supplied cigarettes to our interviewees, making three or four brands available to them. He was always pleased when his subjects smoked, even though the fumes must have irritated him, because he knew it reduced tension and made people more easily accessible to the interview.

In food, as in drink, Kinsey had his strong likes and dislikes; one would hardly have called him a gourmet. He particularly liked ice cream. His strongest dislikes were anything he considered dry—and that included peanut butter, steak and mashed potatoes.

During a grueling auto trip from New Mexico to New Jersey, we were passing through Dodge City, Kansas, at about midnight when Kinsey observed thoughtfully that he would like to try steak once more. Perhaps he had been mistaken about it, he said, and here in the heart of cattle country, if anywhere, we could count on getting a good one. At his insistence, we found a restaurant that was still open, stopped and ordered steak.

The piece of meat the waiter brought was enormous. It was also tough. Discouraged, Prok remarked that he guessed he had been right the first time. It never occurred to him that he always ordered steak well done in his experiments with it, so quite naturally it would always be dry—the quality he disliked so much.

Eleanor Roehr, Kinsey's admirable secretary, once entertained Prok, Mac and a few other guests for dinner one night in her apartment. As a first course she served vichyssoise, which she had made herself, and Kinsey was delighted with it. "Why can't we have this at home?" he asked Mac. She could only look at him with amused eyes. Prok had always declared that he couldn't eat anything made from potatoes.

For all of his scientific nature, in his personal life he was quite ready to do what he would never think of doing in science: reject something on the basis of a single experience. Whenever this happened, as it did so often with a food he had never tried before, I would protest, "Prok, where's your sampling?" He refused to see the connection.

Unfortunately, he was quite likely to employ this unscientific kind of rejection in his relations with people as well. He was inclined to make judgments about them on the basis of one meeting or one thing they might have said.

When we were on field trips and someone in the party had an upset stomach, a not uncommon occurrence considering the hours we worked and the places we ate in, Prok's prescription was invariably the same: orange juice. He probably had these upsets less than anyone else, because his tastes in food were, by and large, quite simple, although there were a few Italian specialties he loved, especially osso bucco. He was also fond of nearly every kind of seafood, particularly oysters, clams and lobsters. Once he took a former Indiana colleague and his wife to a seafood place in New York. He was profoundly shocked when the wife, instead of ordering one of the delicacies on the menu, asked for something she could have gotten just as well in the Middle West.

Although he like fancy desserts and eating in good places, Kinsey was frugal in his daily routine. Working in his office at the Institute, he brought his lunch from home in a brown paper bag. It was usually a handful of peanuts and raisins, a sandwich of some kind, often tuna fish on whole wheat bread, and an apple or an orange. Usually he ate alone, as he worked.

On the subject of chewing gum he was adamant. He never chewed it himself and would have forbidden us to do so if we had displayed the inclination. Fortunately, none of us were gum chewers. Kinsey argued, correctly, that it would have been most inappropriate to chew gum while we were taking interviews.

As a scientist, he saw no relationship between food and sex. He did not believe in food as an aphrodisiac, and would not give any encouragement to those who sought to exploit his knowledge in that direction. To a man in North Carolina who wrote asking for help in compiling a cookbook linking food and sex, Kinsey answered with polite regret that "there is nothing in the data which we have that would be of use to you." But he could not help adding: "I am curious to know what you call 'gastronomical sophistication.' I am something of an experimenter and have delighted in foreign restaurants of many sorts, but I cannot, offhand, see that food types have a particular relationship to anything in sexual histories." Characteristically, because in matters of sex he kept an open mind, he concluded: "Perhaps, however, they do."

Of the foreign cuisines, Kinsey especially admired the Chinese. Harry Benjamin, the New York endocrinologist who was one of Kinsey's long-time friends, remembers Prok's great pleasure when Benjamin's Chinese chauffeur, Tom, arranged a special dinner for him one night in San Francisco's Chinatown, at a restaurant unknown to tourists. "I don't think Prok ever enjoyed a dinner as much as this one that the three of us shared," Benjamin said later.

It was on this same trip that Benjamin introduced Kinsey to the late Mabel Malotte, a celebrated San Francisco madam who had been his patient. She contributed her history and persuaded several of her girls to give theirs. Kinsey once had a long conversation with her and Benjamin in the doctor's hotel room, and as Benjamin recalled, "Prok's cordiality to her and his complete acceptance of Mabel as a person without the least prejudice, although at that time she was in legal difficulties, was touching. He seemed to be going out of his way to show her where he stood."

It was one of Kinsey's most endearing characteristics. He could talk with equal understanding and ease to Mabel Malotte in a San Francisco hotel room and, a few days later, to scientists in his own or some other field. In both cases he expected to get histories.

The world, in effect, was Kinsey's friend, and as he traveled in it he came to know thousands of its inhabitants. Only a few, however, knew him well.

CHAPTER

X

FRIENDS

AFTER MY ARRIVAL in Bloomington, the inner circle of the project was complete except for Gebhard, who did not join the staff until three years later. It was a tightly knit little group, as one would expect of people who spent most of their waking hours together, and although all of us had friends in the University and elsewhere, we were held together by something more than a worker's devotion to a totally absorbing job.

The "something more" was Kinsey. He was the driving force in our lives, around which everything else revolved. The project, of course, was his life and those who were closest to him were naturally involved with it. More than the rest of us, perhaps, he had friends in the University community, since he had been a part of it for nearly a quarter century, but outside the boundaries of Bloomington his best friends were scientists like himself who, in one way or another, were a part of his grand scheme.

If there were any exceptions to his friendships among the scientific community, it was the psychiatrists. He once told me that before he got into sex research he had been afraid of them. Unbelievably, considering that he was a scientist himself, he had the layman's vague belief that psychiatrists were omniscient and could even know his inner thoughts. He felt uneasy with them. Gradually he overcame the feeling, and in time had several good friends who happened to be psychiatrists. Still, he never quite succeeded in completely getting over his early fear. It explains why he was particularly sharp in his counterattacks on the psychiatrists who criticized his book. As they would have been the first to point out, it was compensation, and as they suspected correctly, he held a genuine if suppressed antagonism toward the profession.

Kinsey had a great many friends of every kind, however, and to talk about all of them here, at the length many of them deserve, would make an exceedingly long chapter indeed. A partial sampling, however, would include people like Dr. Frank Beach, then a psychologist on the Yale faculty (Kinsey had known Beach first as head of the animal behavior section of the American Museum of Natural History); Earle Marsh, a San Francisco gynecologist; Dr. Frances Shields, a New York gynecologist; Dr. Benjamin, the New York clinical endocrinologist; and Glenway Wescott, the writer.

One of the first of his particular friends to come into his life was Dr. Robert L. Dickinson, a New York gynecologist and a noted sex researcher in his own right, whose pioneer work in the field Kinsey admired. Dickinson's studies—*A Thousand Marriages* (1931) and *The Single Woman* (1934)—were based on his half century of experience in private practice and drew on the histories of more than 5,000 New York City women patients. His findings had a significant influence on later work, particularly that done by physicians, gynecologists, marriage counselors, students of fertility and similar clinical groups.

No one who knew Dickinson could easily forget him. He was a slim, wiry man who fairly radiated nervous energy. The doctor moved quickly, spoke rapidly and was inclined to be impulsive, but everyone admired his keen, probing mind. None of these characteristics diminished with age, which seemed hardly to touch him except to turn his luxuriant hair and full beard white, making him look like a thin Santa Claus.

I recall seeing him a year or two after I joined the staff, at a conference attended by marriage counselors, psychologists, psychiatrists and other therapists. This affair—held at Pennsylvania State University under the auspices of another Kinsey friend, Dr. Clifford Adams, the marriage counselor, who was in the Psychology Department—was an important one for Kinsey, because it was the largest and most impressive professional gathering he had yet talked to about his work. Still, he was only one item on a full three-day program which included a good many other papers and progress reports.

Dickinson was to talk about a massive study he had made of the physiologic effects of masturbation on the sexual organs of women, to be illustrated with slides showing shots of the vulvas of his subjects. Quite naturally, the lecture hall was jammed to the doors. Dickinson, who was then nearly eighty and looked twenty years younger, began lecturing in his usual brisk, almost headlong way, tapping the floor with his pointer in the customary manner whenever he wished the projectionist to change a slide.

Apparently, however, this unfortunate man, a university employee, had not been told what he was to project, and after he had seen a few of Dickinson's large-size vulvular studies spread across the screen he became so unnerved by the spectacle that he began to have trouble changing the slides. They appeared upside down and sideways, and whenever this happened, Dickinson would bang his pointer on the floor with increasing agitation and cry out in a strangled voice, while dancing about in sheer frustration, "No! No! Not that way!"

In the midst of the confusion, which already had the audience in convulsions, the distraught projectionist somehow picked up from the table a slide which had been left over from another lecture, and momentarily the unbelieving audience gazed upon a peaceful scene of waving wheat in Kansas. Only Dickinson could have survived such a fiasco. After order had been restored, and the slide sequence began to go forward again without incident, Dickinson went on in his excitable way as though nothing more than ordinary chaos had occurred.

Kinsey met this delightful man for the first time early in 1943, after some preliminary correspondence. "It was a rare experience to become acquainted with you," Kinsey wrote after their meeting. He was overwhelmed by Dickinson's personality and his generous offers of help. Their meeting had been an emotional one on both sides. When he learned what Kinsey was doing, tears began to flow down Dickinson's cheeks. "At last! At last!" he exclaimed. "This is what I have been hoping and praying for all these years." Kinsey assured his new friend that Dickinson's work was one of the original sources of inspiration for his own study. Dickinson, in fact, offered to give Kinsey access to all his materials, as well as the benefit of his experience and whatever other cooperation Kinsey might require. Accepting, Prok confessed that he was "capable of considerable immodesty in asking for help in pushing the research." Specifically, he said, he wanted to "come to New York to work in your laboratory or in the room adjacent to it where I may study in detail as much of your material as you want to make available to us."

The relationship between the two men strengthened as time went on, and there is no doubt that Kinsey had a strong emotional attachment to the old doctor. Dickinson was, indeed, helpful to the research in many ways, not only while he was living but even after his death, since he left his models and records to the Institute. Kinsey was on a field trip when he learned of his friend's death, and he hurried at once to New York. Added to his grief was his concern that other interested people might get to the Dickinson materials and remove some valuable items before they could be shipped to Indiana. He called his friend Tripp and asked if he would mind going to Dickinson's office and stand watch over the materials until Kinsey could get there. Tripp hurried over and found Dickinson's daughter, recently returned from China, already there. Kinsey arrived a few hours later, having taken the first plane he could find.

Dickinson's support of Kinsey and the research had been constant and admiring. After a four-day visit to Bloomington in December 1943, he wrote to Alan Gregg, of the National Research Council:

In his offices one was struck with the wisdom of his choice of associates, the hard work done and the remarkable amount accomplished in the time elapsed. . . . In the matter of practical utility, the findings already developed promise very important results in their bearing on early sex education and juvenile sex delinquency, with the elements of new data on the underprivileged, the rural populations and Kinsey's study of criminal law. . . . Whatever portions of my unpublished material Kinsey can use I have placed at his disposition, either now or at my exit. You may possibly be able to imagine the satisfaction of the senior student of one of the most difficult of all researches at the sight of this degree of precision, directness, dignity and freedom from bias or timidity.

A friend completely different, and at the opposite end of the age scale, was Vincent Nowlis, the young psychologist who was briefly a member of our staff and remained an enthusiastic supporter after he departed. Kinsey met Nowlis in 1943, soon after I came. In spite of my addition, Prok was still (and perennially) in need of the extra "hands" he found it so hard to obtain, and having heard good reports of Nowlis from mutual friends he set out to recruit him from the University of Connecticut, where Nowlis was teaching.

In Nowlis' favor was the fact that he was a Bowdoin graduate and a fellow Zete, but nevertheless Kinsey had some advance complaints, as usual, which he expressed with his characteristic bluntness on the first approach he made to the candidate:

I should tell you that your recommendations have been of the highest, on the other hand, I wish you were ten years older, and I wish that your handwriting was better. In securing histories, calculating and manipulating the records, it is imperative that everything be so accurately recorded that there shall be no chance of error; even when a history is examined many years later. I have had so many hours of headache, trying to teach some of my helpers how to write, that this is more than of minor importance to me. Nevertheless I am very anxious to meet you and talk over the possibilities.

Prok did not exaggerate his concern about handwriting, and he might have added that he was especially meticulous about the writing of numerals. New secretaries and clerical workers at the Institute were often astonished to find that on their first day Kinsey would sit down with them and patiently teach them how to make numerals in the way he insisted they be made.

Nowlis was not dismayed by Kinsey's apprehensions and the two met soon after while Prok was on a field trip to New York. By October 1943 a definite job offer was made. Kinsey wanted the new man to concentrate first on interviewing, and at the same time go through all the laboratory operations so he would understand thoroughly what was needed in going after histories. Prok was hopeful that Nowlis, with his extensive training in psychological research, would be able to help in analyzing problems and setting up new research plans.

These hopes were more or less fulfilled. Nowlis proved to be extremely useful, and we all liked this attractive young man. He fitted in quickly with the project's way of life, and it appeared that Kinsey had found exactly the man he needed. Unfortunately, the job was not what Nowlis needed. His training led him in other directions than the history taking which was the major part of his work, and was where we needed the most help. Reluctantly he looked elsewhere and in June 1946 left us to become an assistant professor at the Iowa Child Welfare Research Station, at the State University in Iowa City.

The parting was regretful on both sides. Nowlis wrote to Yerkes: "I know of no other place in the world where I could have learned so much in so little time, and found so many intimations of great things that are coming to enrich biological and social sciences and medical and applied arts."

As for Kinsey, he was really distressed to lose Nowlis, and expended a good deal of persuasiveness in the next few years trying to woo him back. After the first of these attempts, only a year after he had gone, Nowlis rejected Kinsey's tentative feeler in the most sincere and even affectionate way:

Partly with intent and design, I have been slow in getting research started here but by this time I know that I have struck a rich area of investigation and have the tools and enterprise to exploit it, with strong backing. There is also the fact that, despite the trend toward research projects which commandeer the services of many men, of which yours is a particularly bright and productive example, there is something in the very nature of scientific enterprise which demands and fosters individual initiative, which, with all its mistakes and inefficiency, becomes overwhelmingly attractive to a person of my age and potential maturity. For me, Iowa provides this more than any other institution in the country. You have made clear how the expansion of your staff and your activities will provide room for initiative. But there is still a lot of exploration which can be done more effectively close to home in a small fleet of canoes than in a battleship. A salute to you, Admiral Kinsey, from a respectful decliner.

As late as 1949, however, Kinsey was still hopeful. He had tried once more, unsuccessfully, in June 1948 to interest Nowlis in returning, and by the following February he was becoming discouraged in his futile attempts to add another psychologist to the staff. "I have gone long distances to interview possibilities," he wrote to Nowlis, making yet another attempt to persuade him to come back "and what I think about the quality of psychologists to do a job of this sort would not bear print at this present time."

Later in that letter, Kinsey disclosed the anxiety in the back of his mind, a prophetic fear that he did not have much time:

I am increasingly worried over the fate of the research if something would happen to me. If we do not build up a staff of persons who are experienced in research, there will be no one to take over when necessary. The project is too important to allow it to hang as it does now on the life of one individual. It would be very difficult to get together a staff after my passing which could take hold and carry on with anything like the same objective.

In spite of the letter's eloquent arguments, as close as Kinsey could come to a personal plea, Nowlis was not to be persuaded. But the friendship between the two men did not diminish, nor did Nowlis' interest in and support for the project. In fact, he came to Indiana for a week or two and critically reviewed the manuscript of the *Male* volume. Like everyone else, he awaited publication of the book impatiently and in October 1947 sent us a mock questionnaire which he hoped would disclose the publication date. Among the true or false reasons we were to check on why the book "is coming out this early," we found such items as, "Prok finally took unlimited time out from lecturing and history-taking," "Pomeroy decided it was about time to clear the decks for his Ph.D. work," "Biology Hall collapsed under the weight of cynipids and books and histories and punch cards and filing cabinets and reporters," and "Clyde developed writer's cramp and could draw no more figures or charts."

This was the kind of joke Kinsey appreciated. He responded in kind: "I will not return your questionnaire, for we are adding it to our collection of obscene objects. All of your statements are true, even when they are contradictory."

After the book was published, Vincent Nowlis, a psychologist and former member of our staff, was among the first to adopt it as a textbook for an academic course in Social Development. The response was immediate. One Iowa student, whose family lived in a remote rural area, proudly announced in the first class meeting that she was using a copy bought by her mother, who had already read it, although it had been published only a month.

Nowlis, who knew both men, believes that Kinsey and Masters were much alike, in the sense that they were at the very nerve centers of their research projects, and so had to be in absolute control. This impression was never stronger, he recalls, than when he was traveling with Prok and me on a research trip. It was like life on a submarine, moving in a self-contained world with a commander directing every movement, and the crew utterly dependent on him and on each other because the craft was so vulnerable. No one could afford to make a mistake.

On these trips, too, and even earlier, Nowlis was impressed with Kinsey's extraordinary ability to relate to his environment. He felt that Prok could be blindfolded, set down anywhere in the United States, and when the blindfold was removed he would be able to tell where he was by observing the flora and fauna—and then he would deliver a complete lecture on the ecology of the place.

While they were traveling, Nowlis remembers, Kinsey would often gaze out of train windows at the small towns flashing by, and in one way or another express his frustration because there was so much going on in them that he would never know about. Once, watching the crowds mill along the streets in Times Square, Kinsey exclaimed in near despair, "Look at all these people! How can we ever adequately sample them?"

A friendship somewhat more like the one with Dickinson was Kinsey's long relationship with Dr. Abraham Stone, the noted New York physician and marriage counselor, who helped pioneer birth control methods with his wife, Hannah, and later became the first president of the American Association of Marriage Counselors.

Like Dickinson, Stone was an unforgettable personality, although he was quite unlike his older contemporary. Short, with a black mustache and warm brown eyes, he had something of Dickinson's restless energy but his manner was calm and often whimsical. A friend recalls waiting for an elevator one evening with Stone after they had had dinner together and were leaving the apartment. As they waited, a woman's low, musical laugh came from a nearby room and echoed down the corridor. Stone looked up quizzically at his friend and inquired, "Is it amusement, or is it ecstasy?"

As one who had known every major sex researcher from Freud on down, Stone was impressed with Kinsey's work and enthusiastic about him. When Prok went to New York on a trip early in 1945, Stone helped him to get histories, particularly from the Sanger Clinic, the birth control dispensary which his late wife had founded with Margaret Sanger. He also took Kinsey home to have dinner with him and his daughter Gloria. In his thank you note after this excursion, Kinsey spoke warmly: "I appreciate your friendship very much.

The better I know you, the better I like you and I hope we will have a chance for repeated contacts."

Stone contributed his own history at the beginning of the friendship and proved to be continuously helpful in getting others to do so. But as the correspondence between the two shows clearly, the relationship was a warm one on a purely personal level. When they met in New York, Stone sometimes took his friend to dine at one of his favorite small restaurants. He was an habitué of a number of foreign eating places, not always of the first quality, where he was welcomed cordially by the waiters, all of whom seemed to know him, and by the managers or maître d's. The attention seemed to please him as much as the food did.

The letters between Kinsey and Stone were chiefly about matters of common professional interest—for example, Kinsey's taking the histories of 180 women who were sterility cases of a doctor they both knew. Kinsey writes about this episode:

In the course of taking the histories, it became apparent that there were some very distinctive features about these histories. Practically none of the histories represented distinctly erotic women unless the sterility was due to organic defects or difficulty on the part of the husband. These women were quite uniformly restrained and less responsive than the average of the women in our total population who have had children. Dr. H. and some of his colleagues in San Francisco are going to follow up with fluoroscopic studies of tubal spasm during coitus, and the matter is important enough to warrant an extensive investigation.

Since the taking of these histories opened up a new area for Kinsey, he was naturally anxious to get more like them. A ready source was the Sanger Clinic, but he hesitated to approach Stone on the subject because he had recently refused to lecture to the New School class that Stone was conducting at the time. So anxious was he to get the histories, however, that he handsomely offered to withdraw his refusal, an unprecedented action and one contrary to his rigid policies, if Stone would help him get sterility histories. The offer was accepted and Kinsey got nearly 200 histories at the Clinic; added to those already obtained in California, they gave him a total of more than 500 up to that point.

In 1951, when a new edition of Stone's famous *Marriage Manual* was about to appear, Kinsey went over the manuscript in considerable detail, at his friend's request, and offered some specific suggestions. Reading them, one can only marvel again at the astonishing range of Kinsey's knowledge. He attacks, for example, the long-standing tradition that castrated animals appear to be more easily fattened. Nothing in the literature substantiates this idea, he says, and cites the conference he has held recently in Bloomington of several experimental researchers on problems of sexual behavior in animals and in endocrinology. These men rejected the idea.

In the next paragraph he has switched to Japanese art of the twelfth century, and its emphasis on the clitoris. Kinsey believes Stone is wrong to say that recognition of the importance of the clitoris is of recent origin.

On the subject of the hymen, Kinsey is characteristically blunt: "I think any creator who claims that he had a purpose in creating the hymen certainly shows himself incapable of having done a good job. It would seem that it would do less damage to the reputation of the creator if we simply say that the hymen does such and such." Once more assaulting popular beliefs, he goes on to say that his research has shown that breaking the hymen is a relatively painless and simple process, and apparently without any bleeding in younger individuals, particularly preadolescent and young adolescent girls. A good part of any trouble that might occur, he believes, is due to the delay in first intercourse.

Kinsey then brings his biological weapons to bear on Stone's statement that animal species can have coitus only when the female is in heat. The popular belief that this is true, he says, rests on the fact that a few farm animals do exhibit this kind of behavior, but it is not true of anthropoids, and not strictly true of even such animals as cattle, horses and dogs. A more accurate statement, he adds, would be that in some species of mammals the female will not accept the male unless she is in heat.

Kinsey's most severe criticism of Stone's manuscript concerns the section on masturbation, which he declares is right out of the Talmud and has no scientific justification. He is surprised to find Stone providing any support for the idea that procreation is the only justifiable use of sex, and is even more astonished to discover his antagonism to the fact that masturbation forms a legitimate source of outlet, and in any event does no physical harm. Nothing in his study, Kinsey says, indicates that masturbation ever interferes with marriage; the rare cases he has found are so few as to be negligible. On the contrary, he concludes, in women he knows of nothing which more often prepares her for understanding the nature of the orgasm which she hopes to have in marital intercourse, unless it would be premarital intercourse.

Stone took these strictures in good part, and there is no doubt that Kinsey's work had a far-reaching effect on his and other marriage manuals.

Sometimes one friend led to another. It was Dr. Dickinson, for instance, who brought Kinsey together with Earle Marsh, the San Francisco gynecologist, in 1946. They met at the Waldorf-Astoria in New York, where Marsh gave his history. I had planned to be in the city that day, but bad weather brought my flight down in Philadelphia for the night. Consequently Kinsey asked Marsh if he would like to take my ticket and join him at the theater that night to see *A Streetcar Named Desire.*

After the theater Prok took his guest on a tour of the Times Square underworld which lasted until 4 A.M. As they walked, it seemed to Marsh that well over 30 percent (an exaggeration, I'm sure) of the people they met greeted Kinsey with, "Hello, Doc." Nor were these entirely underworld characters; Marsh observed that they appeared to be from all economic and social levels, and Kinsey was as unfailingly kind and courteous to one as to another. In the same fashion, he treated Marsh as though he were an honored guest. "I have never in my life met a man who was so genuine," Marsh said later. He was, the doctor thought, like the comfortable shoes he always wore.

Marsh entertained Kinsey often at his home near San Francisco, and accompanied him to dinners and meetings in the Bay Area. He was constantly impressed by Prok's astounding capacity to absorb information about a locality.

When he was at my house [Marsh recalled years later] the first thing he did was to take a trip all around my yard and up and down the hill and look at the various plants, and at the countryside, drinking it all in, asking questions. Then he would proceed to tell me things about Marin County that I never knew. He had a fund of knowledge about the kind of wood that was used in my house, the kind of furniture that we had. Good God, he mentioned things about my house that I didn't even know. I learned about my own environs from Kinsey, who was actually only a visitor.

As Marsh testifies, he was similarly eclectic in their conversations. When the doctor showed him some films he had made on childbirth, Prok could not only discuss the subject matter, but also talked about photography, filming, editing and sound levels like a professional producer.

From their relationship, Marsh remembers most Kinsey's positive outlook on life: "Somehow nothing defeated him. I don't think it ever occurred to him that life could defeat him. He was able to look through the ugliness to something lovely beyond. I often thought about him as an athlete of the spirit." That spirit faltered only under the worst of the hammer blows of his critics later on, when Marsh noted that he often appeared depressed and exhibited signs of a growing interior irritability. "I noticed a certain sense of isolation that occurred," Marsh says, "and now and again in talking to him I thought I noticed a tear in his eye from time to time."

As so many of us did, Marsh thought of Kinsey as a supreme teacher, even at the Sunday musicales, which the San Franciscan attended when he was in Bloomington. When Kinsey began to talk about a composition he was going to play, it was as though he had suddenly stepped onto the lecture podium. He related the history of a selection and under what circumstances it was composed. Then he spoke about the various recordings of the piece, assessing which one was best and commenting about the solo performances on each re-cord—all this before he put the recording on his high-fidelity equip-ment, which was the best obtainable at that time, and had been put together by a friend who lived nearby. Of these music lectures, Marsh says: "We all felt that we were not lectured at but communed with."

Another friendship, of yet a different character, was the one be-tween Kinsey and Robert Yerkes, of the National Research Council Committee, whose support meant so much to him. Yerkes com-manded respect, not only as a revered member of the scientific establishment, but in his person. He was a benign, solid-looking man, cut on a square pattern, with an appearance of purposeful benevo-lence. Yerkes appeared to look upon Kinsey in a paternal sort of way, and sometimes jokingly offered him "grandfatherly advice," which Kinsey seldom took. As a gentleman of the old school he was alarmed by some of the directions Kinsey's research was taking, but so thorough a scientist was he that he was a bulwark of strength against its critics.

At the very beginning of their relationship Yerkes made an attempt to direct Kinsey's course directly by means of specific advice. He wrote in the fall of 1943:

You are engaged in an extraordinary [sic] difficult and hazardous undertaking. So far as reasonably possible, minimize your risks. Avoid spreading yourself too thin and being, or even seeming to be, over-ambitious, lest you ruin all. This sums up what is in my system, but it may not be entirely intelligible to you.

My advice is to limit yourself for the present to the securing of a reasonably reliable picture of sex-behavior patterns, developments, and adjustments in what might be defined as "presumptively typical and normal male and female whites of our U.S.A. culture and education, between the ages of 12 (?) and 70 (?) years." Postpone inquiry into human variants—racial, cultural, degree of typicalness, etc. etc.—until you have completed your primary task, then let them come as extensions or specialized inquiries.

It was one of Freud's irreparable errors to base his statements of fact, inferences, and generalizations too largely on subjects either on the psychopathic fringe or definitely abnormal. Safety for you, as in my opinion was true for Freud also, lies in limiting your initial inquiry to those individuals who are *modal*, both structurally and functionally.

Forgive the intrusion. I know what I am doing will not seem to you presumptuous because we have the same interest, objectives, and general motivation. My sole excuse is that I have had many more years of experience than you and rather more varied ventures in the conduct and promotion of research!

This advice was about as far from Kinsey's objective as anything could have been, but he was tactful in countering it. His defense was nonetheless firm:

I am very much in sympathy with the idea of getting a picture of the usual portion of the population, before we attempt to analyze the unusual; although such a picture has meant to me, as a taxonomist and a student of variation, securing the picture of the population as a whole. There is no modal portion of a population in curves which are shaped as most of ours. Out of eighteen people who sat around our table in New York [at a recent conference], there are not more than two or three who would fit any one person's notion of what is usual and modal in human behavior. I speak with some knowledge, for I have the histories of most of that group.

Please do not misunderstand me. My first and foremost interest is in the usual picture and I have been concerned with what you have called special groups only because they are, in a way, the experimental material which elucidates the normal controls. I am carefully speaking when I suggest that a study of human behavior which does not take into account so-called variant behavior would be as profitless as descriptive physiology that lacked experimental work. Since experimentation with these aspects of human behavior is practically impossible, we are reduced to examining contrasting types of behavior, as a substitute for an experimental set-up.

Again I want you to be assured that I will give every attention to securing the picture of the average and the usual portion of the population, as the primary objective of our research; and I will give every consideration to the suggestions you have made and to any others that you care to contribute. I value them all, and want you to give us as many suggestions as your experience will allow.

A few weeks later, in a letter concerned primarily with other matters, Yerkes responded briefly:

You took very well my recent critical remarks about scope of undertaking, and I may say in further comment on the subject that I fully appreciate the fairness and wisdom of your defense. The situation is so complex that one must be pragmatic always, and also so far as practicable, logical!

That was the tone of their friendship—respectful of each other, supportive on Yerkes' part, firm yet receptive on Kinsey's. Yerkes did, however, from time to time give Kinsey additional pieces of advice, to be added to the long list of such counsels which there was no possibility Kinsey would ever follow—as Yerkes recognized in a wistful notation: "I hope you will meditate on it even if you are unable to accept it!"

What Yerkes wanted him to consider even if he could not accept was something a legion of grandfathers could not have imposed, although Yerkes was at his eloquent best in advocating it: that Kinsey "take it easy" and not overdo, for the sake of his own health and that of the project as well.

It is my conviction [Yerkes wrote] that your value to the project to which you have dedicated your life will be measured in future decades rather by your breadth of view, prophetic insights and wisdom than by the quantity of your work and its representation in factual reports. I am sure that if in your situation, I should try as speedily as feasible to develop a staff organization which would assure optimal progress of research and reporting while permitting the over-all director to take in good conscience and to the best of his ability profit by frequent periods of vacation. Probably such periods would be most profitable if spent elsewhere than in Bloomington!

Kinsey thanked him courteously and went back to his tireless compiling of histories and his factual reports.

In spite of the great respect he had for Yerkes, Kinsey was no doubt more comfortable discussing his work with another friend, a homosexual contact in New York whom I shall designate here as Will Finch. Kinsey had a great many contacts among homosexuals and every other kind of group, not only in New York but virtually around the world, yet Will Finch was not like the others. A highly literate man with a truly extraordinary sexual history, of which he had kept a detailed record from the beginning, Will Finch was immensely valuable to the research. Not only did he produce a quantity of history givers, as the others did, but he supplied us with a constant flow of letters, diaries, journals and statistical records of his own life, and some others as well, covering activities in various parts of the world. His contributions, begun about the time I came to the staff, continued until long after Kinsey's death, and today are crammed into every corner of a large, locked steel filing cabinet at the Institute —probably the most complete record of a human sexual life ever compiled, and much of it written with grace and style as well as factual accuracy.

In a voluminous correspondence, Kinsey discussed with Will Finch the subjects he talked about with others, but often it had more the sound of one insider talking to another. For instance, on the subject of getting as large a proportion of the population as possible into the research, which Yerkes had raised, how different is Kinsey's response from his relatively circumspect reply to his presumptive grandfather:

The world has a great variety of people in it and their doings vary tremendously. There are too many easy generalizations in the literature which are based upon a few individual cases and which are totally inadequate when one examines a long series of cases. It is this demand for covering the total picture which has led us to accumulate data for seven years practically without publication, and which will keep us at it for another twenty years before we feel ready to generalize on many of the aspects of our problems. Not only does New York differ from Dayton, but Dayton will differ from many another small town. Even in New York there is a tremendous variety of types. The vast majority of the persons with homosexual histories in New York City know nothing of 42nd Street and homosexual prostitution.

Since Will Finch was himself a homosexual, some of Kinsey's most cogent thoughts on the subject were addressed to him, including these particularly perceptive observations:

In the great majority of cases, even in the more obvious of the streetwalking, tavern-frequenting group, I am quite convinced that most of it is acquired. I think I told you of our experience with some of the twelve and fourteen-year-old youngsters whose histories we have caught just as they were going that way. There is a great deal of deliberate and practiced imitation and a larger amount of conscious imitation. Secondly, I am quite convinced that some of these old-timers are still play-acting. I have known of them for several years, had repeated contacts with them, during which they showed all of the traditional stigmata. When they finally became convinced that they would give me a history, they would walk into my hotel room and settle down to a perfectly normal attitude, voice, etc., as soon as they knew there was nothing to be gained by further acting. . . . If one confines one's attention to a homosexual group, of course all the characters which he finds are characteristic of that group, but if one gets as wide a variety of heterosexual histories as we have, he finds many of these things there just as well. This is particularly true . . . of high voice, broad hips, paucity of beard and body hair, so-called feminine deposits of fatty tissue, slight bony structure, softness of skin, late retention of youthful appearance, undeveloped genitalia. It is misleading to talk of these things as characteristic of any group until one knows their incidence in any group. As for mannerisms, you understand that they are much more easily acquired by imitation.
. . . It is possible that it [homosexuality] is on a hormonal basis and it is possible that there are one hundred and one other things involved in the development of the homosexual, but until we have scientifically conclusive evidence that this, that, or the other thing, actually applies, we have no reason for considering that such conclusions as those of Glass, Deuel and Wright [researchers Will Finch has cited] are correct.

After studying behavior patterns of homosexuals and heterosexuals, Kinsey was more than ever convinced that many aspects of the former were not unique. The need for companionship, and heartache over broken and unrequited love, for instance, also appeared in many heterosexual histories, nor could he be sure that these things

happened more often in one group than the other. As for the association of homosexuals with organized prostitution, petty crime and
other underworld activities, these were even more closely paralleled
in the heterosexual. Prostitution, he asserted, did not adequately
portray either heterosexuality or homosexuality as a whole. Kinsey
believed that sex was blamed for a good many things which were not
the fault of either sex in general, any more than they were of heterosexuality or homosexuality in particular. The outcome of most sexual
behavior, he concluded, depended on the way the participating individuals took it, or more often, the way society reacted to it.

Nothing could have proved his point better than the varying
reactions of the small group of friends I have talked about here to
Kinsey's concepts of sexual behavior, and how to study them. In the
great world outside the isolated camp of these scientists and knowledgeable individuals, society's attitude was both ritualistic and un-
predictable, as Kinsey was to prove again and again.

CHAPTER

XI

ANTICIPATING

MASTERS AND JOHNSON

At an early point in the development of our research, Kinsey began to feel a certain impatience with the fact that the data we were collecting was necessarily secondhand. Like any scholar, he yearned for original sources, and while it was true that what we were doing had not been done before, and therefore could be classified as original research, it occurred to him that we ought to observe at first hand some of the behavior we were recording.

In those days, before the advent of Masters and Johnson, this was a revolutionary idea in the field of sex research, and one not easy to carry out. Nevertheless, Kinsey began looking for opportunities to observe. He was acutely aware of the serious dangers implicit in such work and proceeded cautiously, knowing that he could expect little understanding of what he was doing if it was ever disclosed. Those who already believed the project was immoral would be outraged, he knew, and not even many scientists could be expected to condone it. Few people would believe in the scientific purity of his motives. There was always in the back of his mind the clear and present danger that the Institute might be deprived of its support, from the University as well as the Foundation, if it was subjected to the kind of public attack the revelation of such activity would certainly provoke.

In this conflict between his scientific zeal and the strictures of society, Kinsey characteristically decided in favor of science. Considering that the life of the project itself might be at stake, the decision took considerable courage. But even with the decision made, it was not easy to initiate. Our first tentative efforts were in Indianapolis, where we sometimes paid prostitutes to let us take their histories. During the history taking, a girl might remark that her "spur tongue," as she referred to her clitoris, was two inches long. Kinsey might express some disbelief at this figure, but for another dollar the prostitute was willing to let him see for himself.

This observation of anatomical differences—and it typified the kind of research Kinsey knew would be attacked if it was known— was the first step toward observing actual behavior. As Masters and Johnson were later to document, a firsthand understanding of basic structures was essential to acquiring knowledge of behavior.

With the idea of recording what he hoped to observe, Kinsey hired Bill Dellenback, who was Clarence Tripp's partner in a photographic studio in New York. On one of his early visits to New York Kinsey had been photographed by Tripp, and was immensely pleased with the results; he thought they were the best pictures he had ever had taken up to that time.

Photographers who worked with him later were not so fortunate; with them Kinsey was characteristically unsparing. Shortly after the *Male* volume was published, he wrote to a Condé Nast photographer who had taken a picture of him two months before:

It was very good of you to have taken the picture. I appreciate your interest in doing so. I hardly know how to assure you of my appreciation and yet to disapprove as strenuously as I do of the picture. I think it very bad and essentially slanderous. I very much wish you would destroy the negative and all prints of it. If you will do that, I will be glad to give you additional time when I am next in New York to take additional pictures, but again, with the understanding that we will have some control over their release.

I am not sure that you realize the import of a picture of this sort. There are a good many people who would go to any lengths to put a stop to the research we are doing, and publication of the sort of picture you have taken would materially help their cause.

Of course, it was not as dreadful or portentous a picture as all that. Kinsey simply felt much as President Lyndon Johnson did when he was confronted with an oil portrait, executed by a noted artist, which displayed him as something less than noble.

To the end, he remained sensitive about how he was photographed. In 1953, Luther Evans, who was then the Librarian of Congress, decided that the Library should establish a collection of photographs of eminent persons, to be taken by Dr. Albert R. Miller, the well-known Washington photographer. When Miller wrote, in December of that year, to ask if he could photograph him, Kinsey agreed—getting a little tangled in the editorial "we" he usually employed, saying that "we are complimented in having you propose to add my picture"—but cautioned Miller: "I should warn you that I am a difficult subject to photograph and I should want an agreement that our okay would be necessary before you could use any of the photographs you took."

What was this uncertainty about how he looked to the world? A complicated matter, surely, which will emerge in a clearer light, I think, as I tell the story of his life. It had to do with his conception of himself in relation to other people, and was never more apparent than when he was removed completely from his own sphere.

But if Kinsey was positive about himself as a camera subject, he was tentative in his approach to photographing others, particularly when the subject was sexual behavior. In persuading Dellenback to leave his New York studio and come to work in Bloomington, he was well aware that it would not be easy to put Bill on the payroll. The University authorities, who had to approve our budget, quite naturally wanted to know why we needed a photographer. Kinsey told them, truthfully, that he wanted to photograph animal behavior, but he did not add that he included humans in this category.

Dellenback could not have been a better choice for the job. His personality was not only congenial to the staff members, but it was exactly right for what he was to do. In essential attitudes, he was like those of us who did the interviewing. His technical abilities were superb, and if he had a fault, as noted earlier, it was his tendency to be a perfectionist. Except for matters of lighting and angle, however, Bill had little opportunity for perfection in the actual filming—there were no retakes—but he made up for it with the infinite care he took in the darkroom to produce his prints.

More accurately, Dellenback was a cinematographer, although he was equally skilled with the still camera and took photographs for us when they were required. His work was mostly on film, since motion pictures were the only way sexual behavior could be adequately recorded.

His first assignment originated with a trip Kinsey made to New York for the purpose of taking the histories of a homosexual group consisting chiefly of writers, artists, architects and others occupied with creative work. This group held frequent sex sessions, to one of which Kinsey was invited as an observer. For the benefit of skeptics, let me say that Kinsey possessed the ability to observe actual sexual behavior with the same objectivity he maintained during interviews; he was always the scientist, and in this respect so were we all. Another useful aspect of Kinsey's remarkable personality in this situation was his easy way of observing without making the observed feel they were being spied upon.

Dellenback recalls that during these sessions Kinsey seemed much more unobtrusive in his manner than usual, no doubt because he understood the need to move cautiously in this unknown and potentially dangerous territory. He would move quietly around the room, never intruding, occasionally whispering a direction to Bill. He always complimented the subjects after a session and reassured them about the quality and value of what they had done. If they had failed to perform satisfactorily whatever act was involved, Kinsey would say, "You did very well. Just great." He was the absolute observer; there was no personal involvement whatever.

On one occasion his caution and objectivity led to an amusing incident. During a session recording male masturbation, the subject went on and on with the act until the camera began to overheat and Bill knew he was about to run out of film. He made a despairing gesture to Kinsey, indicating what was happening. Prok leaned forward to the subject and said gently, politely, "If you would just come now . . ."

"Oh, sure," the subject said, and immediately came to orgasm just as the film ran out. The man had misunderstood and thought Kinsey wanted a lengthy sequence of masturbation, which he was prepared to keep up indefinitely.

In his utter objectivity about his work, Dellenback could hardly remember who was present in many of the sessions, because he was so busy and had so many details on his mind. As far as he was concerned, the situations were completely nonerotic; it was just a job, to which there was no subjective reaction.

If I appear to be overemphasizing this point, it is because I know how hard it is for the layman, or even the scientist in nonsexual fields, to believe it. But it must be understood that objectivity is attained in such situations when erotic content is removed from the observation—exactly opposed to the attitude of the voyeur, who is sexually stimulated by what he sees. Since there is something of the voyeur in nearly everyone, it is understandable that nonscientists find it hard to accept that scientists may not react the way they do; some would even consider it a kind of condescension. The layman can scarcely imagine viewing a sexual scene without having feelings either of stimulation or of disgust, depending on the state of his inhibitions.

We experienced neither emotion. There was, for us, no more erotic content in viewing the sexual activities of the human animal than in observing any other mammal. If that seems to some readers like a dehumanization of sex, I can only cite again Kinsey's reply to the professionals such as Mead and Menninger who criticized him on this score—that he was not studying emotional or psychological content in sex acts, but only *what* was actually done and *how*. Unlike his critics, he believed the physical elements could be divorced from the others for purposes of study, an idea now much more easily accepted since Masters and Johnson have demonstrated it on a large and convincing scale.

Speaking for myself, I cannot recall a single instance of sexual arousal on my part when I was observing sex behavior, and I am certain this was equally true of Kinsey and the other staff members. We were so busy observing, and recording what we observed, that we had no time to think of anything else.

To return, then, to Kinsey's New York visit: in observing the sexual activity taking place at the group's party to which he had been invited, he was particularly intrigued by the intercourse of a homosexual couple in which one of the partners had an orgasm of such intensity that he was in a frenzy of release, quite unconsciously beating the other man around the shoulders with his clenched fists. With the idea, as always, of getting as much range and variety as possible in his sampling, Kinsey invited the two men to come out to Bloomington, expenses paid, and be photographed in intercourse. They agreed. By this time, they must have been impressed by the attitude

Kinsey had displayed at the party, resisting every attempt to draw him into the activity, but in such a way that no one was offended and everyone understood his purpose in being there.

In Bloomington, Dellenback photographed the intercourse and orgasm Kinsey had observed in New York, while Gebhard, Martin and I joined him.

It was the first of a series of observations. It must be understood that, while they anticipated in some respects what Masters and Johnson were to do later, our films were in no way comparable to what the Saint Louis scientists were able to accomplish. Ours was an extremely small sampling: twenty homosexual couples, ten heterosexual couples and about twenty-five males and females engaged in masturbation—hardly a scientific sample, nor intended to be. We drew no conclusions from what we saw, and the observations were useful only in the way they were intended—that is, for the first time to provide us with firsthand knowledge of what actually occurred in a wide range of sexual behavior. Later the films were studied and data organized from them.

Such experimental work had been done before. Kinsey, who was fascinated by the concept of individual differences, and especially intrigued by physiologic differences and variations in response, had made an earlier trip to Loma Linda, California, where scientists were studying heart rate and respiration during intercourse. He wanted to hire a physiologist to study these phenomena at the Institute, because it seemed to him there was a tremendous lack of knowledge about such matters, but we had no money for an expansion of our activities. It was Kinsey's determination to make some observations of his own, nevertheless, that led him to hire Dellenback and undertake the series of observations which began in New York.

In several ways our work was lopsided and incomplete. For example, we found it easier to obtain the consent of homosexual couples to be photographed, so there were twice as many of them. Further, they were all homosexual males; we were unable to obtain any lesbians. What diversity there was existed mostly in the several types of orgasm displayed.

For example, at one end of the scale, there were both males and females whose orgasms were accompanied by almost no overt body movements. With them, the orgasm was more like a long sigh. Often their partners would not even know it had occurred. At the other extreme, there were those whose orgasms were violent. It was convulsive behavior, almost like an epileptic fit, the body twisting and jackknifing, thrown about in an ecstatic storm. Sometimes these people struck their partners violently on the head and shoulders. In between, of course, were the majority, who came to a more commonplace climax.

We observed directly more human sexual responses than any other scientist before Masters and Johnson. Later, the Saint Louis team showed that on some points we were simply wrong, and they recorded many observations we missed. Making their large body of observations under controlled laboratory conditions, they wove what they saw into a coherent pattern covering the entire cycle of female and male response, and that is the essence of their enormous achievement.

Looking back on this phase of our research, limited as it was, I can see that we were not more successful simply because we were far too anxious and cautious about what we were doing, and consequently missed many opportunities to get subjects because we did not think it safe to ask.

Kinsey was as aware of the potential danger as anyone. When it became known that he was observing homosexual behavior, for example, a few of the scant number of people outside the Institute who knew about it immediately concluded that he must be homosexual himself. Nonetheless, he persisted in following through the observation portion of the research because he believed it was scientifically necessary, and that was enough for him. He set aside space for a laboratory after he returned from the initial photographic session in New York, and began looking for subjects.

As Masters and Johnson have since demonstrated, it is no trick at all, in spite of what the public believes, to obtain people for sexual observation, nor are they prostitutes, exhibitionists, or any other kind of variant from the conventional norm, as is popularly supposed. They are people of every kind, as eager to help the cause of scientific research as the 18,000 who gave us their histories. Our limited observation, overwhelmingly confirmed by Masters and Johnson, as well as by every other available piece of evidence, demonstrates repeatedly that what people will accept and what actually occurs are not necessarily the same thing. The folk belief that no "decent" person will allow himself to be observed is only one more illustration of the vast distance between what Americans say they believe and what they do.

In our case, the public would have been astounded and disbelieving to know the names of the eminent scientists who appeared at the Institute from time to time to examine our work and talk with Kinsey, and who volunteered before they left to be photographed in some kind of sexual activity. It was abundantly clear from our interviewing, furthermore, that there were any number of men and women who would be willing to cooperate.

To cite a single example of the ease with which this could be done, a medical school researcher from another university, who was studying infertility, wanted to find out whether the number of sperm cells per ejaculation, or per cubic centimeter of semen, was lowered in cases where a man ejaculated two or more times in rapid succession. He came to us and asked if we could find subjects in his area who were capable of repeated ejaculation, and who would come to his laboratory. On our next trip to that part of the country we found a number of men willing to cooperate.

The same was true of women. Some who had multiple orgasms, for example, were willing to have coitus under observation when they were told that science was almost completely ignorant of this phenomenon. I remember one woman who was capable of from fifteen to twenty orgasms in twenty minutes. Even the most casual contact could arouse a sexual response in her. Observing her both in masturbation and in sexual intercourse, we found that in intercourse her first orgasm occurred within two to five seconds after entry. She was in her sixties when we made these observations, and curiously enough, had never had an orgasm before she was forty. What we would have liked to explore was the possibility of a physiologic difference between such a woman and one who must experience thirty minutes or more of intense erotic stimulation before she achieves a single orgasm. Unfortunately, we were never able to make the observations that might have resolved the issue of these extreme variations in response.

Another remarkable thing about our multiorgasmic sexagenarian was her ability to achieve full relaxation as soon as her partner did.

Immediately after his ejaculation, she relaxed in complete satisfaction. By that time she might have had twenty orgasms, or only one or two, but in any case, her partner's ejaculation marked a happy termination to her sexual drive.

Sometimes people from whom we had taken histories volunteered to be photographed, and one must suppose that an element of exhibitionism was involved in a few of these cases. That was true of the male partner in one couple who volunteered, though his wife was merely compliant and would never have come forward on her own initiative. Whatever the motive, we were not likely to refuse these fortuitous happenings. We believed we were demonstrating something that would help us better to understand what human sexual behavior, particularly orgasm, was like.

In one instance, at least, a volunteer couple gave us a film of more than ordinary potential usefulness. They had heard of our work and wrote to offer their histories, adding that they also had a film of themselves in intercourse we might like to have. It had been taken by a friend whom they had asked to come in and record their activity. The seven-minute sequence depicted the woman lying on her partner, with her hand palms down behind his head, raising the upper part of her torso from his body so that her face was clearly visible. It concluded with a perfectly photographed orgasm. Obviously a therapist with a female patient who had never had an orgasm, and could not even visualize one, might well show such a film to the woman and her husband, together, so they could see for themselves what intercourse ending in orgasm was like. Of course, one must add, the illustration would have to be in the context of whatever total therapy the case might call for.

Were the couple in this film exhibitionists, or "depraved," or otherwise outside the bounds of organized society? Hardly. Both of them were (and are still) regularly employed in utterly respectable jobs; they have five children; they are regular churchgoers and Sunday school attendants; their life is quite conventional. At the time the film was made, twenty years ago, they were in their early thirties. There were only two unusual things about them. One was their mutual conviction that sex was fun, so much fun that they wanted to record their delight in it, and they were able to do so with a complete lack of inhibition and a feeling of freedom. The other unusual factor was the remarkable range of their sexual life. They had intercourse fourteen times a week on the average, during which he ejaculated two or three times on each occasion, and she had from five to ten orgasms each time. The film made by this couple was one of several amateur records we acquired for the archives.

Since the archives include the most complete record of sexual behavior in the world, the filmed part of it (comparatively a very small part) also includes stag films and commercial films of a more familiar kind. Kinsey was not much interested in them, except as they added to the collection, because while stag films were real enough, in most cases the reactions of the participants were faked and so were of no real interest to the scientist.

In spite of our lack of an adequate physiological laboratory, we did manage to accumulate a substantial body of data on human sexual anatomy and physiology, some of which form the basis for the chapters in the *Female* volume on "Anatomy of Sexual Response and Orgasm," and "Physiology of Sexual Response and Orgasm." This was the small foundation upon which Masters and Johnson later erected their remarkable structure of scientific fact.

Kinsey and Masters were alike in one significant respect—their compelling drive to accomplish the task at hand. Masters works sometimes eighty hours a week, including an entire night, and Kinsey, as I have described, pushed himself in the same way. The two never met, but I am sure Prok would have been delighted to know that at Washington University, only 220 miles away, Masters was just then beginning the laboratory observations that Kinsey himself had hoped to make, but was never able to launch. Masters picked up the scientific trail where Kinsey left it.

With his background in biology, it was natural that Kinsey would be interested in observing sexual behavior in the human animal, and as logical that he should want to make some comparative films of the same kind of activity in other mammals. His desire to undertake this was stimulated further by his realization that so little work had been done in the field—just as he had been directed toward beginning the project by the paucity of material for his sex education class.

The problem in studying animal sexual behavior had been the extreme rapidity of response, and the fact that it might involve every part of the animal's body. Consequently it was very difficult, in fact virtually impossible, to observe everything taking place in the few seconds, or the minute or two, comprising the duration of activity. Moving pictures, however, made it possible to examine and reexamine the identical performance any number of times, studying and measuring the details on any single frame of film if it was necessary. With this kind of record, we could analyze the physiologic bases of the action in various parts of the animal's body.

Before Kinsey died, we had compiled photographic records of sexual behavior in many species of animals. Kinsey, Dellenback and Gebhard began this part of the project with a field trip (followed by several others) to the Yerkes Laboratories in Orange Park, Florida, where we filmed the sexual activities of chimpanzees. Considering the amount of work scientists had already done with the primates, it was astonishing to discover how little was known about the sex lives of these mammals. For example, it was believed (with no evidence to support it) that only female gibbons, among the apes, had orgasm. But Dellenback filmed a female chimpanzee masturbating to orgasm —which she does not experience during intercourse—and doing it with the same clitoral manipulation the human female uses. Watching her perform, one could see why intercourse did not produce orgasm. In chimpanzee copulation, the male approaches, mounts quickly from the rear and the act is over in a moment. Our female chimp took a comparatively long time to produce her orgasm by masturbation.

Kinsey was fond of the chimpanzees, as he was of all animals. After Gebhard had made a later trip to Orange Park to continue the work there, Prok wrote to Dr. Henry Nissen, director of the Laboratories, to thank him for his help, and added: "You have accumulated a very important body of knowledge in your work with the chimpanzees. Dr. Gebhard tells me the chimps like you and I think that is an absolute fundamental in any work with animals."

Kinsey believed firmly that one had to love animals to work well with them, and that it was wrong to be the complete cold-blooded scientist with them that some researchers were. He extended this belief to people, asserting that it was essential to find something one could respect, or relate to, in the object of study—whether it was an animal or a human whose behavior was far outside the ordinary social patterns—before really effective work could be done. It is an idea still not widely believed by psychologists today, in spite of the abundance of evidence to confirm it.

The animal research was full of surprises, not the least of which was the revelation of how little was known about the sex lives of even the most familiar animals. We found, for instance, that homosexual activity was as common among animals as it is among humans. One of our field trips took us to the Oregon State Agricultural College farm, where Dr. Fred McKenzie, head of the Department of Animal Husbandry, helped us take about 4,000 feet of moving pictures of sexual behavior in cattle, sheep, hogs and rabbits. Cattle were being bred there for purposes of artificial insemination experiments, and it was not unusual to see cows mounting cows, which we filmed. But our prize came the day Dellenback recorded a bull mounting another bull, achieving complete anal penetration, and ejaculating as he withdrew.

An eminent sex researcher to whom we showed this film remarked: "Every judge in the country who has to deal with sex offenders should see this film. It might teach him something about what the word 'unnatural' means."

Whenever we learned of studies that would fill the gaps in our own work, Kinsey was quick to acquire whatever motion picture records had been made. He wrote to Dr. John Scott, of the University of Wyoming, when he heard that Scott had made some movies of mating in the sage grouse, and not only got prints of a film showing some of the characteristic mating behavior of sharp-tailed grouse, but also that of the greater prairie chicken.

Perhaps the most unusual discovery we made in the filming of animals was something that had been learned by Dr. Albert Shadle, head of the Department of Biology at the University of Buffalo, who had been studying the life cycles of porcupines, skunks and raccoons. Before he made his studies, it had been widely believed by zoologists that porcupines had intercourse face to face, a supposition reinforced not only by the obvious fact of their heavy quill covering, but by their observed behavior in mating, during which they maneuver around each other, face to face, in a kind of erotic dance, and the male fairly deluges the female with his urine. Yet Shadle discovered that during actual intercourse, the female flipped her broad, spiny tail over her back, disclosing a smooth surface beneath that offered no obstacle to a conventional mounting position for the male. We persuaded him to let us make a film of this act.

On a trip to Swarthmore College, we learned from another scientist something about the unusual factors involved in the copulations of mink. During intercourse, the male mounts the female and seizes the nape of her neck in his teeth. For an hour or more he throws her about in what looks like the cruelest kind of rape, sometimes ruining her pelt (a serious problem for mink breeders) and occasionally even killing her in his frenzy. In an effort to save the females from death or injury, breeders had been experimenting with artificial insemination but found that it did not work. Further study showed that without going through this fierce ritual, the female would not ovulate.

Kinsey pursued the compilation of data on animal sex behavior with the same persistence he exhibited with the major research on humans. One was, of course, intertwined with the other. At a meeting in New York with Dr. Marc Klein, of the Institut de Biologie Medicale, in Strasbourg, Kinsey learned from this distinguished scientist that he had observed orgasm in the female rabbit, a phenomenon most scientists did not know existed. Kinsey was fascinated. At that time he was not convinced that orgasm occurred in any species of mammal except the human female, and to prove it occurred in the rabbit would be of considerable importance His own motion pictures of rabbit coitus did not record that the female reached orgasm, although she was obviously responding erotically.

After their meeting, Kinsey wrote to Klein asking him for some specific references. He meant to cite them in the *Female* volume, then under preparation.

Your descriptions of orgasm for the rabbit female sounded very convincing, but I need to be able to quote authority until I have a chance to see it myself. I have spent some time with rabbit observation this year, although a pitifully small amount of time, and have become very acquainted with the characteristic response of the male rabbit in orgasm but have not seen anything that approached orgasm in the female. I have seen the female raise her pelvis at the approach of the male's orgasm, and give plenty of other indications of erotic response. I have not seen her reach any complete peak of response from which she regressed abruptly into a normal physiologic state. But our observations are so limited that I need the help of you people who have observed abundantly. This is a very important matter, because of the nearly unique or absolutely unique phenomenon of orgasm in the human female.

Klein confirmed what Kinsey wanted to know:

As far as I am concerned, I have very often observed a quite definite peak of response with climax, from which the female falls back abruptly into a quiet state. When the climax is complete, the two partners fall together on one side; at that very moment the female is shrieking and sometimes even the male is shrieking himself. The female thrusts the male aside by a sudden movement of the pelvis and the two animals at once come back to the normal stature on the four limbs. I think that such a climax may be reasonably well called orgasm, the more that it is an individual response of the female which is far from appearing in all females even of a definite strain. . . . Once you know well the sexual behavior in the rabbit, not occasionally but through personal observations of individual cases over months and years, you are finally aware that there are enormous individual differences in this behavior, and that you find patterns of normal and abnormal plays and responses which remind strongly of human behavior.

Dr. Klein recommended several other sources of information on the subject, and one finds Kinsey doggedly following these leads, intent on pinning down the scientific fact—sometimes in an unconsciously humorous way, as when he writes to Dr. A. S. Barkes, of the National Institute for Medical Research, in London, citing him as one who Klein says is "among the people who really know the rabbit."

One of the sources recommended by Klein was Dr. John Hammond, of the School of Agriculture, Cambridge University, and in spite of all he had learned from the Strasbourg expert, Kinsey showed himself not quite convinced:

The very active response which occurs in female cats after coitus, had been somewhat difficult to interpret and we are not satisfied whether this should be called orgasm or whether it represents a reflex response which does not bring the release of nervous tension which is the most distinctive characteristic of true orgasm.

Hammond, too, believed that there was orgasm in the female rabbit at copulation:

There is no possible doubt that there is some nervous connection to the brain which sets free the hormone from the anterior pituitary and so causes ovulation. . . . There is another species of animal which behaves in this way, that is, it only ovulates following coitus; this animal is the ferret. I am enclosing a paper on the ferret which gives some details. A film of copulation in the ferret would, I think, show you by the expression on the face of the female that an orgasm did occur. I have repeatedly seen this.

Besides these sources, Kinsey pursued the subject with Professor H. Hediger, director of the famous Zoological Gardens in Basel, Switzerland, and with other eminent authorities. He came away from the pursuit convinced that the female rabbit did, indeed, have orgasm, not only in intercourse with males but when females mounted other females and exhibited the same kind of "fainting" orgasm Klein had described. Taken together with his observations of chimpanzees, this research showed that there was ample reason to doubt the widely held belief that human females alone of all the mammalian species experienced orgasm.

From filming animals we were able to arrive at more definite conclusions than the films of humans had produced. In the light of subsequent far more detailed studies, notably Ford and Beach's *Patterns of Sexual Behavior,* what we concluded does not now seem so original, although it is still relatively unknown to the general public, much less accepted. Our major conclusion was that the human animal was even more mammalian than we had thought. Every kind of sexual behavior we had observed or known about in humans could be found in animals.

In spite of the importance Kinsey attached to what our cameras were recording, he was constantly apprehensive about this aspect of the research, and fearful of the possible consequences of discovery. Unquestionably, he had every right to be worried. If it had become publicly known, there is little reason to believe the Institute would have survived the publicity. But no one outside the inner circle knew about this phase of our work. We did not talk about it to anyone, and the filming was mentioned only once in the books we compiled—a single cryptic reference in the *Female* volume.

Something of the trouble we might have had could be seen years later when Masters and Johnson's work came to public attention before the publication of their first book. The outrage of the moralists was a serious threat to their work. Nevertheless, these courageous researchers broke the barrier and entered a new era of sex research, just as Kinsey had done.

Some time after Kinsey's death, the Saint Louis team learned of our films and came to Bloomington to see for themselves. To them, as to other qualified researchers, our record of observation, scanty though it might be in sum, was valuable, and so it is to those scholars who visit the archives today and study the film. Only a few sequences cannot be shown to anyone, because there are recognizable persons in them who did not want their identity disclosed outside the Institute.

Perhaps our contribution was small in terms of quantity, but I believe that, in the light of subsequent events, it was not without significance.

CHAPTER

XII

KINSEY AND THE ARTS

W E LIVE a very tight life, working very long days," Kinsey wrote to a New York friend who had frequently obtained theater tickets for him. "The recreation which the theater has brought to us is a lifesaver. We are indebted to you more than you may realize for having tempted us into spending this much time away from our work."

The arts *were* lifesavers for Kinsey. He enjoyed them all, and I think it is quite possible that the time he was able to take off to enjoy them prolonged his life. These cultural experiences were oases of relaxation in the immense desert of his work, the kind of counterpoint to his scientific labors that playing the violin was for Einstein. But even here, he related everything to his research.

Kinsey was far too busy to see many motion pictures, but there was one he saw over and over again, wherever he could find it. The movie was *Quartet*, four short films derived from stories by Somerset Maugham. The episode he liked best told the story of a pianist and his attempts to become a great artist. In the climactic scene, the master teacher tells his student he will never become the great virtuoso he has dreamed of being.

This story simply overwhelmed Kinsey. Tripp recalls that when he saw the picture with him Kinsey cried like a child and blew his nose until people nearby looked at him in amazement. It was then the third time he had seen it. Perhaps he was deeply touched by the way the master delivered this frightful blow with such kindness, or perhaps it reminded him of how he had given up his own promising career as a pianist when he was young. In any case, the scene never failed to move him.

Another of Kinsey's favorites from *Quartet*—"The Colonel's Lady"—depicted a man and his wife living dully together. The man is having an extramarital affair. His wife is a poet, and under a pseudonym has published a book of poems relating the amorous details of her own love affair. Discovering that his wife is the author, the colonel is dismayed. He discusses it with his mistress, declaring that he cannot believe his wife, of all people, would be capable of such a thing. Soon everyone is reading the book and talking about it, a situation the colonel finds so intolerable that he decides he must confront his wife with his knowledge. He does so after dinner one evening.

"Who is this man?" he demands.

"It's you, darling," she confesses quietly. "My poems tell about what we had that is dead now."

Kinsey was overcome by this story, too. No one remembers how often he actually saw *Quartet*, but Tripp, who was with him on the fourth expedition as well, inquired curiously, "How can you enjoy it so many times?"

Kinsey glanced at him. "I don't intend this to be the last," he said.

Busy as he was with his own work, Kinsey took note of what was happening musically on the Indiana campus, and was not above advising those in charge of concerts and theater about what attractions they should try to obtain. Only a year before his death, ill and distracted though he was, he wrote to Dean Wilfred Bain of the music school, informing him that he had heard indirectly that Zabaleta, the Spanish harpist, had been in town and had expressed some interest in giving a concert at the University. Kinsey told the dean that Zabaleta was one of the most remarkable artists he had ever heard, and hoped it would be possible to book him at Indiana.

One of his oldest faculty friends was Professor Winfred Merrill, a pioneer in music education at the University. When Merrill died in 1954, Kinsey was quick to write to his daughter Winifred:

I particularly want to record my esteem for the work your father did in connection with the beginning of music here on the campus. I am afraid that many of the younger faculty and students on this campus have little concept of the considerable significance and sacrifice as well as the brave determination that your father put into the establishment of a program of music for Indiana University. It was not only the establishment of a program in music here, but it was the development of public concerts and an aroused public interest in music that made his contribution of lasting importance.

Kinsey followed the musical life of nearby Indianapolis, and was a friend of Fabien Sevitzky, then conductor of the Indianapolis Symphony. Sevitzky occasionally sent him records, and Kinsey returned the compliment by presenting him with a copy of the *Male* volume. They met socially whenever it could be arranged, which to Kinsey was never often enough.

Although his tastes in music did not go much beyond the early twentieth century, Kinsey did know some young contemporary musicians, especially the composer Ned Rorem, with whom he had an affectionate "Dear Ned" kind of correspondence. Rorem presented him with a set of his *Four Madrigals*, and Kinsey dropped him encouraging notes from time to time, responding both to Rorem's moods and to his work.

Prok's friends, especially those who had attended his musicales, were always sending him records to be added to his magnificent collection, sometimes bewailing the fact that it was a dangerous thing to do because he had everything. Tripp sent him William Warfield's *Ancient Church Music* on one occasion, an item he did not have, and Kinsey responded knowledgeably, remarking that "the Perotinus . . . is one of the most precious things I know out of old music." At another time, Tripp sent him a really mixed bag: a recording by Earl Wild of the Chopin ballades; John La Montaine's recording of the Chopin Sonata in B-flat Minor; and a new pressing of some Gertrude Stein recordings, which Tripp owned and had leased to Caedmon Records. On still another occasion, he contributed the *Early and Late Songs* of Mahler, with the soprano Anny Felbermayer, which Kinsey thought contained "some of the nicest vocal music . . . that I have known." The Sunday evening group agreed with him, he said.

Kinsey intended to make his own record sleeves. Only four months before his death he was writing Tripp to see if there was a source of supply for pockets in New York; a local bookmaker had agreed to make the albums if he could get the pockets. In the same letter Kinsey asked Tripp to get him some records to send to a friend in France—Haydn's *Creation* and *Lord Nelson Mass*, Weill's *Three-penny Opera* and Stravinsky's *History of a Soldier*. In 1946 he sent a gift to his musical favorite Sibelius, through a friend of the composer who lived in Bloomington.

But music was not his only love, although it was his first. He had friends in all the arts, and his correspondence is full of their letters. One whose work attracted him was Tennessee Williams, whom he proposed meeting at the beginning of their acquaintance by mail early in 1950. Kinsey wrote to Williams:

As you may know, we are making an extensive study of the erotic element in the arts. This covers painting, music, writing, the stage, etc. One of the plays we have studied in some detail has been your *Streetcar*. We have been fortunate enough to obtain histories from a high proportion of the actors and two of the companies which have put on the play, and it has made it possible to correlate their acting with their sexual backgrounds. There are a great many points in the play which we should like to discuss with the author, to find out his original ideas and intentions. This is one of the reasons why we should get together.

(Eventually we took the history of nearly everyone in the three separate companies playing *A Streetcar Named Desire* and were able to demonstrate, at least to our own satisfaction, that Stanley, or Blanche, or Mitch, as portrayed by one actor emerged differently when played by another because of differences in the actors' sexual backgrounds.)

Williams replied cordially from Key West, gratified by the attention Kinsey had given *Streetcar*, and declaring that

your work, your research and its revelations to the ignorant and/or biased public, is of enormous social value. I hope that you will continue it and even extend its scope, for not the least desirable thing in this world is understanding, and sexual problems are especially in need of it.

He welcomed the chance to meet Kinsey and discuss his plays, and did so a few months later, in November 1950. It was a cordial meeting, and the beginning of a friendship, carried on mostly in letters. The following year Kinsey wrote that he had seen *The Rose Tattoo* twice in Chicago, and thought it excellent—"a powerful thing." He went on: "Don't call it comedy, it was keen insight into the mixed problems which are the very human concern of a very real and considerable portion of the world. The fine humor in it provides the necessary relief for the other material."

Through Lincoln Kirstein, Kinsey was introduced to the world of the ballet. Kirstein, director of the New York City Ballet, took him backstage after a performance at the New York City Center, and in 1954 Kinsey wrote enthusiastically to say that he had spent four evenings with Kirstein's company in San Francisco, and thought it "a magnificent thing." He added in his flat way: "I think such a thing adds very much to the worthwhileness of life."

Among the dancers Kinsey came to know was Ted Shawn, who helped him get histories of others. With this aid, and that of the people at the Kamin Bookshop in New York, specialists in the literature of the dance, he was able to expand greatly the list of dancers in his files.

In the art world, Kinsey's New York guide was Monroe Wheeler, director of exhibitions at the Museum of Modern Art, who arranged dinners at which Prok could meet people who might be helpful as contacts for his research. As a result he got the histories of a large group of artists.

One of the artists Kinsey met was the sculptor Paul Saint-Gaudens, who wrote to him in 1951 from Vineyard Haven, Martha's Vineyard, to propose the theory that expression in art is an alternative or compensation for the procreative drive. As Saint-Gaudens outlined his theory:

Many children begin to show remarkable imaginative creativity at six or seven, sometimes with an element of sex in it. The expression develops for several years, then usually diminishes toward puberty and vanishes completely in adolescence. (I have seen this pattern in children who were pupils in my clay modeling classes.) It seems to me that free fantasy and undeveloped sexuality combine in the child to make for spontaneous expression in line, form and color. There is no other satisfying outlet at that period, so the creative urge becomes symbolical. With the onset of puberty with its greater factual awareness and full sexual awakening, the artistic creativity turns into the normal adult channel of mature sexuality, romance, procreation and wage-earning.

This would make the artist an emotionally and sexually immature person. Even as an adult he is retarded at, or thrown back to, a phase of development where the sexual and procreative urge is unrealistic and incomplete. He substitutes imagery for reality and artistic fulfillment for sexual and procreative fulfillment. Ordinary everyday work is distasteful to him. This immaturity seems to be part of many artistic personalities, making them incapable of full adjustment to the usual adult business of marriage, regular work, and having children. Their sexual adventures are apt to be peculiar and unsatisfactory. Of course many non-artistic people have these troubles, too. It takes an inherent sensitivity to divert the erotic creative drive into an artistic channel.

My general theory is that all creativity is bound up in one parcel and that sex is part of it. If it is blocked in any way from finding satisfying expression in the usual channels it will find others. I shall be interested to learn to what extent your researches substantiate this.

It was a theory Kinsey could never have embraced. He replied:

I do not like the idea of calling every parallel that occurs between adult behavior and the behavior of children as infantile. It represents an evaluation rather than an objective recording of the fact. I am sure that this procedure has been one of the factors obscuring the real analysis of human behavior. When you record objectively on an individual, either a child or an adult, you are in a much better position to start real analysis of causative factors.

Consequently, we are recording in our histories what sorts of adjustments artists, as well as other people, make. We are also studying children. What our conclusions may ultimately be will depend upon what we actually find in the totality of histories.

Kinsey appeared to encounter more writers than other practitioners of the arts, and they gave him the widest possible variety of viewpoints for his work. After a conversation with Katherine Anne Porter in New York, she wrote:

I was only half joking when I remarked to you that I might have something to say to you on the subject of Sex; but I suspect nothing much is new to you by now. Still, a half-joke can be quite serious, and I did mean it, and shall be delighted to be interviewed on the subject of the erotic element in the arts, including, as you say, literature.

They were instant friends, and they met again soon after. On Valentine's Day, 1952, Kinsey was writing to "Dear Katherine Anne," thanking her for her "very considerable contribution" to the research and "to our thinking on various important matters." He hoped to see her on his next trip to New York, and meanwhile invited her to visit him in Bloomington.

His meeting with another lady, Cornelia Otis Skinner, resulted not only in a friendship and a history, but an article in *The New Yorker* magazine in which Miss Skinner related how she gave her history. When she visited Bloomington on tour with her one-woman show, she came to visit Prok and Mac at their house after the performance—"one of the nicest parties we have ever had," Kinsey called it—and Dellenback took a charming picture of them together.

A writer Kinsey was especially interested in because his work shed some light on the research was Gore Vidal, then at the start of his career. He had just published *The City and the Pillar*, the novel in which he first wrote about homosexuality, and Kinsey thought that he had "done an excellent job with a subject which has been poorly handled in too much of the literature." He continued:

You write very well and have a fine dramatic sense in putting the story together. I am particularly impressed by your balanced understanding of the problems that are involved. There are few treatments of male homosexuality in any sort of literature which allow, as clearly as you do, that many different sorts of factors may be involved in accounting for the development of a homosexual pattern. Your understanding of the diverse social problems which arise with different sorts of cases represents an excellent comprehension of reality.

Kinsey noted that he had heard from mutual friends that Vidal would like to meet him, and suggested some possibilities. They met the following month, cordially, but the Kinsey correspondence discloses no further meetings.

Another writer who became a Kinsey friend was also in time a contributor to the project in many ways. Glenway Wescott visited Bloomington, saw Kinsey occasionally in New York and corresponded with him frequently. It was his literate, informed help that gave Kinsey a beginning on his analysis of pornography, as he acknowledged later.

The two had met at a dinner party in New York given by Monroe Wheeler for E. M. Forster, the noted British novelist, whose homosexuality was not widely known to his many admirers, especially those in America. His homosexual novel, *Maurice*, was still only a rumor to all but a few. (It was reported to be on the way to publication after Forster's death in 1970.)

Present also at the dinner was Joseph Campbell, an authority on Sanskrit, among other scholarly accomplishments, and as Wescott recalls, it was a fascinating evening on that early summer night in 1949. Forster was charmed by Kinsey's personality, and for his part, Prok appeared at first amused by what he seemed to consider an eccentric Englishman, until he came under the spell of Forster's conversation. He had no knowledge of Forster's work.

The point of departure for the conversation was the erotic art of India. Forster knew India; Kinsey was an authority on the art. It was Wescott's first encounter with a scientist, and as he said later, "Kinsey lifted me up out of myself and made me feel, for the first time, a part of a whole. He taught me how to get away from a preoccupation with individual cases."

That evening, Wescott was chiefly interested in Kinsey as the author of a book the whole nation was discussing. But then Prok asked if he would help develop a theory of literature as a key to the sex life of artists, exploring the interrelationships he had already begun to develop through taking histories of the various *Streetcar* casts. It was this invitation that led Wescott to Bloomington, where their friendship developed. The two men disagreed, however, about Kinsey's theory, at least in some respects. They discussed it for hours, argued, but remained friends. Wescott called him Alfred—one of the few who did so. There was a mutual admiration between them, although they could hardly have been more unlike. Kinsey was sometimes disturbed because he could not prod Wescott into writing, a failure which affronted his work ethic. As for Wescott, if there was one quality more than another he admired in his friend it was Kinsey's determination to go farther in his work than anyone had done before.

Frequently they discussed research problems and the strictures of critics, of whom Kinsey once wryly observed, "We've worked all these years trying to find out about sexual behavior, and we've only made a start. Now they want us to consider love. If we started in on that, we'd never finish."

As a writer Wescott admired Kinsey's spare, lean, scientific prose, so refreshingly free of jargon, as clear and direct as his speech. Wescott particularly liked the last five chapters of the *Female* volume, which he termed "dazzling," and he was pleased with what he thought of as the "pervasive optimism" of the two volumes, their generally hopeful tone and the fact that Kinsey was never blasé about his subject.

Wescott says he never heard Kinsey speak moralistically except once, when he remarked, "Tell your sadomasochistic friends to observe great caution. The human body adjusts rapidly and the levels are capable of escalating rapidly." (At the time, however, I believe Kinsey did not yet understand that in such a relationship the masochist is boss.) Kinsey thought sadomasochists were the most frustrated people in the world because of their difficulty in finding each other.

One of Wescott's trips to Bloomington occurred as part of a writers' conference being held at the School of Letters, and Kinsey, with his friend's help, held an open house for the literary visitors, who included Delmore Schwartz and Philip Rahv. Both of these men had been critical of the project before they encountered Kinsey on his home grounds, but after they had met him at the open house, they went out of their way to express approval. Schwartz came to the Institute later and spent several hours in the library. He gave Kinsey the benefit of a long critical talk about T. S. Eliot, and Arthur Mizener, another conference guest, performed the same service, with Scott Fitzgerald as the subject. Mizener and his wife even attended one of Prok's Sunday night musicales.

As a tamer of literary lions Kinsey demonstrated again his ability to communicate with people at every level of human endeavor. They were attracted not only by his personality, his persuasiveness and what he was doing, but by his respect for what they could contribute to the project. After a dinner with Thornton Wilder in New York, for example, Kinsey told him, "It is most stimulating to our thinking to get the reactions of some other persons on some of the problems we are dealing with when those persons have expert backgrounds in totally different fields from our own." So infelicitously phrased, perhaps, as to make a professional writer wince, but the frequent clumsiness of Kinsey's prose style in his letters did not conceal the overwhelming sincerity and honesty of his approach to people, which the recipients understood and appreciated.

Obviously Kinsey's literary contacts were on a high level, but he did not disdain anyone who he thought could contribute to the research. He replied with polite courtesy when Polly Adler, the celebrated madam, wrote to him while she was working on her life story, *A House Is Not a Home,* asking him to write a foreword to her book. It would not, she said, be an exposé of the American male's sex life but a revelation of the causes of juvenile delinquency in America and the world, dealing also with political corruption, a subject on which she was well informed. She offered to pay for the foreword, either to Kinsey himself or to the Institute, and all expenses to California in case he wanted to come out for a conference.

Replying, Kinsey regretted that he could not do what she asked because, as he said truthfully, he had a tremendous number of similar requests, but he wished her "the best of success in your undertaking. I shall, of course, look forward with interest to your finished product."

Miss Adler sent him a copy of the book when it appeared, and Kinsey perused it with interest. "I have read it in detail," he wrote her, "and think it is a definite addition to our knowledge of organized prostitution. We are delighted to put it on our shelves as an addition in our research library." He added that he hoped he would have a chance to meet her personally, perhaps in New York—and one can read between the lines his anticipation of getting her history. She replied that nothing could have pleased her more, not even making the best-seller list, than to know that her book was in the Institute library, and added, "If I have, in my small way, contributed anything to the wonderful work you and your associates do in the future, I will feel my life was worth living, if only to write it down." If he traveled west, she concluded, she would be more than happy to have a visit from him in Burbank. Later, the three of us had breakfast one morning in Los Angeles. Prok and I thoroughly enjoyed her company.

A far more unlikely correspondence was the one Kinsey carried on with George Sylvester Viereck, an extreme right-wing figure whose admiration for Hitler had him in frequent political trouble. In the letters Kinsey exchanged with Viereck sporadically, over a period of several years, there was never any mention of politics, and Viereck did not once refer to his pro-fascist philosophy. The conversation was entirely about erotic books and poetry, some of it Viereck's own, which he sent to Kinsey for evaluation. Prok appeared to have a high opinion of Viereck's erotic writings, and he could swallow the unsavory politics partly because he was so apolitical and partly because he would have done business with the devil himself if it would have furthered the research.

Kinsey's continuing study of the erotic element in the arts led him in every direction, both geographically and aesthetically. It was a tribute to his flexibility where his research was concerned that he bought a book of erotic drawings by the contemporary artist Matta, and even had a good word to say for it despite its abstract style. Ordinarily Kinsey's opinions of nonrepresentational or highly abstract art were extremely caustic, although he tried to conceal the strength of these feelings from all but his intimates. No doubt it was Monroe Wheeler who introduced him to Matta's work.

As always when he pursued a subject, Kinsey quickly became a scholar in the field, and this was true of the erotic element in art as well. In his many letters to his friend Kojiro Tomita, of the Museum of Fine Arts in Boston, he discusses Japanese and Chinese art with his customary confidence and knowledge.

Tomita was helpful to him in evaluating art and in guiding him on occasion in the growth of the Institute's Oriental collection, which is one of the finest sections of its archives. Private collectors sometimes sold him works of erotic art for a fraction of their cost as a gift to the Institute, with consequent tax advantages, no doubt, but also from a sincere desire to help Kinsey's work.

Another Japanese expert who proved useful in this particular quest was Professor Tamio Satow, of the Japan Sex Education Society. P. D. Perkins, an American living in Kyoto, also helped find books in that country. By 1951 Kinsey had acquired for the archives more than fifty scrolls and books of Oriental erotic art. The Oriental art library by that time had three or four hundred volumes, more than half of them Japanese. Kinsey hoped to add a Japanese translator to the staff for a year or two, but that proved to be impossible, and he relied on Dr. Ritchie Davis, a part-time member of the staff who was on the Law School faculty. Davis spoke fluent Chinese as a result of having lived in the country for nineteen years, and also had enough command of Japanese to do some initial translating. Of the printed work on the sex life of the Japanese, Kinsey considered Satow's volume one of the most valuable, and referred to it often.

"If I can get time enough to travel abroad," he wrote to the author, "I think Japan is one of the first places I should want to come." Circumstances made that trip impossible. Kinsey went to Europe instead, on his only trip out of the country (except for Cuba, Mexico, two trips to Peru and occasionally Canada), but until he died he longed for the opportunity to visit Japan.

In his own country he did as much as he could, and got into as many areas of the arts as he could manage, each trip creating a new friend. The actress Uta Hagen, for example, discussed actors and acting with him, and the erotic significance of the actor's part on the stage. Later she took him to watch her acting class.

In making this special study of the erotic element in art, Kinsey used the word "erotic" in the broadest sense of an evocation of emotion more or less related to sexual interest in the subject matter. Hundreds of artists gave him their histories, and scores of them spent considerable time discussing their work with him and helping him judge the erotic content of other artists' work. Some of the best-known artists in the country were his helpers in this respect. The same could be said for those in the other arts, as I have indicated. If Kinsey had lived to complete this aspect of the project, I am certain it would have made a fascinating, and no doubt controversial, report.

CHAPTER

XIII

PRISONS

Our work in prisons was aimed chiefly at getting material for the book on sex offenders, which was published after Kinsey's death, but it was also intended to get information on sex in institutions. He had conceived the idea of the book early in the research, in the days when he was getting histories at the Indiana State Penal Farm and the Indiana State Women's Prison.

I remember the first time I heard him lecture to a prison population, shortly after I joined him. Knowing how poorly educated the inmates were (they had sixth-grade educations, on the average), and how skeptical, hardened and disdainful they might be, I sat down to hear the lecture with some apprehension.

To my astonishment, I heard this university professor speaking openly, honestly and directly to his audience, without vulgarisms, obscenities, or any hint of condescension. With them he demonstrated his striking ability to communicate ideas they not only could understand, but in large measure approved. It was an exhilarating experience. He was able to accomplish this partly because of his personal contacts when collecting gall wasps, but also by reason of his natural ability to use the same simple language his audience employed.

People were never "ill," for example; they were "sick." They were not "injured," but "hurt." If the subject of a history knew the word "prick" but not "penis," Kinsey used it, too, but simply as a term, not in a vulgar or slang sense. And always he sought to simplify —"sex organ," not "vagina." He was constantly working with language, trying to put the proper word in the proper place, and in the course of doing so he developed a fine sense of the use of the vernacular. For instance, the old-time Western prison word for a big shot in the institution was "bonnaroo." We used this word in talking to the older inmates in the West, but since the younger men, even though they might know it, never used it in ordinary speech, we avoided it with them.

Kinsey never used jargon or euphemisms, and he insisted on precise definitions. Someone might ask him, "How many young people have sex relations?" He would reply, "All of them." If an astonished eyebrow was raised, he would add, "If you're talking about intercourse, it would be a much smaller percent." Similarly, if a subject told him, "I slept with ten girls," Kinsey would reply, "All right, how many did you have intercourse with?"

He avoided technical words such as "cunnilingus" or "fellation," even though "mouth-genital contact," used as a substitute, might not be quite accurate in some cases. Prok believed that jargon covered up meanings and was not a proper way to communicate.

In speaking to a prison audience, Kinsey would first explain the project to them, telling them of the need to get more information and stressing the confidential nature of the history taking; he assured them that the prison administration would know nothing of what was said. Getting more information about sex, he would tell them, might make their own sex lives easier in the long run. Then he would go on to talk about the inequities of the nation's sex laws. He never attempted to tell jokes to a prison audience in an effort to put them at their ease, yet he sometimes had a twinkle in his eye, and his talent for making wry remarks was far better than the customary humor of public speakers, especially for that audience.

Another reason Kinsey was able to work with prison populations was the attitude of total objectivity he conveyed to them, the familiar, nonjudgmental approach, which won the confidence of so many of the subjects we interviewed. Prisoners could sense beyond the objectivity a certain sympathy for their lot, engendered by Kinsey's deep conviction that the workings of the legal system, especially in the case of sex offenders, was full of injustices. He once wrote to Miss Edna Mann, director of the New Jersey State Women's Prison, at Clinton: "It is a desperately lonely group of poor little girls who get in trouble with the law, isn't it?"

We were under attack at different times from people who insisted that we should not have included in our sample the history of anyone who had ever been in a penal institution. That, as Kinsey liked to point out, was based on the old fallacy that criminals are made of different stuff from the rest of the population. This notion, he once observed, "fails to take into account that the purer persons who give us histories before they ever get into prison cannot give us any positive guarantee that they will not get into prison at any later time in their lives. Before we or anyone else can ever decide how many persons with prison histories should be included, in any particular sort of general sample, we are going to have to have accumulative incidence figures." Later, we did derive such figures and found that of lower-social-level males, more than 20 percent could be expected to do time before they died.

A large-scale effort to get histories was made at San Quentin, the legendary California prison. The year was 1948, shortly after the *Male* volume was published. Before we arrived, the administration had picked out for us the men they considered to be the prison leaders, such as the most popular prize fighter, the foremost Mexican, the chief Negro, and so on. There were fourteen of them. These men did not necessarily have the best jobs, but they were the power elite.

We met with the leaders and explained why we were there and the need for getting their cooperation. We reassured them, as usual, about the confidential nature of the project, and then they surprised us by disclosing that six out of the fourteen had already read our *Male* volume in prison, even though it was contraband. The others had heard about us through the prison grapevine, as the result of our work in other prisons and among underworld groups.

On that trip we took all fourteen of their histories, and estimated that in the twenty-four hours that followed we could have gotten the histories of 95 percent of the prison population if we had been able to accomplish it physically. As it was, it became necessary to devise a sampling scheme on the spot, instead of simply asking for volunteers at random. We went to the records and got lists of the inmates who were in for various kinds of sex offenses. If the list was short for some offenses—as in incest, for example— we took the history of everybody on it. If it was a long list, as for statutory rape, we might take the history of every fifth or tenth man. Then we cut the pie another way. We would go to a particular prison workshop and get the history of every man in the group, whether he was a sex offender or not.

With the sampling process decided upon, we told the administration that we had to have a place to take histories which would be both soundproof and secure. In prisons there are few places that are confidential. Even the rooms used by psychologists, chaplains and parole officers are only partly partitioned, in most cases. At San Quentin, we were told, there were no rooms available, so we asked if we could use a cell. The only soundproof ones were in what was called the Old Prison, built around 1852 (it was recently demolished). The walls there were two feet thick, and instead of iron-barred doors there were quarter-inch solid steel doors with peepholes about six inches long and four inches high, and even these had a bar across them.

Kinsey and I selected two cells for our work. We had to hang heavy blankets along the walls to keep down the reverberations. Our procedure was to call for a particular inmate to be interviewed, and he would be brought to the bottom of the tier by an officer and there placed in our custody. We were responsible for the man until we returned him.

The administration was nervous about this arrangement and suggested that each of us wear a whistle on a cord around his neck. We scoffed at the idea. Eventually they relaxed so much that they gave us permission to have a bucket of ice with Cokes in it for the prisoners. They were the only bottled Cokes in the prison; such drinks were always served in paper cups. Naturally, when the news of this luxury got around, our prestige with the inmates soared. It also seemed to help our standing that we had chosen to work in a cell rather than an office, although we had no choice.

One day after I had finished a history and was taking the subject back to the guard, I heard a whispered voice coming from one of the cells: "Dr. Pomeroy, I gotta talk to you." I was aware of the urgency and panic in that voice, and as soon as I had delivered my prisoner

I stopped at his cell. All I could see were two wild eyes and a chin through the narrow opening, but I recognized him as an inmate whose history I had taken a few days earlier. He was in a "holding cell," where those charged with violations of prison rules were kept to be tried by the institutional court.

I said I was sorry to see him there and asked what he had done. He had been arrested, he said, on a "sex beef," meaning he had been caught in some kind of homosexual behavior in the prison yard. "Dr. Pomeroy," he whispered, "sometimes when a man gets knocked off on such a beef he doesn't feel like living." And with that, he produced a razor blade and slashed his throat from ear to ear.

Quickly I called an officer. He opened the door with a key that was a foot long, and there the inmate lay bleeding. At that moment my next interviewee appeared and I realized I had sole responsibility for him and would have to leave the injured inmate with the officer.

As I began taking the history, I couldn't help showing that I was upset, not knowing whether the other man was dead or alive. I explained to my interviewee what the trouble was, and he thoughtfully suggested that we sit and smoke until I calmed down a little. Three hours later, after we had finished the history, I hurried to the officers' quarters. They told me the razor was only a fragment of a blade, and the wound was superficial. They had patched the inmate in his cell and had not even bothered to take him to the hospital. I discovered later that this man was a habitual suicide attempter. Once he had slashed his wrists and arms, but these wounds, too, were superficial. Another time he had jumped off an upper tier, a favorite kind of suicide among inmates, but his leap was only from the second tier, not the fifth, and he came down feet first instead of head foremost, as men did who were serious about it.

Sometimes a prisoner wrote to us, expressing his gratitude for the kind of oblique help he was able to get from the interview. One sex offender wrote to Kinsey from San Quentin:

May I take this opportunity to express my sincere appreciation for having been given the privilege of an interview. In the twenty months that I have been in this institution, I have received more personal benefit toward understanding my present situation during the four hours I spent with you, than all other attempts combined. I feel entirely different now toward the entire matter.

Kinsey replied:

Mr. Pomeroy and I very much appreciate the fact that some of the men seem to have gotten help from their interviews with us. Our research has been able to go as far as it has because people have believed it was worthwhile and have been willing to give freely of their time and to disclose things about their own lives which it is time the world understood. I think a great many of the people, like yourself, have found that talking things over has made them seem much more understandable, and, therefore, less of a problem than a person thinks they are.

Kinsey was highly pleased with our history taking at San Quentin. He wrote to the prison's warden, Clinton Duffy, that the material we were getting was the most significant in existence on sex offenders, and was a considerable addition to our understanding of the sexual adjustment of all men in penal institutions. He was full of praise for Duffy's intelligent administration, one that he considered was anxious to understand and do whatever was possible within the framework of contemporary social organization and society's demands. When a bad fire swept part of the prison not long after our first visit there, Kinsey wrote Duffy a letter of sympathy, concluding: "Anything that happens at San Quentin interests me."

Douglas Rigg, who was assistant warden at San Quentin when we first went there to take histories, thinks Kinsey loved being at the prison for many reasons. It was near one of his favorite cities, San Francisco, and the trips enabled him to see the many friends he had on the West Coast. Moreover, few other prisons gave him such enthusiastic cooperation. He had more volunteers, both from staff and inmates, than he could handle. In return, Kinsey was generous with his time, always ready to outline his research and discoveries to staff meetings. It broke the jailhouse routine for both convicts and keepers, who often were as institutionalized as their charges.

The cons were receptive to Kinsey, Rigg says, because they saw in him that rarity, a man who made no judgments about them. They had been lectured to by truant officers, parents, juvenile-court personnel, policemen, boys' club workers, chaplains, wives, sweethearts, probation officers, judges, wardens, parole-board members and cellmates—and suddenly there was Kinsey, the man who did not judge them, who only listened. The clinical effect of that simple act was tremendous.

Just as the *Female* volume was being released, Kinsey fled to San Quentin for a short visit, as though he were making a retreat to a monastery. "This is the last place anyone will look for me," he told Rigg. While he was there, Rigg went with him to San Francisco one day. Kinsey's face and name seemed to be displayed on every magazine cover, yet he was seldom recognized.

At the prison everyone knew him and, better, trusted him. "I personally know some of the prisoners he helped by talking with them," Rigg says. "Some of them were in the awful predicament of being able to trust no one. One had been in death row for years. Each was touched by Kinsey's interest, by Kinsey's obvious, sincere regard for people in deep trouble. He brought out the best in most of us."

Kinsey was clear from the first about what he hoped his prison work would do. As he wrote to a San Quentin official:

We think highly of your whole program at San Quentin. We are impressed with the evidence that an increasing portion of your policy is based on the question of the ultimate readjustment of these men in society. I hope that our work may ultimately make it still more possible for institutions to understand what can be done on the sexual issue. Apart from the question of institutional discipline, there is this issue of sexual readjustment of men after they get back into society, and that is one that we have not reached an understanding of in our own minds. We hope that our research will help point the way on that score.

I was delighted to find that I, too, could make excellent personal contacts with prisoners. I remember particularly a Negro I interviewed at Terminal Island Prison, in Long Beach. He had been sent to San Quentin for one to five years for petty larceny, and while he was there had become involved in a homosexual triangle and stabbed another inmate fatally. He was given one year to life and sent to Folsom Prison. Not long after, a law was passed making the death penalty mandatory for anyone doing a life sentence who was convicted of assaulting an officer in prison, and he was in trouble again. He got into an argument with an officer and hit him on the head with a spittoon, without causing serious injury. Under the law, he was sentenced to death and lived the next six or seven years in Death Row, until through the help of the NAACP and the ACLU his sentence was commuted to life with no parole. He was then sent to Terminal Island, where I met him.

Although he was an aggressive, hostile man, he was also a delightful personality, one I enjoyed knowing. At the noon break we often
played chess, and his moves were always offensive. If one could sit
back and wait, permitting his offense to peter out, it was possible to
beat him regularly. Sometimes when I beat him his hostile behavior
made me a little nervous and I could not help wondering what was
going on behind those bright, penetrating eyes. But nothing ever
happened.

As a result of his work in prisons and his research into the many
ramifications of the laws against sex offenders, Kinsey, as usual, became something of an authority in this field. His scientific training
made him a shrewd observer of the legal process. It was clear to him,
for instance, that the statute law was not the final determinant in the
decision of the judge on the bench. That decision might be determined by a great many things other than the statute.

It is not surprising that he came to have strong opinions on various
aspects of crime. Having spent a good deal of time studying juvenile
offenders, he was convinced that much of the impression that delinquency was on the increase arose from the fact that we had changed
our concept of a juvenile. From the time of early Jewish law until
only a few generations ago, he pointed out, an individual was considered an adult when he became adolescent. By refusing to consider
people as adults until they were eighteen or twenty-one, he said, we
were charging against juveniles all the activity that for thousands of
years was always considered adult, although biologically boys and
girls became adult as early as they ever did.

When FBI director J. Edgar Hoover issued in 1950 one of his
periodic statements (they always came just before Congress took up
the agency's budget) asserting that there had been a "terrifying"
increase in sex crimes, Kinsey scoffed at the idea. His figures, he said,
were based on surveys tending to show what the total population was
doing, while the FBI's figures were based on records of arrests, and
consequently merely reflected police activity. Kinsey pointed out
that what the nation and the FBI were calling heinous crimes against
children were things that appeared in a fair number of our total
histories, and in only a small number of cases was public attention
ever aroused or the police involved. Kinsey numbered himself
among those who contended that, as far as so-called molestation of

children was concerned, a great deal more damage was done to the child by adult hysteria.

The FBI was disturbed by the contradiction between Kinsey's figures and ideas about sex crimes and their own, but there was no open confrontation. Kinsey refused to go into the subject publicly until he had accumulated and calculated enough data to substantiate his generalizations.

Regarding the subject on which he was so frequently quoted, and which outraged so many people—that a substantial part of the population would be in jail under our sex laws if they could be fully enforced—Kinsey was always ready with his facts. He was fond of recalling that more than 90 percent of all males involved in petting were performing breast or genital manipulation, an act which regularly was enough to get men from lower social levels into prison on a charge of public indecency or contributing to the delinquency of a minor.

In addition, more than 50 percent of college males had intercourse before marriage, an act carrying a criminal penalty in half the states under any condition, and in nearly all the states if the girl was under eighteen. We had calculated the homosexual incidence at college age to be about 20 percent—again, a prison offense in nearly every state. Such other sexual activity as mouth-genital contact, exhibitionism and voyeurism, said Kinsey, were in the histories of many more people than the public commonly understood.

"It is interesting," Kinsey remarked wryly, only three months before his death, "that we have had these data in print for all these years and it hasn't gotten under the skin of people until they have to fit the shoe to their own foot."

Kinsey analyzed his histories of sex offenders by studying a cross-section of the population which had never been involved with the law. Most previous studies had failed because they were confined to data on sex offenders alone. To Kinsey it was of primary importance to find out how far the behavior of these offenders differed from that of people who comprised the mass of the population segment from which the offender came. By 1946, he, Gebhard and I had interviewed about 1,400 convicted sex offenders in penal institutions scattered over a dozen states. We had examined, in addition, the records of courts, had talked with police officers, with parole and probation officers, and with other law enforcement groups in large cities such as New York and Chicago, and in numerous smaller cities and towns.

From this mass of material we had come to some conclusions. First of all, as our histories showed, the male matured sexually at an early age, and many boys began their sexual activities before adolescence, most of them reaching the peak in their middle or later teens. Since solitary masturbation and nocturnal emission were the only kinds of premarital sexual activity not contrary to law, everything else was technically illegal. Consequently it was biologically inevitable, Kinsey argued, that the teen-age group of boys should most often be involved in sexual activities which brought them into conflict with the law.

On the other hand, the female developed sexually more slowly than the male, and the involvement of teen-age girls in sex delinquency was more often dependent on their interest in making social contacts than in any sexual drive. Kinsey pointed out that segments of the population differed considerably in the extent to which they accepted or tabooed various kinds of sexual activity. In general, he could say, on the basis of our research, the better-educated portion of the population depended upon masturbation as the chief source of outlet before marriage, while the more poorly educated 85 percent of the population depended primarily on premarital intercourse.

Ultimately, Kinsey concluded, nearly every individual was involved—and most were regularly involved—in sexual behavior which at some point or other was contrary to the law. But only a fraction of 1 percent of this population behaving contrary to the law was ever apprehended and brought before the courts. It was this fraction that concerned him.

Kinsey estimated that about 5 percent of people convicted for sex offenses were involved in sexual behavior differing from the pattern usual at their particular social level. That figure would include those who employed force in making their contacts; the feebleminded or the psychotics, who were not responsible and became offensive in their social deportment; and those who were compulsive in their behavior. All of these, he stated, were people who acted publicly without regard for public reaction, and who offended repeatedly despite the certainty of discovery and the resulting penalties. These were the people, he said, with whom society ought to be concerned, among all of those who were technical violators of the law.

In the treatment of sex offenders Kinsey found himself once again in opposition to the psychoanalysts. Writing to James V. Bennett, director of the Bureau of Prisons, in the Department of Justice, he praised Bennett's system but decried his use of psychoanalytic therapy in the system:

I am afraid your faith in psychoanalysis as a remedy for any high proportion of sex offenders is misplaced. I have had an opportunity to see it in action in some thousands of individual cases. It can do a good deal for a disturbed personality which needs to learn how to accept itself. In a limited number of certain types, psychoanalysis can train the individual into new avenues of behavior. In most instances, however, it does not begin to accomplish what the analysts claim it does, or can do, in changing patterns of behavior.

As far as institutional treatment is concerned, I have a few outstanding cases of where the psychiatrists have done a good deal to help institutional inmates effect subsequent social adjustment. I do have a very much larger number of cases where a well-trained social worker or almost anyone else with a good deal of common sense has been able to do a good deal more for the institutional inmate. The notion that every departure from social custom represents a disturbed personality cannot be substantiated in any scientific fashion. In a much larger number of cases it represents a failure to understand the reality of the world and learning how to conduct oneself without offending society.

Kinsey not only studied the histories of people who had been convicted as sex offenders. He carried on an elaborate study of the procedures involved in the handling of sex offenders in two large jurisdictions; made a statistical survey of the incidences of sex offenses on court dockets; performed a detailed study of police and court procedures; and investigated several other related problems. These studies were made by specialists in the areas involved whom Kinsey brought to the Institute from time to time.

As a result of this work, and the part of it that was reflected in the *Male* volume, Kinsey could point to some concrete results in state legislatures. In California, for example, the lawmakers appropriated $75,000 per year for a study of sex offenders, supplementing his own work, and placed it under the direction of Kinsey's friend Dr. Karl Bowman, of the Langley Porter Clinic in San Francisco. Dr. Bowman's research program made abundant use of our material, and three of his staff came to Bloomington to consult with Kinsey. Consultations also took place at different times in San Francisco. Kinsey himself met with the California legislature's committee on sex laws, and he prepared special documentary material for the consideration of several other committees. Governor Pat Brown, whom he came to know well, worked with him closely in developing the state's program.

In 1952 Kinsey collaborated with an Illinois state legislative committee which was working on a revision of sex laws in that state. He spent much time in gathering factual data for the committee's use. This action followed a pattern he had already established with legislative committees and special research groups set up by the governments of New Jersey, New York, Delaware, Wyoming and Oregon.

All this, said Kinsey, ought to be a lesson to the governor and legislature of Indiana, who could profit from what he was doing instead of being alarmed by the publication of his book.

Of all our prison experiences, of which the ones I have related are only a small sampling, I am certain the most unusual occurred at the Metropolitan State Hospital, in Norwalk, California, an institution unique in the United States in those days. It was a place where some general ideas were offered to the inmate-patients, who were then permitted maximum freedom to discuss and think about things on their own. One could scarcely name a principle of penal institution administration which was not broken at Norwalk.

We happened upon this situation just before the publication of the *Male* volume, when Kinsey got a letter one day inviting him to talk to the sexual psychopath patients there, in return for which he would be able to get their histories. At the time there were about two hundred of these patients in the prison. Kinsey saw the invitation as a splendid opportunity. We had interviewed only a few such people, and he was anxious to talk to more of them, and learn how they were different from other people.

Consequently we found ourselves one day in the office of the superintendent. He was surprised to see us, and told us he knew nothing about the invitation and arrangements for our visit. He surmised that it had been the work of the patient governing body called ESP, meaning Emotional Security Program. Then, to our astonishment, he told us that this body had freedom to invite outside speakers, and was also free to do a great number of other things far beyond what inmates or patients in other institutions were permitted. He, of course, had no objection to our coming, and we took the histories of all but one of the two hundred. The whole situation seemed so unusual to me that I thought it worthwhile to make my own record of what happened there.

Not long before our visit, California had passed a law governing sexual psychopaths which had resulted in simply taking these two hundred inmates bodily and transplanting them to Norwalk, whose administration knew nothing about how to handle them, since this was a standard mental hospital, which did not deal in such cases. Now they had two hundred prison inmates who had been transformed suddenly into hospital patients. These men were in custody for offenses covering a broad range of sexual behavior, including homosexuality, pedophilia, rape, incest, exhibitionism and voyeurism. All of them had been convicted; all had been declared psychopaths.

Since they had no preconceived ideas about what to do with their unexpected patients, the hospital staff began to ask questions and try to find out what should be done. These were some of the innovations they devised to meet their problem:

1. The men wore their own civilian clothing.
2. Wives and family members were allowed to visit the men in their quarters.
3. They were allowed to have privacy with their wives, but after one became pregnant this had to be stopped.
4. Previous patients who had been released were welcomed back to visit.
5. There was unlimited and uncensored correspondence.
6. Work assignments were based on the patient's need, not on what the institution might require. For example, an experienced plumber might be assigned to the kitchen detail on the ground that his homosexuality might be helped by contact with women kitchen workers, even though plumbers were badly needed.
7. There was freedom of movement among the group, and they were even permitted to go into the town of Norwalk under certain controlled conditions. At the beginning there were several escapes, but when the patients returned they were ostra-

cized by the others, and this kind of social pressure ended the escapes.

8. Patients were allowed to have unlimited cash in their pockets.
9. Unlimited gambling was permitted. The administration reported that the professional gamblers among the men quickly won all the others' money, then gave it back so the game could go on.
10. Patients were free to have any pictures they wanted. One large calendar picture hanging in the dining room was the famed nude photograph of Marilyn Monroe. Suppression, said the hospital, would have been worse, and so homosexuality was not suppressed either.
11. Young children came on visiting days, because it was believed that pedophiles must learn to live with them without danger. There were no incidents.
12. A group of Norwalk housewives, known as the Bib and Apron Club, asked if they could help and were told they could come in once a week and give a dance, so that the patients could be taught how to observe the amenities. These occasions would also give them a connection with the outside world.
13. Inmates had the privilege of "firing" any guard or officer they did not like. These people would simply be transferred elsewhere in the hospital.
14. Women therapists were part of the staff.
15. The entire program was therapy oriented, and went on twenty-four hours a day. Formal therapy was developed in what was called the "doctors' group." Eight to ten patients spent about two hours a week in the group with a therapist.
16. There was also a patients' group. No trained therapist sat with these patients, but certain patients from the doctors' group were assigned to it.
17. Inmates often proved to be better judges than the therapists of whether a particular inmate was going to adjust well in the outside world.

Under the program I have just outlined, there was about a 5 percent return rate after the men were released, in contrast to a 20 to 50 percent return in other groups.

One would think that this sensible situation would have been not only encouraged but broadened in the state penal system. Instead California built a $20 million institution to which all sexual psychopaths were sent, and the Norwalk program was ended. The new institution had no such spark, and although some feeble, halfhearted attempts were made to copy the original idea, it was never as successful.

Ironically, the administration at Norwalk had no realization of what a remarkable thing it had done. Its members were not aware that they had been innovators, and that other hospitals treated these patients quite differently. Since that was true, the Norwalk story was never told in its entirety, but I believe it still stands today as a model for treating those whose sexual behavior has been condemned by law.

Kinsey made several trips to Norwalk, and one day invited his old Bowdoin friend Austin MacCormick to come down from the University of California, where he was professor of criminology, and see the program in operation. MacCormick did so, and through a long day listened to Prok talking with sex offenders of nearly every kind, in groups and individually. After the individual interviews he was permitted to observe, MacCormick recalled best Kinsey's great skill in asking questions to which others would have found it all but impossible to get answers. He asked them with the easy manner a family doctor might have in questioning a patient who knew him well. As a consequence, the answers soon became easy and forthright. Prok could do it, as MacCormick observes, because he had a complete understanding of people who had been despised and rejected by most of their fellowmen, which was supplemented by a strong desire to help them understand and resolve their problems. In the bargain, he had the wisdom to know the difference between true aberration and normal behavior.

One can only speculate what good could be accomplished in the world if it were only possible to have a thousand hospitals like Norwalk, staffed by men like Kinsey.

CHAPTER

XIV

TOWARD THE GOAL

AT THE BEGINNING of 1945, Kinsey was forging ahead rapidly toward the point where he would be ready to begin writing the *Male* volume, his first report on the project. He had geared himself to a peak of tremendous activity, and as one who was part of it, I look back on this period with a sense of incredulity that so much could have been accomplished.

Kinsey's own schedule was unbelievable. As the year began, he was planning a New York trip with a program that would have staggered anyone else. He had five lectures before psychiatric groups: the staff and Army psychiatric group at the New York State Psychiatric Hospital; the psychology staff at Columbia University; the staff and Army psychiatric group at Bellevue (two lectures); and the American Orthopsychiatrists Association at its annual meeting in New York (for which he was dinner speaker). Another speech was to be given to a large group of physicians interested in contraception. He planned to take histories at two of the best private schools, by his usual method of lecturing first to parents and teachers. One of the first-rank girls' colleges was also on his schedule, and an organization of psychoanalysts had asked him to meet with them.

All of these groups, of course, would give him their histories as well as make further contacts for him. Dr. Harry Benjamin, the noted endocrinologist and sexologist, had promised to make further contacts with friends and patients, and the newly founded American Association of Marriage Counselors in the city intended to help him get histories. In connection with a survey in progress on wayward minors in New York he expected to obtain histories from the cases going through Bellevue, and in order to help him understand the background of these cases, arrangements were being made to bring him into touch with social settlement groups, with children in the police shelters in the city and with other lower-level groups. Dr. Dickinson had promised to make contact for him with a select group of professional, upper-level and older friends. The scientific staff of the American Museum of Natural History had agreed to contribute.

Across the Hudson, Kinsey had made an arrangement with the Johnson and Johnson Company, in Linden, New Jersey, to take histories from the top executives on its staff. Social workers, a group interested in the blind, and two Episcopal diocese groups were also involved. Back in New York, he had an opportunity to get histories at Cooper Union, if it could be worked in. There were twenty or more physicians and psychiatrists who had agreed individually to contribute histories. (Kinsey once estimated that he could get two or three thousand histories of medical people in New York, if he only had the time and the "hands" to take them.)

By this time we had secured histories from Connecticut to New Mexico, from large cities and from small towns and rural areas. Philadelphia alone had yielded 1,200 histories, and there Kinsey had enjoyed cooperation from psychiatrists, psychoanalysts, Quaker groups, nearly all of the private schools, all five of the medical colleges, students and faculties in several colleges and universities, social workers' groups, the city probation officers, teachers in the public schools, parent-teacher groups, Salvation Army groups of several sorts, and a dozen or more other sources.

Yet we were charged later with concentrating on college-educated, upper-class people in the Northeast!

At the start of 1945, Kinsey could report, his count of histories stood at 7,300, and in the preceding two months he had been given an assurance by the Committee that he could plan on a twenty-year project, with his cherished goal of 100,000 histories.

It is hardly surprising that, by June, Kinsey had worked himself into a state of collapse. In July he wrote to a friend in New York:

I have been exhausted and in bed part of the time for the last several weeks and I am glad that my traveling is over for the first half of this year. Bloomington is remarkably comfortable this summer, and I can settle down and spend most of the rest of the summer on the first book. . . . It has taken three years of continuous calculation on the statistics, and there is a tremendous amount of detail to work into the text that I hope will be rather easy reading. There are endless charts and diagrams for those who want to examine minute details of the data. I have no more long travel until the middle of September. We will be in Chicago, Columbus and Indianapolis early in the fall, and in New York for six weeks beginning the first of November.

As we slowly worked our enormous collection of data into shape for the book, we began to come upon some conclusions that surprised us. We had started out like voyagers on an unknown ocean, not knowing what we might find and, unlike most such travelers, without preconceived ideas of what our destination might be like. Any other approach would have been unscientific, of course. We had no theories of human sexuality, no rigid conceptions of what sexual behavior ought to be, no set beliefs about what it actually was in the whole population.

Taking histories day after day, week after week, month after month, and compiling an immense amount of information from them, ideas began to form, inevitably, and the dim outline of concepts began to emerge from the pile of statistics. We began to see what we thought were differences between social levels, and certain differences between the sexes. But we always had to remind ourselves that often these ideas were inspired by a series of unusual or even bizarre cases, which would make any conclusions drawn from them erroneous.

I learned something valuable from this process. I learned to be skeptical of doctors who advanced theories beginning "Now, I don't have any data to support it, but my clinical impression is . . . " I saw that the clinical impression, without adequate data to support it, could be just as often inaccurate as correct.

For example, I am certain that before Kinsey, if anyone had suggested that the number of males having nocturnal emissions varied by educational groups, the "clinical impression" of most therapists would have been that there was no relationship, nor did we ourselves believe otherwise. But as the correlated data began to emerge from our IBM machines, we were dumbfounded to find that a relationship did indeed exist. Among males who had never gone beyond the eighth grade, only 56 percent had nocturnal emissions. For those who had gone to high school but not beyond, the figure was 71 percent. For college students, it was 91 percent. We believed the reason for these differences to be that the more intelligent males had a greater imaginative capacity, and consequently a richer dream content, which led to more nocturnal emissions.

The most surprising thing to us was that in all our interviewing we had never noticed this remarkable difference, until the histories had been summarized by the machine. It was the kind of thing that would happen over and over again. To take another example, we were conscious as we went along that a great deal of homosexual material appeared in the histories we were taking, but we were entirely unprepared for the startling amount of such behavior that turned up when the records were correlated at last.

At this stage in the research, we were also beginning to penetrate more deeply into specialized categories of histories, two of which deserve attention. Kinsey's success with children is especially worth noting, I think, not only because he was so good with them but because here he was moving in perhaps the most dangerous and controversial area of all.

He had a particular empathy with children. Perhaps one factor in it was the loss of his firstborn, Donald, who died at the age of four. When anyone asked him about his family, he would always say, "I have had four children, Don, Anne, Joan and Bruce." He never failed to include Don. At his insistence, his last three children had been given one-syllable names; nicknames, he believed, could be a psychological handicap, although that had not seemed to affect Prok and Mac.

As one who had a genuine fondness for young children, Kinsey was cross with them only when they disturbed his garden. When my wife and I brought our children on visits to Kinsey's house and we strolled in the garden, he was uneasy and even irritable if my children were not particularly respectful of his flowers and shrubs. Now that I have grandchildren, I understand his anxiety a little better.

In taking a sexual history, we asked people about their sexual behavior from earliest memory—four, five and six—and realized how fragmentary these memories were, and how much we were missing.

At some point Kinsey wondered what would happen if he went to children themselves and asked them about their sex play. Although it was possible to find a few liberal parents who would be willing to have a sex researcher question their young children on this subject, we doubted that we could get an adequate sample unless we got the parents into the act. It would also be difficult and time-consuming to establish rapport with young children, without the parents being involved.

Consequently Kinsey began to create situations with children, with the parents present. These four- and five-year-olds would tell about their sex play while the parents listened, often with surprise. From this preliminary work we discovered an important fact: young children would talk more easily of homosexuality in their histories than about heterosexuality; with adults, the reverse was true.

Kinsey tried to train me to help with interviewing the children, but I found that I wasn't good at it. I was not patient enough, and clearly it was not my forte. For that matter, none of the other staff members was any more successful at this delicate job, and Kinsey had to do nearly all of it alone.

He concentrated at first on the three-, four- and five-year-old levels, working primarily in nursery schools, and always getting the parents' histories first. He also took a scattering of older children, and found that after age eight it was better to exclude parents. There were a few nine- and ten-year-olds who gave histories, but this aspect of the project never really developed. Kinsey had hopes and dreams of exploring in depth such a relatively untouched field, but that part of the investigation died with him.

Nevertheless, we were able to get a fairly broad sampling. When he worked upward into the postadolescent group, Kinsey discovered that he could easily bridge what is now known as the generation gap. These older children got the feeling that he was desperately trying to understand them, and that was enough. He insisted that anyone under eighteen had to get parental consent; this was a firm policy. The exceptions were college students under eighteen, and interviewees in ghetto areas. We seldom had trouble getting permission from parents.

In Chicago we worked extensively in the Francis Parker School and in Chicago University's high school, with grades from kindergarten through twelfth. Kinsey would lecture to faculty, parents and the PTA, getting many histories from these people as well, and never experiencing any difficulty—probably because these were upper-level groups and we had the school faculties behind us.

He once described the procedure he followed in getting children's histories in a letter to Dr. Sophia J. Kleegman, a New York gynecologist.

Our usual procedure is for us to speak to the parents or parents and teachers first, and to go after histories from the parents and teachers. We do not take any history from a child until at least one of his parents has given us a history and has consented to our getting a history from their child. We never take the history of a child under seven unless at least one of the parents is present at the interview. We prefer to take the histories of the children under seven in their own homes, or in some place, such as a school, with which they are familiar. Where the child is not timid, and where the parents find it more convenient, we can, of course, meet them at our hotel.

This children's material is precious. It is giving us more insights into the patterns of behavior than we ever anticipated we could get.

Those who helped Kinsey get these histories were always impressed with the easy way he worked with children, and specialists in the field became immediately aware of his talent. Mr. A. E. Hamilton, a consulting psychologist who headed the Hamilton School, where Kinsey took histories, wrote to him after their first meeting:

That was a nice chat we had about kids. You made me feel that you've got the "way" to go about the job with little people. I'm conceited enough to feel that I know kids about the way you do wasps—and have been on my job with youngsters a little longer, and in somewhat the same way you were with the wonderful stingy folk. And when I come across a fellow who clicks with a child, I'm happy about it.

Mr. Hamilton offered his whole family for histories—"one daddy of sixty, one mama of forty (approximately), one girl of going on thirteen, one boy of seven, one young amazon of three."

Something of Kinsey's approach can be sensed in the letters he wrote to two little girls who had given him (and me) their histories. To Pam he wrote:

Uncle Pomeroy and Uncle Kinsey want you to have a whole letter for yourself while we are sending a whole letter to your sister just for herself. I hope the mailman will ring the bell in a very important fashion and hand you a letter which has your name on it and which is just for your very own.

We are writing you this letter because we want to thank you for letting us come to see you at your house, and for talking to us so nicely while we were there. We think both of you are very nice girls. Tell your mother that we think you are very good girls.

I have just gotten back home, at Bloomington, Indiana. That is why I can write you a letter now. I am writing it so that it will reach you before Christmas. I hope you have a very good Christmas.

And we signed it separately—"Uncle Kinsey" and "Uncle Pomeroy."

To Pam's older sister, Penny, went a different kind of letter:

I am writing to thank you for the very important help that you gave us when you let me talk to you the last time I visited you at your home. Uncle Pomeroy and Uncle Kinsey think you are both very fine girls, and you were very nice to let us talk to you and to draw pictures for us, and to tell us all about the things that you do.

I should have written you this letter sooner, but I went off to talk to a lot of older people after I talked to you and I only came home yesterday. Now I shall be home with all of my own children for Christmas. I hope you have a very good Christmas.

Even when the burden of answering letters weighed him down most, Kinsey always found time to answer a youthful correspondent. A boy in Northfield, Minnesota, a senior in high school, wrote to him and declared he planned to study sexology, but before he made up his mind completely, he wanted to ask advice. Kinsey seriously outlined what he considered the basic requirements.

A little Indiana farm girl wrote:

I am in the fourth grade in school. In science we have studied about bees. We wondered how you found out that nectar mixes with the juice in the bee's stomach while it is flying to its hive. Would you be so kind as to give us this information?

To this Kinsey replied a bit ruefully:

It is quite a compliment to have you think that I can answer questions about honey bees and clover at this time. Frankly, I do not remember who did the original studies which explained how the bees turned nectar into honey, and I am so very busy with the other sort of research that we have been doing in the last years that I cannot take time off to look the matter up. So you have the honor of discovering that a scientist doesn't know any more than you do about some things. Keep up your interest in the outdoors!

Inevitably, Kinsey's work with children led him counter to the conventional wisdom. A few months before he died, he wrote indignantly to Dr. Karl Bowman, of the Langley Porter Clinic, in San Francisco, to deplore two pamphlets issued by the Oakland police force, warning children against speaking to strangers or allowing them to touch them. The pamphlets, he noted, had "gone through the hierarchy and bear the imprimatur of J. Edgar Hoover," and he concluded: "Just where will our world be if all people are raised from here in, never to speak to any stranger? I think . . . we are agreed on the traumatic effects of this sort of thinking."

2

Another group through which Kinsey had to move with care were Negroes. (I say "Negro" here rather than "black" because this was the word used in the context of the times; most Negroes then would have resented being called blacks.) As 1945 began, Kinsey was acutely conscious that his Negro sample at that point was too heavily loaded with poorly educated and economically lower groups, and he was afraid that too many people might take that picture as typical of Negroes as a whole. Obviously there was no way of presenting a true picture of the different social levels among Negroes unless he could get a quantity of histories from the better-educated Negroes. He was especially anxious to be fair and scientifically objective in this area of the research.

That was why we went to Howard University to get histories from educated Negroes, and so round out our sample. Kinsey had been able easily to relate to the Negroes in prison, and he found no more difficulty at Howard. A man who was impatient with racism, he was always able to talk naturally to Negroes, as he could to anyone else.

At Howard the format went as usual—the lecture, followed by history taking. The lecture was given at the medical school, and it went well enough, but we were surprised to find a great deal of resistance to giving histories, a rare occurrence. Kinsey quickly understood why. These students thought Whitey was delving into their lives in his own interest, not theirs; white researchers encounter the same reaction today when they attempt to make ghetto studies.

The students were also against our separating white and black histories at all. We explained that we separated people not only by race, but also by age, religion, gender and a number of other categories, but they were adamant. Finally, exasperated, Kinsey said firmly:

Now, we're going to do this project no matter what happens, and you should know that we already have a large body of histories from lower-level Negroes. When we publish our findings, we will be careful to state that these *are* lower-level histories, but people won't remember that. The only way to correct this impression is for you to cooperate so we can get the whole spectrum.

This speech elicited much more cooperation, but it was still not the 100 percent Kinsey always strove for. In time, however, we did get enough histories of upper-level Negroes to compensate for the others. Their histories, I might add, were much like those of upper-level whites, and vastly different from those of lower-level Negroes, again paralleling the white differences. The figures we obtained were convincing proof that race was not a factor in human sexual behavior.

When we did get down to taking histories at Howard, there was a problem about where to conduct the interviews. We preferred not to use the classroom buildings, so we made an arrangement at one of the dormitories. When it came time for lunch on the first day, we decided not to go all the way back into town to eat and lined up with students in the dormitory cafeteria. The Negro manager came up and told us coldly that we were not welcome to eat there, and thus we learned what racial discrimination was like at first hand. We appealed to the manager of the dormitory. He overrode the cafeteria manager, who, as it turned out, was the only one who did not want us to eat there. The students had no objection. Nevertheless, it was a valuable experience.

As publication time for the *Male* volume approached, we were under constant pressure from Negro publications to disclose specific race data, but Kinsey adamantly refused to take any such approach to his work. He simply pointed out that no Negro data, as such, was included in the book, nor had any such data been assembled and correlated on which to base an article. It would be utterly unfair to Negroes, he argued, to reach any conclusions on the basis of the material available.

Ebony magazine, one of the Johnson publications in Chicago, was the most persistent, and finally offered Kinsey the one kind of bait that would induce him to alter his stand. The magazine's associate editor, Kay Cremin, wrote to him less than a month before the *Male* book was to appear, with a last-minute offer:

In view of the white press's general sensationalism in treating Negro sexuality and the tendency for non-whites to distort facts on the issue, we hope you will give colored reporters an advance view of the material when completed.

Mr. Johnson, our publisher, has authorized me to say that he feels your study is such an addition to the advancement of clear thinking that he will gladly give you or your representatives an opportunity to ask members of our staff for interviews. He cannot, of course, guarantee that they will acquiesce, even with the added inducement of being able to flee their typewriters for a few hours. However, your staff is surely versed in the ways of persuasion, and can win the confidence of most of them. Incidentally, our staff is largely female, and mostly colored. I am white, and pretty busy during office hours, but will talk with an interviewer at my home if you still need data on white women. It is also quite likely that, once started interviewing here, you can gather many names from staff members and from Mr. Johnson for other interviews.

Replying, Kinsey made the smallest possible concession, granting permission to quote a paragraph from page 223 of the book, and then accepting the invitation to take histories.

After the *Male* book appeared, Kinsey still had the inadequacy of the Negro sampling on his mind, and that was the motive for our approach to Howard, and the interviewing there which I have described. In asking permission of Dr. Mordecai W. Johnson, the university's president, to make the trip, Kinsey made his position clear:

Our first published volume was confined to the white male, even though we did have the histories of more than a thousand Negro males, and more than a thousand Negro females. We have refrained from any publication on the Negro because we are very anxious that there be no misinterpretation by basing conclusions on anything less than a thoroughly adequate sample of all social levels. Our first volume reports considerable differences of patterns of behavior between the better educated and more poorly educated white males, and we are very conscious of the fact that too many of the generalizations on the Negro have been based on lower-level groups alone. It is because we are anxious to secure the histories of better educated and socially upper-level Negro groups that we are coming to Washington.

The enterprising *Ebony* sent out a questionnaire early in 1952 to Negro college students in an attempt to get data on their sex lives, and sent a copy of it to Kinsey, asking for his comments on the replies they had received, which were at variance with his figures.

Since the questionnaire method was anathema to Prok, his reaction was predictable, but his reasoning was sound. He replied:

If you are getting something like 20 per cent response, you are left completely in the dark as to the 80 per cent of the persons who fail to answer the questionnaire. This is very different from our 100 per cent sampling, where we get the histories of everybody in a group that we work with, and is a very much higher refusal rate than we get even among the so-called volunteers. . . . This will account for the first difference between your figures and ours.

Secondly, your results are going to differ from ours because of the difficulty that anybody has in understanding any sort of written questionnaire. Your very first question, "how old are you?" is not going to be closer than within one year of accuracy because there are persons who calculate as of their past birthday and there are persons who calculate as of their forthcoming birthday. This is one thing we always have to clear up in taking our histories by personal interview. We also note that you ask about premarital intercourse and about homosexual activity but you do not ask a point-blank question concerning masturbation.

Thirdly, you are going to get more cover-up on written questionnaires than you are on an interview where an interviewer has won the rapport of a community. People, even when guaranteed anonymity, will not commit themselves on socially taboo and legally punishable activities like premarital intercourse and homosexual activity, when they have to put it down in black and white. Practically all previous questionnaire experience indicates that they come out with figures very much lower than personal interviews.

Getting what could be reasonably considered as a complete sampling of the Negro population remained one of the unfulfilled objectives of Kinsey's life, another of the hopes that he died without realizing.

3

In the pivotal year of 1945, the Second World War ended—and in remembering that fact I am aware that once more it may be difficult to understand how anyone could have lived through one of the cataclysmic events of human history without being affected by it. It was not, I am sure, that Kinsey was unconcerned about the issues of the war, or that he was indifferent to its outcome in any way. Rather, his scientific dedication to the project and his overwhelming involvement with it simply placed a wall between him and the events that were shaking the world. It impinged on him, since his son was not old enough to be endangered, only when it concerned his work, as in the early days, when he made every effort to get draft deferments for his staff members, and later, when the Army made some tentative use of his work.

The war was virtually over before that occurred, much to Kinsey's disgust, since he had hoped to be able to make studies of men in the Armed Forces while the services were still at full strength. It was April 1945, however, before he was called to Washington for a two-day conference with the head medical and psychiatric staffs of the Army, the Navy, the Public Health and Selective Services—forty, all told, of the top men from these agencies. He took up the entire two days presenting summaries of his data and answering questions, and concluded that these leaders in the field understood what he was talking about but that they were having difficulty explaining to ranking officers in the services, who still thought in terms of right or wrong, normal or abnormal.

With the war over, Kinsey continued to advise the Army in various ways, particularly on the venereal disease problem, working with the Surgeon General's office. It was his opinion that much of the public campaign against VD had been directed toward the segments of the population least often involved in promiscuous intercourse. His figures showed that a fifth or less of illicit intercourse was with prostitutes; the other four-fifths included neither professional prostitutes nor amateurs accepting pay. Consequently, with 80 or 90 percent of some of the largest segments of Americans participating in such intercourse, he said, it indicated the extent of the problem in controlling venereal disease.

When the Surgeon General's office proposed making a film on VD and sent him the scenario for comment, Kinsey answered:

I wonder about the scientific accuracy of laying emphasis upon sterility and on the fact that there is no positive cure for gonorrhea. Technically both statements are accurate. Technically it is just as accurate to say that there is no positive safety in walking across any street anywhere and that one should, in consequence, confine himself to his house for the rest of his life. What would a statistical comparison show between the danger of being knocked down by automobiles in the course of one's life and the danger of never being cured of a case of gonorrhea?

Kinsey also resisted any attempt by others to apply his techniques in making Army studies. A young Army doctor wrote to him in 1948, reporting that he was going to set up a Mental Hygiene Consultant Service at Camp Pickett, Virginia, and it had occurred to him that he would be in a unique position to administer the Kinsey questionnaire to the many new draftees he would examine. Kinsey was aghast at the idea. It took a solid year to train a new man for the project, he said, granting that the interviewer was qualified, and in any case, the essence of his approach was to win the interviewee's confidence and get him to give his history for the sake of the project. Even the most skilled interviewer, he believed, would never get comparable material from persons who were forced to contribute histories. Besides, he considered what the young doctor proposed as an abrogation of the Constitutional rights of the draftees, which the public would not tolerate if it were found out.

In setting forth these opinions, Kinsey recalled that at the end of the war some internationally known investigators had tried to reproduce his study with a group of men in Biarritz, but the project lasted less than two weeks because the commanding officer put a stop to the whole thing.

While the Armed Forces' medical leaders were much in accord with Kinsey, it was obvious both during the war and after that in the conflict between conventional morality and medical fact, the services in the end came out on the side of morality, with what to Kinsey were lamentable results. For example, the Army's Section of Troop Information and Education had made a study of factors influencing men in their sexual behavior in the Army, but influential members of the Chaplain's Corps and some other officers did not like what the report revealed, and locked it up in Washington without public disclosure. The report showed that the attitudes of whole groups of men influenced individuals more than the moral lectures they were given, and that matter-of-fact scientific presentation of data had about as much influence as any formal education. Kinsey saw this as a hopeless confusion of moral issues with practical medical problems. He pointed out that his figures showed that only 5 percent of males changed their behavior after they were sixteen, and there was no evidence that Army influence altered this figure.

As for another popular belief, that Army life developed homosexuality, Kinsey scoffed at the idea. Nearly 30 percent of the males who were inducted into the Army, he said, had already had some homosexual experience. He estimated that not more than 5 percent of those who had homosexual activity while they were in the service had had their initial experience after joining. Among women, he asserted, the exceedingly severe stand that the WACs and the other women's services in the Armed Forces took against heterosexual activity was probably a greater factor in the homosexuality which existed in these branches than the lack of recreation in the USO sense. In or out of the Army, the prime factor in the development of homosexuality, as his data showed, was the failure of society to approve premarital heterosexual relations, and that was true of both males and females.

If the Army and the end of the war were only minor factors in Kinsey's life as 1945 came to an end, the major factor was the shortage of help as the project moved rapidly toward its first climax, publication of the *Male* volume. He resisted attempts to persuade him to hire psychiatrists. That was not the kind of help he was looking for. Psychiatrists, he believed, were trained in a technique of interviewing which was inadequate for obtaining an overall picture of sexual behavior in any large number of persons. His experience with subjects who had been interviewed by psychiatrists indicated that he could get 95 percent or more of the factual data in an hour's interview which a psychiatrist was accustomed to taking several hundred hours to obtain. This was not an attack on psychiatric method as a therapeutic technique, he said, but simply to say that it was impossible as a means of obtaining data for an overall survey. A properly trained psychiatrist, indeed, would have found it extremely difficult to adapt himself to our short interviews. Kinsey also believed that not many of them would be willing to spend the long hours in the field; we were interviewing fifty or more persons a week at the time.

This is an explorer's job [Kinsey declared], in which the ability of the man to meet people of diverse social levels and quickly win confidence is fully as important as any professional background that he may have. . . . The work is too difficult for anyone who does not have an enthusiastic conviction that it is worth doing whatever the obstacles. I am skeptical of the man who says he will be interested if the salary is not less than thus and so. That is the wrong point from which to begin.

The problem of "more hands" was a critical one, and Kinsey was near despair about it as 1946 began. Making a progress report to Yerkes in February, he noted that we had passed the 10,000 mark in histories near the end of January, and in spite of increased time given to preparing the book and the lack of field staff, he would be able to report an accumulation of 2,500 histories during the past year when he made his annual report in April—more than in any previous year.

Nevertheless, Kinsey wrote to Yerkes:

I am discouraged about additions to our staff. I know how to persuade people to give us histories, to get a fair portion of the record from them when we get their histories; and Mr. Pomeroy and Mr. Martin have helped splendidly in their jobs, and Nowlis in the laboratory analyses; but there are all sorts of factors that enter in making it difficult to find additional persons. There are several people who would be suitable if they were willing to travel, but that factor holds back some of them. There are some who do not have personalities that would make it possible to win confidence from people quickly, there are some who are opinionated in regard to certain matters of sex so that they would be useless in getting histories from many of our subjects. I have interviewed perhaps twenty persons since seeing you last.

Salaries were a difficulty. In the job market after the war, young beginners could get four and five thousand dollars a year—nearly as much as Kinsey himself. Even if he did hire one of these aspirants from a list that was long and kept growing, it would take years of training before the newcomer could take over any major part of the work, and Kinsey was still worried about what would result "if something should happen to me."

The problem of the library was also pressing upon him. He had been accumulating it from the beginning, at his own expense. The University had urged that he sell it to them, to be added to the general collection, but Kinsey argued that it should be a part of the project. There were many items in it, he pointed out, that would cause consternation if they appeared on the routine orders of the University library. By 1946 he had succeeded in persuading Dean Fernandus Payne that the library belonged with the research, but the expense was making it impossible for him to keep up with it.

For one thing, it was growing at a considerable rate. Large collections and even whole libraries had been given to the project; in most cases the donors had asked to remain anonymous. It was attracting attention, too, among psychiatrists and other specialists in the field, who realized that it was already one of the best collections in the country and were beginning to consult it.

Originally Kinsey had hoped to finance the library himself, but it had now grown beyond his means and he had to ask the National Research Council, the source of our funds, for permission to use some of the annual appropriation for books. The expense Kinsey himself was bearing could be judged by the fact that not long before he made this request he had paid $435 for a specialized library of about ninety volumes. He had learned that it was for sale just before one of the largest medical libraries in the country had tried to buy it. He was able to get it for the original cost price, probably not more than 60 percent of the current market value. But in order to secure it, he had been compelled to buy it on the spot and pay for it personally.

He proposed to Yerkes that he would turn over all the books he had accumulated to the research, to be the property of the project and to go wherever it might go. He estimated that he had bought with his own money 450 volumes at an original cost price of about $2,500, and the remainder, which had been given to him, he labeled as the property of the project. These gifts were increasing, and as Kinsey noted in soliciting Yerkes' support for an Institute library, the Institute had been designated as heir to large collections, of more than ordinary value. Yerkes agreed with him.

Meanwhile, Kinsey's other problem, the help he needed, was becoming acute in 1946 as he was compelled to center his efforts on getting the book written. He hoped, with wildly misplaced optimism, to finish by the end of the summer. He had guarded himself as much as possible against distractions, particularly the out-of-state visitors who were capable of taking several days out of the working week, but he was reluctant to neglect the interviewing for the book.

Help was on the way, however. Paul Gebhard was just around the corner.

CHAPTER

XV

GEBHARD ARRIVES

Until the early spring of 1946, Gebhard had never heard of Kinsey. He had been immersed in work at the Harvard Graduate School, where he was finishing his requirements for the doctoral degree in anthropology under the distinguished Professor Clyde Kluckhohn. As his doctoral struggle drew to a close he anticipated a summer of relaxation, but Professor Kluckhohn took a different view. "You should not assume that you know everything merely because you are getting a degree," he admonished Gebhard. "There are gaps in your knowledge, and you ought to spend the summer plugging them up."

Gebhard looked skeptical, a frame of mind natural to new holders of the doctorate. "What, for example," Kluckhohn challenged him, "do you know about symbolic logic?" Abashed silence from the successful candidate. "Well, then, what do you know about Dr. Kinsey's work?" Kluckhohn demanded. Gebhard admitted he had never heard of Kinsey, and as any scholar would, asked for the references.

"He hasn't written anything yet," Kluckhohn said, "but he is doing extremely important work in sex research and he often comes to New York. You would be well advised to go down there and talk to him next time he's in town."

Kluckhohn went on to argue that anthropologists are always trying to make cross-cultural comparisons, which are not easy with many kinds of research. Sex research was different, however, be-

231

cause it did not get bogged down, like the others, and offered an ideal vehicle for such comparisons, as Ford and Beach were to show later in their *Patterns of Sexual Behavior.* Kluckhohn concluded: "If you're going to be an anthropologist, you ought to know what Kinsey is doing."

That, as Gebhard remembers the conversation, was his introduction to Kinsey. Taking his mentor's advice as seriously as it was intended, he wrote at once to Prok, who agreed to see him if he would give his history. They were to meet at 7:30 P.M. in the Hotel Astor, where Kinsey would be interviewing.

Arriving in New York by train, Gebhard went to the Astor and announced himself from the lobby. He had to wait for a time because Kinsey was occupied with another visitor, but eventually sat down with Prok and began by giving his history. During it he unwittingly put Kinsey through torture. Gebhard was (and is) an obsessive pipe smoker, as I am, but on this occasion Prok made no comment on the hated tobacco smoke, while his subject puffed away during the history.

After the interview was completed, Kinsey talked to Gebhard about his attitudes toward different kinds of sexual behavior. How did he feel about homosexuality? It wasn't a crime, Gebhard declared blandly, but an illness, probably endocrine in origin. What was its incidence in the population? Kinsey inquired. Rare, Gebhard told him. If it had been common or even prevalent, as an anthropologist he would have noted it. Kinsey's face was impassive as he listened to these remarkable statements.

"How did you come here?" he asked.

"By train," Gebhard said.

"What did you do as soon as you got in the station?"

"I went downstairs to the men's room and urinated."

"Did you notice anything unusual there?"

"No."

"Come with me," Kinsey said.

It was after midnight when the two men left the Astor and shuttled across town to Grand Central. They started down the stairs to the men's room, but Kinsey held out his hand and they stopped halfway down.

"Gebhard," he said, "how long does it take a man to urinate?"

"Thirty seconds or so." Paul estimated.

Kinsey pointed out two or three people in the rest room below them and said, "Keep your eye on them."

As he watched, Gebhard realized that these men were not coming out, as the others were doing, although he and Kinsey stood on the stairs for several minutes. Prok then took his new friend back to Times Square and showed him the male hustlers at work there, and then they went back to the Astor. By this time Gebhard was properly astounded, and aware that he had a good deal to learn about homosexuality.

Kinsey had gone to so much trouble because he had somehow come to the conclusion during the earlier interview that Gebhard might be the answer to his staff problem. By this time it was two-thirty in the morning, and Paul realized he had no hotel room yet; they were not easy to get in 1946, as a result of wartime shortages. When he mentioned his plight, Kinsey said, "I have two beds. You can stay here."

Gebhard recalls that Kinsey snored so hard he had trouble falling asleep, and had no more than closed his eyes, so it seemed, when Kinsey was shaking him and saying, "Get up, Gebhard. It's eight o'clock and I've got to take a history in an hour." Kinsey always called him Gebhard, rarely Paul.

Two weeks later the newly graduated anthropologist got a letter inviting him to come to Bloomington. It indicated that Kinsey was interested in him as staff material. He came out at the end of June and spent four days during which, as he said later, "I was grilled in a nice way." Even while he was interrogating Paul, Kinsey was also subtly lecturing him on the aspects of sex about which he was uninformed. I was with them through much of this procedure—"always behind my shoulder," Paul says now. I was there because Kinsey had asked me to help him in assessing the candidate's reactions.

When Kinsey returned from New York following that first encounter with Paul, he had told me the whole story and I had asked him what the young man from Harvard was like. "He's cut on straight lines," Kinsey said. "Straight shoulders, straight up and down —almost Oriental." He appeared not to notice any discrepancy in this description.

At the time Gebhard came to Bloomington for his interview,

Kinsey was considering four people for a staff job. He and I had drawn up score cards on each candidate, with plus and minus checks according to the individual's reaction to erotica, his education, his attitudes about sex behavior, and so on. When the scores were added up, Gebhard came out well ahead of the others.

Offered the job, Paul came to Bloomington again with his wife, and after further discussion they retired to the Student Union building to talk it over and decide. Overriding other considerations in Gebhard's mind was his feeling that he was getting in on the ground floor of something big. He liked both Kinsey and me; Martin was an enigma to him, and remained so. There was also the question of salary, as there had been with me.

"What are they paying you now?" Kinsey asked.

"Four thousand, two hundred," Gebhard said, referring to his pending job in Nebraska, where he proposed to go on an archaeological dig for the Smithsonian Institution.

"I'll give forty-four hundred," Kinsey said, and no doubt thought he was being generous.

So the deal was concluded, and the Kinsey-Pomeroy-Martin-Gebhard team, whose names were to be identified with our published work all over the world, was complete at last. Paul and his wife went off to Maine for a vacation before he started work, but Kinsey kept sending him letters and wires wanting to know, impatiently, when he could come to work, so that finally he cut his vacation short and returned to Bloomington.

At first Gebhard did little interviewing. He accompanied Kinsey and me on a field trip to New Mexico and another to Philadelphia, but he felt useless on these expeditions. His "breaking in" period was in Bloomington, where he took student histories, as I had done. During my apprenticeship Kinsey had given me lectures in his office, telling me what he knew about the research. With Gebhard he was satisfied to sit in while the new man was taking histories, which made Paul feel, as he recalled later, that he was taking his oral examinations for the doctorate all over again. He was acutely conscious that he was not doing as well at taking histories as Kinsey, nor as well as he expected to do when he had done more of it, and that made him feel uncomfortable. After the sessions Kinsey would tell him what he had done wrong, which only added to his discomfort.

But he learned by trial and error, as well as by Kinsey's instructions, just as I had done. Interviewing a woman in Chicago, when he reached the section dealing with frequency of intercourse, she answered, "Four or five."

"Per month?" Paul inquired.

"No, per day," she answered, greatly embarrassed.

From that response Paul learned not to put words into people's mouths.

From the beginning, it can be admitted now, Gebhard felt some hostility toward Kinsey, although a large part of it was due to a misunderstanding. Paul thought he had been hired as an anthropologist, to study social structures and patterned behavior in their relation to Kinsey's research. In fact what Kinsey wanted was an interviewer. When he realized this, Gebhard was disappointed and angry, feeling that he had been taken in under false pretenses. He was shocked to discover that Kinsey did not really care how anthropologists felt about sex. In retrospect, Gebhard believes he should not have sounded off on the subject until he knew more about sexual behavior, but he still thinks Kinsey was wrong to feel as he did. In any event, the initial mood was one of disillusionment on Gebhard's part.

I shared Paul's feeling that Kinsey did not want or intend to give either of us any autonomy. We were in the position of workhorses, harnessed to the project under Kinsey's direction, and we resented it, Paul perhaps more than I. There were many evidences of Prok's suppression. For example, Gebhard had been on the staff for two years before Kinsey permitted him to give a lecture. Again, when letters came from those who had given histories, asking questions of Paul or me, Kinsey took them over and answered them himself. The habitual editorial "we" in his correspondence could almost always be translated as "I."

Gebhard's reaction to his new situation was understandable. He had been well formed and directed in another discipline at Harvard before he ever came to Bloomington. He had the union card, his Ph.D., and he expected to be treated as a colleague, according to academic usage. And it was true that Kinsey did treat me as a colleague, which I found extremely satisfying. Moreover, Paul had gone through years of training under older, authoritarian men, and he had

had quite enough of that atmosphere; he felt himself ready to start out on his own.

Consequently it is not surprising that Kinsey appeared to him as simply another older, authoritarian figure, of the same kind he had known, who acted as if he were a research assistant. Yet on other occasions Kinsey would appear to soften, and Paul would instantly respond. This alternation, blowing hot and cold, left Gebhard a little groggy. Actually he and I and Martin could have united and outvoted Kinsey, but as Gebhard remarked later, "It never came to a vote." The sense of hierarchy was always there, and Gebhard found it difficult to adjust to, as well as to Prok's quick switches in attitude toward him.

A small but significant sample of the kind of thing that caused tension between them occurred one day when the two men were talking and eating peanuts. The subject of the talk was the problem of Gebhard's getting out of the university housing where he and his wife had been living, and buying a house. To do that, Gebhard observed, he would have to borrow the money and he did not know if he could do it.

"Don't worry," Kinsey said, "I'll lend you two thousand dollars, interest free."

But then, only a moment later, he turned on Paul in seeming exasperation and exclaimed, "Gebhard, you've eaten up three-fourths of those peanuts."

It was not that he begrudged the peanuts. What he was trying to say was that he thought Gebhard had not been paying attention—like those guests at his musicales who were not invited again—and it bothered him.

On another occasion, during a trip to Texas, Gebhard had eaten something that gave him diarrhea, and Kinsey told him that he should eat only citrus fruits, which was exactly the wrong advice. Not knowing that, Paul began virtually to live on orange juice, while his diarrhea grew worse by the day. Meanwhile, he was getting extremely hungry, and when we stopped one noon at a roadside restaurant he gave in and ordered a hamburger.

Kinsey obviously disapproved, but he said nothing until we were in the car again, when he upbraided Gebhard for going off his liquid citrus diet. Thinking to pass it off with a little levity (always a mistake with Kinsey), Gebhard said, "Prok, those bacteria are always eating on me, so I thought I'd give them something to eat on."

Prok's reaction astonished even me. He turned on Paul and said very seriously, "Gebhard, sometimes I despair of you as a scientist."

Fortunately, Paul and I hit it off extremely well and became good friends. It was much easier for us to communicate with each other than with Kinsey. As soon as we discovered that we were both chess addicts, an intense rivalry began which was somewhat resented by Prok, who thought our chess playing a waste of time, like any other game. Although we had to stop playing chess because the competition became too intense, we continued to compete in other, less serious ways, as in the miniature golf contests we had in Miami, while Kinsey watched us, incredulous that two scientists would so dissipate their time.

There was also a certain amount of practical joking between Paul and me. Gebhard was scheduled to leave on the Miami trip a few days before I did, and when he got to the airport discovered that the plane's departure would be delayed for an hour. Whiling away the time, it occurred to Paul that I knew when the plane was supposed to leave and would presume he had gone. He called me, disguised his voice, gave a fictitious name and said, "I am calling from the lobby, and I am ready to give my history. Shall I come up?"

"Just a minute," I said, and Paul knew I was looking through my appointment book.

"I don't seem to find you listed here at all," I said after a time.

Gebhard pretended to be annoyed. "Look here," he said, "I'm a very busy man and I've driven quite a distance today to get here in time for the interview," and he went on with escalating rage until he finally broke down and admitted the hoax.

Later, in Bloomington, Gebhard wrote a letter to the Indianapolis *Star*, protesting something from a very right-wing viewpoint, and signing the letter, "W. A. Pomeroy, Bloomington." When I saw it in the paper, I wrote a painstaking letter to the *Star*, pointing out that I was W. *B.* Pomeroy and had no connection with the writer of the letter. The joke was not revealed until the following Christmas, when Gebhard sent me a card signed "W. A. Pomeroy," in his unmistakable handwriting. On the following Christmas, Paul got a large box from me. It was filled with gravel for his driveway.

While we amused ourselves with this innocent fun, Christmas remained a serious thing for Kinsey. We had long since decided that the whole business of the holiday had become so commercial that it was ridiculous, and had quit giving any but humorous presents to staff members. But Kinsey insisted on being more than generous, as though he saw himself in the role of Lord Bountiful. He seemed to enjoy distributing largesse, and appeared in the staff members' doorways on Christmas Eve carrying hampers full of gifts.

Arriving at the door, he might open up a liquor hamper filled with expensive bottles of the best beverages and say, "Pick out any two bottles you like," and then go on to the next stop. He expected nothing in return, and indeed would have been embarrassed if gifts had been offered to him. He wanted to be the one to give. Paul and I found this merely uncomfortable, but Martin was in real distress because it was psychologically difficult for him to accept gifts, and Kinsey was especially generous to him because he had always insisted on treating him as a son.

Paul saw Kinsey as a driven man, who considered any attack on the research an attack on him personally. If Gebhard or I were opposed on some phase of the work, we would defend ourselves if we could, and if we couldn't, would say in effect, "Well, maybe we did make a mistake. We're not infallible." Kinsey, however, viewed any disapproval as an assault on his integrity, and thus he was especially vulnerable to criticism when the books emerged.

Kinsey's peculiar defensiveness extended itself to the smallest incidents. We were sitting one night in a restaurant with some other scientists, talking about sex loudly enough to be overheard at adjacent tables. The waitress told us that some people at another table had complained about the conversation. The others accepted this rebuke and lowered their voices, but Kinsey said grimly, "Well, they didn't have to listen." On the occasions when Kinsey made an extreme statement at some meeting, Paul and I were often put in the position of cleaning up after him, so to speak, defending and qualifying what he had said.

A further explanation is needed here. We were not an unhappy, quarreling research team by any means. We did our work together, and in general got along amicably, except when the inner tensions surfaced in the ways I have described. Other research teams experience the same thing, as the evidence, literary and otherwise, shows. In our case it may have been aggravated by the nature of the project, which compelled us to work so closely together for such long hours.

In any event, whatever Paul's initial reservations may have been, his coming solidified our research group. The work was put on a more solid institutional basis at about the same time by the incorporation of the project as the Institute for Sex Research, on April 8, 1947.

While the incorporation was being discussed, Yerkes wrote to suggest several possible names, including Indiana Sex Research Institute, Kinsey Research Institute, Institute for the Study of Human Behavior, and the name which was finally adopted, although Yerkes himself preferred Sex Research Institute.

The papers were duly drawn and the corporation came into existence. As before, appropriations were made to Indiana University, but for use by the corporation instead of Kinsey's personal use, as had previously been the case. The University continued to do the accounting. Kinsey transferred the library and the collections to the corporation almost immediately, for "$1.00 and other considerations." It had been understood that he would be recompensed for what he had spent as a purchasing agent, in effect, and he now put in a claim for about $6,000 spent from his own pocket.

The move toward incorporation had been initiated by the University itself. President Wells believed that if the research was officially organized as a special project, with its own records, the problem of access to sensational materials would be solved. It also gave the University a certain protection. President Wells could say to the legislature, or whoever else might complain about what Kinsey was doing, that the project was an autonomous, separate institute which happened to be based at Indiana. The University gave it heat, light and rent and paid Kinsey's salary, but its work was a separate entity.

Kinsey suggested, and his proposal was adopted, that all the earnings the books made and everything we might earn by lecturing should be turned back to the Institute. In that way he could not be charged with profiting personally from the project. Those who accused Kinsey of exploiting sex for money were taken aback when they learned the truth, because obviously if he had wanted to he could have made a small fortune. Oddly enough, while the two books did make a substantial amount, it was only a fraction of what was made from books *about* the Reports by those who capitalized on them.

Not long after the incorporation, Kinsey was offered another job. Dr. Carl Hartman, head of the Zoology Department at the University of Illinois, wrote to say that he was leaving and wanted to know if Prok would consider succeeding him—at $9,000 annually, plus summer school salary and a 7 percent contribution toward his annuity. It would have been a tempting offer to anyone else, but Kinsey was not to be tempted. He replied:

I have only one job from now on to the end, and that is carrying through this research project. I am practically free of teaching here and without administrative responsibilities other than the not inconsiderable one of managing this research. Consequently, I shall not be available for any other but a similar research position anywhere at any salary.

The truth was, too, that Kinsey felt comfortable at Indiana. By this time he had been there for more than a quarter century and his roots were deep. Although his work had made him some irreconcilable enemies on the faculty, they were extremely few, far outnumbered by his friends, including those who did not agree with him. When Professor Fowler Harper, of the law faculty, announced that he was leaving the University, Kinsey wrote to this man with whom he had so often disagreed:

I can't let you go without telling you that I have very much appreciated your friendship and the amount that you have contributed to my thinking during these many years. I appreciate the several specific things that you have done for us, especially in connection with this sex behavior research. Whether or not I agree with your reactions and thinking on some social problems that you have tangled with, I am sorry that you are leaving here. For I think your thinking has been a stimulation to everyone and particularly to those who disagreed with you.

Social reactions are realities which have to be accepted as realities whether they are what we like or not. I differ from you primarily in believing that social changes come very slowly and as the result of a greater complicity of processes than we academic people usually realize. I hope that you can contribute to spurring on social evolution on some of these matters in which you are interested without being so badly hurt that you actually become not only ineffective but actually detrimental to change. . . . Your independence of thinking is far too valuable to have it lost.

The tribute may have been nearly lost in Kinsey's sometimes tortured prose, which was worst when he was trying to express something not directly connected with his work, but the letter said as much about Kinsey as it did about Harper.

As we moved toward publication of the *Male* volume, it seemed to me that Kinsey's temper grew shorter under the pressure. For example, a defensiveness was sometimes apparent at the weekly Friday morning staff meetings which were held between research trips. Kinsey would give us complete and detailed accounts of everything that had happened since the last meeting, dramatic lectures in which he often personalized his conflicts with those he thought were impeding progress.

At these meetings it was Martin, in his quiet, stubborn way, who sometimes provided his own obstruction and challenged Prok's absolute authority, particularly when he thought it was necessary to defend someone or something Kinsey had attacked. At other times we would be asked for suggestions about how to deal with a problem, and when Martin came up with an idea which Kinsey subsequently rejected, Clyde often continued to advocate it until Kinsey turned on him as though he were a member of that invisible army which was costing us thousands of hours of delay, and accused him: "You're obstructing the project!" Gebhard and I were occasionally the objects of these accusations as well. Because he realized he had such an enormous amount of work to do, with small likelihood he could ever finish it, Kinsey was impatient with even the smallest detail that might be considered an impediment to the research.

Since the kind of outbursts I have described were relatively rare, living with Kinsey was not difficult, and we came to understand that they usually occurred when he was either frustrated by something or ill. The worst of them came in the last two or three years of his life, when he was increasingly unwell. Dellenback recalls a night in 1954, in Peru, where Kinsey had gone to explore pre-Columbian erotic art, some of which Bill was to photograph. Unfortunately, Prok became ill not long after he arrived and had a difficult time before he got home. Meanwhile, the Kinsey party were house guests in the hacienda of their Peruvian host. Bill and Gebhard shared a room while Kinsey had the adjoining room, in which he was lying ill a good part of the time. One night, after everyone had gone to bed, Bill sat at the desk in his room writing a letter with a pen, under a single small light. Paul had assured him that the light would be no bother, and was quickly asleep. As he wrote on, Bill heard Kinsey get up and go down the hall to the bathroom. When he returned he paused in the doorway and Bill peered out at him, with a smile, but Kinsey said in a fierce whisper:

"Bill, for heaven's sake, you're keeping the entire household awake with the scratching of that pen!"

It was an irrational outburst, and Bill was both hurt and angered. Next day, Kinsey had seemingly forgotten about it.

Back home, working in the laboratory, Dellenback had always been aware how difficult it was for Kinsey to engage in casual small talk. He would never drop into Bill's photo department during the day for a minute or two of social conversation, although he passed the open door frequently. His work ethic prevented that. But at night, when he came back to the office to work and found himself alone in the Institute with Bill, he would sometimes stop to talk. Even then he had to have an excuse.

"Look at this, Bill," he might say, bringing in a picture. "Isn't this extraordinary?" Then, having established a purpose for relaxing, he could sit down and talk.

These were not everyday occasions. Mostly he was so involved in his work that he had no feeling for the passage of time. Mac would call him at six o'clock and tell him it was time to come home to eat, and after he had gone back to work in the evening, she would call him again at eleven o'clock and tell him it was time to come home and get some sleep.

Except for their infrequent night chats, Kinsey and Bill seldom talked about anything except business. In Oregon, however, at a time when Bill was photographing animal sexual behavior, they drove around for two days in a rented car, and just as he occasionally did with me on our long trips, Kinsey spoke about the past—especially about his childhood, and about the rigid morality of his father, which he could neither forget nor forgive.

At least one point of conflict was avoided between photographer and scientist. Their chief difference was Kinsey's complaint that Dellenback, a perfectionist, was not turning out enough work. But Kinsey did not do with Bill what he did with so many other people—that is, become an expert in his field. Not that he would have found it particularly hard. He had done photography in his earlier days, exceptionally good amateur work. For some reason, however, he made no effort to dominate Bill's domain; he trusted him, and for the most part let him do things his way. On occasion he might become overly enthusiastic when a good salesman had finished talking to him about the virtues of a new piece of photographic equipment, but Bill could always talk him out of it if he thought it was something the laboratory did not need.

On the other hand, Dellenback had to be certain that if it was something *he* wanted to buy Kinsey would have no opportunity to try it out himself. For Prok was a clumsy do-it-yourself man. His long, slender pianist's hands were hopelessly incompetent to cope with mechanical gadgets. Once Bill brought him a slide viewer which he had borrowed, intending to buy it after Kinsey had looked it over. When he came into the office next morning, expecting to get Prok's quick approval, he found Kinsey ready to throw the viewer out the window. Trying it the night before, he had jammed a slide in it and concluded the whole apparatus was a pile of junk he intended to have nothing to do with.

Dellenback was one of those on the staff whose admiration for Kinsey did not waver, no matter what their difficulties might be. Indeed, Bill believed that Prok's faults, particularly his dogmatic and aggressive nature, were essential to getting the great project off the ground and sustaining it through its many vicissitudes. Bill overlooked the arguments and remembered Kinsey's genuine warmth, how he would return from a trip and greet those who had been left behind with a quick, eager smile and, "Well, hello. How *are* you?" It was not perfunctory; he meant it. His kindliness came through particularly to women and children. Bill's wife, who saw only that side of him, would not listen to the slightest criticism of Prok. Those who spoke to him on the telephone, or casually in person, were always impressed by his warmth and were consequently surprised when they heard from him by letter. These, with only a few exceptions, were rather formal

But there was a little less warmth and charm in Kinsey's manner during those tense, nervous days before the *Male* volume was ready to be sent to the publisher. A hint of worse things to come was apparent in his attack on Marynia Farnham, the New York psychiatrist, who had just published her book *Modern Woman: The Lost Sex*, written in collaboration with Ferdinand Lundberg.

The point at issue was one that advance publicity on the book was soon to bring to a boiling point—that is, the use made of Kinsey's material. Kinsey and Dr. Farnham had been corresponding since May 1945, when he had tried to dissuade her from quoting material, some of which had appeared in professional journals, before his first book was published. At the time she had seemed to agree with him, as he reminded her later, and had written that she thought it quite possible to get along without the material, and in any case would not quote anything precise or use any figures.

Nonetheless, as Kinsey wrote to her in 1947, after her book was published:

contrary to all scientific courtesy and custom in such matters, you went ahead and published our material contrary to your agreement not to publish it. I would further point out that the use you have made of the data which you ascribe to us involves gross inaccuracies in nearly every case.

He demanded that she either put an errata slip in every copy— and he listed fifteen errors—or eliminate all references to his research in the book as distributed. If she did not, he concluded irately:

I shall follow the practice which is customary in science, namely that of publishing all of these corrections in scientific journals, particularly those that go to psychiatrists, to psychologists, to biologists, to sociologists, and other professional groups, and in the leading Negro magazines of the country in order to correct the misuse you have made of our data on that group. It will also be necessary to correct each and every one of your misstatements in each of our own forthcoming publications.

A rather innocent letter from Dr. I. W. Gittelson, of the Veterans Administration Hospital in Lexington, Kentucky, drew from Kinsey a short lecture on the scientific method. Dr. Gittelson wrote that he was planning a research project which would attempt to establish homosexuality as a factor in schizophrenia. He asserted that he had a sufficient number of patients with this psychosis who had also exhibited strong evidences of "latent homosexuality." Gittelson, who had been a student at Indiana, and to whom Kinsey had once given a reprint of something he had written on homosexuality, asked if any other reprints were available, and if it would be possible to get any data from the forthcoming book. Kinsey replied:

As a scientist, I am shocked and disturbed at the opening sentence in your letter. You indicate that you are "planning a research project which will attempt to establish homosexuality as a very frequent etiological agent for a schizophrenia." Scientists do not attempt to prove anything. They attempt to discover what the facts of the universe are, and they accept these facts whether they are in conformance with anyone's preconception or no. As a scientist, it has been my duty to point out where previous bias has led to erroneous conclusions in this field of human sexual behavior, and I hope that you are not going to add to the list of things which I shall have to critically analyze on that score some day.

I would point out two other problems in scientific method. In the first place, the frequent association of two phenomena is not a sufficient demonstration of cause and effect. This is one of the most elemental things in logic, but one on which scientists too often make mistakes, especially in the field of medicine. In the second place, a study of either schizophrenia or the homosexual, which is confined to persons who are examples of schizophrenia and the homosexual, is like running an operative experiment without any controls.

The data on homosexuals in the *Male* volume might be useful, he added, but warned: "I should point out to you that there is a considerable proportion of the persons with homosexual experience who are never disturbed enough to land in clinics, and which the psychiatrists, in consequence, rarely know anything about."

After this virtual tirade, Kinsey closes characteristically: "Come to me again if I can be of any use."

There were, at the same time, the usual distractions. One was the constant effort of the nudists to involve him in their cause, once they had sensed him as a champion of freedom. Kinsey seemed to have trouble making his position on nudism clear, particularly to its exponents.

Ilsley Boone, a leader in the movement and editor of *Sunshine and Health,* its chief magazine, was his constant correspondent for a time. Just before the *Male* volume was published, Kinsey wrote to him:

We have inevitably been interested in the nudist movement in the course of our study. Attitudes toward nudity are a very important adjunct of all sex codes and the approach which your group is making to these attitudes is, of course, something to note and to be objectively studied by any scientific student of human behavior. Consequently, I should like to come to meet you personally and in the course of time learn more about the nudist movement. . . .

You understand that as scientists we neither approve nor disapprove of any sort of human behavior. We are neither for nor against you as a movement, but I can assure you that we are desperately anxious that the nudist movement be understood objectively and without the prejudice which old traditions introduce into the attitudes of some people toward your group. I am sure you will find, when our volume is published, that we will have done a great deal to help people to consider all of these matters of human behavior more objectively and with greater tolerance. I think you will find that we can contribute to a fuller acceptance of your nudist movement through that same sort of scientific analysis of it.

The nudists, however, tried in various ways to take Kinsey's name in vain in support of their movement. Only a year after he had written to Boone, Prok felt compelled to admonish a Chicago nudist leader, who had talked with him on the subject, for quoting him out of context, quotations which some newspapers had eagerly seized upon. He should limit himself, Kinsey said, only to what was published about nudism in the *Male* volume. He reiterated that the Institute neither approved nor disapproved of the movement.

Privately, to his attorney, Morris Ernst, Kinsey gave a more specific view of his opinions about the nudist movement.

We have a minimum of data on nudist camps, but what we do have is unanimous in indicating that they are the most asexual situation that we have ever found in our society. We do have data on nudity in the household circle, and certainly we have no indication that exposure of children to nudity, either in the household or elsewhere, has ever been the cause of sexual delinquency. As you know, I have avoided all appearances in court in all specific cases. I fear that if we once appear anywhere that will establish a precedent that will lead others to make life a perfect nuisance for us in demanding our appearance in other courts. We can be of more use if our time can be devoted to objective research. Nevertheless, I am quite sure that our local authorities are off on the wrong foot when they attempt to suspend a nudist camp on the grounds that it contributes to the delinquency of the child who attends it, or for that matter, that it is a source of delinquency for anyone.

But nudism and its problems occupied only a small corner of Kinsey's mind as the great day approached when the *Male* volume would appear, in January 1948. There was little to forecast the furore that was soon to erupt—the international publicity, the fight with the press, the breaking of old friendships, the sudden fame that would make him a household word. I think of this when I read the cordial exchange of letters, only three months before publication day, between Kinsey and his friend Dr. Lewis Terman, of the Stanford Psychology Department.

I can hardly wait to see your first volume [Terman writes], and shall be just as much interested in the second one. From all I have learned about your investigation I feel sure your data will be by far the most valuable that anyone has published. Your material on homosexuality among boys is convincing evidence that rigid classifications of the traditional kind are simply not valid. As you probably know, I have myself come to the conclusion that homosexuality is largely a matter of conditioning, although it may well be that glandular conditions are at the bottom of some cases.

And Kinsey's warm reply:

I am honored by your interest in our research and I hope you will be pleased when the data begin to be published. . . . Certainly I shall make a point of coming to see you as soon as our paths come anywhere closer. I do get West occasionally and I will make a visit to you one of my prime objectives of such a trip.

Who would have thought, reading these letters, that the two men would soon be locked in a bitter quarrel? But that was only one of the prices Kinsey would have to pay for the fame that was about to envelop him.

PART THREE

MALE AND FEMALE

CHAPTER

XVI

KINSEY AND THE PRESS—I

N EVER TELL YOUR hopes or dreams to a journalist," Kinsey once remarked to Bill Dellenback. He was bitter about the press in general, but warm and complimentary toward specific writers and publications. This ambivalence, in its many aspects, provides a perfect case history in the long conflict between science and the press, and illuminates the formidable difficulties of finding a common ground between them satisfactory to both.

In considering Kinsey's controversy with the press, one must remember two major factors influencing it. One was his profound ignorance of how the press works, and his resistance to criticism of any kind, particularly when it was what he considered uninformed. The other factor was the general inadequacy of science reporting at the time the *Male* volume was published. There were excellent science writers extant who knew how to handle Kinsey's data, but they were few in number, confined to the major wire services and perhaps a half-dozen major newspapers and magazines. Science writing had not yet become the well-developed specialty it is today; the atomic blast at Alamogordo had only recently ushered in that new era when our first book appeared.

The conflict between scientist and reporter, at best, resists easy solutions. A newspaper reporter or a magazine writer comes equipped for the task, if he is not a qualified science reporter, with nothing more than his intelligence and his general background knowledge, neither of which may be adequate. Interviewing a scientist, or dealing with scientific data, he must try to understand what a specialist is telling him, extract from it what will be of most interest to his mass audience and write it in a way that will inform them—and possibly, in the case of magazines, amuse, titillate, or otherwise entertain them as well.

On the other hand, the scientist usually finds it exceedingly difficult to talk on a comprehensible lay level. If he is obliging enough, he will try to explain or interpret what he is doing in the most simplified way he can manage. In doing so, he cannot document or support his ideas in the detailed, technical manner he would employ if he were writing a paper himself for a professional journal or lecturing to an audience of colleagues. Consequently, when the newspaper story or magazine article appears, he sees his work interpreted in the broadest possible way, without documentation or qualification, and his immediate worry is that his fellow scientists will think him a publicity seeker or guilty of making loose, unscientific statements. Science writing is the bridge, when it is done well, which both informs the lay reader accurately and satisfies the scientist. This small miracle is not always brought about.

In the case of the Institute's work, the problem was immeasurably complicated by the fact that the subject was the scientific consideration of sex, about which it is extremely difficult for the lay public to be scientific, since its attitudes are wrapped up in layers of religion, morality and emotion. It could have been virtually guaranteed that the press reports of our data, for the most part, would not be able to satisfy both the readers and Kinsey, and so it proved.

A fair summary of the pre-Kinsey attitude toward sex in the press was provided by Professor Donald G. Hileman, of Washington State College, who analyzed "The Kinsey Report: A Study of Press Responsibility" in *Journalism Quarterly*, the professional magazine of journalism educators.

Before 1948, the problem of sex so far as the press was concerned centered around how much attention should be given sex matters and in what way they should be emphasized in the news columns, in radio, television, movie and theatrical productions, in novels and other books, and in advertisements. By and large, the approach was a negative one—one of how sex should *not* be handled for fear that readers, viewers and listeners might be offended.

The Kinsey report on men was to give the press its first real opportunity to consider sex in a positive light. Sex had graduated from a backroom discussion to the front room parlor in acceptance and the new approach was centered around education and understanding.

The press met this challenge in varying ways, and with varying results. For his part, Kinsey was at first amazed and then utterly dismayed by what happened. He was not interested in fame (although he was human enough to enjoy it); he wanted only to make a progress report on his research and establish its validity as a scientific project.

In his innocence of the press, Kinsey believed that he could lay down ground rules and satisfy public curiosity about the *Male* book in a dignified, controlled way. In early autumn preceding publication, he responded to the advance interest that was rapidly building up by inviting writers to come to Bloomington, where they would be permitted to read the galleys under certain conditions, and only after they had signed a contract agreeing to these conditions. The contract stipulated that the writers must submit their manuscripts to him for factual corrections before they could be published. Another paragraph declared that the use of data must be in accordance with the spirit of the copyright laws.

There was some grumbling from the press—more from the newspapermen than the magazine writers. Newspaper reporters are not accustomed to submitting copy for approval to anyone except their editors and the copy desk; traditionally they regard such an action as another intrusion on the jealously guarded and constantly infringed freedom the press is constitutionally guaranteed. Magazine writers are more accustomed to the practice. Kinsey did not know these facts about the press, and he was further laying himself open to trouble in the contract clause citing the "spirit" of the copyright laws as a guide for using data. The interpretations of that word were potentially as wide as a barn door. And most important, he did not yet understand the depth of the gulf between the scientific and lay interpretations of his work.

By the time the first manuscripts began to come in for factual correction, early in September 1947, Kinsey's education began. He was so alarmed by what he read in the initial batch of stories that he sent out at once a form letter to those he had not yet heard from:

I am writing to advise you that some serious questions concerning the first manuscripts that have been submitted to us for magazine presentation of data from our research have arisen. I am writing to forewarn you in case you may be falling into the same error in the preparation of your own material.

The manuscripts which we have seen have been very largely confined to direct quotation or paraphrasing of bald conclusions drawn from each and every part of the book. They have paid a minimum of attention to the history of the research, the basic implications of the material, and they have not made any attempt to develop the background on which any of the bald conclusions are based.

You will realize that we are very much concerned with the presentation of this delicate material to the public in a fashion which will not bring offense. The presentation of a long succession of bare conclusions which have been selected primarily because they will startle the public, is bound to offend a great many persons before they have any opportunity to look at the specific data and the elaborate argument out of which those conclusions are reached. This can do irreparable damage to the whole future of the research. After a consultation with the publishers and their attorneys and our own staff, we have had to restrict the articles which have already been submitted to us to a minimum of such presentation. We will have to restrict your own article if it has made the same approach.

We can allow a limited use of such summary conclusions and have no objection to discussion of the general background of the research, its social and scientific significance, or to a presentation of two or three items in more detail.

While these restrictions may have seemed reasonable and necessary to Kinsey, to several journalists they were the red flag flaunted before the bull. Some were in trouble with deadlines, others with their editors. There was little possibility that any writer getting this letter would have been happy about it.

Ironically, the first, and in Kinsey's opinion the worst, offender was the Science Service syndicate, which Kinsey had looked on most favorably before it began to distribute anything about his own material. He wrote to Watson Davis, then its head, in as much sorrow as anger, commending him for the "many good things" he had accomplished, and then after the inevitable "but," letting go a full salvo:

The headline of your first press release—"50 per cent of married men unfaithful"—has caused us more trouble than all of the other press and magazine releases combined. It has been the subject of adverse editorials from newspapers from Miami to Detroit and the Pacific Coast. It has been objected that the word unfaithful does not represent scientific objectivity, and the emphasis upon this single item from the whole body of research has made some people feel that this is all there was to the research, and that the Rockefeller Foundation had wasted its money when it meddled into the affairs of married men. . . .

The Associated Press and the United Press checked with us before they released their material, and all of the magazine articles were submitted to us in manuscript before they were published. It was a mistake that we did not ask you to follow this procedure in the case of Science Service.

Earlier that year, Kinsey had outlined his program for dealing with the press. As he described it to Gerald Wendt, editor of *Science Illustrated*, it seemed clear enough to him:

There are actually scores, and possibly a hundred or more of the magazines that have been at us for material. There will be no exclusive rights and we ourselves will do no writing. We will cooperate with any magazine that wants to write up any of our material on two conditions: First, that no data be used prior to the time of its technical publication. Second, that we have an opportunity to check the scientific accuracy of the material used. We will not attempt to dictate anything concerning the style, or point of view, or interpretations.

Kinsey no doubt meant it sincerely, but obviously, in his first reactions to what had been written, he was attacking both point of view and interpretation. Perhaps he was already wary on the basis of sensational articles about sex published by *Collier's* earlier that year, during the magazine's flamboyant but fatal attempt to save its own life, which ended three years later. Writing to Hannah Lees, a magazine writer whose work he knew, who had asked for permission to look at the galleys of the *Male* volume, he had *Collier's* much on his mind:

Our offer stands to any magazine that will handle the material in a sober and honest fashion. We have to record that *Collier's* has published within the last year some of the most despicable articles on sex that have appeared in any journal for a decade. One of them almost completely wrecked the Friends' work for homosexual cases in the New York City courts. We should have to be very sure of the way in which *Collier's* did anything before we would give them access to our material. I still have some faith in you, but I wonder what the actual policies of the managers of *Collier's* would be. Our research is no material for yellow journalism.

Not all the dismay was on Kinsey's side. Magazine editors and publishers, surveying what their writers had wrought from the *Male* galleys, were uneasy both about the omnipresent Post Office Department and their more conventional readership. Macfadden Publications, for example, had a piece about the project scheduled for the December issue of *47* (the magazine's title was to change every year), but the management was so disturbed by the proofs that they insisted on several changes, which were made at the printer's, and even then they were worried about Post Office reaction. Dan Senseney, a free-lance writer who reported this episode to Kinsey, told him he was afraid that the story about the book he had written for Macfadden's *True Story* might suffer the same fate. Kinsey wrote him indignantly:

Our society is in a sorry state if your publishers can be so intimidated by the post office that they hesitate to publish as inoffensive an article as yours. I quite understand their position and blame no one except the original source of the intimidation.

It was the misuse of statistics, taken out of context for their obvious public interest, which appeared to cause the most trouble. Perhaps the worst example was a story that appeared in Hearst's San Francisco *Examiner* on December 6, 1949, which quoted Kinsey as saying that 5 to 10 percent of sex offenders needed clinical help, and the rest should go to prison. We were then getting histories from inmates at San Quentin, and what we had actually said was that 95 percent of all sex offenders had nothing in their histories different from the rest of the population. The *Examiner*'s story caused considerable consternation among the San Quentin inmates and made it difficult for us to regain rapport with them.

Kinsey's version of how all this had happened provides further insight into his troubled relations with the press. To Dr. Norman Reider, a San Francisco psychiatrist, Kinsey wrote:

The *Examiner* reporter, who is located at San Rafael [in other words, a "stringer," meaning an out-of-office correspondent], came to me for a statement on these sex offenses against children. We had recently prepared a careful statement for the Associated Press, and consequently I gave him a statement which was very carefully worded with an additional sentence or two to cover the immediate California situation. I have dealt with this reporter before, and he had seemed to be appreciative of our research and desirous of reporting it accurately. After he left me, he rewrote his notes and brought them back to me in typewritten form for okay. The statement was excellent and entirely accurate.

The article in the *Examiner* the next morning was inaccurate in each and every sentence without exception. In a high proportion of the cases, it was diametrically the opposite of what we had said. The headline read that we recommended imprisonment for 90 per cent of the sex offenders. The original statement given the reporter, which was a statement we had made in many quarters before, was to the effect that not more than 5 to 10 per cent needed imprisonment. Obviously, the article was deliberately distorted some time between the time I okayed the reporter's draft and the time it came into print.

To anyone familiar with newspaper practice it was obvious what had occurred. The reporter had filed his story either by wire or by phone, and in the *Examiner*'s city room it had been rewritten, as is often the case with a stringer's story. The distortion had occurred in the rewrite, no doubt to accord with the paper's Hearstian style, and the erroneous headline based on the rewritten story.

Several years later, when Carl Lindstrom, then executive editor of the Hartford *Times*, was assembling an article titled "Kinsey and the Press," he queried the *Examiner* for its version and got a rather puzzling reply from Linton von Beroldingen, the managing editor. Von Beroldingen had checked the paper's library and found the story filed with a special note that it had got into the paper with an incorrect statement and was not to be picked up for further use under any circumstances. The following week, said the editor, another article was printed setting forth Kinsey's position correctly at roughly five times the length of the original.

As for our contention that the story had been sent in accurately and been deliberately changed by someone "higher up," which the reporter himself had told us, Von Beroldingen considered it a gross misstatement. There were few editors, he declared, who would deliberately change facts in stories. He did not say whether this truism could also be applied to Hearst rewrite men.

It was no wonder, then, that Kinsey was cautious about the press, and even hostile on occasion. A few months after the *Male* volume appeared, when he was about to address the Pennsylvania League for Planned Parenthood, he was so worried about any information leak that he wrote to the program chairman:

My speech as a whole must not be mimeographed, or, in any other way, reproduced. If I cannot be guaranteed that, I will have to cancel the engagement. It is worth many thousands of dollars to the press to get ahold [sic] of such material from us now, and everything that we say will be printed in a garbled fashion before we ever put it in print, if the press is not controlled. I will either have a short mimeographed report for their use before the meeting, or else hold a press conference with them.

If he was wary about the written press, he was positively terrified of electronic journalism. Once, in San Francisco, the noted foreign correspondent Marguerite Higgins called him at his hotel room and asked for an interview. He consented, but when she appeared accompanied by a television camera crew, about which she had not informed him, he refused to let her in the room.

I think one of the things that annoyed Kinsey most about press treatment of his work was the half-humorous tone of so many stories and articles, typical of the way in which sex is discussed so often in mass publications. Kinsey noted this fact in agreeing to speak to the University of California Press Club in 1949 on "The Press and the Kinsey Report." He wrote to the program chairman:

I will lay considerable emphasis on the responsibility that the press has in a sober treatment of a subject which has been too often involved with emotional reactions, of which sexual humor is, to a considerable degree, a measure of unresolved emotional conflicts. If the rest of your program is traditionally humorous, either you will be out-of-place, or I will be out-of-place at the meeting. There have been endless centuries of consideration of this problem in humorous fashion, and that is not how we are handling a scientific research project which considers such significant human problems.

Yet certainly Prok was not entirely humorless about his press relations. When John C. O'Brien, who was president of the National Press Club in 1949, wrote to ask him to address the members, with the understanding that his remarks would be off the record, a privilege usually accorded generals and statesmen, Kinsey at first refused, but then consented when a concession was made: "I come to the Washington Press Club with the understanding . . . that 'no newspapermen will be present.' "

Furthermore, he could be generous when he thought a publication had done a good job. He went out of his way to compliment one paper, the Monterey *Peninsula Herald*, for its coverage of a lecture he gave in Salinas, and a little later in Carmel. The stories on these lectures, he said, "were excellently written, were factually much more accurate than most newspaper material, and obviously caught the point of the total presentation as well as details. Frankly, it is so unusual to get these things combined in newspaper reporting that I wanted to tell you that we thought you have contributed to the understanding by the public of the material we were presenting."

After his first round with the press Kinsey was bruised and in some cases very angry, but I feel sure that he did not believe he had been treated unfairly, on the whole, as some newspaper executives and magazine editors imagined. With his ability to get quickly into other professions and disciplines, I think he began at least to understand the problems involved. Unfortunately, his difficulties with the press over the first book were as nothing compared with the storm that broke over the publication of the *Female* volume. Even though he was better prepared for it, the shocks were violent. But this story must wait for a later chapter.

CHAPTER

XVII

THE MALE VOLUME IS BORN

In the fall of 1947, as Kinsey got closer to publication of the *Male* volume, he was doing little else but work on the book, as he had from the beginning of that year. He took occasional business trips, and made short history-taking journeys to San Francisco and Philadelphia. But chiefly he devoted himself to the tremendous task of getting the statistics put together and writing what he hoped would be a readable book.

Kinsey's literary method was unique, to say the least. He made his superb speeches from the scantiest of notes, little more than headings, and he put his books together in something of the same way. He carried the general outline of each volume, topic by topic, in his head, and filled in this skeleton with the data emerging from the machine, what was usable from the bibliography, and the material supplied by our special consultants in various fields.

This method was completely contrary to the orthodox procedure, in which the writer examines the literature first, absorbing it and taking notes. Kinsey approached each topic with a completely fresh look, based on his own original research, then he went back to the literature (if any existed) to see whether it confirmed his findings. If it did not, he would simply say that the previous research was wrong —and it was, almost invariably.

The only difference in compiling the two books was that in the *Female* volume he had the advantage of an established outline to follow from its predecessor. In general structure they were alike, with some additions and differences which will be made clear when I come to describing them.

Kinsey did the actual writing himself, dictating the last portions of the *Male* volume to a stenotypist imported from Chicago. Both the books ended as very personal statements, but that was particularly true of the first. The rest of us read every word, of course, several times over, but relatively few of the suggestions we made were taken. Kinsey always listened attentively to us, and occasionally he nodded his head and agreed, but more often he was convinced that he was right and we were wrong. He took more advice from us on the *Female* volume, but that was because he was working with extra care and caution as a result of the controversy over the first book.

In both volumes his work was as meticulous as one would expect from a scientist. I might, for example, suggest that he substitute the word "usually" for "inevitably" in a sentence, and Kinsey would answer impatiently that I was nitpicking, but he would nevertheless consider the matter seriously, and then, in most cases, attempt to convince me that he was right. "Don't you see how much better this sentence reads with 'inevitably' in it?" he would ask earnestly.

On larger matters the four of us worked together. We would take for consideration tables loaded with correlated figures from the IBM machine—for example, the frequency of masturbation, broken down by age and completed education. As we contemplated them, Gebhard might say, "See how those frequencies diminish by age," and then Martin might point out that at one educational level there were inconsistencies in Gebhard's generalization. To this I might add that these inconsistencies were minor and statistically insignificant. Then Kinsey, having listened to us, would observe that it was clear to him the tables showed decreasing frequency by age, and after further discussion of the question he would take this concept at which we had more or less mutually arrived and put it into prose form. Later, we read and criticized what he wrote, with the mixed results I have described.

Martin was in charge of all charts and graphs, but Kinsey was as meticulous with this statistical material as he was with the prose. He planned every detail, down to the spacing, the thickness of the graph lines and the titles.

With such attention, and so vast an amount of material, it was hardly surprising that each book took the better part of two years to write, although it would be difficult to define the exact beginnings, since Kinsey was carving out small pieces of the projects well in advance of actually sitting down to serious, virtually full-time work. As early as 1946 he was writing on the *Male* volume, and in 1950 we had started coding our data and putting them on IBM cards, so that early in 1951 Kinsey could begin to write the *Female* book.

President Wells had urged Kinsey, for policy reasons, to seek out a medical publisher. The book would then, he thought, go into the hands of the most reputable people, those who needed it for scientific purposes, and consequently would have little other circulation and so not be misinterpreted. Wells, like Kinsey, had no idea of what was going to happen, but he did take what seemed to him a sensible presidential precaution. He asked Kinsey to agree that, in fixing the publication date, he would not publish anything during the sixty-one days the Indiana legislature would be in session, or immediately before it began. It had been Wells' observation that the Assembly was subject to agitation while it was in session and likely to deal heatedly with whatever was agitating it, while the same matters would never even be heard of if they happened fifteen days after adjournment.

Since few people knew what Kinsey was up to, there was no rush of interested publishers when it was time to market the *Male* volume. Lippincott, which had published Kinsey's work in biology, displayed some interest, and Macmillan, apparently having heard some rumors about what was going on in Bloomington, made a rather tentative inquiry. But Kinsey, feeling that Wells was right on this subject, turned them down as not being primarily medical publishers.

He was also pursued, with somewhat more enthusiasm, by McGraw-Hill, which had apparently heard about the *Male* volume through the publishing grapevine. Kinsey respected this house and thought its medical department might well develop, but as he finally wrote to the McGraw editor with whom he had been discussing the matter:

We do have a special problem in keeping the book identified as a very sober, scientific contribution which is very much needed in the medical field and which has been supported by the medical interests, and it will be of considerable concern to the medical groups. To keep the book so identified, it seems desirable to publish with one of the companies which has been recognized as a medical publisher for a longer period of years.

In the end he found his publisher by sheer accident. He had gone to Philadelphia to lecture before fifty invited guests, among whom was Lawrence Saunders, president of W. B. Saunders, one of the oldest and most respected medical publishing houses in America, whose offices were in that city. Like everyone else, Saunders was tremendously impressed by the lecture, and afterward asked Kinsey if he had made any arrangements to publish his work. The resulting conversations between the two men led to a contract.

After the book was published and Kinsey was famous, he could have had his choice of publishers, and it seemed that half the houses in the industry were trying to get him on their list, but Kinsey was an intensely loyal man and he saw no reason to desert Saunders, who had treated him fairly and published the *Male* volume to his satisfaction. For his part, Larry Saunders must have found Kinsey a most unusual author in other respects. He refused to take any advance royalties on either book, and in fact was opposed on principle to any such arrangement, no matter how customary it might be. He believed in submitting the entire manuscript, presumably ready for copyediting and the press, and he did not approve making changes either on galleys or on page proofs.

With the *Male* volume, however, he submitted the first part of the book to the publisher, and Saunders assigned one of its best editors, Helen Dietz, to go over with Kinsey the usual editorial queries and help plan the book's layout. Their first meeting, in Philadelphia, was an occasion Miss Dietz later recalled vividly.

It took place in the old library of the Saunders Company [she wrote], and we sat down together to go over the first portion of the manuscript. . . . We remained at the office long after everyone else had gone home—my first inkling of his disregard of "normal" working hours. And as we parted, he asked what time we began work in the morning, and looked his obvious disapproval of such a late starting hour as 8:45. But even more revealing to me was a small incident connected with our work. We were both engaged in drawing rules down the left-hand side of the manuscript pages as a sign to the typesetter that that particular material was to appear in smaller type size. Since these rules were for the eyes of no one but the typesetter, I was

drawing them rapidly and crookedly in our usual style, but Dr. Kinsey carefully drew each one with the aid of a ruler. When I commented on his
unusual care, he looked at me in gentle rebuke and assured me that everything worth doing was worth doing precisely and carefully.

This meticulousness carried over in all Dr. Kinsey's work with his manuscript, and made him an ideal author for an editor to work with. His care
extended to the quality of the manuscript paper used, and the type of pencil
with which he made the few corrections appearing on the finished manuscript. He was extremely conscious of his writing style, and believed that a
book should read well aloud, paying special attention to the cadence of his
sentences. I recall several times finding him sitting at his desk in Bloomington reading the manuscript aloud to himself.

Recollected in tranquillity and with kindness, Miss Dietz's estimate of Kinsey as an "ideal author for an editor to work with" was
not exactly a fair summary of what went on in Bloomington as we
neared the deadline with the first volume. Although their personal
relations were cordial, Miss Dietz and Kinsey had endless editorial
arguments, nearly all of which she lost, as they labored together on
Prok's home grounds to get the manuscript in final shape. Kinsey
could be quite brutal about these arguments. "This is the way it has
to be," he would say flatly, ending an argument with total finality. I
must say that in the majority of cases I felt he was correct. We were
accustomed to having our suggestions treated this way as the book
was being written; it was a new experience for Miss Dietz. She fought
bravely for a while against the overwhelming force of Kinsey's personality, until in the end he gave in to her on a few of the minor
points she raised, and she returned to Philadelphia with a rather limp
moral triumph.

But at last the long task drew to an end. The very big chore of
proofreading was finally accomplished, and by late October 1947 the
final part of the job, the index, was completed and sent in. After that
there were only a few plate proofs to correct. By then the presses
were actually rolling on the first pages of the book, with the publication date set as January 5.

There had been some discussion about the title, *Sexual Behavior
in the Human Male,* but nothing compared with the postpublication
argument raised by critics, both literary and scientific, about the use
of the preposition. It was amazing how impassioned people got about

that small word "in." They were, of course, completely wrong. As Kinsey patiently explained, the title did not imply that we were reporting on *all* human males, but on behavior occurring *within* the human species; consequently, as any good dictionary would confirm, "in" was the correct preposition.

Before publication, Saunders had made a market research analysis to determine the potential sale of the book, and on the basis of the figures produced, had ordered a first printing of 10,000. This was one of the more spectacular publishing mistakes of the decade. As public curiosity built up rapidly, Saunders increased the first printing to 25,000, but even this was far from enough. Within ten days after the first printing had been officially released, the publishers had ordered their sixth printing, bringing the total in print to 185,000, and the book was making its way up the best seller lists everywhere in the country, to the complete surprise of all concerned.

Now it was possible for the general public to see what the magazine writers and newspaper reporters had been translating for them in millions of words of reporting and analysis. The impact of the book on these laymen could only have been numbing. What they saw was 804 pages (including the index) of tightly written scientific prose, interspersed with numerous charts and tables which could not be understood except by those with at least some background in statistical analysis. The same sense of frustration must have struck the eager readers of Masters and Johnson, two decades later, who found the sober technical contents no match for the intriguing title *Human Sexual Response.*

Nevertheless, *Sexual Behavior in the Human Male* was as much a landmark in its field as Freud's first work had been. It was divided into three main sections: "History and Method," "Factors Affecting Sexual Outlet," and "Sources of Sexual Outlet." We began by setting forth our objectives and describing how the study had been developed, summarizing the difficulties we had encountered, from the organized opposition of other scientists to the hotel manager who would not let us take histories because, as he said, he didn't intend to let anyone have his mind undressed in *his* hotel. At the same time we listed those who had cooperated with us and it was an impressive compilation—twenty-six medical and psychiatric groups, seventeen penal and correctional institutions, seven other related institutions, thirty varieties of social and civic organizations.

Carefully Kinsey described the taxonomic approach he had used, citing its roots in biologic research and in the applied and social sciences. Then he analyzed the nineteen studies of sexual behavior which had preceded ours, noting critically how they had obtained their data.

With this historical introduction out of the way, Kinsey plunged into the long, extraordinary chapter on interviewing which I have discussed. That was followed by an exposition of the statistical problems involved in the work. Kinsey described our coding process as far as he could without impairing its confidential nature, even reproducing a sample history, but this was done largely as a general indication to other researchers of how they might proceed in developing their own codes. Embedded in the highly technical discussion of sampling procedures that constituted most of this section was the twelve-way breakdown we employed in sorting out our histories: by sex, race-cultural group, marital status, age, age at adolescence, educational level, occupational class, parents' occupational class, rural-urban background, religious group, religious adherence and geographic origin. Kinsey then rounded out his discussion of method by examining in detail the problems involved in validating the data.

Turning to the factors affecting sexual outlet, Kinsey began to disclose our findings, bolstered with statistical graphs and charts, about early sexual growth and activity, total sexual outlet, age and sexual outlet, marital status and sexual outlet, and age of adolescence and sexual outlet. In this part of the study we were concerned with erotic arousal, orgasm and sex play in preadolescence and in adolescence itself. Here was the later much discussed material on total sexual outlet and the factors affecting it, the relationship of age to various kinds of outlet, the sources of sexual outlet among married males and among adolescents.

Kinsey came to some definite conclusions about this part of the study. Males who were early adolescents, he observed, usually began sexual activity at once and maintained higher frequencies for at least thirty-five or forty years, and the factors contributing to this early adolescence continued to operate over that time span. Exercising one's sexual capacities did not seem to impair them, he went on. It was theoretically possible that very high activity rates might contribute to physical impairment, or relate indirectly to diseased conditions or other difficulties in certain cases, but this outcome was observed in "exceedingly few" high-rating males.

Males who were late adolescents, Kinsey concluded, more often delayed the start of their sexual activities and recorded minimum frequencies both in early years and through the remainder of their lives. Those who deliberately chose low frequencies to conserve their energies for later life appeared never to have found enough justification for using them as they grew older. Kinsey believed that most of the low-rating males were not capable of higher rates, and could not have increased their rates to match the more active segments. In general, the boys who were the first to mature were those who most often turned to masturbation and to premarital sociosexual contacts, engaging in heterosexual and homosexual relations more frequently than boys who were last in maturing.

Kinsey thought there was some reason to believe that these early-adolescent males were often more "alert, energetic, vivacious, spontaneous, physically active, socially extrovert, and/or aggressive individuals in the population" than the late adolescents, who were inclined to be "slow, quiet, mild in manner, without force, reserved, timid, taciturn, introvert, and/or socially inept." This correlation was a surprise, Kinsey observed; we had no indication that we would find it before we began analyzing the data. He was careful to point out, too, that there was much individual variation, and no inevitable correlation between personalities and rates of sexual activity.

Kinsey concluded:

There is evidence that the late-maturing males have more limited sexual capacities which would be badly strained if, through any circumstance, they tried to raise their rates to the levels maintained by the sexually more capable persons. If further studies show that some physiologic quality, such as metabolic rate, works together with or through the hormones to determine the time of onset of adolescence, it may become a matter of clinical importance to exercise some control over that event. If this were done, would the subsequent sexual performance then be affected? Parents and clinicians may properly be concerned with such questions.

Discussing the relation between social level and sexual outlet, Kinsey observed that upper-level people rationalized their patterns of sexual behavior on the basis of what was right or wrong, and so all sociosexual behavior became a moral issue, while lower social levels rationalized on the basis of what was natural or unnatural. These matters, he said, "lie deeper than logic," and most of the tragedies developing out of sexual activities result from the conflict of attitudes between different social levels. The study spelled out the differences in attitudes toward sexual activity at various social levels, and established statistically the patterns of behavior at each level. It also explored the differences resulting from an individual's rural or urban background, and his religious background, in terms of sexual outlet.

The final part of the *Male* volume was taken up with the sources of sexual outlet, beginning with masturbation. Kinsey observed that masturbation and heterosexual coitus involved far more people than any other kind of sexual activity, and so it was a question "whether activities which are as important as these can be altogether ignored, easily regulated, or completely ruled out of the lives of any large number of people." He reviewed the long, sorry history of conflict over masturbation, and reaffirmed, on the basis of our 5,300 male histories, in which 5,100 recorded masturbatory experience, that no measurable damage was done except in the rare compulsive psychotic. But our records did show thousands of boys living in continual conflict and in some cases even attempting suicide because of what they had been taught about masturbation. For the others, masturbation was a regular sexual outlet alleviating nervous tension, and in many cases these boys lived more balanced lives than those who practiced some degree of abstinence.

In this section, Kinsey attacked prevalent teachings that while the harm done by masturbation had been greatly exaggerated in the past, no young man would want to accept it as part of his life pattern. These teachings also warned about "excessive" masturbation, but since the word was never defined, and the individual had no way of knowing how his own rate compared, the result was a kind of subtle and indirect condemnation as damaging as the more extreme views of an earlier day. Many of the people responsible for these "compromised attitudes," Kinsey charged, were physicians, and he added that even the psychiatrists were divided on the question. He pointed out that European-trained psychiatrists brought with them the orthodox Freudian viewpoint that masturbation was an infantile substitute for heterosexual intercourse, and were astonished to find it persisting in the adult lives of American men. When it occurred in the history of a married male, they looked upon it as pathologic—which was merely, Kinsey added, "a rationalization of their own European mores."

However, he concluded, the relationship between masturbation and sociosexual adjustments remained to be determined. Kinsey stated that it was clear masturbation was relied on by upper-level males because they did not have enough outlets through heterosexual coitus, and consequently to a degree this represented an escape from reality. "It is to be noted," Kinsey reminded his readers, "that at age fifty-five the college-bred males derive only 62 percent of their total outlet from marital intercourse, and that 19 percent of the outlet at that age is derived from the dream world which accompanies masturbation or nocturnal emissions. Any final assay of the significance of masturbation should take these and still other specific data into account."

While some of these views were certain to arouse the moralists, Kinsey was on more dangerous ground with the nonscientific public when he came to heterosexual petting and premarital intercourse. In the matter of petting, he made what must have been one of the first shrewd observations forecasting what would later be called "the new morality." He noted that the prevalence of marriage manuals in the previous two decades, and the courses in psychology, home economics, marriage and child development in the schools, helped to explain why young people even then were more or less oblivious to the widespread criticism of their petting behavior. Many boys and girls might pet only for the immediate satisfaction, he said, but a surprising number were consciously aware of the relationship between these experiences and their subsequent marital adjustment.

Nevertheless, Kinsey went on, "It is amazing to observe the mixture of scientifically supported logic, and of utter illogic, which shapes the petting behavior of most of these youths." They were particularly careful to avoid genital union, yet they made erotic contacts which were just as effective and in some cases even more taboo. "By petting, they preserve their virginities, even though they may achieve orgasm while doing so," Kinsey wrote. "They still value virginity, much as the previous generation valued it. Only the list of most other activities has had new values placed on it."

We found, as the book reported, considerable evidence that premarital petting experience contributed to the effectiveness of sexual relations after marriage, a conclusion which ran contrary to the usual statements in the literature of sex education, although some researchers had already come to the same view. Once more, in his summary, Kinsey made it clear that whether premarital petting was right or wrong was a moral question that a scientist could not decide, but its relationship to subsequent marital adjustment was something that could be measured.

That distinction did not satisfy the moralists, of course, and they were even more upset by Kinsey's following conclusions about premarital intercourse. The general impression that the middle class were the most rigorous upholders of the social tradition against such intercourse was based on that class's expressed opinion and not on the record of its actual behavior, Kinsey declared. A "not inconsiderable" part of the population would openly defend the value of such intercourse, he said, and there was an increasing opinion among professional groups in America that "there are social values to be obtained by pre-marital experience in intercourse."

What these values might be were determined, he added, by such factors as the nature of the partners, the situations under which it took place, its relationship to venereal disease and the success or failure in avoiding an unwanted pregnancy. Our figures contradicted the common assertion that everyone who had premarital experience subsequently regretted it. Few among the males did so; the female figures were not yet ready.

In his final conclusion on the subject, Kinsey displayed once more a breadth of view his outraged moralist critics so often denied he had:

For the individual who is particularly concerned with the moral values of sexual behavior, none of these scientific issues are, of course, of any moment. For such individuals, moral issues are a very real part of life. They are as real as the social values of a heterosexual adjustment, and the happiness or unhappiness of a marital adjustment. They should not be overlooked by the scientist who attempts to make an objective measure of the outcome of pre-marital intercourse.

As for marital intercourse, the *Male* book's data provided some insight into man's sexual capacities and the great variation occurring in such activity. But more remarkable, Kinsey declared, was the fact that so much of it was stereotyped, "restricted to the age-old patterns which are an established part of the mores. The variety that is recorded does no more than allow the scientist to glimpse the extent of the variation that might occur in the human animal's sexual behavior."

After the book was published, a substantial part of the moralists' objections to it was centered on the statistics for extramarital behavior, which showed how prevalent it was in the population. Yet the volume itself proposed far more questions on this subject than it attempted to answer. Kinsey observed that only a relatively small proportion of the population accepted unlimited extramarital intercourse, and even those who defended this activity most strongly usually had little of it in their own histories.

Whether this is a tribute to the effectiveness of the mores in controlling the behavior of persons who think that they are emancipated, or whether it is evidence that extra-marital intercourse entails difficulties that they did not anticipate, or whether it merely indicates that successful extra-marital relations are carried on with difficulty under our present social organization, it is impossible to say at this time. Certainly the psychologist and social scientist, and society in general, need a great many more specific data before there can be any final evaluation of the effects of extra-marital intercourse on individuals and on their relations to their homes and to the society of which they are a part.

Few of the critics appeared to have read this reasoned paragraph.

In studying prostitution as an outlet, Kinsey was amazed to find how much of the world's literature had been devoted to the subject in proportion to the relatively small proportion of the male population indulging in it. Our figures showed that in the United States the number of males going to prostitutes was not as high as generally believed, and the frequency with which they went was very much lower than anyone had realized until then. Only about 69 percent of the total white male population had experience with prostitutes, we found. Many had no more than one or two experiences, and no more than 15 or 20 percent had such relations oftener than a few times a year over as much as a five-year period in their lives. To put it another way, nearly a third of the males never had any kind of sexual contact with prostitutes. Not only that, but the incidence and frequency of intercourse with prostitutes was rapidly decreasing in each subsequent decade.

More shocking to many people than the data on premarital and extramarital intercourse were the statistics Kinsey produced on the high incidence and frequency of homosexual behavior in the male population, particularly its coexistence with the heterosexual in the lives of a large part of the male population. In view of these statistics, Kinsey concluded, "it is difficult to maintain the view that psychosexual reactions between individuals of the same sex are rare and therefore abnormal or unnatural, or that they constitute within themselves evidence of neuroses or even psychoses." Needless to say, the controversy these remarks renewed is scarcely settled even now, nearly a quarter century later. Kinsey believed that homosexual activity would appear in the histories of a much larger portion of the population if it were not for existing social restraints. If it were possible to do what some advocate and eliminate homosexuality from society by isolating and "treating" all those with homosexual tendencies, Kinsey observed, it would mean isolating at least a third of the male population, and if those predominantly homosexual (4 to 6 on the scale he introduced in this book) were to be treated, it would mean isolating at least 13 percent of the male population. Altogether that would mean about 6⅓ million males. There were many readers —or rather those who read about it in the popular translation—who found themselves profoundly shocked by that figure. Kinsey concluded:

If all persons with any trace of homosexual history, or those who were predominantly homosexual, were eliminated from the population today, there is no reason for believing that the incidence of the homosexual in the next generation would be materially reduced. The homosexual has been a significant part of human sexual activity ever since the dawn of history, primarily because it is an expression of capacities that are basic in the human animal.

At the end of the *Male* volume, Kinsey was able to sum up his findings in three short paragraphs.

Viewed objectively, human sexual behavior, in spite of its diversity, is more easily comprehended than most people, even scientists, have previously realized. The six types of sexual activity, masturbation, spontaneous nocturnal emissions, petting, heterosexual intercourse, homosexual contacts, and animal contacts . . . all prove to originate in the relatively simple mechanisms which provide for erotic response when there are sufficient physical or psychic stimuli. . . .

There is little evidence of the existence of such a thing as innate perversity, even among those individuals whose sexual activities society has been least inclined to accept. There is an abundance of evidence that most human sexual activities would become comprehensible to most individuals, if they could know the background of each individual's behavior.

The social values of human activities must be measured by many scales other than those which are available to the scientist. Individual responsibilities toward others in the social organization, and the long-range outcome of behavior which represents the individual's response to the stimuli of the immediate moment, are things that persons other than scientists must evaluate. As scientists, we have explored, and we have performed our function when we have published the record of what we have found the human male doing sexually, as far as we have been able to ascertain that fact.

We appended a long list of tables which we believed would be of great help to clinicians in comparing the sexual histories of people who came to them for help with the averages for others of the same age group, educational level and religious or rural-urban backgrounds. But these reference tables, summarizing the outlets, proved to be a failure for reasons that were never clear to us. People simply didn't use them, although I (and I presume some others, at least) still find them extremely helpful today. Kinsey was so disappointed by this rejection that we did not include comparable tables in the *Female* volume.

There was an immediate reaction from the public as soon as the book was published. In the first month we got more than a thousand letters, and of these only six were from cranks or otherwise unfavorable. Naturally one remembers the adverse comments. I recall a Brooklyn woman who wrote in a rage to assure us that men were nothing but a bunch of leering, prancing goats, and we should be ashamed to have written such a book. Another man wrote—the first of a legion—to say that he was an autograph collector, and now that Kinsey was famous he would like to have his autograph. Kinsey told him it was against his policy to give autographs—and carefully signed his name.

By this time, too, there were some outraged cries from the bookstores. Saunders was unaccustomed to having a trade book on its list, and indeed had never considered ours as one, so it was being sold to the trade at their customary 20 percent discount, known to booksellers as a "short discount," instead of the usual 40 percent for the general books sold by nonspecialized publishers. But old houses change with glacial slowness, and it was not until publication of the *Female* book that Saunders modified its policy.

Kinsey was gratified later to find out that much of the continuing sale of the book had been to professional people. A survey of these buyers was conducted by Basic Book Service, of New York, in a 10 percent sampling of American members of various professional associations that was designed and conducted by Dr. Irving Lorge, of Columbia Teachers College. Psychiatrists proved to be the largest group of buyers and readers, followed by sociologists, psychologists, anthropologists and psychiatric social workers. Dr. Lorge's figures showed that only a fraction of all his interviewees had bought but not read the book, while substantial percentages had read but not bought it. Among those who neither bought nor read, the psychologists and anthropologists were almost equally disdainful, but the psychiatric social workers surpassed them both by a substantial margin.

There was one immediate move toward censorship. Early in May the Health League of Canada, the Quebec Catholic counterpart of the Health League in America, petitioned the Postmaster of Canada to prohibit distribution of the book through the post office in that country. The petition called the volume obscene, garbage fit only for the sewer. Saunders' attorneys wrote a letter to the Canadian postmaster defending their right to use the Canadian mails, but no action was taken.

The book was soon being translated into several languages. The Dutch version was particularly good, correcting errors and misinterpretations in the original text. In England, nearly 10,000 copies of the book had been sold by 1950. The English edition was printed from the American plates by Saunders' London branch.

All told, by the time Kinsey died there had been eleven printings of the *Male* volume. Sales continued steady at a high level for a year or more in America, and the book was translated into French, Spanish, Swedish, Japanese, Italian, Dutch and German.

In America the book was the basis of a thriving industry. Not only was it near the top of the best seller lists in its own right, but it touched off a spate of books attempting to capitalize on it, not to mention the national controversy that embroiled laymen as well as scientists. The book itself was one of those occasional phenomena in the publishing business, a little-read best seller, much like Masters and Johnson's first volume. People who read the reviews or heard about the controversy rushed to buy the book and found themselves holding three pounds and 804 pages of scientific prose and statistical charts, for which they had paid $6.50. The simple fact of the matter was that few lay readers would have had enough background knowledge in psychology and statistical method to grasp any more than the essentials of what Kinsey was talking about. Only the idea of a massive "sex book" could explain the phenomenal sales of more than 200,000 copies in the first two months.

A cartoon in *The New York Times Book Review,* showing a suburban housewife quietly reading at home with her husband, the *Male* volume tucked securely inside a magazine called *The Home Gardener,* was a clue to its primary readership, which appeared to be urbanites and college students. A few colleges did not encourage reading it. At Wellesley, according to *Time* magazine, the local bookstore told students they could not buy a copy unless they had the written approval of a professor. *Time* also reported other reader reactions, which I would not guarantee as authentic. In Kansas City, the magazine said, a grain merchant gave his mistress a copy inscribed on the flyleaf, "I hope this will help you to understand me better," and in Miami Beach a playboy was said to have bought fifty copies and sent them to all the women he knew. Librarians told us that the book was constantly being stolen.

Kinsey's name became that amorphous thing, a household word. The certain proof was its prevalence in the scripts of radio and nightclub comediar.s. A typical gag: "He's at the awkward age—you know, too old for the Bobbsey Twins and too young for the Kinsey Report." People referred to the Institute as "the Sex Center," and the phrase "hotter than the Kinsey Report" became a national figure of speech.

In Bloomington one of the first results of this great wave of publicity was a deluge of letters. Kinsey labored through them conscientiously for a time. Many were requests for him to make speeches, prepare papers, or write other books. His replies became shorter and shorter, and he began to resist the pressures, but it was months before he could make any real adjustment to the new situation. He had believed before publication that his work might attract attention, but he had no idea it would be so sudden and of such overwhelming proportions.

In the early days he had tried to be helpful to students who requested information for term papers, but after 1948 he could no longer do this, except in rare cases. I'm sure many people thought him short and curt in his replies, particularly those who requested information and were turned off by Kinsey's brief, stock (and true) answer that what the inquirer wanted to know had not yet been developed in our research and he would have to wait for further publication.

We were compelled to get extra secretarial help but could not afford all we needed; still, every letter was answered, with the exception of those from cranks, which were marked in his files by a red seal. Often Kinsey's replies would be apologetic. His files are full of letters beginning, "I am sorry not to have replied before, but I have just returned from a field trip."

Form letters for the most common inquiries soon became a necessity, and soon there were about twenty of them. One was for letters beginning "I have a sexual problem," in which Kinsey explained that we were not clinicians. Another was for those that began "Congratulations on the book," and came from strangers. There was a different letter to answer those who wrote, "I thought this was a terrible book," or more usually, "It is a good book, but . . ."

Crank letters never comprised much of the total volume. Mostly they were based on religious objections, condemning Kinsey for going against God's word, or declaring him an enemy of good morals. As one might expect, a large proportion of these letters came from California, where paradoxically he had been so well received, but his interviewing in that state was never subjected to any undue pressure from the kind of people who write crank letters.

Even with a flood tide of correspondence, Kinsey went right on in the old way, initiating more of it on his own. He often wrote to a scientist, "I have just read your article in [naming a professional journal], and I would be grateful if you could send me a reprint."

Many times he went on, "I wonder if you have thought of . . ." and then offer criticism. Anything written by anyone else, no matter in what field, interested him if it had anything to do with sex. His urge to investigate every aspect of sexuality, intending sometime to write about it, led us briefly into a good many unexplored areas—sex among the blind, or among epileptics, for example. We went into these areas a distance, but not far.

Kinsey would, for instance, ask people who had suffered heart trouble about their lives and sex problems as a result of the disease. For a time, too, we worked with the feebleminded, recording their histories. But these, like other specialized explorations, were never summarized; no papers were ever written about them.

The mailbag brought letters of every imaginable kind. Often they were grateful letters, which Kinsey naturally enjoyed reading. Typical of these was one from a reader in upper New York State, who wrote:

I am a professional man slightly past middle age and have three grown up children. I wish that I and others could have read your book years ago. With the exception of Homosexualism, for which I have never had the least desire, and extra-marital relations, I believe I have indulged more or less in all of the main class perversions, if they are such, which you describe in your book.

As a result of such episodes I have always felt that I was a moral pervert, a pariah or outcast and thereby developed a degree of Inferiority Complex which has been a deterrant [sic] to me in my profession.

Now when I find such a high percentage of others in the same boat, I have been mentally relieved and now can hold my head a bit higher and meet life on a surer basis. I am offering no brief or extenuation for this moot conduct except that the primary urge was more than my inhibitions could withstand. I am deeply grateful to you for presenting to the world facts that are unquestionable.

By contrast, one might find in the morning's mail a letter from the distinguished French philosopher René Guyon, writing from Bangkok to thank Kinsey for sending him a copy of the book, and adding:

I have tried for so many years to introduce some clarity and reasonableness in those sexual matters, entirely distorted by prejudices, that I enjoy deeply books of information which induce sophisticated persons to think over those questions and to select the way they think the best. May I add that I have really no doubt that the sexual attitudes which I advocate in my set of Sexual Ethics will become commonplaces within some thirty or forty years, especially amongst free thinking people.

Another kind of letter that pleased Kinsey came from people who had noted that on page 74 of the book he had asked anyone who had calendar records of their frequency of sexual outlet to place the data at his disposal. Many people responded, and hundreds more of these records were added to our files. Dr. John C. Hamon, then secretary-treasurer of the American Society for the Study of Sterility, in San Francisco, wrote to offer the records of nearly 2,000 patients, extending from one month to several years, who had recorded their menstrual dates, intercourse dates and basal body temperatures.

A great many other letters, of course, were attempts to use Kinsey in one way or another. Some of them were well-meaning, like that from the lady representing a hospital ladies' auxiliary unit in Milwaukee who asked Kinsey to contribute something bearing his name to be auctioned off at a benefit, to which Prok answered politely:

We have assiduously avoided doing anything which would seem to indicate any attempt on our part to get publicity. We are attempting to do sober scientific research, which, however, we think should be accessible to the general public. We must, therefore, abstain from accepting the sort of thing that you offer.

Yet one of the most common accusations made during the public hysteria about the book was that Kinsey was only a publicity seeker!

There were, as one would expect, letters from old friends who had known him in the early days and now hastened to congratulate him. One of them, a New York doctor, seeing Kinsey's picture in *Time*, wrote to him:

Dear Al: That was a helluva picture of you in *Time*. It seems to be the style nowadays for these monkey photographers to get a good view of your nose holes and incidentally, anybody who shoots us old buzzards from below upward sure gets the eyebags and the chin slack at their best. We are still pretty goodlooking guys you know (when taken from the right angles)!

I think Kinsey may have been most taken aback when he read a letter one day from a Hollywood agent who declared he had found a motion picture producer who would be interested in making a movie out of the *Male* volume—certainly the most unlikely consequence anyone could have thought of. Kinsey replied that he couldn't conceive of any such happening, but on the other hand he was willing to discuss the matter. The agent was delighted to see that he did not have a closed mind, and said what he proposed was a semidocumentary, like an illustrated lecture. At that, Kinsey wrote a reply so discouraging that anyone but a Hollywood agent would have given up. To further importunities Kinsey replied with his usual bluntness:

I hope you understand that we are not at all interested in the possibility of doing our book into a picture. I told you in the previous letter that we do not understand how it can be done. Unless you can sell us on believing that a motion picture would contribute something to the advancement of scientific investigation in our field, we would not agree to having any picture made.

More obvious attempts to capitalize on his fame Kinsey simply dismissed, as when Mae West sent him a telegram at the Commodore Hotel in New York when he was staying there. "Anxious to meet you. Please telephone me Warwick Hotel." Kinsey considered that a transparent publicity attempt. He did not come up to see Miss West, then or ever.

Another consequence of his fame was the customary deluge of books about sex sent by promotion directors of publishing houses who hoped for a quote to be used in the publicity. Instead, what they got in most instances, if not a brief refusal, was a sour critique of the book, unsuitable for framing. When Knopf sent him a copy of Simone de Beauvoir's *The Second Sex,* the philosophical precursor of Women's Liberation, Kinsey replied first with an adroit piece of oneupmanship by noting that "we have, of course, known the French edition and the translations in other languages," and then he continued with this devastating critique:

We have constant demand on us for the certification of everything from bras to religious books, and we have to confine any public statement to books that are strictly scientific productions or which contain original data of interest and importance to science. De Beauvoir's book does not fit into either of these categories, even though it is an interesting literary production of the sort that France has been writing about women ever since the days of Eleanor of Aquitaine, in the fourteenth century.

Longmans, Green had no better luck when they sent Kinsey a copy of *English Life and Leisure,* by Rowntree and Lavers, which they reported the British critics were speaking of as "the English Kinsey Report." Kinsey answered that he had already bought a copy of the book, and so he was returning the gift copy, about which he remarked:

As far as sex is concerned, the material in the book is contained in fourteen pages. That is a rather thin contribution to be labeled the "English Kinsey Report." Those fourteen pages represent no original contribution with the exception of half a dozen individual case histories. There is nothing approaching the sort of public opinion sampling which present-day surveys ordinarily utilize. I should think that there are some other parts of the book which may represent a more specific contribution, but that is outside of my area for expert judgment.

What really annoyed Kinsey, however, were the books about his book. The first was a serious symposium, edited by Kinsey's friend Albert Deutsch, called *Sex Habits of American Men*, published by Prentice-Hall. Most of its thirteen contributors were friendly, and Kinsey was grateful for this support, but he was angered by the statement from Dr. Robert P. Knight, a Yale psychiatrist, that the common cold had about the same incidence among Americans as homosexuality, as reported in the *Male* book, but the prevalence of colds did not make them "normal."

Another book attempted to "translate" Kinsey for the average reader. Written by Morris Ernst and David Loth, *American Sexual Behavior and the Kinsey Report*, published by Greystone Press, was the *Male* volume in simplified terms, for $1.95. While Kinsey considered this book a help, there was an implied criticism nonetheless in his letter of thanks to Ernst:

The magazine articles and commentaries on this first book undoubtedly helped interest the public in our work. On the other hand, we have found too many hundreds of people, and there probably are hundreds of thousands, who thought they were getting an adequate condensation of our whole book from these other articles, and have not attempted to see the book itself. This is even true of professional men, and we find that we have been criticized more often for what our commentators have said than for what we, ourselves, said in our book. All of these are things that we will want to take into account in handling the publicity on our second book.

The book that upset Kinsey most was *The Sexual Conduct of Men and Women*, by Norman Lockridge, published by Hogarth House, which asserted on its dust jacket: "We did not plan to publish the contents of this book for some time to come . . . [but] excitement caused by the recent appearance of the Kinsey Report has suddenly brought most of these doubtful factors into a maturity of public interest."

Kinsey was outraged by this spurious volume, which he exposed in a coldly furious letter to Ernst:

There is no Norman Lockridge, and there is no Hogarth Press. The author of the book is really Sam Roth, who is the publisher. He was thrown out of business and given a penal sentence for publishing obscene books when he was running the Falstaff Press. There was another charge of sending obscene literature through the Post Office. He is a book pirate, who has facsimiles of books published by Doubleday, Dutton, etc. etc. etc. A couple of days after they published the book about us, the Post Office descended upon Sam Roth and closed up his business. As I understand, he was prohibited use of the U. S. mails . . .

His present volume . . . is utter trash, mainly borrowed from earlier writings, and it would have had nothing to do with us if it had not been for the chapter by [G.] Legman, which is so vicious in its attack upon us that it is quite unbelievable. When the Post Office did Sam out of business this last week, he had to rush the printing of the book about us over to Citadel Press . . . a fairly respectable reprint house from which the book may now be obtained.

Kinsey chose not to sue, believing that public dissemination of the story about Roth's book would do the Institute more good. Ernst agreed.

Inevitably, along with fame came an invitation from the A. N. Marquis Company to appear in a new *Who's Who* volume, *Who Knows—And What?* There was, however, an indexing problem. Wheeler Sammons, the editor, reported to Kinsey that they did not know whether to list him as an authority on human sex behavior, sex crimes, gall wasps, or perhaps all three. Kinsey admitted that he might be a problem because he had done special research and published in the fields of gall wasps, edible wild plants, high school biology and human sex behavior, and in each field he had done more work than anyone had accomplished before.

Sammons decided eventually that he would list Kinsey in all four areas, and with a twist of bibliographical humor told Kinsey he had "pleaded with the compilers not to run amok and add a listing to 'sex behavior among edible wild plants.' "

Thus fame came to Alfred C. Kinsey, professor of zoology, and he found himself known everywhere in the world as a symbol of sex. At first he was pleased by the immense success of the book itself, and by the general reception it enjoyed. Shortly after it appeared, he gave an enthusiastic report to President Wells, who was then doing a tour of duty with the Office of the Cultural Adviser, Headquarters of the European Command. Kinsey considered that 95 percent at least of press comment, in magazines and newspapers, had been objective and definitely favorable. Publications that had wavered at the beginning, apparently not knowing exactly how they were going to treat the book—*Life* magazine and *The New York Times* were examples—had finally joined the chorus of approval. Bookstores were having difficulty keeping the book in stock. Three weeks after publication it was on the best seller list. No complaints had been registered with the University except by one faculty member (Thurman Rice, no doubt), or with the publisher or the National Research Council. The Rockefeller Foundation had received only one expression of dissatisfaction, from Harry Emerson Fosdick, whose brother was then its president. Dr. Fosdick had complained that the advertising was not dignified enough, a cavil Kinsey thought groundless.

"There will be complaints ultimately, without doubt," he concluded, "nevertheless the flood of approval seems clear evidence that the public wanted such an objective scientific study of sex made. As scientists and educators, I think we have under-estimated the public's capacity to look facts in the face."

A more serious underestimation was the capacity of the scientific community to turn on its own, especially those who felt their specialties threatened. Within a few months Kinsey found himself embroiled in a running battle with critics which never really subsided until he died.

CHAPTER

XVIII

THE CRITICS

Approaching the controversy which swirled around Kinsey and the *Male* volume I find myself with no inclination to refight old battles, no urge to prove that Kinsey was everlastingly right and his critics wrong. That was not the case, in any event, and I have no wish to join the ranks of those numerous generals who have been revising past wars to suit their egos.

Nevertheless, it is a subject that can hardly be ignored. Kinsey's reactions to attacks upon him tell a great deal about the man, just as some of the critical onslaughts tell much about the critics. There is also the fact that there were two wars going on against Kinsey, the one that appeared in the public prints and that many people knew about, the other a much more cutthroat struggle among scientists which came to the surface only in the professional journals. It was the latter arena Kinsey cared about, because it was there he considered his professional reputation and the validity of his work to be at stake.

There was little question about how the public at large felt. In a poll taken by George Gallup's Public Opinion Institute following the book's publication, 58 percent of men and 55 percent of women thought Kinsey's research was a "good thing." Only 10 percent and 14 percent respectively thought it a "bad thing." A division of 3 and 5 percent each qualified their opinion, and there was the usual apathy or ignorance—29 percent of men and 27 percent of women with no opinion. When this result was broken down between those who had heard or read about the book and those who hadn't, the results were not significantly different, except that there were more—73 percent of both sexes—who thought the research was a good thing, and only 10 percent who thought it bad among those who had heard or read about it.

But the scientific community was a different matter. Four months after the book was out Kinsey was writing to his friend Dr. Carl Hartman, by this time director of the Ortho Research Foundation in Raritan, New Jersey:

It is going to be interesting in the course of the years to see which of the so-called scientists and clinicians expose their emotional selves in their attack on our work. Making allowance for all such corrections as any scientist must make on any such work, I am still confident that we have an approximation to the fact. I must admit, however, that I am surprised at some of the persons who would like to avoid facing the fact.

There lay the somewhat complicated key to Kinsey's reactions. Those who attacked him, he believed, were "exposing their emotional selves" by attacking his work, and there was enough truth in this idea in some cases to justify his feeling. But Kinsey insisted that this was true even of good friends who criticized his work. Reviews that praised him and the project in a broad sense, and admitted that he had indeed reached "an approximation of the fact," he nevertheless condemned (and their authors as well) when they went on to take exception to some of his conclusions. They were all, he was convinced, unable to "face reality," one of his favorite phrases. Thus he wrote to Dr. H. M. Parshley, head of the Zoology Department at Smith College, who had given him a favorable notice in the New York *Herald Tribune:*

Reactions to our book are going to constitute a most interesting chapter in the history of science. It is amazing how many people have been willing to base generalizations about human sexual behavior on general gossip and a handful of clinical cases, while they now object strenuously to an adequate and carefully selected 5,300 cases. It indicates, of course, that there are emotional factors involved, and not an objective desire to face the fact. Your favorable review, and those of some of the others, are, consequently, worth a great deal at this time.

There was a certain amount of rationalization, too, in his reaction to criticism. "We are not disturbed about the people who have been criticizing," he wrote to Dr. Roland E. Mueser, of the Ordnance Research Laboratory at Pennsylvania State. "We shall always be glad to sit down with anyone who has seriously considered the questions he asks. I worry about these supercilious criticisms only because I think they may confuse the public, and delay their utilization of our material."

I must hasten to say, however, that Kinsey had good reason to be angry and impatient with some of the criticism. Often we could only shake our heads in wonder at what we read, and for one accustomed to intellectual in-fighting, it was not difficult for us to identify the critics who had personal axes to grind—usually, as I have said, because they felt their own work was threatened. Much of the criticism, too, was based on a simple lack of knowledge of what we were doing, which the critics could hardly admit, or were else completely unaware of.

Critics attacked us for things we had not done and for things we *should* have done. Sometimes the list seemed endless. They thought we should have described the total sample, recorded the number who refused, listed specific questions, measured the resistance in each interview, compared the histories of volunteers and reluctant contributors, and measured the reliability of the coding of the interviewers. They claimed we needed more attitudinal data. Some complained that we did not list the questions our subjects asked, and had failed to provide a complete description of our procedures and methods. Others argued that the figures based on all our histories should be accompanied by corresponding figures for only the histories used in the specific report. We were accused of neglecting to differentiate statistically insignificant differences from differences statistically significant but not large enough to matter. It was commonly asserted that we needed a psychiatrist or an analyst on our staff. Some were upset because we had no data on whether subjects, or their parents, were immigrants.

The list went on. We needed geographic breakdowns. We told what but did not tell why. We should have published case histories. We had ignored European experimental research. More physical data were needed. Some cases should have been psychoanalyzed as a check. We had failed to take cognizance of transference during the interview, in the classic pattern of psychoanalyst and patient. We had neglected to get at latent factors. We had been unconcerned with the subject's emotional state. Unconscious motivations had been ignored. We should have studied morality scientifically. The influence of will-power had been overlooked. Our special vocabulary had not been defined.

There were more, but these will provide an idea of the formidable range of omissions and commissions with which we were charged by the critics.

All of this alternately disgusted, amused, irritated or disappointed us. Kinsey's first reaction was to rush into print with answers, but after sober talks with our advisers and consultants, he took their advice, for the most part, to remain silent, to adopt the position that what critics said did not matter in the long run, and meanwhile we still had an enormous amount of work to do. It was hard advice to take, especially for Kinsey, but it was right. To have gone on the attack ourselves would only have meant precipitating new storms, which would have interfered with our work.

The critics could be divided broadly into five categories. There were the moralists, who were upset because the study had been done at all. Because they were often well-known people, they seemed to constitute a larger force than was actually the case. They were in fact a distinct minority. Then there were those who took advantage of the importance and worldwide recognition of our study to call attention to themselves by criticizing it. A third group were conservative people devoted to the status quo in science who did not like Kinsey because he was an innovator. A fourth class consisted of those who did not realize how much Kinsey knew about subjects outside zoology, and so attacked his generalizations based on materials we were not able to include in the book. Finally, there were those who pointed to the real mistakes we had made, but sometimes did not allow for the fact that the *Male* volume was really a progress report, which unquestionably had faults. (It is surprising, however, how well it has stood up. Even where the statistics erred, the percentage of error was small, and as later research has proved, the conclusions we drew from them were correct.)

So much for the generalities. The specifics were a different matter.

2

One may begin, I think, by dismissing the moralists, who made their expected remarks, to which no one but the already convinced paid any attention. In this category would be Mrs. Clare Boothe Luce, the National Council of Catholic Women and (for the *Female* volume) such thinkers on scientific matters as Kathleen Norris, Fannie Hurst, George Sokolsky and Dorothy Thompson.

There were some surprises in this category, however. It seemed grotesque that an eminent university president such as Harold W. Dodds, of Princeton, could be guilty of the unacademic fantasy of his much-quoted comment: "Perhaps the undergraduate newspaper that likened the reports to the work of small boys writing dirty words on fences touched a more profound scientific truth than is revealed in the surfeit of rather trivial graphs with which the reports are loaded."

Even more incredible was the view of a Yale zoologist, Professor George A. Baitsell, who wrote in the *Yale News:*

I don't like Kinsey! I don't like his report; I don't like anything about it. Kinsey is not trained to do work in this field. The work should be done by a sociologist. In his interviews, Kinsey employed a thoroughly objectionable technique. The interviews often have a serious effect on the subject's nerves. Children, reluctant to be questioned, have been virtually forced to submit because of the possibility of being labeled "deficient." The Kinsey Report might well be called the "Kinsey Inquisition."

Behind the expected clerical words of the Reverend Dr. Henry P. Van Dusen, the noted New York divine, lay a chilling forecast of what might happen to our financial support. "Few have raised ethical queries," he wrote, "regarding the sponsorship of this study by a national research body, and its financing by one of the great Foundations dedicated to promote the well-being of mankind throughout the world." Dr. Van Dusen was not only president of Union Theological Seminary but a leading member of the Rockefeller Foundation. Already the handwriting was on the wall.

While reading these criticisms, Kinsey learned that a critic nearer home was doing his best to undermine him. It was Thurman Rice once more. The feud between them had simmered along for years, sometimes rising to peaks of the ludicrous, as when Rice, attacking the value of the research, wrote to Kinsey that he was particularly grieved because he was frequently mistaken for Prok, since, as he said, they were both interested in sex, were both about the same size and of rather florid complexion. Kinsey could not think of a reply to that one.

Soon after the book emerged there were reports from the Pennsylvania State campus that, in speaking appearances there, Dr. Rice had charged that President Wells was greatly concerned about Kinsey, and expressed his opinion that the research would set back sex education in the United States at least twenty years.

Kinsey did not take this attack very seriously. He was confident that President Wells and the trustees would support him, as indeed they did. He was more concerned about the possible effect of the nationally printed criticisms on his standing at the Rockefeller Foundation, the source of the Institute's income. Consequently he was at pains to communicate frequently with his friend at the Foundation, Alan Gregg, who had been one of his firmest supporters from the beginning. Reviewing the critical situation with Gregg, four months after the book's appearance, Kinsey wrote:

Certainly the most serious and authoritative reviews have been unanimously for us. This has meant a great deal in the public acceptance of the material, and you may know that the Gallup poll indicates that five out of six of the population believe that such research should have been done. There is a long series of scientific reviews and journals in many fields which are very encouraging. . . .

In contrast to the above, there are certain people in the sciences and in clinical practice who are very bitter in their attacks on us. These are only beginning to appear in print but you will see more of them within the next month. The emotional intensity of their attacks provides evidence that something more than scientific objectivity is involved in their criticisms. Compare, for instance, the newspaper review which you have seen by Geoffrey Gorer and the more vicious one which he is planning to publish in the *American Scholar* this summer, with a careful analysis of our statistical method made by Leo Crespi of Princeton, who is a statistical advisor to the Gallup Poll. . . .

Jealousy animates some of the other reviews from persons claiming scientific standing. The psychoanalytic objections reached their climax in a review that Dr. Kubie will have in an issue of *Psychosomatic Medicine*, in which he calls upon the Rockefeller Foundation and the National Research Council to take the project out of our hands and put it in the hands of psychoanalysts who can do the job properly.

There is no organized church nor religious move against us, but there are inevitably persons who object that we have no right to publish and distribute results which threaten our moral system as much as this book does. The most specific move in this direction will center in articles to be published in June and July issues of the *Reader's Digest. . . .*

You will also be interested to know that we have even been the object of jealousy with certain sections of the underworld which is involved in the distribution of obscene books. . . .

With all, the reactions have been much more favorable than we could have had any right to expect. Nevertheless, the emotional intensity of the moves against us needs to be understood and everyone concerned with this project needs to stand firm on the scientific and social desirability of this study and our right to make the results available to the public.

Gregg told Kinsey that he was neither surprised nor disturbed by the reviews, except for the one written by Dr. Lawrence Kubie, the New York psychoanalyst. Most of the criticisms, he thought, did not carry much weight, and few would have any bearing on what might be done in the next volume. All the Institute staff, he said, deserved appreciation for the equanimity with which they had received "splashes of everything from molasses to vitriol, and still not become obviously embittered or pontifical. Nothing cheers me so much as your determination to keep learning and trying."

As the battle between Kinsey and his critics went on, however, year after year, Gregg's confidence was shaken. Early in 1950 he confided to Dr. George Corner, of the National Research Council:

It is probably best for me to write you in terms and at a level I do not particularly relish. . . . I would point out that the most copious and the most cogent criticism of Kinsey's first volume has been mathematical. I would think that issuance of the second volume without explicit and effective attention to staff needs in this direction, especially if Volume 2 turns out to contain mistakes that could have been forestalled by the addition of a competent statistician, runs the risk of appearing to some of us here as headstrong and indefensible. Though this would reflect most on Kinsey, I think it reasonable for me to forewarn you that trouble could come in the continuing Rockefeller Foundation support to the National Research Council Committee if Kinsey did nothing to meet the statisticians' criticisms when he could have done so.

It would be helpful for me to be able to tell our Trustees what are the uses of the royalty income thus far from Volume 1, since there are many speculations as to why we need contribute at all to such an obvious success.

The most bizarre rumor thus far is that the Kinsey report has made millions for the Rockefeller Foundation, which I add for comic relief.

The one review that appeared to concern Kinsey most was Lewis M. Terman's long sixteen-page analysis in the *Psychological Bulletin*. The Stanford University psychologist had been Kinsey's friend, as I noted earlier, but there was more to Kinsey's feeling about it than the breach of a relationship which had been cordial but not particularly close. Perhaps more than the others, Terman's review symbolized for him the moralism and prudery of so many of his worst critics, wrapped in a blanket of professional criticism, most of it directed at his statistical methods.

It was maddening in another way, too, being one of those "yes, but" reviews so common in book reviewing, particularly among academicians. It began, for example: "Like others, the reviewer has been deeply impressed by the magnitude and potential significance of Kinsey's research. From the first volume of his projected series it is obvious that no one has ever obtained so much information from so many persons regarding the most secret phases of their sexual histories." And it ended: "The reviewer fully agrees with Kinsey that the facts about human sexual behavior should be brought to light, and he regards this investigation as so important that he sincerely hopes it can be carried through to completion. But he also hopes that the many faults of exposition and interpretation to be found in this volume will not be repeated in those which follow."

The key to the review, however, in Kinsey's opinion, was in the paragraph just before the close, where Terman observed: "Notwithstanding Kinsey's frequent reiteration that his job is to report facts rather than evaluations, it has been possible to quote numerous passages in which recklessly worded and slanted evaluations are expressed, the slanting being often in the direction of implied preference for uninhibited sexual activity."

In a copy of the review Kinsey had underlined "evaluations" and the phrase "often in the direction of implied preference for uninhibited sexual activity," opposite which he had written on the margin, "Moral." Underlying Terman's criticisms was a moralistic attitude toward sex, which Kinsey could not abide.

There were other things, however, both good and bad about the review. On the bad side was the probability that Terman had been hurt by our summary of his work in the *Male* volume, which had also raised a fundamental difference of opinion. Kinsey had written: "The data would have been more reliable if they had been obtained by direct interviewing [Terman had used a questionnaire], and the conclusions would have been totally different at certain points if the analyses had been confined to particular educational levels."

Kinsey had also discussed Terman's prediction that premarital intercourse was increasing with such extraordinary rapidity that "intercourse with future spouse before marriage will become universal by 1950 or 1955." These figures, Kinsey said, had been accepted widely by psychologists and sociologists, and he was convinced that Terman had felt his prestige threatened by our challenge to his data. Terman, who was eighty years old at the time, did not live to see his prediction fail to come true.

Some of Terman's objections, however, bordered on the ludicrous. For example, he complained that in asking interviewees about nocturnal emissions, Kinsey had obtained a 100 percent higher frequency in his interviewing than I had in mine. It was true. Kinsey's figure was .06, mine was .03, a difference of one ejaculation per year —but a 100 percent difference.

On the other hand, Terman had some legitimate criticism to make. A central point in this criticism, as well as in others, was the method of sampling we used, and the sample size. This is a technical problem of absorbing interest only to psychologists, sociologists and statisticians, and I will not belabor it here. But it *was* a fundamental element in the dispute, and Kinsey was much concerned about it. Raymond Pearl, the noted statistician, had spent some time with us at the beginning of the research, advising on the problem, as Lowell Reed did later, and we had had the benefit of other statistical advisers. Still there were some admitted deficiencies in the method, which Kinsey stated clearly enough in his defense, so that anyone could have understood it:

Our sample is not as adequate as could be obtained from a stack of cards, or a pile of coins, or from some other simple physical situation. It is not as adequate as I was able to do with my gall wasp material. I do not believe that any sampling of human material can ever obtain the adequacy that pencil and paper statisticians work out on the basis of physical phenomena. That is why we have indicated what sorts of errors should be allowed for in any and all of our figures. We will insist, however, that nowhere in psychological or sociological literature has there ever been a sample which approaches the adequacy of ours. Certainly in a study that has dealt with sex or any other aspect of human sociology or psychology, there has never been any such widely distributed sample involved. The Public Opinion and the Market Research people are the only ones who have ever used such samples. Terman certainly did not have anything like a distributed sample in his marriage clinic cases on which he based his conclusions on marital happiness, nor his jail cases on which he based his conclusions on homosexuality.

While he defended himself ably on technical grounds, Kinsey could not forbear to attack the motives and personalities of his critics, beginning with Terman, as when he wrote:

I think we are objective and fair when we say that the animus of the whole review is jealousy and a considerable prudery. There have, of course, been a good many psychologists who have resented the fact that a biologist has had anything to do with this study. We got considerable ill treatment from them early in the study, and never did get any sort of acceptance from them until some of the top people put us on their program in Philadelphia a little over two years ago. Like sheep, the lesser fry then decided they had better plump for us. We have had no outright trouble with them since.

Kinsey based his charge of jealousy on the fact that Terman was one of a score or more people to whom the National Research Council had appropriated money for a long period of years to get a survey of human sex behavior done, and in Kinsey's opinion all had failed or stopped short. His friend Carney Landis had failed, Kinsey argued, but it had not prevented him from becoming an ardent supporter of the Institute. But Terman and Dr. Adolph Meyer, of Johns Hopkins, were among those who had failed and consequently criticized him from the beginning, Kinsey said.

Always Kinsey returned to the endless debate about the samples. One of his most pungent observations on the subject was made to his friend, Dr. H. M. Parshley, of Smith:

You ask about the percentage of our histories who were sex offenders and other low characters. I will tell you as a good friend exactly why we did not publish the exact figures of the constitution of our population. We anticipated that there would be a good many people like Terman who would have their own ideas as to the exact percentage of barbers and college professors of one rank and another rank who should be included. We anticipated that we would spend the rest of our lives arguing exactly who should be accepted as a normal individual, and who should be ruled out as a low character. I know perfectly well that some people would suggest that all persons who have ever been convicted and done jail sentence should be ruled out. By the same token, one would have to rule out anyone who ever will do a jail sentence. For our part we have felt that a man who has lived sixty or seventy or eighty years without going to jail and then is arrested on a drunk charge after his wife has divorced him, or some other similar thing, is a normal individual, the same as a thirty year old who has not lived long enough to prove that he will never be caught by the law. We have had suggestions from a number of psychologists of Terman's generation that we should confine ourselves to a good, normal, middle-class group, such as college professors. In actuality, the histories of this group represent one of the widest departures from anything that is typical of the mass of the population.

Oddly enough, the correspondence between Kinsey and Terman after publication of the review was polite and restrained on both sides. As the controversy grew, however, Terman apparently felt he should explain himself further, and after sending a copy of the review to President Wells, he wrote:

When I sent the reprint to you, I should have made it clear that I regard Kinsey's investigation as very important and that I hope it can be continued to completion. I am strongly of the opinion, however, as are also my psychological colleagues at Stanford, that Dr. Kinsey should take account of some of the criticisms in preparing his later volumes. Some of his sources of error and confusion present in the first report could easily be avoided in those which are to follow.

This seemed to be the judgment even of some of the strongest Kinsey supporters, notably Yerkes. When Kinsey asked him what he thought of the Terman review, Yerkes replied with his customary forthrightness that he thought it was the first one he had read which contained serviceable adverse criticisms. It must be remembered, however, that the two men had been close friends for many years, and that Yerkes had the highest opinion of Terman. If Prok expected sympathy and support from Yerkes, therefore, he could hardly expect to get it in undiluted measure.

In Yerkes' opinion, Terman had written with reasonable objectivity, impersonally and with every effort to be fair, but he did not agree with all of his friend's critical statements, nor had his high opinion of the project and the book been changed by them. Yerkes pleaded with Kinsey to accept the idea that his work must be an approximation of the scientifically satisfactory. He advised Kinsey not to reply in print, but to write a conciliatory letter to Terman which would convince him of Prok's "breadth and hospitality of view and eagerness to improve his technical practices and to gain in wisdom." He also advised Kinsey not to be oversensitive to well-meant adverse criticism, and he concluded: "My chief hope and object in writing this letter is to help to bring Kinsey and Terman together as able and honest fellow biologists who should work as friends in spite of disagreements."

It was not to be. Kinsey remained convinced that Terman had betrayed him, through jealousy and a basic prudery.

Second on Kinsey's new list of enemies after publication was Geoffrey Gorer, the British cultural anthropologist who was at the time consultant to the Columbia Research Project on Contemporary Cultures. Gorer's review in the New York *Herald Tribune* Sunday book review section was one of the first notices in the mass media, and I must say that it dismayed all of us. Perhaps it was because we were not familiar with the kind of reviewing it represented, which is common in the quality London Sunday newspapers, where British intellectuals would count it a weekend lost if they did not dismember each other with the literary elegance for which they are celebrated. The amount of academic bloodletting between rival dons is a gory thing to witness, and the merciless slaughter of American writers, especially academicians, chills the blood of visitors from this country.

Gorer's chief complaint, aside from his general condescending attitude, which Kinsey found infuriating, was the issue of the sample, which he deplored at length. He, too, was a disciple of the questionnaire method, which he was still using to measure sexual behavior as late as 1970, when his survey of British attitudes and practices was published in the London *Sunday Times*.

In private Kinsey attacked Gorer on a personal basis. He wrote to a New York friend:

His objections to the quality of our sample would have been valid if we had done proportionate sampling, that is, if we had intended to get an overall average from the whole population with a sample in which each element of the population was represented in the same proportion that it occurs in the United States Census. In Chapter 3 of our book we clearly point out that we have used stratified sampling, which depends upon securing approximately equal samples from each segment of the population, in order that we shall have enough cases even in the less common groups to make a good statistical calculation. Statisticians are largely agreed that this is much the better method of sampling. By simple arithmetic it is then possible to weight the results, obtained from these several groups, and reconstruct the picture for the total population. . . .

Gorer was either incapable of understanding the differences between proportionate and stratified sampling, or else he had ulterior motives.

Probably Gorer had no ulterior motive; that was simply part of Kinsey's feeling about his critics. There was a profound difference of opinion about sampling, surely, and this coupled with Gorer's infuriating style was what stirred Kinsey to such anger.

Little if any damage was done by his reviews, in spite of Kinsey's exaggerated fears. The newspaper review was quickly forgotten, and a later one in the *American Scholar* was so unimpressive by any standard that few took it seriously.

Some reviews were merely curious, such as Lionel Trilling's "Sex and Science: The Kinsey Report," out of which this well-known Columbia University critic and professor of literature was able to get considerable mileage. Originally published in the *Partisan Review* for April 1948, it next appeared in the *Bulletin* of the Menninger Clinic for July 1949. Trilling included it in a volume of his essays, *The Liberal Imagination*, published by Viking Press in 1950, and in London by Secker and Warburg in 1951; there was also a paperback Doubleday Anchor Books edition in 1953. The review made its final appearance in a 1954 New American Library paperback, Donald P. Geddes' symposium, *An Analysis of the Kinsey Reports on Sexual Behavior in the Human Male and Female,* where it was termed "the classic essay on Kinsey."

The essay itself, however, only demonstrated that a literary critic, however distinguished in academic and other intellectual circles, is not a qualified judge of matters outside his competence. It was full of such simplistic judgments as: "Surely the problem of the natural in the human was solved four centuries ago by Rabelais." Trilling was quite unable to grasp the scientific nature of the book, but he did raise the question of the social uses of science, a legitimate enough inquiry. Kinsey's view on this subject was expressed succinctly several years later in a letter to René Guyon:

I think there is wisdom in keeping a research investigation rather separate . from clinical or social application. When one becomes interested primarily in the application of data, it is too liable to warp one's interpretation of the data, and certainly is liable to play too large a part in the decision as to what ends of the research should be undertaken. Consequently, we rather strictly abstain from reaching decisions on social policies growing out of our own data. You must not, however, believe for a moment that we are at all disinterested in seeing such social interpretations made. We think it better for them to be made by persons like yourself and others, rather than by ourselves. We are ready to call attention to the importance of your interpretations, and certainly should give them a prominent place if we quote the interpretations of anyone on these social issues. You have approached these problems with a clear logic which, moreover, has a considerable amount of human experience to support it. I refer to the Napoleonic Code, for instance, and to the experiences of Scandinavia in reducing its sex laws to the level of social importance.

Where the social implications of the Report rubbed against the scientific establishment hardest was among the psychoanalysts and the sociologists; consequently some of the most adverse reactions came from these specialists. Here the scientific fact in which Kinsey dealt came into hard conflict with the metaphysical concepts inherent in psychoanalytic theory—two opposed approaches to human behavior.

Kinsey's chief antagonist here was Dr. Lawrence S. Kubie, whose review appeared in the *Journal of Psychosomatic Medicine.* It was not enough for Kinsey that Kubie should write:

The courage, patience, humility, and above all the broad humanity of those who for the last ten years have devoted themselves to this colossal undertaking must command profound respect. . . . The result is the most important statistical addition which has ever been made to our information on the incidence in a total population of various patterns of overt sexual behavior; and although several important types of behavior are omitted, the report merits detailed study by everyone who is concerned with human nature.

That much would have constituted a rave review, if it had not been for the nearly sixteen pages which came after it. Kinsey was offended by Kubie's well-meant statement that none of his criticisms were aimed at the authors; the analyst considered every mistake a result of their lack of experience with the phenomenology and psychology of illness. His chief arguments were that more cases were needed, that representative individuals ought to be studied in great detail and that experts in psychopathology were needed to give meaning to the study. This was the burden of Kubie's perennial crusade—to make psychoanalysis the only answer to the world's problems.

Kubie sent Kinsey a copy of the review, with what would no doubt have seemed to anyone else a conciliatory letter:

It is a two-fisted review, I am afraid, but I hope that you will realize that my frank criticisms of what seem to me to be the deficiencies of the report are offered in a spirit of profound respect for the groundwork which you have laid. My review is a crusade to induce you to expand this study in directions which seem to me so absolutely essential, no matter how difficult they may be.

Kinsey in his reply began by assuring Kubie: "Your criticisms, pro and con, are so eminently sincere and your attitude so fair that it is a pleasure to tangle with you," and then he tangled with him for three tightly written pages. It was one of Kinsey's milder rebuttals, but it was clear then and later that Prok, on the basis of our history taking among psychoanalysts and psychiatrists, did not believe that Kubie's viewpoint represented the profession.

Kubie's review became a subject for evaluation by Karl Lashley, of the National Research Council Committee, in the course of his recommendation for further funding of the project. Lashley rejected Kubie's criticisms of our interview technique and our statistical procedures; attacked his concept of "normality," which had occupied so large a part of his review; but supported him on his objections to some of our interpretations as oversimplified. He rejected further the idea that the Committee should try to influence Kinsey's program in view of Kubie's criticism.

In this report Lashley cast doubt for the first time on the wisdom of supporting the project to the point of getting 100,000 histories. Continued accumulation of data by the same methods, he argued, could be expected to give diminishing returns. "The important general principles can probably be derived from the first 15,000 cases," he wrote. "Accumulations beyond that are likely to be taxonomic and ultimately extend to descriptions of the sexual patterns of widowed Baptist missionaries in Afghanistan." He noted that Kinsey had never presented a clear program to justify 100,000 cases, but nevertheless he recommended that there was every reason to encourage the study for another five years until present projects were brought to completion, after which future plans could be discussed and evaluated. Unfortunately, the Kubie review proved to be an important factor in the Rockefeller Foundation's withdrawal.

The controversies with Terman, Gorer and Kubie were the main attractions in the big tent of the Kinsey Controversy, but there were some fascinating, puzzling and occasionally frightening sideshows. In the puzzling category I place, for example, his battle with Albert Ellis, the New York therapist and writer on sex problems. Ellis was actually a rather strong Kinsey supporter, yet he was the subject of one of the sharpest, most blistering attacks Kinsey made on anyone. "Puzzling" is the only word to be applied to such an attack on a man who began his review of the book in the *Journal of General Psychology* by calling it "undoubtedly the most important collection of sex facts ever printed . . ." and went on:

Kinsey and his associates are doing a study that is broad and comprehensive enough to make all previous sex surveys look feeble by comparison. They are doing it, moreover, in a manner whose incisiveness and preciseness must commend scholarly respect. They are not only conducting a significant pioneering search for the facts of sexual behavior, but they have also taken care to equip their expedition with carefully planned and selected research techniques. Theirs, in a field hitherto little known for objective investigation, is a truly scientific venture. Whatever its ultimate execution and outcome, its spirit can hardly be too highly praised.

But Ellis followed with an attack on what he considered to be the book's inadequacies, and Kinsey responded with a tirade which exposed the raw nerve that was causing him so much anxiety—fear that the assaults on his work might cause enough concern at the Rockefeller Foundation to cause them to cut off the money which made the project possible. It was a fully justified fear, for this was exactly what happened. The assault on the *Male* volume was not enough, because the bulk of the controversy was on a scientific level, but when the *Female* volume brought every moralist to the barricades, the end of

Foundation support was certain, and Kinsey could sense this far in advance. I am sure that his abiding fear that he would not be able to continue the work lay behind much of the seemingly irrational anger in his attacks on his critics.

Consequently he viewed with alarm, and renewed anger, the large-scale effort by the American Social Hygiene Association to examine his work at its annual meeting in New York, March 30–31, 1948, at the Hotel Pennsylvania. Convinced that the Association meant to discredit him, Kinsey confided to Dr. Dickinson his belief that the program was the work of a

group of malcontents who will then issue a pronouncement, as coming from a sober scientific session, against our book. The plan is to discredit it by insisting that the sample is inadequate. Gorer, a fanatical moralist in the Sociology Department at Harvard by the name of Zimmerman, Father Cooper, who writes on chastity from the Catholic University of America, and groups of others of the sort are the speakers at the meeting.

Social Hygiene has a great deal at stake. It does them no good to have our data show that there has been little change in sexual behavior in the past twenty-two years, in spite of the millions of dollars Social Hygiene has spent, and the millions more that has been spent by other agencies under the stimulation of Social Hygiene. Social Hygiene has had a great deal of money cut off by the Venereal Disease Division of the United States Public Health Service, in consequence of our statistics. They will have to fight to discredit us, or else adopt new policies. I have it on good authority that there is some division in the Social Hygiene Association as to which they should do.

However much truth there may have been in this, the meeting of the Association was not exactly the public lynching Kinsey imagined it would be. He was attacked but he was also defended before the 250 or so social workers, statisticians and other interested people present. Some of the speakers and listeners, including his strongest critic, Margaret Mead, protested the fact that Kinsey himself was not there to defend himself. The chairman of the meeting told the audience that the Association had considered inviting him but had decided against it, at which renewed protest broke out.

The list of speakers produced a kind of rehearsal of the whole Kinsey controversy. George Corner sketched the history of the report and defended it wherever he thought it was necessary. Dr. Jules Eisenbud, associate in psychiatry at the College of Physicians and Surgeons, Columbia University, a practicing psychoanalyst, declared the report to be highly biased. Dr. Clyde V. Kiser, statistician of the Milbank Memorial Fund and the Institution for Population Research at Princeton, disagreed with most of Kinsey's statistical method. Dr. Louis Dublin, of Metropolitan Life, defended Kinsey against Eisenbud. Dr. John W. Riley, Jr., of Rutgers University, a sampling expert, criticized the report because it was not a random sample.

So it went. Margaret Mead, the most accomplished speaker on the panel, amused the audience and startled some of them by asserting that the Report was puritanical. As Kinsey had expected, Dr. Carle C. Zimmerman, the Harvard sociology professor, attacked the Report as an assault on American family patterns, and Corner duly challenged him to produce any evidence from the book that Kinsey had actually recommended changes in sexual mores. Zimmerman declined. The visiting clergy were equally divided, the Catholics against, the Episcopalians for.

Through and around the discussions buzzed the energetic figure of Dr. Dickinson, who was active enough to take the place of a dozen defenders. Helen Dietz, the Saunders editor who had worked with Kinsey on the book, attended the sessions, too, and wrote a private report in which she concluded that the criticisms, while numerous, were on a high level, and pointed out that every speaker took pains to praise Kinsey's long years of work and the importance of his contributions.

3

These were the major battles with the professional critics, and if Kinsey responded most sharply to them it was because he cared much more about the opinion of the scientific community than about that of the rest of the world. Among the lay critics, however, he made one exception, and again because he feared, with reason, that the sources of our funding would be influenced. This exception was Fulton Oursler, then an editor of the *Reader's Digest*. Oursler had created his reputation as a mass magazine editor in the twenties, when he made *Liberty* magazine one of the most popular periodicals in the country. In this job and others Oursler had become a successful exploiter of sex and sensation, before he made a complete turnabout in the thirties and went to the Presbyterian precincts of the *Digest*, joining as a top editor two ex-clergymen and an ex-missionary on a magazine which had been founded by a missionary's son. In this ecclesiastical atmosphere, abetted later by his own conversion to Catholicism, Oursler became a deadly enemy of sin.

When the *Male* volume was published, he was outraged and wrote an article so vitriolic that DeWitt Wallace, the publisher, refused to print it. The original article advocated suppression of the book. In the compromise which followed this unsuccessful effort, Oursler's name disappeared and a far more subtle, and much more dangerous, attack was launched under a blandly clever editorial device not unknown in the magazine business.

The device was the loaded symposium. In June 1948 the *Digest* published as a lead article a collection of opinions titled "Must We Change Our Sex Standards?" and subtitled "A symposium on one of the most vital questions of our time." The editorial matter preceding the quoted opinions gave away the show to knowledgeable people, unfortunately a small number of the magazine's millions of readers.

"Is the love of man and woman merely an animal function?" the *Digest* inquired rhetorically, then continued:

Are spiritual ideals of mating, of fidelity and chastity no more than irrational and sentimental nonsense? Have our conventions and moralities—and what we have always held to be simple decency—been outmoded by findings of modern science?

All over the land, people are asking these questions. Because of newly published polls and cold, detached, scientific surveys, many people have come to fear that old anchors are being swept away, old foundations destroyed. They have just been told that practices long held in abhorrence must now be regarded as acceptable. Science, so it is said, does not recognize any expression of sex as "abnormal"; except for "maniacal" deeds, pretty much anything is all right.

From parents as well as young people, pleas for guidance are pouring in, not only to pastors, priests and rabbis but to family doctors, editors, psychologists, authorities in many fields. Some of the most repeated inquiries have now been brought before a selected group of educators, scientists and religious teachers. Their comments, which follow, prove that there is a body of competent scientific and intellectual opinion that holds fast and firm to the long accepted ideals and ways of virtue.

Of course it proved nothing of the kind. It proved that the *Digest* had sent a loaded inquiry to a hand-picked group of people who could be guaranteed to give the right answers. This "selected group" included a rabbi, a professor of moral theology, an Episcopal rector, a small collection of writers, Norman Vincent Peale, Father Flanagan, the National Commander of the Salvation Army and J. Edgar Hoover. There was a smattering of psychiatrists and doctors, and one legitimate scientist, Dr. Robert A. Millikan, a Nobel Prize winner—in physics. Some of the statements from these people were so vague as to constitute little more than a high-minded defense of virtue and antimaterialism.

It was an obvious piece of trickery, and the *Digest* followed it three months later with another symposium on the same subject, composed of letters from readers who had read the first symposium, thus getting additional usage from the idea. These carefully selected replies included one from an anonymous professor who appeared to fear for his tenure, and another from Henry C. Link, head of the Psychological Corporation of New York, who took the occasion to quote from his own book, *The Rediscovery of Morals*. Other correspondents were Harold Dodds, of Princeton, whose opinion I have quoted; an economics professor from Heidelberg College in Ohio; Jackie Robinson, a Brooklyn Dodgers infielder; and the general director of the Health League of Canada, which had been so active in trying to ban the book from the Canadian mails. As a pretense of impartiality, the symposium included statements supporting Kinsey from a woman in North Carolina, and from Kinsey's friend Philip Wylie, whose *Generation of Vipers* must have already stamped him as immoral in the eyes of many *Digest* readers. These were two out of thirteen. The first "symposium" had been a 100 percent attack.

As another part of the sideshow in the *Male* book controversy it was instructive to follow the attitudes of the church. They were not all as negative as one might have expected. The comments of Catholics, from Bishop Fulton J. Sheen on down, were predictable. Less so was the conclusion of Reinhold Niebuhr, the Protestant theologian, who found Kinsey's point of view "distressing." Niebuhr's complaint, in *Christianity & Crisis,* was essentially a defense against what he considered the Report's assumption that the churches had failed to set up adequate sex standards, although he was also disturbed by what he considered the implication that new norms could be created by a statistical study of sex practices.

The lesser clergy were far more supportive in their opinions. The Reverend Carlton Babbs, minister of the Westwood Methodist Church, in Cincinnati, sent Kinsey a paper titled "The Significance to Religion of the Kinsey Report" and asked for comment. Kinsey replied:

In the midst of emotional and illogical expression that has come to our book from some church leaders, it is refreshing to know that there is a segment of Christian leadership that believes it is desirable to face the truth. Frankly, I have more faith in the leadership of the Church than would be warranted by some of the statements that have come out against scientific research in the field of sex from certain quarters of the Church. One cannot be optimistic about the future of the Church unless one can be sure its leadership will pass into the hands of persons like yourself, who can face realities without becoming so emotionally upset as some persons are. Consequently, for the sake of religion in our culture, I hope that your article may have considerable circulation.

To a man in Washington who had sent him a favorable review and a sympathetic letter, he wrote:

You are mistaken in believing that the Church is the chief source of opposition in our research. In actuality there has never been any organized opposition to our research since it began, and none of it since our book has been published. A good many persons in high positions in the Church have given very specific assistance to the research. Right now the only persons who are objecting in print are persons who are scientifically employed, although their objections are obviously animated by deep emotional conflicts, rather than by scientific evaluation of our material.

Often criticism came from people who had read not the book, but only magazine articles reporting on it. Kinsey's answer to this kind of opposition was typified by his reply to the Reverend Joseph E. Haley, of the Department of Religion at Notre Dame:

I thoroughly agree with you that it is not the function of a scientist to make moral evaluations, and I strongly feel that a scientist is not qualified to work out moral codes. There is a statement in the introductory pages of our book to that effect, and the conclusion of the book comes back to a similar statement in the last paragraph of the final chapter. We have tried very hard to report the objective fact . . . and have repeatedly emphasized throughout the book that interpretations of these facts must be left to others.

The particular statement which you quote from the magazine articles report interpretations of the authors of the articles and not our own. I hope you will take the opportunity to go through our book and judge our work on the basis of our own report rather than upon the accounts of the book written by others.

Churchmen of several faiths held symposia on the Report, joining with scientists, laymen and assorted other groups. Holding a symposium on the *Male* volume became almost fashionable, as the Browning Clubs had been in the 1890s. By the end of 1949 there had been more than two hundred seminars and symposia, to our knowledge, but very few of them, Kinsey observed, had managed to get anywhere, and he was weary of emotionally charged reactions, whether for or against the book. He was also discovering that some of our interviewees had tried to save face with other people by deliberately misrepresenting what they had told us, and some even denied ever giving us a history although we had it down in detail and filed away.

His friends and well-wishers, naturally, had rallied around in the reviewing media. Karl Menninger wrote a letter of protest to the editor of the *American Journal of Psychiatry* over an adverse review of the volume, which Menninger called "probably the most important book published in our lifetime." To Kinsey he had written: "I want you to know that I think you have done a job of monumental importance and I shall say so at every opportunity. I urge you not to be discouraged and disheartened by the criticism."

Probably the most bizarre of the criticisms against the book were made by Dr. Edmund Bergler, an irascible New York psychoanalyst who was a strong proponent of the notion of vaginal orgasm, an idea since completely discredited and then well on its way to being so. The controversy began with a Bergler article on "Premature Ejaculation" in the August 1950 issue of the *International Journal of Sexology*, to which Kinsey replied with a scathing letter in which he said, among other things:

You have not fairly represented our position in regard to so-called vaginal orgasm. I have emphasized abundantly that orgasm involves the whole nervous system and not merely the vagina, which happens to be an organ that is least supplied with nerves. Similarly, your statement that the woman is normally vaginally frigid, is your own invention and nothing that we have ever said or thought. Your suggestion that we think orgasm is derived primarily from clitoris manipulation digitally performed, again has no basis in our statement of the situation.

Your suggestion that we think that orgasm is not to be expected because the penis does not come in contact with the clitoris, or that intercourse consists of rubbing the penis interlabially against the clitoris, is a travesty which you have invented for your own ulterior purpose of our understanding of the anatomy and physiology involved in coitus. Your article contains other similar misinterpretations and distortions of our position.

If you claim to be a scientist, you are under some obligation to be sure of the accuracy of the statements you make. It is also the function of a scientist whose data are thus misrepresented to see to it that such misrepresentations are not propagated in the literature.

Your treatment of the material smacks much more of a dogmatic effort to win a point than a scientist's effort to discover the fact. Your evident disdain for the significance of science, especially biologic science, is one more reason for believing that you are not interested in seeing psychoanalysis established scientifically.

Thus began an acrimonious controversy which resulted in the publication in 1954 of an entire book attacking the Report, *Kinsey's Myth of Female Sexuality,* which Bergler wrote in collaboration with Dr. William S. Kroger, a Chicago gynecologist. No other critic had gone so far (194 pages), or expressed himself so violently, but that was characteristic of Bergler, who far surpassed Kinsey in his inability to stand criticism and contradiction.

At risk of exhausting the subject and the reader, one further criticism ought to be noted. A common complaint of the moralists was that the Report would be "damaging" to young men and women. An attempt to measure the effect of the book on this group was made by Leo P. Crespi, associate professor of psychology at Princeton, and an undergraduate assistant in the department, Edmund A. Stanley, Jr. The results of their survey were published in *Public Opinion Quarterly.* A majority of the college students surveyed believed that the ultimate effects of our study would be beneficial, and they were familiar with the criticisms made by both scientists and moralists. The report concluded:

The students who read the book felt that its effects would be more on attitudes than on practices. They felt in general that these effects would be more good than bad, and they were overwhelmingly against withholding the content of the report from the public. A majority of them also agreed that the Kinsey study would have the effect of increasing the moral acceptability of sexual practices which were found to be prevalent. Finally, they found the work moderately "surprising," but on the whole "scientific" rather than sensational. In short, the majority of the students exposed to the report remained with the conclusion that it was a straightforward presentation of facts by conscientious scientists, the effects of which will be socially constructive.

Not even Kinsey could have asked for a fairer, or more prophetic, assessment of what we had accomplished.

By the end of the following year, 1949, he had survived the worst of the battles over the book, and was already looking forward to the next round in a somewhat more philosophical mood. Just before Christmas he wrote to a fellow zoologist, Dr. E. E. Jeffers, of Montana State:

We have hoped that the world would be more comfortable as a result of the discovery of the facts, and we have reason to believe that there are a great many people who have found our report a source of comfort. We hope to have another book out in a year or so and a string of them thereafter. There are still a lot of things that will surprise people when we get them into print.

CHAPTER

XIX

BETWEEN BOOKS

IN THE MIDST of controversy, life went on at the Institute. More working space was needed as preparations for the second Report began, and early in 1950 we moved from the old, dreary quarters in Biology Hall into the remodeled basement of Wylie Hall. It was to be our home until the final move to a new building, which was accomplished when Jordan Hall opened in 1955.

But life was not quite the same on campus. After the *Male* volume was published there was a subtle change toward Kinsey in some quarters at the University and in the community. Much of the veiled hostility came from religious groups who were offended by what he was doing. Some faculty members were unfriendly both to him and to the research because of their restrictive family backgrounds; Kinsey had outgrown his, they had not. One of them remarked to him after publication of the *Male* book, "You did a fine job, but I wish you had written a book I could read to my wife."

There was much more opposition to Kinsey in the community, a conservative small town in a notoriously conservative state. The townspeople were always a little suspicious of the academic community, but the gulf between town and gown widened when it became known that this particular professor was involved in sex research. "A queer duck," was the verdict.

As for Kinsey, he was alternately depressed by the continuing battles with his critics and buoyant in his usual manner. Three weeks after the *Male* volume was published, he made a friend who was both loyal and helpful in a great many ways, and this must have been some consolation. The friend was Clarence Tripp, now a New York psychotherapist. At that time, Tripp had no thought of studying psychology. He was only twenty-eight years old and working in the photography business in New York with Bill Dellenback. Having read the *Male* book with mounting enthusiasm, Tripp called Kinsey in Bloomington. This conversation between strangers ended with Kinsey's inviting Tripp to Bloomington for a day's visit. About five hours later, the young photographer got a wire from Kinsey: "On thinking it over, one day is out of the question. We need at least three."

Tripp was astounded. Though he had told Kinsey not much more than that he was interested in sex research and wanted to write about the subject, somehow Kinsey had sensed not only a friend and supporter but someone worth knowing and helping. As it turned out, Kinsey extended the invitation because he had decided to give his visitor the grand tour, at the usual price of a history, which Tripp had no hesitation about giving. In fact, as the history progressed—it was the first order of business; Kinsey took no chances—Prok was plainly delighted to find a subject who had no inhibitions about discussing any kind of behavior. He not only gave Tripp a detailed tour of the laboratory but invited him home and introduced him to Mac.

After dinner, Kinsey remarked "Why don't we go back to the lab?" and at that point Tripp unwittingly made a gross blunder. Instead of gratefully accepting the invitation, he launched into a complicated theory of his own about sexual behavior, to which Kinsey listened with a mixture of growing discomfort and disbelief. He was shocked because it was heavily psychoanalytic, an approach he abhorred, and because it opposed nearly everything he believed.

When Tripp had finished, Kinsey looked dumbfounded. "Where did you get *that?*" he inquired. Tripp told him, confessing the derivation of his theory from other sources. By now Kinsey had recovered himself. With his usual thorough teacher's manner, he reviewed the biology of the theory Tripp had expounded, comparing it disdainfully with Lysenko's. He was still clearly shocked by the low psychoanalytic level on which Tripp had approached him, but in correcting him he seemed to be consciously moving the dialogue back to his own level.

It was characteristic of Kinsey, however, that he did not correct Tripp simply by opposing his own views. The next day he invited a professor from the biology department to talk with him and Tripp about his theory, and it was the visitor who presented the major counterargument. If Kinsey was given an outrageous idea to consider, it was his habit to invite another professor to argue against it for him. Although he was a formidable man, there was a gentleness about him, an unwillingness to damage somebody else's ego, that led him to resort to such psychological maneuvers.

After this there were many contacts between the two men and a number of events flowed from the meeting—the beginning of our filmed behavioral studies, the coming of Dellenback to the Institute and Tripp's usefulness as a supplier, among other things, of both contacts for histories and materials for the archives.

Kinsey needed all the friends he could muster at the time he met Tripp. As he had feared, there were already rumblings in the Rockefeller Foundation that his grants might be affected. President Wells had talked to Alan Gregg by telephone, and Gregg had suggested for the first time—this was April 1949—that it might not be possible or advisable to persuade the board of the Foundation to make further appropriations for the support of our research, on the spurious contention that we now had funds of our own from the book's royalties.

Informed of this, Kinsey protested to Gregg with all his eloquence. Such an action, he argued, would be taken by the public as a vote of no confidence. The original plans had called for expansion considerably beyond anything possible during the war years, and now, for the first time, men with research experience would be available. Expansion of the histories and utilization of the data already accumulated would be possible only if the present staff were expanded, Kinsey asserted, and four or more additional staff members were needed for history taking. If the critics were even partly correct, the project also needed strengthening in psychological and statistical areas, besides which there were basic physiologic, neurologic and other biologic problems in which we ought to be doing research. In the critical area of sex offenders the staff would also have to be expanded, not to mention the further research to be done on the erotic element in art.

Clearly, or so it seemed to Kinsey, the necessity was for the financing to be on something more than the year-to-year basis which the Foundation had established. Theoretically, Kinsey admitted, the research could support itself through lecturing and popular writing, but that would be a last resort.

Temporarily his arguments were at least partly successful. Gregg was able to talk the Foundation into a promise of continuing the grant for three years more, and secure in that knowledge, Kinsey could plunge into fieldwork again. In spite of the extraordinary new burdens fame had brought him, he was still inexhaustible. In the summer of 1949, for example, we spent two months taking histories in the San Francisco Bay area. We got 460 of them from these sources: parents, teachers and children, chiefly between two and four years old, in a nursery school; 100 percent of all the persons, chiefly older women, in a summer training course for high school and college counselors at the University of California; 100 percent of all the people, chiefly women, in a similar course at San Francisco State; a group of amputees, whose sexual behavior following amputation provided remarkable experimental data on the nature of erotic response; 180 women representing the sterility cases of Dr. John Hamon, the leading sterility specialist in the area; two groups of actors playing in national companies in San Francisco; and prisoners interviewed during three weeks of intensive work at San Quentin.

Dr. Hamon's cases, I might add, showed a high correlation of sterility and sexual unresponsiveness in the female; the contrast with women who had had children was remarkable. Kinsey thought this finding might correlate with the spastic Fallopian tubes so often found in these cases. Dr. Hamon and other specialists in the Bay area cooperated with us to secure data that might ultimately contribute additional knowledge to the understanding of sterility.

Our three weeks at San Quentin produced some of the best material we had yet been able to obtain on sex offenders. Kinsey meant it to be the beginning of a long study of inmates of the state's institutions, undertaken at the request of the California Prison Commission.

He was as adroit and assiduous as ever at getting histories. After a lecture in Saint Louis, he asked one of his friends, Edgar Anderson, director of the Missouri Botanical Garden, for his history, and Anderson agreed amusedly:

Of course, of course, I shall be glad to be one more statistic in your invaluable collection. I must say I was amused by the ellipticity of your approach. Is this Method number 14A in your bag of tricks, or a new sub-modification of the old original number 1-B?

Later in the same letter, Anderson wrote plainly and prophetically:

As for me, I am deeply concerned about the future of your program. It hinges on you, more than I think you can realize. Unless you mend your ways you cannot carry on in this fashion for very much longer. It is time you let your Scotch-Presbyterian conscience drive you into taking a real vacation for the sake of your most important program. I am *not* an M.D. but I am a trained observer and I have been observing you for some years. It is later than you think.

But Kinsey could not even consider easing his driving pace. Besides dealing with the critics and the Foundation, and making field trips for more histories, and analyzing data, he was now running a substantial establishment in Bloomington. As of June 1, 1950, we had a staff numbering eleven, including a librarian, a photographer, an executive secretary, a translator, a statistical calculator and special research assistants. The library, too, was growing. It had 8,000 volumes and was valued at $150,000, undoubtedly a low valuation. The Institute budget was $100,000 a year, and Kinsey planned to expand it to $160,000.

Our program at this point gave priority, as always, to the compilation of more histories. But we were aiming directly at getting additional material from the youngest and oldest segments of the population, from lower social levels, rural groups, devoutly religious people, Negroes and other racial groups.

Some of the applications of what we had already done were becoming evident by this time, too. There were, besides the reevaluations of sex offenders which lawyers and judges were beginning to make, new assessments of the *Male* volume's impact on other fields, of which education was a good example.

Professional educators, analyzing the Report, saw in it several points of significance. The whole question of sex education in the schools was being examined in many places, leading directly to the controversies over this subject which embroil schools and parents today. Some educators were asking how schools could contribute to the changes in customs and prejudices which the Report had forecast by implication. Guidance workers had been given much useful information for dealing with troubled adolescents. Juvenile officers, teachers and social workers had received a clearer understanding of the sexual needs of delinquents, predisposing them to develop a tolerance for sexual codes in conflict with their own. Schools were also challenged to consider departing from the traditional chronological groups, and to make allowances for physical as well as mental maturity in organizing classes. These were only a few of the possibilities for educators raised by the Report.

In Bloomington, Kinsey spent a certain amount of time answering his mail and keeping in touch with the million and one things that interested him. New problems, too, had been raised, of which one of the most annoying was the increasing appearance of impostors. A woman in Falls Church, Virginia, to take a typical example, wrote to say that she had just received a telephone call from a "Dr. Lucas of Indiana University," who told her he was with the Kinsey Research Foundation, and that he was working on a report for a new book called *Married Life*. He had asked her such questions as "How long have you been married?" wanted details of her appearance, her husband's occupation, what she considered the greatest problems in marriage, how much of a part sex played in her married life, how she would rate herself and her husband sexually, and whether her husband was passionate. The call had seemed legitimate, but the lady wrote to inquire if it really had been.

Kinsey gave her his standard reply to such inquiries, denying that any member of our staff ever worked in such a manner and telling her how the research was conducted. He identified the caller as an impostor and urged the correspondent to report fake telephone calls to the police. The problem of impostors was so annoying by 1951 that the National Research Council felt it necessary to issue a press release on the subject, quoting Kinsey's stock response.

Reading over Kinsey's shoulder, so to speak, in those troubled years between the two books, I am astonished anew at the range of his mind and the diversity of his activities. For instance, in a letter to Sally Kamin, of the Kamin Dance Bookshop, in New York, he appears in his role of art expert, which he had become as a collector of erotic materials for the Institute collection. He doubts if there is an erotic Japanese scroll worth $500. "I have probably seen more of them than anybody else," he tells Miss Kamin, "and I certainly have seen the best that are known. They range anywhere from $25.00 to $300.00 for the best. Few of them are worth more than $150."

He took the time to congratulate a fellow student from the days of the Bussey Institute at Harvard, Dr. Harold H. Hagan, associate professor of biology at City College of New York, on the publication of his book *Embryology of the Viviparous Insects.* "I watched your work start," he wrote, "and inevitably followed it as any Busseyite follows another," and added wistfully: "Unfortunately, I am out of insect research now, as you must know. I become a bit homesick for that kind of thing when I see a nice job like yours turned out."

I doubt if anyone ever had a more fascinating ingoing and outgoing mail box than Kinsey. On a single day, where else would one find in the incoming box this blunt missive addressed to "'Dr.' (ha) Kinsey: Hey, Kinsey, all my women and men friends, and I, think you're full of Bull shit, and hope you rot in hell, which we figure you will in due time. You're just a frustrated old codger, who doesn't even know which 'end' is up. Laughingly yours."

And in the outgoing, a note to Alice Roosevelt Longworth, thanking her for a pleasant luncheon with her and her guests.

Kinsey's mail was full of excursions into every conceivable aspect of sex, from the commonplace to the esoteric, demonstrating once more the wide-ranging capacity of his mind. On so ordinary a subject as masturbation, he not only took every opportunity to clear away the remaining cobwebs, but he meant to be precise about the matter. Thus, when a third-year medical student at the University of Wisconsin wrote to ask whether it was true that 2 percent of males did not masturbate, or whether all of them did at some time in their lives, Kinsey was happy to give him an answer which knocked down one more myth:

Our survey indicates that ninety-six percent of the males masturbate at some time in their lives. The popular opinion that one hundred percent are so involved is not based on any statistical study and is very clearly incorrect. The four percent not involved includes a certain number of apathetic individuals who are satisfied by an occasional wet dream, a larger number of persons who have nocturnal dreams with such frequency as to provide considerable outlet, and a still larger number of persons, particularly from lower social levels, who begin intercourse with considerable frequency at an early age.

He was particularly severe with writers who appeared to accept the facts about sex but then condemned them without saying that their objections were moral. Discussing a sex education pamphlet written for young people by a fellow scientist, Kinsey says in an indignant letter that the pamphlet does the "damnable thing" of

insisting that sex is something that should be freely accepted and frankly faced, and then systematically [goes] through each possible form of sexual outlet and [condemns] every one of them with the possible exception of nocturnal emissions. Concerning masturbation, he does very well in admitting that it does no harm and that it is well nigh universal, but then he undoes the whole thing by warning that it is very likely to lead to the development of an asocial personality. He condemns petting as likely to lead to something worse, and he condemns pre-marital intercourse in pages and pages and pages of the most obvious sort of rationalization, which is based upon wishful thinking rather than upon any record of the fact and which should, in actuality, be summed up with the thinking that is really in his heart—namely, that pre-marital intercourse is morally wrong. If he were to say that, I, as a scientist, would have no argument with him one way or the other. . . .

Kinsey concludes sarcastically that since the writer has not condemned either nocturnal emissions or animal intercourse, "I take it that the unmarried youth is to find all of his outlet from those two sources. . . ."

He had positive ideas about how information on such subjects as masturbation should be given. Writing to a Bronxville, New York, doctor who was planning a questionnaire survey of eleventh- and twelfth-grade high school boys or college freshmen to measure the effect of telling adolescent boys the truth about masturbation, Kinsey had some things to say that would have confounded those who did not understand his attitudes. He does not, of course, approve of questionnaires as a method (refusing to answer one, he condemned them as "too easy a way for one person to make hundreds of other persons do work for him"), but having disposed of this objection, he tells the doctor:

Telling a boy that masturbation will do him no physical harm is giving him the peace of scientifically established information with which I should concur. Advising a boy to masturbate or advising a boy that masturbation is a better source of outlet than pre-marital intercourse whether it is with companions or with prostitutes is a totally different matter that involves evaluations and a minimum of any science. As a fact-finding scientist, I can not agree with you on your policy nor disagree with it.

I would remind you, however, that there are a great many people, including half or more of the psychiatrists, who would strenuously disagree with you. You may be interested to know that we have the personal histories of over two hundred psychiatrists; and on this issue of masturbation I find that the European group, which is the larger group, objects rather consistently against masturbation and against the lack of pre-marital coitus, while a larger number of the American bred group would agree with you.

In another letter Kinsey discussed the subject of male fertility with Dr. Frank K. Shuttleworth, of the Institute of Child Welfare, University of California at Berkeley. He believed that students in the field had all been "too prudish" to make an actual investigation of sperm count in early-adolescent males. His own research for the *Male* volume had produced some material, but not enough. He could report, however, that there were mature sperm even in the first ejaculation, although he did not yet have any actual counts. The research showed further that males were rarely responsible for pregnancy until they were in their late teens, even though they might have an abundance of intercourse earlier than that without making ary attempt at contraception. This subject was one of the detailed studies Kinsey hoped to make later but never completed.

Even in a fellow professional such as Shuttleworth he would not olerate departures from the scientific method. He writes: "Your statement that the human male finds it easy to reach an orgasm 'because his contribution to the reproductive process requires an orgasm in order that seminal fluid may be discharged,' belongs in the realm of purposive philosophy."

Another correspondence concerned spontaneous orgasm. Dr. Phillip Polatin, of Columbia University, asked Kinsey for information on this subject, about which we had acquired a considerable amount of information. Kinsey pointed out to Polatin that spontaneous orgasm while awake is a little more common in the female than in the male, but masturbation in the female is more often without fantasy. He believed it would not be impossible to find a patient who reached spontaneous orgasm without fantasy, but it might be difficult to explain theoretically the source of the actual stimulation.

Kinsey thought that women who most often experienced spontaneous orgasm were those who were most generally responsive, in a sexual sense, with high rates of outlet. (Kinsey once defined a nymphomaniac as "someone who has more sex than you do.")

There was nothing wrong with spontaneous orgasm, in Kinsey's opinion. On the contrary, as he pointed out to Dr. Polatin, some of these highly responsive women who had occasional spontaneous orgasms were among the socially most significant, most efficient and energetic women in all his female histories. Many of them were professionally trained in medicine or psychiatry, or some other field.

One of the more esoteric subjects Kinsey discussed by mail was sex and social dancing. A researcher at the University of Chicago, undertaking a project to determine the role of social dancing in the lives of adolescents, wanted to know if Kinsey had any information on its erotic aspect. That kind of information was in all our histories, but it had not been analyzed and Kinsey had to give a conjectural answer. Social dancing might lead to some erotic response on the part of the male, he thought, but rarely in the female, although there was a tremendous difference in the response at various social levels, more occurring in the better-educated segment of the population. In any case, he concluded, the amount of erotic response in dancing was certainly much less than the moralistic literature would lead one to believe.

(Kinsey, we must remember, lived in the pre-rock era. What he would make of today's social dancing, with its surface appearance of eroticism and its lack of touching, I can only surmise.)

More specialized by far than sex and dancing were Kinsey's observations on lesbianism and the clitoris. One of Kinsey's good friends, Dr. Carl H. Moore, of the Zoology Department at the University of Chicago, once asked what some might have thought a naïve question. He wondered if Kinsey could define exactly what a lesbian was. The popular definition might not be accurate, he suspected, and speculated as to whether lesbianism had anything to do with the length of the clitoris. The women of Lesbos, he reminded his friend, were reputed to have clitorises as long as two inches.

In his answer, Kinsey noted that Sappho's homosexual experiences were no different from those enjoyed by most other ancient Greeks, both male and female. Her name attached to sexual relations between women was purely a literary consequence, and had nothing to do with the size of the clitorises of the ladies who lived on the island of Lesbos.

There is a tradition, Kinsey noted, that female homosexual histories are often correlated with the size of the clitoris, and our research was trying to determine what truth there might be in this notion, but unless a clitoris was of unusual size, the subject was not able to provide us with an estimate based on her own observation.

In fact, measuring a clitoris is an extremely technical matter, as Kinsey pointed out, even for the best-trained gynecologists. We spent considerable time checking with these specialists on the technical problems of securing exact measurements. We were convinced in the end that it was nearly impossible to do so because of the amount of fleshy material and the position of the material in the prepuce. A woman could certainly get no clear estimate of her own clitoris without technical training on how to take a measurement— and even then it would be difficult except in the case of very large organs.

I might add that taking penis measurements is much easier, obviously, and we had the largest body of penis measurements in existence—another Kinsey collection. It included more than 4,000 sets of measurements made by those who gave us their histories, and more than 1,200 others made by a scientist who turned his records over to us. For the curious, the maximum authenticated record in our files was ten and a half inches in erection, although there were in existence unofficial reports of longer ones. For the worriers, the average length was nearly six and a half inches—and I should note that there is no correlation between length of the penis and sexual ability.

The clitoris, however, is a more complicated organ. Kinsey pointed out to Dr. Moore that there were evidently racial inheritance factors involved in its size. Clitorises measuring more than an inch are apparently very rare in whites, but may occur in 2 or 3 percent of blacks, or at least they did so in the limited number of black histories we took. Long clitorises are well known among black prostitutes, and measurements of three inches and more were obtained from perhaps one out of 300 or 400 black women. Circus sideshows often exhibit individuals with clitorises that may measure as much as four inches. In some of these cases erection is possible, but in many such cases it is not. It is in only a small portion of these cases, then, that coitus could be had both as male or female.

Kinsey said in conclusion that all the records he knew about of females with enlarged clitorises also showed them to have well-developed vaginas and all the other characteristics of females. Many of them had histories of childbearing. Consequently he rejected the idea that they were hermaphrodites.

As we prepared the data for the *Female* volume, it was logical that Kinsey should extend his interest in the field of gynecology. We had the cooperation of several specialists, one of them an English gynecologist who was among the doctors making tests for us of awareness of tactile and pressure stimulation in women.

Writing to a doctor in San Francisco about this man, Kinsey reported that our English colleague found between 70 and 95 percent of the women he examined aware of tactile stimulation in every part of the vagina, which disagreed with all the other tests. For a while Kinsey corresponded with this doctor and could not discover the source of what he knew must be an error, because there are no nerve endings in the vagina. This was an important question for Kinsey to be certain about because the idea of the vaginal orgasm was still believed in by many psychoanalysts—and in fact this was one of the points on which he was later severely attacked.

The answer was discovered when the Englishman came to America and Kinsey was able to observe him actually making tests. It developed that he was not placing the speculum as deeply as any of the other gynecologists, and consequently was testing only the forward areas of the vagina. Under these circumstances, it was impossible to touch any area in the deep vagina without simultaneously touching vulvar areas.

What seemed most significant to Kinsey was that the English doctor had been holding the speculum with his hands through all these tests. Exploring further, Kinsey found that stimulation of the vagina without touching the speculum brought no response, while moving the instrument without touching the vagina did elicit a response, obviously because external areas were stimulated. That was the answer, Kinsey said. While the doctor held the speculum, thus stimulating external areas, it was inevitable that every test would record interior awareness of tactile stimulation.

It was Kinsey's knowledge of physiology, learned through his studies in biology, that enabled him to grasp these problems in their most technical details. As a consequence he was capable of discussing such a question as the sexual response in women as measured by the secretion from the Bartholin glands. (The secretion is measured by absorption in a tampon.) He informed an inquiring sociologist from Graz, Austria, that he had found a tremendous individual variation in the amount of secretion from these glands within a single individual. It might be correlated with the individual's level of arousal, he said, but was not so correlated between individuals. Kinsey could cite cases of women who were highly responsive sexually but were almost completely lacking in Bartholin and cervical secretions.

Here, as in other areas, Kinsey was always ready to challenge previous conceptions, particularly those held by psychoanalysts. One of the psychoanalytic theories he particularly disbelieved was that the vagina must become the prime site of stimulation in order to achieve a satisfactory sexual life. In this theory, clitoral stimulation is denounced as infantile and inadequate for any mature adjustment, although it is admitted that the clitoris is the prime source of sensation in preadolescent years; the mature individual transfers the site of sensation to the vagina. This is the essence of the controversy about whether nerve endings exist in the vagina.

Kinsey employed a half-dozen good gynecologists to make experimental tests of a long series of patients—the English doctor was one of them—to determine the extent to which women were aware of tactile and heavier stimulation in every part of the genitalia. This single aspect of the research led Kinsey into an area where no one had ever explored with any such thoroughness before. When the results were published, there were still those who refused to believe them, notably Dr. Bergler, the New York analyst. Subsequent research, however, most particularly that of Masters and Johnson, has confirmed that Kinsey was right and his critics wrong.

Among the inquiries Kinsey received, one of the most unusual came from Professor Dennis Strawbridge, of the Combat Analysis Group, Institute for Air Weapons Research, Museum of Science and Industry, University of Chicago. Strawbridge was studying the relationship between aggressiveness and sexuality, and cited recent studies of fighter pilots in Korea which indicated that one of the principal characteristics distinguishing aces from non-aces was aggressiveness. The theory had been advanced that combat aggressiveness was reflected to some extent in the pilot's sexual history, and the professor wanted to know if Kinsey believed a man's aggressiveness was reflected in his sexual history, and whether he felt he could select the most aggressive individuals based on sexual histories.

Kinsey refused to put it on that basis. There was reason to believe, he said, that there was a high correlation between efficiency of reflexes and other neural responses, and the intensity of sexual response. We did have some significant data on that point. But sexual behavior, Kinsey pointed out, is like any other biological phenomenon: it is influenced by a great many factors which make it impossible to expect any simple and unvariable correlation with a single factor. Consequently, as he says, we saw cases of dull and slow-reacting individuals who nevertheless exhibited an intense sexual response.

The majority of persons with a high capacity to respond to a variety of stimuli, to respond with immediacy, and to respond frequently are certainly not monogamous. Their rates of activity, both heterosexually, homosexually and masturbatory, are usually high, but I should want to see the specific data on any large series of cases before I could be convinced of the generalization which you say the studies of fighter pilots in Korea have given. Frankly, as a result of the Army's monumental failure to carry through its extensive study of sexual behavior of military personnel in the Second World War, I should need to be convinced that any study being undertaken now went to the actual root of the matter.

As the result of a lecture given at Bloomington by Dr. Victor Vogel, then head of the Public Health Hospital for Narcotics, Lexington, Kentucky, Kinsey was able to share in correspondence some of the information we had gathered from hundreds of histories of narcotics addicts, correlated with sex histories.

Kinsey found that there was a considerable difference in the effect of different drugs on sexual behavior, and that there was, in the bargain, some variation in individual reaction to the drugs. Generally speaking, he told Dr. Vogel, he discovered that opium derivatives reduced erotic responsiveness, and in the case of long-time addicts completely eliminated any responsiveness or interest in any sort of sexual activity. Cocaine, on the other hand, had an erotic effect. Marijuana had no effect appreciably different from alcohol; there was a lowering of inhibition, apparently due to the first effects of the depression of the central nervous system, which might stimulate an individual to express interest in sexual activity and try to have sexual relations. On the other hand, said Kinsey, the research showed that marijuana slowed up response, usually prevented orgasm and in some males prevented erection.

There were individual variations in all of these responses. Kinsey, for example, followed the case of a man who was a drug addict and an alcoholic besides, who was nevertheless very active sexually. But that, as he pointed out, was a most unusual combination, one seen in only a few rare cases.

Kinsey told Dr. Vogel that he was aware of the hypersensitivity of the addict to sexual stimulation when drugs were removed from his reach. In both males and females, spontaneous orgasm occurred on the slightest provocation, including nocturnal dreams to the point of orgasm in both sexes, although it was more common in the male.

These were all generalizations, Kinsey warned Dr. Vogel, and needed hundreds of additional cases to confirm. A final report, he predicted, would emphasize the importance of individual variations.

From drugs and sex, Kinsey found it easy to turn to a discussion of literature. His views of classic writers, from his special standpoint, were refreshing. He was disdainful, for example, of the kind of scholarship which glossed over the homosexual elements in the work of men like Plato, Shakespeare and Michelangelo, among others. He wrote a congratulatory letter to Professor Ronald B. Levinson, who had sent him a copy of his new book about Plato, and complimented him on doing a franker and more honest job. "Obviously," he says, "we have had to spend considerable time with Plato's writing in the course of our own research"—something no one would have thought "obvious" who did not know Kinsey.

But he had a point of disagreement with Professor Levinson:

I am not sure I can follow you in ever believing that there were many Greeks, outside of sexually worn out old men, who subscribed to a regime of idealized love without physical contact. Knowing what I do of the human animal, I cannot believe that the love and affection which the older males bestowed upon Greek boys, and their aesthetic admiration for the bodies of Greek youth, could have failed to arouse specific sexual response which found their outlet in overt sexual relations. Such things do not happen in either heterosexual or homosexual histories among beings today, and the drunken Alcibiades to the contrary, I do not believe it happened in ancient Greece.

Although Kinsey's research in literature was directed toward its sexual elements, the hunt for new materials to be examined and later added to the library led him into antiquarian paths. Thus I find him writing to the Right Honorable H. L. Willink, Master of Magdalene College, Cambridge (there was some discussion in the office about how to address him), asking about the best extant edition of Pepys' *Diary*. Behind the inquiry lay the hope that he would have an opportunity to examine the unexpurgated Pepys manuscript in the College library. Kinsey told the Master that he was especially interested to know the extent to which the sexual material in the original text was available in any of the published editions. If these editions did not help, he added, he might try to arrange someday to get more direct access to the original.

The Master gave him a cool British reply:

There is no doubt that the Wheatley edition is the best at present published. The College is not prepared to make any of the excluded passages available. I understand that the Pepys Librarian has recently received a request similar to that in your letter, and has replied to this effect. I cannot usefully add to what he wrote.

(An unexpurgated edition of the *Diary* was published, for the first time, in 1970.)

Kinsey's expertise in collecting erotic literature led him, at least once, to become a literary detective. A man in Maryland questioned the authorship of *Sadopaideia*, a sadomasochistic classic noted in the *Female* volume, and Kinsey hastened to acknowledge that he had, indeed, made an error, which would be corrected in the next printing. He added that one of the people who had worked in the Institute library had left behind a penciled note in the book that Lefourcade had ascribed it to Swinburne. Reexamining Lefourcade, Kinsey failed to find any such reference. Further, he took time to search through Swinburne's works and found no mention of *Sadopaideia*. Nevertheless, he sought out the researcher who had left the note and made a further effort to identify the authorship. The attempt ended in failure, but no doubt if Kinsey had had the time, he would have been in a position to write a monograph on the subject before long.

There was no avenue of research Kinsey was unwilling to explore. As early as 1948 it occurred to him that it might be useful to get histories from the social levels represented by the Communist Party in New York City. He wrote to his attorney, Morris Ernst, asking him to raise the possibility with J. Edgar Hoover, director of the FBI, to make sure that there was no objection, and that there would be no trailing of subjects or attempt to secure information obtained in the interviews. We did take the histories, and there was no trouble with the FBI. Three years later, Ernst told Kinsey he was doing an article for *Look* magazine on the necessity of treating the membership of the Party from a psychological rather than an economic angle. It was Ernst's belief, after talking to some two hundred ex-Communists, that an extraordinarily high percentage of them had come from broken homes, and had extreme sexual difficulties.

Kinsey was unable to help him. Although there had been rumors in the press that he had found links between sex and Communism, in reality he had too few histories of Communists to warrant making any kind of generalizations. All he could say was that those he had interviewed came from low educational levels and were frequenters of Eighth Avenue taverns and the waterfront in New York. Only a few had completed college or graduate school, and there was a sprinkling of college faculty. As for conclusions, however, the number was simply too small to warrant any.

On another tack, since there was little research material on transvestism available when he began his research, Kinsey made every effort to find out more. When people asked him for sources so they could study the phenomenon, there was nothing in the scientific literature he could recommend. Naturally, Kinsey soon became the foremost authority on the subject because he deliberately sought to get as many histories as he could from these people. As always, he was anxious to sweep away the myth from the reality, particularly when the research began to show that there was no truth in the widely held belief that homosexuality and transvestism were the same phenomenon. By 1948 Kinsey had compiled nearly 2,000 homosexual histories, and there were only a few isolated cases of transvestism among them. Similarly, among the transvestite histories he took, homosexuality rarely occurred.

Here again, Kinsey found himself at war with the psychiatric establishment, which, as he said, concentrated on the behavior of abnormal people and tried to explain it with elaborate theories. To Kinsey, as his own research went on, it seemed that the explanations were much simpler. "I think that much of human sexual behavior," he wrote to an Oklahoma transvestite, "is no more complicated than a person's likes or dislikes for particular foods, books, amusements, or anything else. Through it all, association is a very important factor. This means that what a person happens to do one time is avoided or repeated another time, depending upon the pleasure derived from the first experience."

By the summer of 1951, pressure was beginning to build at the Institute once more. The worst of the quarrels over the *Male* volume had died down, but now Kinsey and the rest of the staff were beginning to get the manuscript of the *Female* book into shape. That summer he curtailed visitors, even good friends of the project, and brought his attention to bear on this second Report. The knowledge that it was going to appear had already stirred ripples of interest, which would mount before long into a tidal wave.

CHAPTER

XX

TOWARD THE FEMALE
VOLUME

The combination of publicity from the *Male* volume, which continued without much abatement, and advance speculation about the new one was causing agitation in other places besides the Rockefeller Foundation in the summer of 1951. President Wells had to counter restless stirrings in the Indiana legislature and among some vocal alumni. He was a master hand at this kind of thing. For some time, whenever the State Budget Committee made its annual one-day visit to the campus, he had insisted on taking the two state senators and two representatives who made up the committee on a tour of the Institute.

Wells was quite aware of the state of mind of these visiting firemen. They had heard lurid tales in Indianapolis about the goings-on in Bloomington, gossip fed by the Indianapolis *Star*, a right-wing organ which lost no opportunity to put Kinsey in a bad light, no matter what the facts might be. Arriving in Bloomington, the Budget Committee would be torn between curiosity and moral fervor. Wells deftly defused them by showing them the Institute, which removed any aura of eroticism that might surround our work. Certainly the quarters we worked in were anything but erotic, and Kinsey looked as far removed from being a sex maniac as a Baptist minister. His friendly, persuasive manner and the scientific lectures he gave the visitors as he conducted them about the place left them convinced that the University was not in the hands of the free-love movement after all. They returned to Indianapolis in an authoritative position to put down wild rumors among their colleagues. Wells gave the same treatment to inquiring newspapermen and visiting clergy. The reaction was always favorable.

Still the rumors persisted. In June 1952 Wells felt compelled to write to Governor Henry F. Schricker, who would be arriving soon for the commencement exercises:

A couple of nights ago I attended a meeting of the First Methodist Church Board of which I am a member. Following the meeting, I walked into the pastor's study and noticed a copy of Dr. Kinsey's book on the book shelf. I asked the pastor why the book was there. His reply was to the effect that he used it day after day in counseling parishioners who are having marital and moral problems. He stated that the book had been of great assistance to him since it had been published and he believed that it had forced us to come to grips with certain unpleasant aspects of our lives which for generations we have tried to solve by refusing to recognize their existence. Naturally such a method made no more progress than it would in any other area of life. Problems of this type cannot be solved by refusing to recognize their existence.

Wells enclosed a supportive letter from the Bishop of California and a copy of the alumni magazine, which described our research and explained the reasons for it. The president noted that the magazine contained stories about other campus research projects—Kinsey's was not the only one.

But Wells had no illusions about which one of Indiana's projects was the most significant. He could not forget—and often told about —the incident which occurred during his tour of duty in Berlin with General Lucius Clay, when he flew to Paris to see Julian Huxley, then director general of UNESCO. Instead of talking about the business at hand, Huxley wanted to gossip about his old friends and colleagues in genetics and biology at.Indiana, where he had once lectured. When he inquired about Kinsey, and heard that he was doing well, Huxley pulled out of his desk drawer a copy of The New Yorker and opened it to a cartoon depicting a man and his wife reading, with the wife inquiring of the husband, "My dear, is there a Mrs. Kinsey?"

Wells chuckled, but Huxley regarded him intently and seemed to be waiting for an answer. "Well, is there?" he asked impatiently.

The president assured him there was, and they went on to talk about Kinsey's work. "You know what the French say about the book," Huxley remarked. "They say statistics may be all right in the counting room, but not in the bedroom."

At home, Wells had a difficult problem in dealing with the trustees, who were subjected to emotional attacks on Kinsey from all kinds of people. The question of the project was raised many times in the board's deliberations, but never in the context of whether it should be suppressed, according to Wells. The members only wanted to know how to answer the questions that were raised with them. Kinsey was always ready to give them answers. Occasionally he came and talked to them. Few people hearing Kinsey talk about his work remained unpersuaded.

To their great credit, the trustees stood firmly with Kinsey through the storms of controversy. They fully accepted the president's policy, namely, that they had formally declared themselves in their statements on academic promotion and tenure as guardians of academic freedom, of freedom for scientific research, and in favor of following the search for truth wherever it led. Kinsey's work was the ultimate test of that policy. Wells told the trustees that if they could meet this test the others would be easy, and on this issue would be determined whether Indiana was to be a university of the first rank or simply another teachers' college. The trustees squirmed occasionally in pain, Wells recalled after his retirement, but they never retreated.

As 1952 ended, their severest test lay before them. It had been one thing to publish research about the sexual behavior of American males, but as one might expect, to discuss the behavior of American women was quite another thing. Publication in August 1953 of *Sexual Behavior in the Human Female* was to bring our work to a climax.

More than ever, as we began to correlate the data for the *Female* volume, we experienced the exciting feelings of discovery in a relatively unexplored field that had occurred as we prepared the first volume. Our preliminary runs on the figures for females indicated a wider difference between men and women in their sexual responsiveness than later emerged from the total figures for both sexes, but we were much more impressed with the increasing number of similarities between the sexes. Long before Women's Liberation made a national debating issue of the subject, we had come to some significant conclusions.

Summarizing our research in anatomic structures, for example, Kinsey wrote in the *Female* volume:

In brief, we conclude that the anatomic structures which are most essential to sexual response and orgasm are nearly identical in the human female and male. The differences are relatively few. They are associated with the different functions of the sexes in reproductive processes, but they are of no great significance in the origins and development of sexual response and orgasm. If females and males differ sexually in any basic way, those differences must originate in some other aspect of the biology or psychology of the two sexes. . . . They do not originate in any of the anatomic structures which have been considered here.

Later in the same volume, Kinsey added:

In spite of the widespread and oft-repeated emphasis on the supposed differences between female and male sexuality, we fail to find any anatomic or physiologic basis for such differences. Although we shall subsequently find differences in the psychologic and hormonal factors which affect the responses of the two sexes . . . males would be better prepared to understand females, and females to understand males, if they realized that they are alike in their basic anatomy and physiology.

Kinsey was well aware that in making such statements, and in approaching the subject of female sexuality at all, he was running counter to strongly held popular beliefs and traditions. Beginning his discussion of sexual response and orgasm in the *Female* volume, he wrote:

In view of the historical backgrounds of our Judeo-Christian culture, comparisons of females and males must be undertaken with some trepidation and a considerable sense of responsibility. It should not be forgotten that the social status of women under early Jewish and Christian rule was not much above that which women still hold in the older Asiatic cultures. Their current position in our present-day social organization has been acquired only after some centuries of conflict between the sexes. There were early bans on the female's participation in most of the activities of the social organization; in later centuries there were chivalrous and galante attempts to place her in a unique position in the cultural life of the day. There are still male antagonisms to her emergence as a co-equal in the home and in social affairs. There are romantic rationalizations which obscure the real problems that are involved and, down to the present day, there is more heat than logic in most attempts to show that women are the equal of men, or that the human female differs in some fundamental way from the human male. It would be surprising if we, the present investigators, should have wholly freed ourselves from such century-old biases and succeeded in comparing the two sexes with the complete objectivity which is possible in areas of science that are of less direct import in human affairs. We have, however, tried to accumulate the data with a minimum of pre-judgment, and attempted to make interpretations which would fit those data.

This declaration failed to save us from even a fraction of the wrath of moralists and other critics, but time has vindicated us. Subsequent research, especially that of Masters and Johnson, has amply validated our observations.

It was understandable, however, that many people would be outraged by our findings about women, particularly in such areas as premarital and extramarital intercourse. As we began to correlate these figures for the *Female* volume, we raised some questions of our own—of a different kind, of course—and realized that we were in new and probably dangerous territory.

I remember how fascinated we were, for example, when it appeared that the incidence and frequency of premarital intercourse was greater in males than in females at the same age and social level. We had been eager to get the calculations from the IBM machine for the females, so that we could compare them with the figures for the males. But when the comparison was made, our initial assumption that the statistics would be almost identical if good samples had been taken of each, and both were equally truthful, turned out to be wrong. In fact, there were large discrepancies in the figures, and those for males were higher.

We began to ask ourselves searching questions about the meaning of these statistics. We examined again the figures for mean frequency of premarital intercourse for women with a grade school education between sixteen and twenty years old. They showed that the incidence was 0.3 per week, while the comparable figure for men was more than five times higher, 1.6. For high-school-educated females of the same age, the figure was 0.2, and for men 1.9. At the college level, it was 0.1 for females, 0.2 for males—only twice as high.

There were several possible reasons for the discrepancy. Our samples of males and females might not have been quite comparable, especially at the lower social levels, where the difference was greatest. It was true, too, that females tended to cover up more than males because of social taboos. Another possible source of error was that our male samples included prison inmates, but the female did not, and we knew with some certainty that the incidence of premarital intercourse among men who had done time was higher. On the other hand, none of the activities females had experienced as prostitutes were included, but male intercourse with prostitutes had been. Still another possibility was that white males, in 1940, had more intercourse with Negro females than the reverse, and Negroes had not been included in our calculations because of insufficient data. Another thing that might have escaped us was the fact that some males had intercourse with females outside the United States, and we had no comparable female samples who had been outside this country. Finally, the coital frequencies of males were based on orgasm, so if multiple orgasm had occurred it would increase the frequency count, whereas in the female figures intercourse was based on the experience itself rather than orgasm.

Each of these factors, we concluded, had probably affected the cumulative total to some small extent, and we spent some uncomfortable hours mulling over this situation and trying to rationalize it.

It is understandable, I think, that we almost never thought in terms of total sexuality in men or women, because we observed such great variations between age, marital status and social levels that it seemed impossible to put them all together as a whole. How, for instance, could we add the individual who had thirty sexual outlets per week to the one whose record was once a month on the average? What comparison could be made with a grade school dropout who had more premarital intercourse than a twenty-four-year-old graduate student? Still, after the books were published, people seized on figures like those for extramarital intercourse to categorize people as a whole, without any regard for the questions we raised and the reservations we made.

In several ways the *Female* volume was a different book, although it covered in general the same kind of material the *Male* survey had encompassed. For one thing, the *Male* volume had been purely Kinsey's work, notwithstanding the contributions each of us had made to compiling the data for it. The *Female* book was more a group project, salted down with qualifications, and like a good many other products of mass creative effort, I am not sure it was better.

The structure was somewhat different, too. After a preliminary section on history and method, the major part of the volume dealt with our findings on types of sexual activity among females. The third part, five chapters, was devoted to something we would not have been able to do in the first book, that is, comparing male and female responses and behavior. These chapters, covering anatomy, physiology of sexual response and orgasm, psychologic factors in sexual response, neural mechanisms of sexual response and hormonal factors in sexual response, were perhaps the book's outstanding contribution, since they constituted a body of original scientific research not available anywhere in the literature before.

Something of what Kinsey had learned from the first book could be seen in the way he began this one, not only with the usual historical background but with a clear statement of his scientific objectives and a defense of the right of the scientist to investigate, as well as the individual's right to know. There was a good deal of other material which showed how far we had gone beyond the first volume—an examination of problems of marital adjustment, a discussion of the sexual problems of unmarried youth, the sexual education of children and the social control of sexual behavior.

There was, again, a chapter on the sample and its statistical analysis, in which Kinsey once more defended his methods, and another chapter on the sources of the data, in which he repeated his methods of obtaining histories and the various checks we made on them. He was able to add a section on recorded data as sources of information, since by now we had accumulated a large collection of calendars, diaries, correspondence, scrapbooks, photographic collections, artwork and other erotic materials which had become a part of the study. Once more, too, Kinsey reviewed previously published studies, dividing them this time into anthropologic, legal, statistical and other surveys.

Then came the heart of the book—types of sexual activity among females—which was to precipitate a national furore and nearly wreck the project financially even as it made Kinsey more famous. It was not that there was anything intrinsically sensational in the material, but only the American double standard operating again. We might make disclosures about men that were shocking to prevailing middle-class morality, but after all, they merely confirmed the conventional wisdom that men were no better than they should be. To talk of girls and women as sexual beings, however—that was too much.

We covered the same ground as in the first volume, fundamentally, but with the advantage of much more material and more experience in evaluation, the material was a great deal richer. In discussing masturbation, for example, we were able to talk about mammalian and primitive human backgrounds, to discuss how girls learn to masturbate, and to make summaries and comparisons of male and female masturbation.

In his remarks on the social significance of masturbation in females, Kinsey laid the groundwork for some of the criticism that was about to descend on him. Declaring that "the vagina . . . in most females [is] quite devoid of end organs of touch" and was therefore "incapable of responding to tactile stimulation," he flew in the face of the psychoanalysts who believed masturbation interfered with the "vaginal responses" which resulted in the mythical "vaginal orgasm," the sign of "sexual maturity." Kinsey asserted flatly what is now believed by all but a few, that "the areas primarily involved in the female's sensory responses during coitus are exactly those which are primarily involved in masturbation, namely the clitoris and the labia." He went on to point out that there was evidence to indicate that premarital experience in masturbation might actually contribute to a female's capacity to respond in marriage. Inexperience in orgasm before marriage, he noted, was often responsible for her difficulty in reaching it in marriage.

Similarly—and once more the moralists were outraged—Kinsey recorded "a marked, positive correlation between experience in orgasm obtained from pre-marital coitus, and the capacity to reach orgasm after marriage." While he was willing to admit that selective factors might have accounted in part for this conclusion, he pointed out that there are "psychologic and sociologic data which show the importance of early experience in the establishment of habits of thought and attitudes which are very difficult to alter or counteract in later years."

In studying marital coitus, Kinsey took the broad view:

Sexual adjustments represent only one aspect and not necessarily the most important aspect of marriage. No balanced program for American youth can be confined to preparing them for sexual relationships in marriage. But it is inconceivable that anyone who is objectively and scientifically interested in successful marriages should fail to appreciate the significance of coitus in marriage, or wholly ignore the correlations which exist between pre-marital activities and the sexual adjustments which are made in marriage.

When it came to extramarital coitus, however, Kinsey was once again in hot water with his critics, as events proved. He was careful to point out that we did not yet have enough data to undertake an overall appraisal of the problem, but he was willing to set down some conclusions based on the experiences of the females who had contributed to our histories.

He observed, for example, that extramarital coitus attracted some people because it gave them a variety of experience with new sexual partners who were sometimes superior sexually to their marriage partner. At times the motivation in either male or female was a conscious or unconscious attempt to acquire social status. In other instances, the female had accepted the experience as an accommodation to a respected friend, even though she might not be particularly interested in the relationship. There were occasions, too, when it was done in retaliation for the partner's extramarital activity, or for some sort of nonsexual mistreatment, real or imaginary. Sometimes both females and males had used extramarital affairs as a means to assert independence. Some of the females, Kinsey noted, had discovered new sources of emotional satisfaction in extramarital relationships, while others had found it impossible to share such a relationship with more than one partner, and were involved in guilt reactions and consequent social difficulties.

Among Kinsey's other conclusions about this kind of activity was his notation of a "not inconsiderable" group of cases in which husbands had encouraged wives to engage in extramarital activities, most of them in an honest attempt to give their wives the opportunity for additional sexual satisfaction. Thus, in 1953, Kinsey pinpointed the existence of an interest in what came to be widely known as "mate swapping," out of which have grown the group sex behavior patterns of the present day.

Summarizing his data on extramarital sex, Kinsey observed that they only emphasized the fact that "the reconciliation of the married individual's desire for coitus with a variety of sexual partners, and the maintenance of a stable marriage, presents a problem which has not been satisfactorily resolved in our culture. It is not likely to be resolved until man moves more completely away from his mammalian ancestry."

The report's section on homosexual responses and contacts drew critical fire, particularly from laymen, who did not understand or could not accept the fact that, as Kinsey put it, "there are individuals who react psychologically to both females and males, and who have overt sexual relations with both females and males in the course of their lives, or in any single period of their lives." Some people read this for the first time in their lives, in the popular versions of the book's contents. But many of the others, who were academically aware of this fact, Kinsey observed, "still fail[ed] to comprehend the realities of the situation." To fortify his observations, Kinsey at this point reintroduced and amplified his 0–6 heterosexual to homosexual rating scale, which had appeared in the first volume.

As to the extent of female homosexuality as compared with the male, Kinsey noted that it was much lower among females, with the accumulative incidence of homosexual response in females ultimately reaching 28 percent, compared with 50 percent in the males. There were, he added, only about a third to a half as many females who were, in any age period, primarily or exclusively homosexual. This contradicted the widespread opinion held by both clinicians and the general public that homosexual responses and completed contacts occurred among more females than males. Kinsey attributed that notion to the fact that females are more openly affectionate toward each other in our culture, and to wishful thinking on the part of some heterosexual males.

As I have said, the final five chapters of the book were outstanding. Kinsey began with a chapter on the anatomy of sexual response and orgasm, whose material had come from several sources. Females who had given us histories had attempted to describe and analyze their own sexual reactions; that accounted for a substantial part. There was also the record obtained from scientifically trained people who had observed human sexual activities in which they themselves were not involved. We drew, too, on the observations we and others had made of other mammals, particularly the library of documentary film we had accumulated in studying animal behavior. Besides published clinical data, we also had available a body of unpublished gynecological data. There was the published data on gross anatomy of the parts of the body involved in the sexual response, and some special data on the detailed anatomy of some of these structures. We had access to published records of physiologic experiments on sexual activities among lower mammals, and on the human animal as well, although not as much. Here too, finally, we brought together the work that had been done for us by the anatomists, physiologists, neurologists, endocrinologists, gynecologists, psychiatrists and the other specialists who had helped us interpret the data.

The following chapter dealt with the physiology of sexual response and orgasm, and I doubt if it has ever been so thoroughly or so clearly described. In the summary at the end of the chapter, Kinsey made his point that orgasm was essentially the same phenomenon in male and female. At the time, this conclusion was somewhat surprising, since orgasm had appeared to occur only infrequently in female mammals lower than man. Another surprise was our discovery that not only did females appear to be capable of responding to the point of orgasm as quickly as males, but some responded even more rapidly. We found no data to support the common belief that females are slower in their capacity to reach orgasm. It was Kinsey's conclusion that females might not respond as quickly or continuously because they were less often stimulated by psychologic factors. In general, too, we found that the aftereffects of orgasm were not essentially different from the male. Although ejaculation is a male phenomenon, Kinsey concluded, it depends on a minor anatomic difference between the sexes and not on any fundamental differences in physiology.

In a chapter on psychologic factors in sexual response, we were able to present thirty-three bodies of data which agreed that the male is conditioned by sexual experience more often than the female. Males, we found, share vicariously the sexual experiences of other people more often. They frequently respond more sympathetically when they see other people in sexual activity, and they may react to a great variety of objects associated with their sexual activities.

So far, not surprising. But we also discovered tremendous individual female variation. Perhaps a third of the females in the population, we estimated, were as frequently affected by psychologic stimuli as the average of the males. In fact, 2 or 3 percent of the females we recorded were not only psychologically stimulated by a greater variety of factors but were stimulated more intensely than any of the males in our sample. They had responded to the point of orgasm with frequencies far exceeding those known for any male. A few were being stimulated regularly by psychologic factors to the point of orgasm, and that almost never happened among any of the males.

The data in this chapter effectively disposed of a centuries-long accumulation of mistaken ideas derived from attempts to explain differences between the sexual responses of females and males. Kinsey ticked off these old ideas: differences in the abundance or distribution of the sensory structures in female and male bodies; differences in the roles females and males take in coitus; the different roles that females and males play in connection with reproduction; differences in the levels of "sex drive" or "libido," or even innate moral capacities; differences depending on basic differences in the physiology of orgasm in females and males.

Wrong, all wrong, said Kinsey:

We have already observed that the anatomy and physiology of sexual response and orgasm do not show differences between the sexes that might account for the differences in their sexual responses. Females appear to be as capable as males of being aroused by tactile stimuli; they appear as capable as males of responding to the point of orgasm. Their responses are not slower than those of the average male if there is any sufficiently continuous tactile stimulation. We find no reason for believing that the physiologic nature of orgasm in the female or the physical or physiologic or psychologic satisfactions derived from orgasm by the average female are different from those of the average male. But in their capacities to respond to psychosexual stimuli, the average female and the average male do differ.

The possibility of reconciling the different sexual interests and capacities of females and males, the possibility of working out sexual adjustments in marriage, and the possibility of adjusting social concepts to allow for these differences between females and males, will depend upon our willingness to accept the realities which the available data seem to indicate.

Kinsey went on in the following chapter to explore the neural mechanisms of sexual response, particularly the physiologic role of the brain, and concluded this remarkable section with a long chapter on hormonal factors in sexual response. In his highly technical thirteen-point summary at the close, Kinsey's first and final points provided special illumination for hitherto dark or shaded corners. There were patterns, he said, which could not be explained "by the known anatomy or physiology of sexual response," or by "known differences in the capacities of females and males to be aroused by psychosexual stimuli." These patterns, he noted, included

the early development of sexual responsiveness in the human male and its later development in the female, the location of the period of maximum responsiveness for the male in the late teens and early twenties and for the female in the late twenties, the subsequent decline of the male's sexual capacities from that peak into old age, and the maintenance of female responsiveness on something of a level throughout most of her life.

As for hormones themselves, Kinsey was willing to believe that hormonal levels might affect levels of sexual response—that is, the intensity and frequency of response, and the frequency of overt sexual activity—but, he went on:

there is no demonstrated relationship between any of the hormones and an individual's response to particular sorts of psychologic stimuli, an individual's interest in partners of a particular sex, or an individual's utilization of particular techniques in his or her sexual activity. Within limits, the levels of sexual response may be modified by reducing or increasing the amount of available hormone, but there seems to be no reason for believing that the patterns of sexual behavior may be modified by hormonal therapy.

As the manuscript neared its final form, several of Kinsey's friends, specialists in their fields, gathered to help him. Bob Laidlaw, a New York psychiatrist, and Emily Mudd, head of the Philadelphia Marriage Council, for example, came out to Bloomington and spent a week going over the final draft. They worked in separate rooms at the laboratory, each going over the same chapter, making notes. Then they met with Kinsey and the staff, raising questions and making suggestions for additions or changes to existing material. Laidlaw recalls:

I was deeply impressed with the way in which Kinsey handled this. Here was a manuscript on which he and all of you had worked so diligently and here were the two of us bringing in a point of view from the outside which at times differed quite markedly from the text. In this situation, Kinsey admirably demonstrated his scientific objectivity. If he felt that he was right and we were wrong, he staunchly defended the text, but in many instances where we were able to make a reasonable presentation, he instantly accepted it and made appropriate changes in the text. His kindly, sympathetic, unassuming manner persisted through the seven days of intensive work where . . . we were going at it morning, noon and night.

As he had with the *Male* volume, Kinsey wrote the *Female* book himself. He used all the editorial help that was available, but in the end it was the product of his own hand. To the lay audience the result was less than absorbing. Although the typographical presentation of the second volume made it seem more readable than the first, the prose was the same, and in it Kinsey made no concessions to popularity. On the other hand, as scientific prose it was wholly admirable and has often been cited as a model of clear, scholarly writing in science.

The writing of the book was a triumph of intellect over pressures that would have overwhelmed lesser people. Laidlaw had observed the powerful effect the attacks of the critics had on Kinsey, even though he was able to put on a convincing front of external calm. He could not stop thinking about critical opposition after he had gone to bed, and he had trouble sleeping. Soon, with the publication of the *Female* volume and the even more violent onslaughts upon it, he was to be in worse trouble. Laidlaw remembers meeting him on a day in 1954 when he was to speak at an evening round-table meeting of psychologists. He looked worn and his eyes were red-rimmed. He was having difficulty sleeping, he said, and was utterly exhausted. Laidlaw persuaded him to go to bed, although it was only ten in the morning, and kept everyone away from him for the remainder of the day.

These, then, were the ingredients that went into *Sexual Behavior in the Human Female,* the book that it appeared the whole world was waiting to read. As with the first volume, it was to be viewed first by the press. The ordeal of the press and the critics now awaited Kinsey, and it was to be far worse than he could have imagined.

CHAPTER

XXI

KINSEY AND THE PRESS—II

By THE TIME the *Female* volume was ready to appear, the advance interest was so great that we were in a state of siege from the press. More than 150 magazines and newspapers asked to see the book before it was released to the public. We selected about thirty of those Kinsey considered the most reputable and representative, and provided them with prepublication galley proofs. To have done more would have been an exercise in chaos and meant a stoppage of our work. In any case, it would have been physically impossible to handle more people. As it was, the operation consumed a good deal of time and energy.

Ground rules were laid down. Each writer was permitted a maximum of four days in Bloomington with a choice of three periods during late May and early June of 1953. The Institute provided free access to the pre-publication proofs in return for an agreement that there be no release before August 20, each article to be a single publication not exceeding 5,000 words. Kinsey held three separate briefing sessions for the writers, and also gave them the guided tour of the Institute. As before, he secured their signed agreement permitting him to check what they wrote for factual errors.

Thus Kinsey hoped to reduce and control the publicity on the second book, but again he underestimated public interest—particularly great in this volume because it was about the behavior of women, a constant subject of debate, controversy and interest in American magazines and newspapers since their beginnings.

Because of the extreme advance pressure, even review copies had to be protected. The security problem was so extraordinary that it was impossible to send out galleys or review copies more than two weeks before publication of the book. To have done otherwise would have meant that the entire book would have been pirated, reprinted and published in condensed versions months before. Within a year of publication of the *Male* volume, in fact, we had received letters from nationally known writers and publications asking for complete copies of the *Female* manuscript.

To a certain extent Kinsey's plan to limit advance publicity worked. Publicity *was* reduced in quantity, and a more responsible presentation to the public was assured, but the impact of simultaneous articles about the book in thirty mass-circulation magazines was so great that it gave a somewhat different impression to the reading public, and lent credence to the charge that we were seeking publicity.

Another unexpected consequence was the flood of books which presented themselves as commentaries on or summaries of our work. There were nearly fifty of them. Some misrepresented the research, others misreported specific data and nearly all were inaccurate in some degree. People often told us they had read our Reports in paperback, meaning that they had read a condensation or summary; the *Female* volume was never in soft covers until recently, and the *Male* volume not at all. These were the people most likely to quote a statement attributed to us which we never made, one that was usually either wrong per se or judgmental. Even some scientists assumed that we had authorized these publications, and the mistakes in them were forever laid at our doorstep. The inevitable errors we actually made in the Reports were enough without having to bear the burden of what others wrote.

Later we were afflicted by a rash of fiction about sex researchers, which only served to confirm bigotries and fears about what we were doing. Needless to say, none of them bore the slightest resemblance to reality, and fortunately for Kinsey most were published after his death. The Institute library has a shelf full of them, fifteen all told, ranging from Irving Wallace's *The Chapman Report*, which was a best seller, to such transparent deceptions as *The Love Investigator,* by Ernest Gebler; *Bucks County Report,* by Stuart James; and *The Sex Probers,* by Hilton Smyth. One, *Sex Behavior of the American Housewife,* by W. D. Sprague (his real name was Bela von Bloch), had the consummate gall to carry a dedication to Kinsey, although the book was a hoax, a compilation of old material gathered from here and there and simply thrown together. Another of these books, *The Man from O.R.G.Y.,* was made into a motion picture in 1970, long after the event that inspired it.

While the authors of these books nearly always disclaimed any comparison with the Institute—the "any resemblance is coinciden-tal" ploy—thus avoiding a libel action, the inevitable parallels with our research were made. I cannot think of another research project in any area which was subjected to this kind of misrepresentation and harassment. Masters and Johnson, whose books are also controversial, have virtually escaped.

In anticipating the onslaught of the press with the publication of his second volume, I do not think Kinsey underestimated the poten-tial danger of what was going to be said. There was the experience with the first volume as a precedent, and now the added peril brought about by our precarious commitment from the Rockefeller Foundation. Beyond that there was the fact that a book costing eight dollars and covering more than eight hundred pages might again reach the best-seller list, but the majority of people, unable to afford it or not equipped to read it, would be getting their ideas about the work solely through the mass media. In other words, their reactions would be based on press releases, not the book itself.

A dramatic evidence of this danger was the comment of Repre-sentative Louis B. Heller of New York, a New York Democrat, who in August following the book's publication denounced it as "the insult of the century" and urged that it be barred from the mails until Congress could investigate it. Heller, as it turned out, had never seen the book but formed his opinions entirely from what he termed "extensive reports in the press." Most Americans, one must presume, got their opinions about it in the same way. Kinsey could control to some extent what was printed before publication, but afterward the press could say what it liked.

Even the prepublication treatment of the writers who traveled to

Bloomington became a story in itself. *This Week* magazine, a Sunday newspaper supplement, called the activity there "The Great Kinsey Hullabaloo," and the subhead promised "the fantastic story of how waves of reporters stormed Bloomington, Indiana, after the hottest secret in publishing history." Grace Naismith, science editor of the *Reader's Digest*, declared: "I have just participated in the most amazing publishing event in my editorial career. I'm not at all sure but that it is the most amazing event of all time." Some magazine called the release date, August 20, "K-Day."

In the most thorough analysis of the magazine coverage, Professor Donald Hileman, whose *Journalism Quarterly* article I have mentioned earlier, commented that the pocket magazines, which might have been expected to be more sensational in their treatment, were not in fact. One, *People Today*, attempted to improve on the original model with an article titled "Franker Than the Kinsey Report on Women," but the piece itself was quite sober.

Professor Hileman concluded that the big magazines seemed to play down the book's results. *Ladies' Home Journal*, for example, gave little attention to "infidelity," which was the subject of most of the sensational treatments. *Cosmopolitan*, a Hearst-owned publication, was the only one of the major magazines to come out solidly against Kinsey's interpretations, on the ground that they were plainly slanted against chastity and in favor of free love. This virtuous conclusion did not prevent *Cosmopolitan*'s editors from illustrating their article with two nude female pictures, one displaying the back and the other a head-and-shoulders shot.

The fifteen magazines Professor Hileman studied handled the book for the most part in an intelligent and educational manner, with no attempt to be lurid or obscene. Generally they were "favorable" to the study, some calling the Report "reassuring" and a help to "understanding of our sex lives." *Cosmopolitan* was the only one to argue that it might lead to the destruction of the moral code. Nine magazines mentioned the limitations and possible "questionable" areas in the method we had used in collecting data.

Among newspapers, press reaction on the whole was muted. Some buried the digest of the Report that was issued, and others left it out entirely. A few editors and publishers denounced the book. The overwhelming majority, however, shared the reaction of Carl E.

Lindstrom, executive editor of the Hartford *Times*, who reported in the *Bulletin* of the American Society of Newspaper Editors:

My own embarrassment over having printed the Kinsey digest was that, having braced for a tumult of criticism and outraged sensibilities, the silence that followed was deafening. Not a single phone call disturbed the tranquility of my hours at home; not a letter nor a personal visitation. The following day, in the presence of an Episcopalian minister and a Jewish rabbi, the subject did not come up. When their reaction was asked for, both approved the publication of the digest from which not a dozen lines had been removed.

This embarrassment of mine is beginning to crystallize into a sort of foolish dismay that once again [as in the 1948 election] newspapers have been somewhat out of touch with what the people are thinking and talking about.

Kinsey was pleased with some of what was printed. He went out of his way to compliment both the United Press and the Associated Press on their handling of both books, and he even thanked Walter Winchell "for your friendly reporting," although he could not resist pointing out some "factual errors" in Winchell columns. (These, I should add, occurred before the *Female* volume was published.)

However, Kinsey carried over to the press the same attitude he took toward those in the scientific community who had attacked him. Not long after the *Male* book was published, he had written to Dr. John C. Whitehorn, psychiatrist in chief at Johns Hopkins:

The inside story that lies back of the journal and newspaper articles is, in many instances, much more important than the material that was actually published. The backgrounds of the individuals who have done the writing very often supply the key to the attitude in the published article. There are, for instance, employees who have been fired from positions for having collaborated with our research; there are persons who are notorious for their promiscuous activities who have suddenly become religious converts. There are persons who thoroughly are in accord with our work, but who have been placed in awkward positions, amounting sometimes practically to blackmail, who have been forced to make public statements against us. There are many other complicated situations which we are carefully recording for our own files, and which will be available someday for writing a complete history on the public reaction to this scientific work in a field that involves such intense emotional disturbances.

Unfortunately for the cause of documentation, no such file was ever kept.

One could understand Kinsey's suspicious attitude after his first experience with the press, when in truth there were a good many distortions of his work, and nothing that occurred in the frantic effort to anticipate the second volume was calculated to soften him. In fact, the first offense was the worst. It occurred three years before the *Female* book was published, and to compound the case, the authors were his attorney, Morris Ernst, and Ernst's collaborator, David Loth, who had published the generally favorable symposium on the *Male* volume.

Their article was printed in the May 1950 issue of *Redbook* magazine, and what apparently precipitated the quarrel was not so much what Ernst and Loth had written but the fact that the magazine had labeled the piece on the cover a "preview" of the *Female* volume, and changed the introductory material to give the same impression. When Kinsey got an advance copy of the magazine, he was angered and disturbed enough to put out a press release denying that any "preview" had been given. The release declared:

The authors of the *Redbook* article had not been given any special access to our material on the female. Nearly all of the accurate data in the article have been available in print ever since the publication of our volume, *Sexual Behavior in the Human Male*, and most of the further predictions in the article are certainly not based on data which we have in our files. Many of the predictions will certainly not be substantiated by our final calculations. This is equally true of similar predictions which have appeared recently in other magazine articles.

The release then went on to deny specific statements.

Soon after this release was given to the press, Ernst wrote an anguished, apologetic letter to Kinsey:

I am terribly disturbed and I have learned my lesson. I think it is dangerous for anybody to write anything relating to your great project. With the best of motives I thought I would reduce the idea that your project is so scientific that the public would have nothing to do with it. In the article we wrote we used nothing except material that you have uttered in speeches or previously in print. The newspaper pickup distorted the entire situation because of your great fame. A paper like the New York *Post*, which we happen to represent, went further than some of the others. I don't know why this all happened in view of the other material of a similar nature that came out in *Pageant* and elsewhere. Personally I am not disturbed and I hope you are not too much disturbed. After all, these are all one-day wonders. I tried to think of what could be done to slap these people down, but I can find no formula that would be effective.

Later in his letter, Ernst put the blame directly on *Redbook*.

What made all the trouble was that *Redbook* put on the jacket [*sic*], *directly counter* to our order, the phrase "preview." They also changed the introductory caption [*sic*] over the article. Maybe I am really peeved because believing that I am a tough guy, I let people like *Redbook* put one over on me. Although we had advised them that we must see all publicity, I had not thought it necessary to put that into the contract. As a matter of fact, even if it had been in the contract and they had violated the terms of the contract we could not have done much about it. Incidentally, *Redbook* tried to get the piece put into the *Reader's Digest* and we immediately scotched that.

If *Redbook* had not tried this cheap, dishonest stunt, I think the article would have been of real value to your great work. Above all, however, it should make doubly clear to you and your associates my suggestion that you should get out serial, popular versions and all other versions of your future work. . . . Incidentally, *Redbook* came to us and indicated that they had some other people, not too friendly to your movement, who were going to do a piece.

Kinsey responded with unusual restraint:

Do not be disturbed over the whole matter. We are still getting long distance calls, telegrams, and other correspondence about it, and only yesterday we had to stop three journals that were planning some sort of reprint or condensation of your article. We will keep alerted and hope we can control the situation.

Wade Nichols, the young editor of *Redbook*, who had taken the nearly moribund magazine and radically changed its audience from elderly ladies in Kokomo to "young marrieds," wrote two letters of apology to Kinsey, but Prok was not mollified. He told Nichols that he appreciated the letters and also "the spirit in which you have written us now on two occasions and shall be glad to meet you some time," but then he went on:

By some interesting coincidence, I find that you are quoted in *Quick*, our Bloomington local paper, and in some other quarters as saying that you were "sorry the article had met with Kinsey's disapproval." We are beginning to get considerable comeback from this to the effect that we are finicky and unfair to you in disapproving of your article.

The statement that you are sorry that the article met with our disapproval is a long way from admitting that you did not check your sources of information and were responsible for a considerable amount of material which was diametrically opposite to the fact.

Ernst had written that he had "scotched" an attempted pickup of the *Redbook* article in *Reader's Digest*, but Kinsey, sensing a possible new attack by Fulton Oursler, wrote sharply to Grace Naismith:

You and your whole office should understand that the Ernst and Loth article was published without any authority from us, and we promptly disclaimed any responsibility for it in a press release which both United Press and Associated Press carried on the same day that *Redbook* reached the news stands. . . .

You will note that nearly all the guesses which were made in the article are either incorrect or go way beyond any information which we on this research project have. The only accurate statements were those that were based upon data which were already published in our first volume. *Redbook* has apologized and repeated their apology, but we are still in deep water because of the people who thought we allowed a particular group to have a scoop. There will be no information available from our data on the female until we are ready to publish our book, and that cannot be in 1950.

I write you because I trust your judgment to use as much, or as little of this as is necessary around your office.

With the *Redbook* experience rankling in his mind, and conscious of the hot wind of publicity already blowing on him, Kinsey understandably resisted any effort to get him further into the public eye. Fearing and distrusting television, he turned down flatly the most prestigious programs. Larry Spivak, enterpreneur of "Meet the Press," invited him for the second time, early in 1950, to be on the program, and also inquired whether Kinsey would not like to publish one of his "questionnaires" in the *American Mercury,* which Spivak still owned at the time. Kinsey gave him his standard refusal, without further elaboration.

After the *Female* book appeared, Edward R. Murrow wrote to say he was starting a new interview show—it would be "Person to Person"—and invited him to be one of the first guests. Again Kinsey was curt: "It is a policy of the Institute that we never appear on radio, television, or in movies. We feel that for the present our best medium for reaching the public is through our publications." Unconsciously underlining his sense of removal from the communications world,

Kinsey addressed his letter to *Edgar* R. Murrow.

Friends as well as strangers were refused. Bruce and Beatrice Gould, the husband-and-wife team who had so successfully edited the *Ladies' Home Journal,* were friendly to Kinsey, and had even invited him to take histories from those on the magazine's staff willing to give them, which he had done. But when Bruce Gould wrote Kinsey a long letter inviting him to contribute an article to the *Journal* about how he was interpreting his work to his own daughters, Kinsey refused. It may have been the bitter memory of what Dorothy Thompson had written about his work in the magazine that caused him to reply:

I am distressed . . . that you so completely miss the point of our research. We are exploring research scientists and we are not publishing in your *Journal* or any others, advice to others on what they should or should not do. Moreover, we keep all personal information confidential including the information that we have on Anne and Joan as well as the histories of your staff.

If you want somebody else to do advising on the basis of our data, we should be glad to list you among the journalist groups that we will notify ahead of publication of the book and they can come here to Bloomington and learn enough at first-hand of our work to give them some basis for whatever application they wish to make. I am sorry that Dorothy Thompson did not do that before she wrote about it.

One of the major newspaper writers on sex (among many other subjects) was Max Lerner, with whom Kinsey had a long and friendly correspondence. In July 1950 Lerner wrote a series of articles on the homosexual situation in Washington, for which Kinsey had the highest praise: "I think these represent as well written articles on sex as I have seen in magazine or newspaper writing." He did, however, have some significant cavils, and they represented the kind of viewpoints that elicited attacks from the moralists.

I think you are a bit confused about the compulsive homosexual being the socially dangerous individual. Again, as your articles so well pointed out, it depends upon the way in which this compulsion works out. If it results in rape, promiscuous forcing of relations upon minor children, etc., it is the dangerous thing that society needs protection from. If it simply leads to frequent sexual relations or to promiscuous relations in circles where such promiscuity is readily accepted (and there are many such situations where such promiscuity is mutually welcome), it is a very different matter socially.

Moreover, our specific record on blackmail in connection with the homosexual probably places the police as the most frequent blackmailers. The police and the underworld group known as "dirt" would account for practically the whole of blackmail. "Dirt" are males who are usually in their teens or twenties who search for a homosexual relationship, enjoy a homosexual relationship, and get paid for a homosexual relationship, and then satisfy their guilt complex and their inclination to live without any work by threatening disclosure if the person will not pay money to keep their mouths shut. There are tens of thousands of young males in our population who consider this the simplest and most pleasant way of making a living. We have the histories of hundreds of them.

The racket could not exist if it were not for the fact that police and courts cooperate with them by prosecuting the person who is exposed and not prosecuting the "dirt." New York City does better than some of the other cities in prosecuting these people. San Francisco and Berkeley, California, have practically put an end to the racket, but it thrives in most cities. These young males are not interested in international espionage, so naturally they confine their activities to older males of social position who make the mistake of picking up these boys as strangers on the streets. Consequently, the males who are most often blackmailed are not the compulsive homosexuals but the promiscuous, older homosexuals of social position who make their contacts with street-walking young prostitutes in cities where the police departments and courts condone the blackmail racket.

Kinsey was so sensitive to whatever appeared in the press that even in the midst of intensive work on the *Female* volume, and the imminent arrival in September 1952 of a considerable group of consulting editors which would tie him up every day for the next month, he could still find time to write Harriet Pilpel, a partner in Greenbaum, Wolff and Ernst, who had taken over the legal work with the Institute from Ernst, about the introduction of a "Dr. Pinsey" character in the comic strip "Abbie 'n' Slats." He was sure the strip would do him a great deal of damage, and wanted to know if there wasn't a way of forcing the artist and the syndicate to cease and desist.

What disturbed him in this instance was the fact that "Dr. Pinsey" had started out as a rather mild character in the strip, but by this time was making sexual advances to those from whom he was trying to get information. Kinsey believed, with reason, that this might very well color the reactions to his research of a considerable segment of the public, besides being a total perversion of what the Institute was doing.

Mrs. Pilpel was a little taken aback by this development, since her firm represented, from time to time, the strip's owners, Capp Enterprises. She discussed the problem with the Capp brothers, who assured her they could not kill off "Dr. Pinsey" before the third week in October (it was then mid-September) because the strip was already in metal for release through October 20, but they promised not to use "Pinsey" or anyone like him in the strip after that date. There the matter ended.

Kinsey was most outraged, however, by the references to him in *Washington Confidential,* one of the series of sensational gossip books written by Jack Lait, a veteran Hearst editor, and Lee Mortimer, a nightclub columnist for Hearst's New York tabloid the *Daily Mirror.* In *Washington Confidential,* published in 1951, a chapter called "Garden of Pansies" asserted: "Dr. Kinsey wasn't appalled by the 6,000 fags in government jobs. According to his calculations, 56,787 Federal workers are congenital homosexuals. He includes twenty-one Congressmen and says one hundred ninety-two others are bad behavior risks."

Responding irately to this nonsense, Kinsey wrote to Harriet Pilpel:

We never made any calculations on the number of Federal employees who might be homosexuals, even if our national averages apply to that group. We never made any calculation as to how many congressmen might be involved. These calculations were made by other journalists on the estimates for the national average. I can well believe that this published statement can do us no harm, but on the other hand, it might very well do some. I wish that somebody who had a stronger case against these two authors would do something to remove them from their position as prime social menaces.

Yet Kinsey wrote quite civilly to Lait himself, correcting him and saying he would appreciate a note indicating the correction had been received, and would be appreciative, too, if any further printings contained the corrected statement. There is no indication that it was ever corrected, and Kinsey continued to believe, with justice, that the book was "the most vicious sort of gossip from end to end." No doubt he would have appreciated a snide story making the rounds at the time that Mortimer had been beaten up in the men's room of a nightclub, and there were a thousand suspects.

Sometimes it seemed to all of us that there was no end to the distortions that sensationmongers would inflict on the books. Another of the purported "previews" of the *Female* book, similar to the *Redbook* affair, occurred in England, where the nation's largest Sunday newspaper, *The People,* carried what it called an advance notice of the book in its issue of May 4, 1952. This was by far the most outrageous such attempt to capitalize on public interest in the forthcoming volume, and Kinsey wrote at once:

You should be informed that the entire article is a hoax. Neither Harold Albert [whose by-line appeared on the piece] nor any other person has had access to the manuscript, and the actual manuscript does not contain any of the quotations which Mr. Albert purports to have seen in it. We should be indebted to you if you will make corrections to the above effect in some forthcoming issue of your journal.

Stuart Macflour, the managing editor, purported to be puzzled by Kinsey's letter. He could not really understand how it could be that Albert had led him to believe he had secured actual quotations. Albert had told him, he said, that he had every reason to believe he possessed factual information contained in the book, although he did admit himself in error in enclosing certain sections in quotation marks. Macflour added blandly that he did not construe from the use of quotation marks that Albert was implying that he was actually quoting from the book. In any case, he concluded, the information was factually correct and the general trend of Kinsey's findings had not been misrepresented.

Kinsey did not let him get away with it. He answered:

Whether Mr. Albert was misled or whether he intended to mislead, he was equally responsible for the fact that he did not have material of the validity which he claimed for the article. He states specifically in the article that he is one of the few who have been privileged to have a preview of the manuscript. The fact of the matter is that there is no one who has ever seen the manuscript and had the capacity for previewing it. There was a report by Ernst and Loth in this country that they had secured information about what was to be in the book and that too was false.

Consistent use of quotations throughout the article not as quotations coming from us personally but as though they were quotations directly from the book would make him legally liable in this country.

As for the last remark in your letter, I should inform you that in actuality many of the statements in Mr. Albert's article are as diametrically wrong as anything could be. They do not accord with the material we shall publish.

Probably the most formidable opponent, if it could be called one, that Kinsey took on was *The New York Times*. The trouble began with the *Male* volume. The *Times* at first refused to accept advertising for the book, reportedly on the insistence of an elderly member of the board of directors who was shocked by it. Then there was a long delay in reviewing the book, although it had been given the major attention of reviewers in every other medium. Kinsey's suspicions were voiced in a letter to Philip Wylie, in Miami:

The accurate statement concerning the New York *Times* would be that they had reviewed our book in their section only after several months of debate as to whether they should or should not. They have refused, down to date, to accept any advertisement on the book [it was then a year and a half after publication]; although it was listed in second, third, and fourth place for many months in their own list of Best Sellers. They have carried only a very small portion of the news stories about the book and the research, in comparison to what practically every other paper has carried, and in practically every instance, the stories have been definitely slanted against the research. For instance, in reporting the Symposium of the American Social Hygiene Association, their reporter had given a faithful account of the papers presented by all of the people on the Symposium; but the *Times* published only the account of the papers which were directed against us. The issues of the *Times* in which this was carried were dated March 31 and April 1, 1948. The full and complete report of the American Social Hygiene Meeting is now in print so it is possible to see exactly what the New York *Times* did in slanting their report of the meeting.

A careful reexamination of the relationship between the *Times* on the one hand and Kinsey and the Reports on the other shows rather clearly, I think, that this was a case in which an atmosphere of mutual distrust escalated as time went on. There is no doubt that powerful opponents of the research somewhere in the upper echelons of the *Times* successfully succeeded in refusing advertising for the book and delaying the reviews. That this was a policy judgment seems incontrovertible. In such an atmosphere, the much more debatable question of the news treatment of the American Social Hygiene Association meeting can be seen in a different light, and it is not hard to understand why Kinsey was only too ready to see discrimination against him. A paper certainly has a right to refuse advertising; every newspaper exercises that kind of judgment. It also has the right to review a book whenever it likes, or not at all, although the moral aspects of this right can become questionable, and surely they were in the case of the Report. But coverage of a news event is an entirely different matter, particularly in the *Times.*

In putting together his article on Kinsey and the press, Carl Lindstrom, the Hartford editor, sent his version of the Hygiene Association coverage to Turner Catledge, then managing editor of the *Times,* along with a comment on the incident from me (a year after Kinsey's death). I had told Lindstrom that the *Times* reporter (it was Lucy Freeman) had done an excellent job in covering both sides of the argument, but by the time it had passed over the metropolitan desk and into the paper, all of the "pro" material from the convention speakers had been deleted and only the "con" portions retained.

Kinsey and I believed this to be true, but there was a shade of doubt. There is no question that the story was cut, but the *Times* reporting of the events for the two days show that nine of the twelve speakers were quoted, and most of them supported Kinsey at least in part, although nearly all criticized him, too. The reports of what these speakers said were fair summaries, as Catledge argued in his reply to Lindstrom, and there was pro-Kinsey comment in the stories as well as criticism. The three speakers who were omitted, however, were entirely pro-Kinsey.

As Catledge asserted, editors and copyeditors would normally leave both sides of the debate in the story, and so they did, and it was equally true, as he claimed, that they would have no editorial interest in cutting out any material favorable to Kinsey. Nonetheless, something had been cut for reasons not established, and what had been cut was all pro-Kinsey. Naturally, we were sure that it was deliberate slanting. Prok would not accept the fact that the stories, on their own merits, were substantially fair. Were the cuts made for space or policy reasons? Were the omitted quotations legitimate material for cutting in any case? Who can say?

In any event, it is not hard to see why the mutual suspicion developed. Consequently, when Kinsey repeated his demand as the *Female* volume was about to appear that writers must agree by contract to permit him to see their manuscripts and check them for factual accuracy, the *Times* refused to abide by this rule. Catledge's argument was that he strongly advocated a reporter's submitting his story to a scientist he had interviewed for a check on factual material, but if the scientist made it a condition for getting the story, the reporter would have to make his own judgment as to whether he would accept on those terms. In the case of the conditions for the *Female* volume, Catledge thought Kinsey's requirements went beyond good newspaper practice and were intended to usurp responsibility which the *Times* felt it must keep.

On this point there could be no compromise. Kinsey was adamant and the *Times* stood on what had long been accepted newspaper practice. From this history of misunderstanding Catledge came away with the feeling that Kinsey and our staff had developed a thorough dislike for the press without sufficient basis. He thought there was more irritation than distortion involved. Kinsey, on the other hand, remained convinced that, for reasons he could not fathom, the *Times* had chosen to oppose him.

It was not true, however, that Kinsey had a thorough dislike for the press as a whole. His relationships were excellent, for the most part, but in the light of the several incidents I have cited in this chapter and the previous one on the same subject, perhaps it is understandable that he sometimes had reason for anger and suspicion. As for the rest of us, as I told Lindstrom: "We still feel here at the Institute that on the whole we have been treated as fairly by the press as could be expected."

The sticking point in nearly all the arguments with newspapers was Kinsey's insistence that stories be submitted to him for review of factual error, no matter what the circumstances. As I have said, newspapermen were always reluctant to accept the condition. This became an issue once more, and a nationwide controversy in the bargain, on October 16, 1953, when Kinsey was to address a group of psychiatrists in Indianapolis. The chairman of the meeting had told him that it would be a closed session, for psychiatrists only, but just before he was to speak Kinsey learned that instead it was to be open, except that newsmen would be barred. He protested, refusing to lecture under such an arrangement and saying that if the meeting was to be open, newsmen should be allowed to attend and take notes. He only requested that he review the stories, as usual. When this story emerged on the AP's trunk line, it made it appear, in Kinsey's opinion, that he was attempting to censor the press and to keep newsmen from open meetings.

In fact Kinsey had once more hit on the reporter's most sensitive spot, and the AP's insistence that it had not "garbled" the account, as Kinsey charged, was true—except that it had also not told quite all the story. Its first night lead out of Indianapolis on October 15, 1953, did not mention Kinsey's insistence that newsmen be allowed to attend his lecture, but instead began: "Newsmen who cover a speech here Saturday by Dr. Alfred C. Kinsey will be required to submit to the Indiana University sex researcher any articles they write so that he may check them for factual errors before they are published."

Perfectly accurate, as I say, but not the whole story; not garbled, simply incomplete. Quite possibly, however, the Indianapolis bureau did not know about the behind-the-scenes argument over Kinsey's insistence on admitting newsmen, nor apparently did it know that the agreement to submit copy was a standing rule at the Institute, applied for many years. The story made it appear that this rule was being invoked for the first time.

A small storm blew up over the incident. The Indianapolis affair was denounced by J. R. Wiggins, managing editor of the Washington *Post* and chairman of the Freedom of Information Committee of the American Society of Newspaper Editors. Then, the following night, Kinsey agreed to permit newsmen to cover the speech, whereupon the sponsoring organization closed the meeting to reporters entirely. Further protests came, from the National Association of Science Writers. In a telegram to Kinsey its executive committee observed that some newsmen viewed Kinsey's attitude as "a publicity stunt" and "an insulting gesture toward the newspaper profession," and went on:

Those of us who know you as a sincere scientist, often unfairly attacked, do not attribute such motives to you. However, we do regard the condition you lay down as tantamount to censorship and a violation of freedom of the press. If pre-publication approval is granted you, the same privilege can be demanded by anyone from a Nobel prize winner to a quack, by politicians and police chiefs, by lawyers and labor leaders, by both parties to an automobile accident. The principle at stake is the peril of coloring a news story for self-interest. The public must always know that news articles are objective reports of unbiased newsmen.

Anticipating a counterargument, the Association said it had agreed to submission of their reviews of the *Female* volume because of the special circumstances surrounding copyright ownership of the advance proofs which were made available. But the present demand raised an issue of broader implications, the wire concluded, and the Association urged Kinsey to withdraw it.

He did not, of course, and the storm soon blew over. But Kinsey continued to feel until his death, as did I, that checking articles for accuracy was not censorship of the press, and that the press was making a mistake when it did not utilize the opportunity to get the facts straight. On the other hand, I could agree with Lindstrom that in the relationship between scientists and the newspapers there were faults on both sides, and it did not profit anyone to try to determine who was most to blame.

I would not want to leave the impression, either, that Kinsey had no cordial relations with reporters. Sometimes, however, they were unlikely. One would have thought, reading the material about Kinsey in *Time* magazine, that he would have been irritated by the application of *Time* style (notwithstanding their denial that such a thing existed) to his research. On the contrary, Kinsey was much pleased by most of what they wrote, and when Gilbert Cant, who did the story on the *Female* book, duly submitted his copy to be checked for accuracy, Kinsey wrote him appreciatively "I think your account will contribute definitely to the public understanding of the work we are doing. I am even more interested in the possibility of getting together with you personally, and even some day, of having you hunt birds in our backyard."

Nevertheless, there were a few little points Kinsey wished to raise with the writer's copy, and he did so for several pages. It is an illuminating letter. In it Kinsey disputes Cant's opening argument that he has attacked clinicians, anthropologists, sociologists and psychoanalysts, and that they in turn have not accepted his work as contributing to their fields. For every attack in each category, he says, he can produce a long list of men from the same discipline who support him, and in fact the research has had its chief support from such medical groups.

The list of supporters Kinsey draws up is impressive, beginning with the medical divisions of the Rockefeller Foundation and the National Research Council. Then there is the almost universal cooperation from gynecologists, and Kinsey goes on to note that he was asked to give the Biggs lecture for 1949 at the Academy of Medicine in New York, one of its higher honors, and was invited to give it again in February 1954. Support has come, too, from the American Association of Marriage Counselors, of which Kinsey is an affiliate. The United States Public Health Service has conferred with him repeatedly on the problem of venereal disease. He has lectured to psychiatric groups all over the country, and a similar array of medical groups. He has been making a basic study of factors in sterility in connection with sex behavior, and has had the active cooperation of medical groups in San Francisco and New York for years.

Cant's manuscript also referred to the relationship between Freud's work and ours, and Kinsey calls his attention to an affinity which many people had overlooked:

It would be interesting to note that the relations between our work and Freud's depends upon specific recommendations that Freud made in the middle 1920's to the American group that was first organizing the National Research Council's Committee for Research in Problems of Sex. He very definitely saw the need for gathering the sort of factual record which we have accumulated. Dr. Yerkes, who was chairman of the National Research Council's Committee when Freud first made these suggestions, summarizes the relation between Freud and our work in the Foreword to the present volume.

With publication of the *Female* book Kinsey attained *Time's* cover, the American equivalent of the Queen's Honors List. Prok was immensely pleased with Boris Artzybasheff's portrait of him. He asked Cant if he could have the original, and Otto Feuerbringer, the assistant managing editor, sent it to him, in a mutual exchange of compliments.

If there were rifts in the relationship between Kinsey and the *Time* organization, they were trivial and momentary. One interchange, however, is worth remembering for reasons which will become obvious. I quote in full a short colloquy between Kinsey and Nicholas Samstag, *Time's* director of promotion. It needs no further ornamentation.

Samstag to Kinsey, June 30, 1952: "Have you amassed any data —or are you planning to do so—on the liquor consuming habits of Americans? I would appreciate a brief description of any projects along this line which you have on hand or are contemplating."

Kinsey to Samstag, July 7: "We have no data on the liquor consuming habits of Americans. We are, of course, doing research on human sexual behavior, and are getting data on drinking habits only as they have a direct bearing on sexual activity. None of these data have yet been tabulated. The most intensive scientific study of alcoholic drinking is being done at Yale."

Samstag to Kinsey, August 7: "Thanks for your prompt reply to my letter. Is there any way to see a précis of the findings on alcoholic drinking at Yale?"

Kinsey to Samstag: "The alcoholic study is located at Yale University. The address of Yale is New Haven, Connecticut, and not Bloomington, Indiana."

While it was a minor matter in the context of the whole, I think that Kinsey was most irritated with the attempts by those in the press who wanted to exploit his work and his fame for reasons of their own, even when it might possibly be well meant. After the *Female* volume, he was impatient because there were so many of these attempts, and his temper grew a little shorter with each one. He sought, for example, to stop a producer from distributing a cartoon film titled *Report on Love,* which used his name frequently and otherwise appeared to capitalize on his research. Kinsey wrote to Harriet Pilpel about this, saying that he was "increasingly disturbed at the number of journal articles which start out with a title to the effect: Dr. Kinsey says. We meet hundreds of people who subsequently refer to such articles as *our* articles which *we* wrote for such and such a journal."

Fifteen years after his death this is still going on, principally in the advertising for pseudo-documentary sex exploitation films, and in the films themselves, where poor Prok is still being credited with saying things he never said, is still being quoted out of context, is still cited as advocating things he never advocated.

He fought this kind of thing almost to the day he died. A little more than a month before his death, an editor of *Modern Man,* describing itself as "the Man's Picture Magazine," wrote to say he was planning a serious, straightforward article on the existence of erotica in the fine arts through the ages. He asked Kinsey to orient the magazine's approach to the subject. Utterly exhausted and ill as he was, Prok found the strength to answer one more time:

We have spent some hundreds of thousands of dollars and many years of energy in accumulating the data which will ultimately go into a volume on the erotic element in art, and an additional volume on the erotic element in Peruvian art. What proportion of this total expense is your publication ready to underwrite for pre-publication privileges on our years of research?

In spite of the earnest efforts of Carl Lindstrom and others to find some common meeting ground for science and the press, it was never wholly achieved in Kinsey's lifetime. In his particular case, the ground he stood on was narrow, and always embattled.

CHAPTER

XXII

AGAIN THE CRITICS

A FEW MONTHS before publication of the *Female* volume, Kinsey wrote half jokingly to a Philadelphia psychiatrist, Dr. Eleanor Steele:

At this moment we think we have a great volume on the female and that you will find it even more useful than the male volume. By the time the objectionists get done with the book I haven't the least idea whether even we will still be able to believe in it. It contains, nevertheless, a tremendous amount of information which has been analyzed as carefully as our augmented and more experienced staff can handle it and as top statistical, neuro-psychiatrists and other experts have been able to help us.

As matters turned out, by the time the "objectionists" were done with it, we had lost our foundation support and Kinsey was precipitated into the physical decline which led to his death. The objections were far more irrational and emotional than in the response to the first volume, as I have said, because the subject was women, and the total effect on the public consciousness was that Kinsey had been roundly condemned. It did no good to assert that more of the clergy were for us than against us; the big ecclesiastical voices in the major pulpits had spoken. Nor did it help to cite the overwhelming support we got from the scientific community; people remembered the vociferous and well-publicized voices of a relative few. Then, of course, there were the laymen who simply felt that the honor of American women had been trampled upon—judging by what they read about the book, although they would never have sinned by reading it.

It was even widely believed that the *Female* volume was a commercial disaster, a rumor originating in the ardent desire of some people to believe it was true. Actually, in a little more than two years after it was published, the *Female* book's total sales reached 75 percent of the total attained by the *Male* volume in six years. At the end of 1955 it was still selling so well that 749 copies were shipped in October and November alone of that year—a figure roughly double that for the *Male* book. Because of the tremendous concentration of publicity just before and after publication, a large proportion of its sale was compressed into a period of a month or two after its release. Its translation record was also excellent. It appeared in Hebrew, French, Portuguese, German, Spanish, Norwegian, Finnish, Italian and Dutch. English copies were shipped to eighty-six foreign countries.

As for fan mail, the publishers got a total of about five hundred letters on the two books combined, almost evenly divided between serious observation and crank letters. Nearly four hundred of these were about the *Female* volume, and contrary to the response on the first book, the majority had something unkind to say.

Kinsey's friends were as stunned as he was by the emotional intensity of the attack. One of them, Sophia Kleegman, a New York gynecologist, wrote initially:

There is an enormous difference in the quality of the reception the "Female" is receiving! I am surprised and, of course, gratified that so many of the established conservative editorial opinions have been not only laudatory, but actively protective and defensive of your work.

But then, not quite three months later, she was writing:

Are you holding back on me? Have you written two books on the Female—? From some of the recent reviews I have been reading, it seems to me they must be reviewing a book other than the one you so kindly had Saunders send me. Certainly some of these reviewers could never have gotten their material from your book as it is. Some of this recent tripe must be pretty annoying—but I do hope that by now your skin has developed the necessary degree of impermeability to the vitriolic attacks of certain of our "learned psychiatrists."

Kinsey responded, "Actually, the more insane the adverse criticism is, the simpler it should be to make a reasonable segment of the public understand what its animation may be," but in reality he was puzzled and much disturbed. These reactions are apparent in a letter to his old supporter Dr. Carl Hartman, to whom he wrote a year after the *Female* volume appeared:

I am still uncertain what the basic reason for the bitter attack on us may be. The attack is evidently much more intense with this publication of the Female. Their arguments become absurd when they attempt to find specific flaws in the book and basically I think they are attacking on general principles. There is a segment of the church that believes that sex morality is the most important thing in all morality. Honesty, charity, plain ordinary decency toward one's fellows and a hundred and one other virtues sink into insignificance when they are considering sexual morality.

I have no doubt that the attack in the Newark *Star* is a Catholic attack. I think you will never see a more open Catholic attack on us for they do not want it to become apparent that they, as a church, are against us. I lectured only a month ago at Rutgers and the administration was specifically warned that there would be disturbances and picketing by church groups if they carried through their engagement with me. I suspect the Newark *Star* attack is an aftermath of their failure to keep me off the Rutgers campus.

There is nothing that disturbs me more than the fact that there is practically no scientist outside of yourself and the National Research Council's committee that has commended any aspect of any single item in our volume on the female. [This was not the case, in general, as time proved.] I have no doubt that there are many scientists who have seen some importance in what we have done but the only ones who have bothered to go into print are those who are objecting. These objections are on the same philosophic grounds as those coming from the Newark *Star*.

Having just lost the Rockefeller Foundation's support when he wrote this, Kinsey was naturally in a much discouraged frame of mind. Actually, the reception of his work was not nearly as negative as it seemed to him then. Erdman Palmore, who studied a total of 124 published reactions, noted that 64 percent were mostly or completely favorable, 31 percent mostly or completely unfavorable, and 5 percent neutral. Our old friend Glenn Ramsey, surveying 295 fellows of the Division of Clinical and Abnormal Psychology of the American Psychological Association, learned that about 95 percent of these scientists thought the project sufficiently worthwhile to be continued to completion, and only 2 percent registered overall disapproval of the research.

In the popular press, the moralistic condemnations of such writers as Kathleen Norris, Fannie Hurst and George E. Sokolsky were more than balanced by medical and other writers, as Albert Deutsch, Dr. Lena Levine, Max Lerner and the noted medical columnist Dr. Walter C. Alvarez, who was one of Kinsey's most enthusiastic supporters from the beginning. The conservative New York *Herald Tribune* not only gave its readers a splendid factual report on the *Female* volume by its science editor, Earl Ubell, but also declared editorially:

There is an honesty in science which refuses to accept the idea that there are aspects of the material universe that are better not investigated or better not known or the knowledge of which should not be available to the common man. We believe that happiness is not furthered by ignorance.

Some of the specific charges were easily refuted, among them the notion that the Kinsey books in the hands of young people would make them feel that the old sexual morality was dead, and thus lead to sexual promiscuity, perversion and crime. The old sexual morality was in fact beginning to die at that moment, but not at Kinsey's hands. A transition period was commencing, coinciding with the vast upheaval in American morals and manners which is still taking place; our two volumes were only signposts, pointing in which direction the parade was going to anyone who cared to examine them. Study after study of college students disproved that those who had read our work had suffered a corruption of their personal moral codes.

Nevertheless, there were those who seriously advocated that the *Female* volume be restricted from public sale. It was not so surprising to find some of the more vociferous clergy in this category, but it was shocking to read Margaret Mead proclaiming the book should not be permitted to become a best seller because "the sudden removal of a previously guaranteed reticence has left many young people singularly defenseless in just those areas where their desire to conform was protected by a lack of knowledge of the extent of nonconformity."

This kind of attack centered on the belief expressed by a well-known psychiatrist, Dr. Milton R. Saperstein, who, in a review of Donald Webster Cory's *The Homosexual in America* in *The Nation*, launched a gratuitous attack on Kinsey and on Drs. Clellan S. Ford and Frank A. Beach, the authors of *Patterns of Sexual Behavior,* on the ground that their publishing of sex materials had an "anxiety-producing effect."

Countering this criticism, Albert Ellis and Cory himself asserted that the idea that

the publication of truths may produce anxiety in individuals in our culture who have not been accustomed to accept such truths is a dangerous, anti-scientific, freedom-destroying assumption. It is essentially the doctrine that has motivated all anti-democratic regimes, from the Inquisition to modern totalitarian states. If it were consistently applied, any fact which failed to support the existing mores of any culture—whatever they might be—would automatically be branded "anxiety-producing," or "non-Aryan," or "unpatriotic," or what you will. And any falsehood, presumably, that supported existing *mores* would be considered "good" and "true."

Where the most serious attacks on the *Male* volume had been centered on the techniques of getting the interviews and the statistical interpretation of them, the center of the storm in the *Female* volume was, as one would expect, among the moralists, and particularly the clergy, both Catholic and Protestant, with the support of a few rabbis as well.

Clerical condemnation of the book was international in scope. Adverse articles appeared in all the prominent Italian Catholic publications, in Rome, Bergamo, Naples, Milan, Palermo, Bologna and Ancona. In America, the opposition came close to home when a concerted attempt was made by organized Catholics in Indiana to end our research by putting pressure on President Wells and the trustees. The instrument employed was a letter that nominally emanated from the National Council of Catholic Women, and was signed by the Indiana Provincial Director and by the president of the Indianapolis Archdiocesan Council of Catholic Women. It read:

In the name of more than 150,000 women—most of them mothers, many of them with sons and daughters of college age—we, the Indiana Provincial Council of Catholic Women, seek some reassurance from you that Indiana University is still a place fit for the educating of the youth of our State.

How representative of Indiana University is the thinking of Dr. Alfred Kinsey? We have not, of course, read his latest book, but we have seen the sensational reports of it in magazines and newspapers, and these are frightening, indeed.

The letter went on to attack Kinsey at length and concluded:

If you, Dr. Wells, do not recognize how dangerous it is to popularize incendiary suggestions like these, we tremble at what may happen to our sons and daughters entrusted to the care of Indiana University.

To the president, the message was clear enough. If he did not end the University's support of the project, or at the very least renounce it, these Catholic women would see to it that no more daughters of Catholics attended the University, which had always had a very large Catholic enrollment because at that time there were few Catholic colleges in Indiana.

Wells answered with a reply that was at once firm and conciliatory. He noted, first, that the University never approved or disapproved of the findings of its experimental scientists, whether the results were popular or unpopular. The endorsement given to any research project at Indiana, he said, concerned the right of the scientist to investigate every aspect of life, "in the belief that knowledge, rather than ignorance, will assist mankind in the slow and painful development toward a more perfect society. To deny this right and this objective would seem to deny the belief in a divine order as it pertains to man and the universe."

Kinsey could not help being dismayed by the virulent denunciation poured upon him by some of the Protestant clergy, all the way from Billy Graham to Reinhold Niebuhr. In light of the changes in social attitudes of the past fifteen years, many of these criticisms may seem merely absurd today, but their cumulative effect was a potent one at the time.

Graham, the fundamentalist, surely spoke only to the already converted when he proclaimed: "It is impossible to estimate the damage this book will do to the already deteriorating morals of America." It was more difficult, however, to assess the damage done by the attacks of an intellectual like Niebuhr. As in the case of Lionel Trilling's essay on the *Male* volume, Niebuhr's review of the *Female* book, which appeared orginally in *Christianity & Crisis* on November 2, 1953, had a long reprint life. It was summarized in a Philadelphia publication, *The Lutheran,* two days later; republished in the *Quarterly Review of Union Theological Seminary* in January 1954;

summarized again in *Information Service*, the publication of the National Council of Churches of Christ, on March 27, 1954; the original Niebuhr summary was reprinted in the *St. Lucas Herald*, of Evansville, Indiana, in June 1954; and the original review printed again in Geddes' 1954 symposium, *An Analysis of the Kinsey Reports on Sexual Behavior in the Human Male and Female.*

Thus wide dissemination was given to a series of views and attitudes which had no relation to what was actually said in the book, but merely reflected the theologian's own moral philosophy and his deep anger at Kinsey for supposedly advocating a doctrine he would not have dreamed of advancing. It was the old, tiresome argument of the physiological versus the emotional, in which it was always declared that it was not possible to examine human sexual behavior on a physiologic basis alone. This led to the attack on Kinsey as one who believed in the "human animal" idea, which offended not only the religionists who had never believed in Darwin, but everyone who was devoted in his own calling to explaining behavior solely on some other basis. Then, too, many people simply could not accept the reality of what people actually did, as disclosed by our figures, but insisted on believing the mythology of what they publicly said they did, or the moral imperative of what they ought to be doing.

Niebuhr, at least, argued his convictions with honesty and skill, even though he simply lacked understanding of what we were doing. Not as much could be said, however, for some of the others. How, for example, could one find a reasonable reply to Dr. John W. Wimbish, pastor of Calvary Baptist Church, in New York, who asserted: "The professor from Bloomington would lead us, like deranged Nebuchadnezzar of old, out into the fields to mingle with the cattle and become one with the beasts of the jungle." Or how respond to the "Spiritual Crusade with Mary to Christianize the Christians and to Marianize Everyone," a pamphlet of instructions issued by the Franciscan National Marian Commission in December 1953, which urged its followers to conduct a crusade against Kinsey and all his works.

Eventually, too, the clergy saw Communism in the book. Dr. Jean S. Milner, minister of the Second Presbyterian Church in Indianapolis, preached a sermon, "The Celestial Fire," on October 18, 1953, in which he said:

My first comment this summer when, on vacation, I read this review of the Kinsey Report [in *Life*] in discussing the matter with my family, was that there is a fundamental kinship between that thing and Communism and that the influence of this report, though it may seem to be a thousand miles from Communism, will in time contribute inevitably toward Communism, for both are based on the same basic naturalistic philosophy.

Ironically, the Communists did not agree with him. D. Y. Leonov, writing in the *Soviet Magazine,* declared that Kinsey's writings served the ends of "American reaction." We were "imperialists," he said, and also "apologists for the imperial principle of exploitation." If he had taken it seriously, Kinsey would have been dumbfounded to find Leonov numbering him among the "sociological Darwinists and Freudians."

So the theological criticism went. The core of it was expressed in a *Christian Advocate* editorial, which said the Report was "still inimical to accepted moral standards and unacquainted with the religious viewpoints on sex." That was what no church could swallow—that, and the idea propounded by the Reverend Robert J. McCracken, minister of the Riverside Church, in New York, who declared in a sermon:

The charge is not that Dr. Kinsey treats sex simply as a biological function but that he treats it solely as such. . . . He conveys the impression that his facts are the only real facts, the important facts, hedged around unfortunately by taboos and conventions that are superstitious, uncritical and outmoded. From the point of view of ethics this is the crux of the matter.

Some of Kinsey's old enemies from the reviews of the *Male* volume returned to ride again. Dr. Henry Van Dusen renewed his attack, but this time did not mention the project's sponsorship by the Foundation. Harold Dodds was not heard from, but a variety of other educators took up the torch. Dr. Millicent C. McIntosh, the president of Barnard College, expressed her concern about the effect of the Reports on young men and women of high school and college age. President Raymond Walters of the University of Cincinnati condemned the *Female* volume as merely a new expression of an old materialistic tenet that man is no different basically from other animals. President Clarence E. Ficken of Ohio Wesleyan University asserted forthrightly in his opening chapel remarks when school began in September 1953: "You can either contribute to the moral fiber of this campus or you can merely be a statistic in one of Mr. Kinsey's animal books."

Karl Menninger, who had supported the first book so strongly, now turned against us and said he was "disappointed" by the *Female* volume. Here was revived once more the prejudice of the psychologist against the biologist. Menninger declared that Kinsey the biologist had not made enough allowance for margins of error involved in changing from observing insects to observing persons. "Kinsey's compulsion to force human sexual behavior into a zoological frame of reference leads him to repudiate or neglect human psychology, and to see normality as that which is natural in the sense that it is what is practiced by animals," Menninger wrote in his review.

The psychoanalysts were once more on the march. Dr. Franz Alexander was vehement in his denunciations; Dr. Bergler soon appeared with his book upholding the sanctity of the vaginal orgasm; and Dr. Theodore Reik, who deplored applying statistics to individuals, charged that Kinsey had ignored emotional reactions. Dr. William Kroger, Bergler's collaborator, maintained in a magazine article that Kinsey equated a good husband with a stud animal. Perhaps the most fanciful of these excursions was the prediction of Dr. Karl Stern, chief of the Department of Psychiatry at the University of Ottawa, that Kinsey was the herald who would usher in the 1984 Orwellian world in North America. It was not "the gentlemen from the cloak and dagger department" who would bring about this sinister development, said Dr. Stern, "but the friendly canvasser who accumulated samples of 'sexual outlet' and samples of virginity, threw them into the computing machine and presented the Formula of Truth to the reading variety of the species."

Kinsey turned with considerable relief from such fantasies to the letter of a young girl from Illinois who wrote to say that her father had just obtained the *Female* book, and as a science teacher had been asked to review it. Everyone in the family wanted to read it, she said, but her father had hidden the book, saying it was not a good thing for teen-agers to read.

I am seventeen [she concluded] and soon will be eighteen. If it isn't wise for teenagers to read the book, it shouldn't be on the market. But I firmly believe that it should be on the market. The days when sex as "one of those things you shouldn't talk about" are past, or at least should be. The sex problem, if there is one, should be brought out of the closet. The worst problems we have today are the ones we don't understand. I think you are doing the right thing when you bring sex out in the open.

Kinsey's reply was a masterpiece of subtlety: "Legally your father still has responsibility for you, and consequently he must determine what is to be done in the present matter. Certainly you should be able to find the book in your public library or in bookstores in your town."

There were other small bits of relief. *Variety*, the show business publication, reported that the Omaha papers had blasted the report editorially, and *Variety*'s book reviewer had written as an individual to the "Public Pulse" column, setting forth a rebuttal. In the same issue it was noted that Bob Hope had opened his first radio show that year with the gag "Kinsey came back, and so did I." But, *Variety* commented, "Where Kinsey didn't let his devotees down, Hope did." Senator Robert S. Kerr, of Oklahoma, was quoted in the Minneapolis *Tribune* for October 7, 1953, as remarking, "Dr. Kinsey and Senator [Joseph] McCarthy have one thing in common. They both claim to have uncovered a lot of domestic disloyalty."

In February 1954 Kinsey spent two days with the psychiatrists at the Veterans' Hospital in Little Rock, Arkansas, where he found most of the professional audience on his side. The sessions came to a dramatic close, however, when Franz Alexander, who had been a speaker earlier on the program, rushed to the platform before adjournment, strongly denounced everything Kinsey had done and urged all psychiatrists to reject every one of his conclusions. This emotional outburst shocked more than it converted any of the professional men present. It convinced Kinsey that he had spoken truly when he wrote to Dr. Alvarez only a few months before: "It is amazing what emotional disturbances there can be in this day and generation when science attempts to enter a field which has heretofore been considered primarily a matter of moral philosophy."

One surprising development was the return of Dr. Kubie to the Kinsey wars with what he obviously meant to be a conciliatory, peacemaking approach—indeed, he called the special article he wrote for *Psychosomatic Medicine* a rapprochement. Kubie said:

An impression has developed that the points of view represented by Kinsey on the one hand and by the medical profession on the other are irreconcilable. This is unfortunate both because it is not true, and because it can hinder a constructive meeting of minds. Furthermore, the apparent controversy has led many lay observers of the dispute to take sides where there should be no sides. It is for this reason that before discussing the report on the study of women, I will consider the controversy itself.

I believe that many of Kinsey's implicit and expressed criticisms of medical education and of the medical profession are justified. At the same time, much of the criticism which physicians, psychiatrists included, make of Kinsey's methods and assumptions are equally justified. In other words, to this commentator it seems that each expresses valid criticisms of the deficiencies of the other. These mutual criticisms are relevant to an objective evaluation of the accuracy and usefulness of Kinsey's studies only insofar as they have introduced a confusing element of distrust and animosity into a discussion which should be objective, friendly, and scientific. If we can shed our defensiveness, it should become possible for each side to use constructively those criticisms which are valid. Therefore I will begin this effort at a rapprochement by voicing some of my own misgivings about the medical profession in areas which Kinsey has rightly criticized—sometimes explicitly, sometimes by implication.

Yet the article itself did not bind up the wounds. It only reopened the old ones, and concluded with the hope that Kinsey would continue his work with his customary zeal and dedication, but only as "a member of a team of mature men and women of equal stature and authority in the sciences and of much greater sophistication than his in all of the behavioral sciences"—which Kinsey could not be blamed for finding patronizing and even insulting.

Finally, at this time there was another controversy over the statistics, centered on an examination by the American Statistical Association. This report, known as the Cochran-Mosteller-Tukey Report, which covered the *Male* book only, became a rather famous document in the scientific world—debated, argued about, supplemented, commented upon and reprinted endlessly. Originally titled "Statistical Problems of the Kinsey Report," it was written by William Cochran, Frederick Mosteller and John W. Tukey, with the assistance of W. O. Jenkins, and was published by the Association in 1954. It was, in reality, a symposium, and besides the four men mentioned, there were included papers by Kinsey himself and a summarized discussion of the criticisms by nine other scientists, including Terman and Paul Wallin, a Stanford sociologist, who had been so critical of the first Report. Because of its lengthy title, the Association's document became familiarly known as CMT, just as our staff was conveniently abbreviated to KPGM.

On the whole, the report was very favorable. The writers declared that the statistical and methodological aspects of the work were outstanding in comparison with other leading sex studies, and termed the interviewing "of the best." They criticized Kinsey for not indicating which statements in the book were undocumented or undocumentable, and declared he should have been more cautious in drawing precise conclusions from a limited sample. Some of the findings were questioned because of possible bias in the constitution of the sample, but the writers noted that no previous study of any kind had been able to avoid that difficulty, and bias could not even be reduced by a probability sampling program.

As for the statistical help we had used, the writers noted that it had been limited in part because of wartime shortages, and concluded that the kind of assistance that might have resolved some of the most complex problems would require a knowledge possessed by perhaps not more than twenty statisticians in the world. They then went on to recommend a probability sampling program in future work and made other technical suggestions.

One would have thought that Kinsey would consider the report a moral victory, even if it did not completely vindicate him, but he wrote in his customary vein to George Gallup, after a meeting with the writers of the report.

Our conference was a considerable success from our standpoint, thanks in part to the help which your group gave us. I think the statistical group had not really intended to say some of the things their words really meant, and they seemed amazingly unaware of the public relations problem that such a report, by its inept phrasing, would present. We understand each other better now, even though they would not back down on their insistence that probability sampling was the only perfect thing, and they very well understand that we do not intend to engage in any such program, and that we will explain to the world why we are not engaging in it.

In a more confidential assessment, he told his friend Dr. John Hamon, in San Francisco:

You will be interested to know that in the report of the statisticians whom the American Statistical Association sent out to investigate our methods, they reached the amazing conclusion that there are two sex studies which have shown more caution in verifying their results before publication; one of these being the work by Katherine Davis, which we find utterly contradictory in any detailed analysis, and the other being by Faris of Philadelphia. They are evidently enamored of the fact that Faris attempted to compare the value of reported data on behavior, and observed data by asking 200 men to estimate the time it took them to reach orgasm and then getting them to go to the toilet of the Wistar Institute to masturbate while they checked the time with a stopwatch. Most of them took longer in the experimental performance than their estimates would have indicated. The fact that there were psychological factors which delayed these men in actual performance is the thing that neither Faris nor the statistical committee take into account. Neither do they note the abundance of observed data which we have published in Chapter V in the Male volume, nor the additional abundance of data which we will have in the Female volume.

George Corner, of the National Research Council, issued a statement on the Association's report. Statistics, he said, was not the whole story in this kind of research, and his own Committee had been much impressed by the experience and knowledge Kinsey had accumulated in the previous fourteen years. Much of this, he observed, consisted of facts which could not be put into figures—facts bearing on social adjustments, sex physiology and education, and the laws governing sex offenses.

In his own comment on CMT, Kinsey wrote that

most of the suggestions made in the CMT report were distinctly useful, and we utilized a large number of them—specifically something more than a hundred of them—in preparing our second volume. We disagree with the CMT report on only one major issue, namely the practicality of obtaining a probability sample in our area of research. Because of the sensitive nature of the subject involved, we do not believe that probability sampling is practical in any extensive study of human sexual behavior which attempts to survey the whole population of a large city, a state, or the United States.

There is no major area of human physiology, psychology, or psychiatry in which our knowledge has been less adequate than in the area of sexual behavior. For this reason, we never intended to confine our research to a study of the incidences or the frequencies of the various types of behavior in these United States. From the beginning we have attempted to secure data on the anatomy and physiology of sexual response, on the relation of hormones to sexual response, on the factors which account for particular patterns of sexual behavior, on the significance of each type of behavior in the social organization, on the problem which society faces in attempting to control the social behavior of its individual members (sex laws and sex offenders), and on still other matters. Not more than 20 per cent of the information which we have so far gathered has been brought together in the two volumes which are now published. Data which we already have will be the subject matter of later publications on sex law, on sex offenders, on juvenile sexual delinquency, on prostitution, on transvestism, on homosexuality, on the relation of drug addiction to sexual activities, and on still other matters. In all of these areas we should be able to add to our knowledge, but in every one of these areas other investigators will have to make the more extended studies which we, in one lifetime, shall not be able to make. We have chosen, in view of our present lack of knowledge on most of these matters, to make a general survey of the whole area of human sexual behavior.

In retrospect, the controversy over the two Kinsey Reports seems slightly incredible. Harmful to youth? The present generation would consider their conclusions old-fashioned in the climate of freedom which now prevails. Shocking to the general public? How unmoved would a much larger part of that public be today, when nudity, four-letter words, explicit sexual situations and utterly frank discussion of sex are the characteristic of every medium of communication except newspapers and television. Debatable in its conclusions? They are nearly all accepted as a matter of course now, and Masters and Johnson have gone on to break new grounds of controversy and knowledge.

Yet the world has not changed as much as it appears. If the books were published today, one could be quite certain that the moralists would be as vehement as ever, the religionists would still decry the consideration of man as mammal and the followers of Freud would still find the decaying mansion of orthodox psychoanalysis under siege. I believe the scientific community might be much less opposed, although the statisticians still quarrel about method and the sociologists mistakenly consider empirical studies like Kinsey's outmoded.

In 1953, however, the combined effect of the critics was devastating and it profoundly affected the fate of that grand project Kinsey had begun fifteen years before.

CHAPTER

XXIII

ROCKEFELLER QUITS

In THE AFTERMATH of the first wave of assaults on the *Female* volume, George Corner undertook to gain the Rockefeller Foundation's renewed support for our work. Late in November 1953 he sent to it the National Research Council's formal request for new funds.

He was eloquent in his argument. During the first quarter century of the Council's Committee for Research in Problems of Sex, he said, the problems that seemed most hopeful of solution had been in the physiology of reproduction. Histology and endocrinology were the specialties used to approach these problems. In the past decade, however, as he pointed out, the study of sex behavior in animals and man had developed rapidly, and in the next quarter century, he predicted, the most urgent as well as the most feasible problems would concern the mechanisms for controlling sex behavior. For these the techniques required would be largely endocrinological, neurological and psychological experimentation.

Corner reminded the Foundation that the Committee had been unanimous in its allocation of grants to our program, and believed that its continued support would help Kinsey as a sign of scientific recognition, as well as make his work possible. Informing Kinsey of this initiative, Corner admitted frankly that he could not predict the outcome.

Although the royalties from the *Female* volume were not yet certain, Kinsey believed that the Institute could support itself for a time on royalty income, but not long enough to make the next volume possible. In fact, he doubted if it would finance the study of sex offenders which was next on the agenda, much less his planned investigation of physiologic and neurologic problems involved in sexual responses.

In February 1954 Corner heard from the Foundation, and the news was not good. Dean Rusk, the new president, was worried about a possible congressional investigation of Kinsey, in which an issue might be made of the Foundation's relation to his work.

The origin of Rusk's concern was a classic case of congressional response to a small pressure group for purely moralistic ends. The pressure had come from a particularly virulent group of our critics, unofficially led by Dr. A. H. Hobbs, assistant professor of sociology at the University of Pennsylvania, who not only had bitterly assaulted Kinsey's statistics, which he seemed to fear would prove that homosexuality was normal and premarital relations a good thing, but complained loudly that the prestige of the Foundation had given unwarranted weight to these implications. While no organized conspiracy was involved, people like Hobbs and Harold Dodds, Harry Emerson Fosdick and other eminent moralists were forever writing protest letters, sending copies to each other and to their congressmen.

Some of these letters eventually reached a congressman who was ambitious enough and sufficiently simplistic to do something about them. He was Representative B. Carroll Reece, an ultra-right-wing Tennessee Republican highly influential in the Eisenhower administration, who later became Republican National Committee Chairman. In 1953 Reece decided to form a House Committee to Investigate Tax-Exempt Foundations and named to it Angier L. Goodwin (Republican, Massachusetts), Jesse P. Wolcott (Republican, Michigan), Gracie Pfost (Democrat, Idaho) and Wayne L. Hayes (Democrat, Ohio). The nice balance between Republicans and Democrats, with Reece himself there to tip the scales in the event that voting divided on party lines, proved to be an illusion. Only Wolcott, nearly as reactionary a backwoods figure as Reece, could stomach the subsequent bizarre occurrences.

Having established his committee, Reece permitted himself to be interviewed by the press, whereupon the real reason for this investigative body emerged. "The Congress," Reece announced blandly, "has been asked to investigate the financial backers of the institute that turned out the Kinsey sex report last August."

Rusk, an astute politician long before he took up residence in Foggy Bottom, understood these signals clearly. Obviously a "get Kinsey" move had been launched, and in getting him, the Rockefeller Foundation, always a target of the more backward congressmen, would certainly be attacked as well. Rusk was worried, which no doubt accounts for his rather strange meeting with George Corner in February 1954, about a month after Reece had officially announced his committee. Corner's account of this meeting was transmitted in a letter to Kinsey:

My first piece of news is that the president of the Rockefeller Foundation, Mr. Dean Rusk, asked me to see him a few days ago. The reason for this was his concern about the possibility that the Reece Committee may make an issue of the Rockefeller Foundation's relation to your work. Evidently he was looking me over to see whether I would be a suitable witness before a Congressional committee, and he finally asked if I would consent to being named by him if he is asked questions relating to the work of the Sex Research Committee. I told him I would gladly testify. He then said that he would like very much to see whatever press clippings are available that are favorable to your work. Since neither the Committee nor I have kept clippings, Mr. Rusk asked if I would find out whether you have done so and whether you would send him a batch of them. If you can do this, I suggest that you send them to him directly, letting me know that you have done so.

The other piece of news is that the Committee's application for renewed support was modified by deliberation at a long and earnest meeting, so that we are now asking for $50,000 instead of $80,000.

Corner told Kinsey that he thought Rusk was personally favorable to sex behavior studies and did not think he would dodge responsibility for the Foundation's support of the Institute, but apparently he misjudged his man. A few days after Corner wrote his letter, the Foundation turned down the Committee's request and began to extricate itself as completely as possible from the embarrassment of having Kinsey as a client.

When he heard the news Kinsey wrote an almost despairing letter to Rusk, promising to send along magazine and newspaper clippings commending the research (although it was already too late) and a sampling of his total file, which "runs into many thousands of published comments." He regretted not having had a chance to meet Rusk and hoped he could persuade him to come out to Bloomington. Royalties from the two books would be enough to carry on research for about three years, he said, but

it should be made clear that those funds are not sufficient to carry the studies through to conclusion and publication. Moreover, to use up all of the visible income in the next three years would threaten the continuation of the research beyond that point. To have fifteen years of accumulated data in this area fail to reach publication would constitute an indictment of the Institute, its sponsors, and all others who have contributed time and material resources to the work. The discontinuation of support from the Rockefeller Foundation and the National Research Council at this time makes it imperative, therefore, that we seek other sources of income before our immediate resources are gone. Is there any chance that we can get you out here to Bloomington some day?

This statement of the Institute's financial needs was made only for the record, at Corner's request. Kinsey knew the Foundation would not be likely to change its mind. That was confirmed by Rusk's response, which indicated that the only thing on his mind was Reece's forthcoming investigation. Rusk wrote that he had tried to telephone Kinsey about his impressions of the pending investigation but could not get him because Kinsey had already started on his trip to Peru. The University's lawyer in Washington had reported that the Reece committee had shown no official interest as yet, but Rusk was certain this was not the end of the matter, because within the week he had had a letter from a committee staff member inquiring about the Foundation's policy toward publication of scientific materials. The question, as he said, might arise.

When he returned from his brief trip to Peru, Kinsey found a letter from Norman Dodd, the Reece committee's research director. It was a "fishing" letter, and Dodd was so badly informed that he addressed it to the "Kinsey Institute for Sex Research." He inquired the amount of the grants that the Institute had received from the Foundation through the National Research Council's Committee, whom they had come from, and their significance in the work of the Institute. He also asked about the origin and history of the Institute, and any other facts concerning its operations and aims.

Kinsey replied politely, setting forth the information and noting that support had also come from the University and royalties on the books, and that all the money had gone to the Institute, not to any individuals. He described the research, pointed out that the Institute had never proposed any policy toward the sexual behavior of individuals or any social policy concerning control of it. But, he observed, the Institute had served many agencies concerned with the social application of scientific knowledge by supplying them with data when they asked for it. He listed them, and it was an impressive list: specialists in psychiatry, psychology, social work and similar fields; church groups; legislative committees concerned with the revision of state laws; state and local law enforcement officers, penal administrators, courts and others who had to consider problems of sexual behavior. Kinsey enclosed various documentary records, a copy of the articles of incorporation and a marked copy of "Twenty-five Years of Sex Research," describing the history and program of the Council's Committee.

For what happened then I have drawn on Dr. Tripp's research, which will be published in a forthcoming book. Reece's committee began its public hearings on May 10, 1954. Twelve witnesses appeared during the sixteen sessions that were held, and it was obvious that they had been handpicked, as the two dissenting committee members, Hayes and Pfost, charged later. Their testimony was directed against foundations in general, but particularly the Rockefeller Foundation, specifically in its connection with the Institute. Professor Hobbs, who had been one of the chief instigators of the action, appeared at the May 19 session and made a series of serious and completely unsubstantiated charges against the research. The dissenting members demanded that the charges be investigated and Kinsey given a chance to answer, but Reece overruled them. He had already made it clear, publicly, that he had no intention of hearing Kinsey, or of hearing testimony from anyone else who might be familiar with the research.

At the sixteenth session of the hearings, on June 17, a new set of unusual events began. The twelfth witness, who had been scheduled to speak against foundations, instead began to give factual evidence directly contradicting staff testimony. Furious, Reece interrupted him and closed the hearings to the public. He would hear no witnesses for the defense, he said, not even in private. If the foundations wanted to make sworn statements and mail them in, they could do so.

What followed was described in a stinging 6,000-word minority report issued by Representatives Hayes and Pfost. The majority report had to be written by Reece himself, since no one else on the committee would help him. He did so with the aid of his New York lawyer, Rene A. Wormser, and the help of frequent quotations from Professor Hobbs, but in the end the "findings" were no more than a recapitulation of Reece's original charges. Reading it, no one could have known that there had even been any hearings.

In their minority report Hayes and Pfost asserted: "There is no evidence that the majority even read the Foundation Reports, let alone that they allowed them to influence the 'final conclusions' that were drawn before the hearings ever started." As for the "factual" material in the majority's findings, said the minority report, it was a "curious mosaic formed by the staff [but not the body] of the committee under [the pen of] Rene Wormser." The minority described the proceedings as "barbaric" and the majority report as "a crackpot view by persons who are ill with a fear sickness."

There was a missing piece in the puzzle. How did it happen that Representative Goodwin, without whose vote Reece would not have had a majority, had voted as he did, against his own public statements on the matter? *The New York Times* reached Goodwin at his home in Melrose, Massachusetts, and asked him. He had signed the majority report, Goodwin explained, only on the promise that a long list of exceptions and qualifications be included in the final report. They were not, in fact, included.

When this discrepancy was disclosed, parliamentarians in the House raised the question as to whether the Reece report was legitimate. Goodwin, learning of the omission, declared it was not a majority report. As usual, however, nothing was done about it and the report, illegal though it obviously was, stood in the record.

One might have thought that this development would have encouraged the Foundation to reconsider its position on the Institute grant. The danger from Congress had been removed and made to appear as ridiculous as it was. Moreover, the position paper the Foundation had submitted to the House committee, while Reece had ignored it, had been circulated in the press and constituted a public vindication, since nothing had been developed to contradict it. During the battle with Reece, furthermore, in defending the Foundation, Rusk had made a number of high-minded statements about the principles on which its giving was based, and if taken at face value they would lead one to believe that no other course than to support the Kinsey research could be taken. The Foundation, Rusk said, had put its confidence in a number of social and scientific studies which it had not only backed but planned to continue. It would not give up its intellectual freedom under government pressure, and scientists and scholars must not be interfered with in their work, the result of which must be intellectual achievement. "We believe," said one of these statements, "that a free society grows in strength and in moral and intellectual capacity on the basis of free and responsible research and scholarship."

How to explain, then, the sudden cutting off of support for the Institute? A much harder question to answer was why, at the same time, the Foundation gave one of the largest grants it had ever made, $525,000, to Harry Emerson Fosdick's Union Theological Seminary, one of the primary critics of Kinsey's research. The grant, it was announced solemnly, was "to aid in the development of vital religious leadership."

Some explanation, obviously, had to be made. When it appeared on August 24, 1954, it was enough to make the angels and all of us in Bloomington weep. In announcing forthcoming grants, including the one to Union Theological, Rusk said: "Some of the projects formerly supported [by the Foundation], including that of Dr. Kinsey, are now in a position to obtain support from other sources." We would have been happy to know about those other sources.

In reporting this story, the *New York Times* writer must have felt that those who knew better would find the statement too much to swallow. He interjected at this point a reminder that Kinsey had warned the American Psychiatric Association that "religious and other groups are exerting pressure on . . . the Rockefeller Foundation to end its support of [our] studies in human sexual behavior."

Observing that a further explanation was required, another Foundation spokesman, Dr. Keith Cannon, asserted that "the funds for Dr. Kinsey were dropped as of midsummer because [the Kinsey Research] did not request a renewal of support," and "the presumption was that Dr. Kinsey's work was now well endowed and did not need further help from the Foundation."

As Corner's letter which I quoted earlier confirms, there was no truth whatever in the statement that we had not requested a renewal. It was a matter of record, as was Kinsey's affirmation that it was far from the case that we needed no further help. There is no slightest question that the Foundation understood our financial position, in detail.

The truth was that the Foundation had simply quit, under pressure and out of fear, in direct contradiction to its frequently reiterated principles. As President Wells recalled later, its staff wanted to continue support but the Foundation board could not take the heat. To avoid further adverse publicity, the withdrawal was not even disclosed publicly as such, but was mentioned almost casually in the Rusk announcement of new grants—a little masterpiece of public relations.

Wells then had to go to his own trustees and tell them what had happened. They would have to stand alone on this issue, or not, he told them. They stood. No announcement was made by the University, either; it quietly took up what it could of the financial burden.

In 1963, when the Foundation was celebrating its fiftieth anniversary, Wells was among the six hundred guests at a dinner in the Plaza Hotel in New York. Rusk was the principal speaker, the Rockefeller family was present, and the guest list included, among others, university presidents and scientists from all over the world. Robert Sproul, who had recently retired as president of the University of California, sat next to Wells, and as the two men chatted amiably together, Wells inquired, "Do you know why we're here, Bob?" Sproul said he assumed it was because their universities had been involved with research grants which the Foundation had made and considered important.

After dinner, Wells repeated this conversation to Dr. Robert S. Morison, head of the medical division of the Foundation. "Yes," Morison agreed, "I can tell you exactly why you're here." He went on to relate that each division had been asked to look over its records for the fifty years and determine what grants had been most significant. A young assistant in Morison's division had brought him the Institute records and inquired, "Dr. Morison, just what is the significance of this?"

On his desk that morning Morison happened to have the newest and best gynecology textbook for medical students. He turned to a chapter and said, "Look here," and then went on to another chapter and still another. 'Young man," he said, "this is pure Kinsey. It couldn't have been written before Kinsey, and it has profoundly affected this branch of medicine." After relating the anecdote, Morison said to Wells, "You're here because we consider the Institute financing one of the most significant things we ever did."

Wells agreed. He still believes that the project was one of the monumental scientific ventures of the twentieth century in America. How ironic, then, that it could have been virtually destroyed by one reactionary congressman, a tiny band of fanatic moralists and a foundation president who talked about principles that he and his board readily abrogated under pressure.

This was the turning point in the project. I believe that the loss of foundation support, coupled with the severe strain of trying to find more money, added to his already impossible schedule, hastened Kinsey's death. The Institute did not die with him, but when his driving, commanding genius was removed from it, the character of the project could not help but change, and the grand design he had begun could never be carried out.

PART FOUR

THE LAST YEARS

CHAPTER

XXIV

TOWARD THE END

AFTER THE ROCKEFELLER DEBACLE, life went on at the Institute. It was the same, yet it was not. I think I can illustrate the difference by contrasting Kinsey's approach to the people and problems he encountered before and after the climactic period. Before, he was as he had always been. Afterward, the tension, anxiety and, I believe, the subconscious worry that he had not long to live were plainly evident in many of the things he said and did.

For instance, I cannot imagine that in the last two years of his life he could have carried on with such remarkable equanimity the unlikely 1950 correspondence with John Sumner. The executive secretary of the Society to Maintain Public Decency, successor to the New York Society for the Suppression of Vice, was now an elderly man, with the wars against sin well behind him, yet one would have thought that he and Kinsey would not have been able to communicate at all. However, the correspondence between them is calm, even friendly. Kinsey wrote first, observing that they should have met before. He has heard that Sumner is about to retire and hopes that "we may have an opportunity to meet some day." He asks for copies of all the Society's annual reports that may be available, to be placed in the Institute library.

In earlier times, I am sure, Sumner would have conducted an immediate investigation of the Institute, if it had not already felt his wrath. Now he replied pleasantly that he had had the pleasure of hearing Kinsey and others speak at a symposium on the *Male* book in the New York Academy of Medicine, and admitted he was thinking of retiring at seventy-three, after thirty-seven years with the Society. He would be glad to send all the annual reports he could find, and added, "I hope that they may prove of interest to those who may have occasion to look them over. There is no charge in connection therewith." And he concluded astonishingly: "Hoping that your studies may prove of some benefit to the human race . . ."

Sumner sent along forty-seven of the Society's reports, and a grateful Kinsey, in thanking him, suggested that they meet in New York, which he said had been suggested to him by mutual friends (although I cannot surmise who they might have been). Kinsey thought it would be profitable to them both to get together and was sorry he had let it go so long. There is no record that they ever met, and posterity was deprived of a conversation that could only have been historic if it had been reported.

In small things, too, Kinsey behaved in his customary way. A man in Jefferson City, Missouri, who had made a nature film called *Sunrise Serenades,* about birds, sent him a print of it to document his censorship trouble and got a sympathetic reply:

In spite of the fact that I appreciate your cooperation in the matter, I think that as scientist to scientist, I should tell you that I think it damnable that they should have expurgated the film. If in a scientific age you are not allowed to show even birds copulating on a film, things are going pretty bad.

Kinsey remained calm, too, through a minor episode with Christine Jorgensen, whose Danish operation first brought sex change to the attention of the American public. Miss Jorgensen had visited the Institute in the spring of 1953, at Kinsey's invitation, but because of the publicity that surrounded her every move in public, we had taken the utmost care to protect both her and us from the inevitable sensation the meeting would have provoked in some magazines and newspapers. We could easily anticipate the headlines: CHRISTINE MEETS KINSEY.

Miss Jorgensen came to Bloomington without any fanfare, stayed at Kinsey's secretary's apartment to avoid notice, visited the Institute and proved to be most cooperative. Just before she left, however, under circumstances which were never quite clear, she encountered some reporters in the lobby of the local hotel and talked with them briefly. Later, she asserted that she gave them a simple statement:

I have met Dr. Kinsey and admire his work immensely. I gave to him, just as thousands of other people have given to him, a case history for use in his very important research. If more people would cooperate with scientific research such as this the world would find better understanding of many complex problems.

What emerged, at least in a few newspapers, was something quite different. Miss Jorgensen wrote Kinsey a penitent letter, admitting that she had made a mistake in giving the interview, but pleading her youth and the difficulties of having fame thrust so suddenly upon her. She was deeply grateful to Kinsey for the help he had given her, declaring that she felt now that she could cope with her problems. She denied the "ridiculous statements" attributed to her.

Perhaps it was partly because he knew something about what it meant to achieve sudden fame that Kinsey wrote to "Dear Christine" cordially and politely, thanking her for her help and the spirit in which she had cooperated. He did not even mention the unfortunate interview.

In this period just before publication of the *Female* volume, with the hard work of preparation nearly done and the severe weather still to come, Kinsey could appreciate an amusing memory elicited by Alton Blakeslee, who had succeeded his father, Howard, as science editor of the Associated Press. After inquiring whether it was true that Kinsey had written a book which had sold 440,000 copies (he had; it was the high school biology textbook), Blakeslee recounted an incident whose authenticity he wished to establish.

One day Kinsey happened to be in a bookstore dealing in rare books and, after browsing around a bit, fell into conversation with the proprietor. He happened to mention his name, which at that moment was familiar all over the world. "Kinsey?" the proprietor inquired, and then, in sudden recognition, "Oh, yes, you're the author of *Edible Wild Plants of Eastern North America*, aren't you?"

The story was true. As it turned out, the dealer regularly stocked that book because it was in constant demand, although it had no relation to his regular stock.

During the period preceding publication of the *Female* book with all its difficulties, there were other serious problems. The notorious Customs case was beginning to take shape, leading to a landmark decision on the right of the government to seize materials purchased abroad and shipped into the United States for scientific use—in Kinsey's case, pornography and materials about sex. A large shipment had been seized in 1953, and Kinsey, through his legal counsel, had appealed immediately to the Treasury Department, under which United States Customs operates. The Treasury was in an awkward position. If they gave a favorable decision, they were certain to get strenuous objections from Kinsey's congressional enemies, such as Representative Heller. If the decision was unfavorable, they were equally certain to get a bad press, at least from the newspapers, which were aware of the dangers to all from the censorship of one.

The only way to escape direct responsibility for a decision was to force Kinsey to take the case to court, but even that meant giving an initially unfavorable decision. Not surprisingly, this was the decision ultimately taken, but the whole affair dragged on for years and was not settled (in our favor) until after Kinsey died. It was a constant irritant, added to others. Prok saw other institutions importing all kinds of material with sexual content, unopposed by Customs, while a state university's imports were subject to seizure.

Kinsey believed the issue was clear: whether Customs could use its own judgment in denying a scholar the right to any sort of material. Nor was it only his own interests that were in jeopardy. Art material was being denied to museums in other American cities, and Harvard had been unable to import contemporary Russian literature. Other institutions were involved as well. But it was only after the *Female* book and the Foundation affair that Kinsey's indignation about the Customs action boiled over.

After the *Female* volume was published, it must have seemed to him that the gates of irrationality had been opened everywhere, not only in Washington. The book appeared to have stirred up every kind of exploiter, every moralist, every psychotic in the country. Some of the events were bizarre, to say the least. The chairman of the Civic Affairs Committee of the New Orleans Council of Churches wrote to us in October 1953, wanting to know if we had heard about a kind of national road show that was taking advantage of the book. The committee had been sent some publicity issued in Houston which promised that a panel of two movie stars, a lecturer and an "authoress" would appear at the Music Hall there to discuss the Report on women. The stars were said to be Joan Blondell and Reginald Owen, and in addition to them and the panel, it was advertised, four women, all masked, would appear on the stage. Supposedly women who had been interviewed by Kinsey, they were from Los Angeles and included an unwed mother, a former gun moll for a gangster, a former prison inmate and a streetwalker. Audience participation would be encouraged and a special question-and-answer period would be set aside.

This remarkable assemblage did not appear in Houston, or even in Dallas; the promoters were forbidden by both cities to stage the show. Then it was promised for New Orleans, but after a protest the mayor intervened and had it canceled. The New Orleans ministers wanted to know whether Kinsey knew about or approved of this traveling circus. Kinsey said he had read about it in the papers, but of course denied any connection with the group. Nothing more was heard of it, if it in fact existed.

Kinsey was wearily impatient with the flood of letters suggesting, or even requesting, that he do specific things with his research. His mood showed through in a barely polite letter to a woman in Sussex, England, to whom he wrote: "It would, of course, be interesting to run the correlation you suggest between sexual performance and childbearing. There are several thousand other things that have been suggested to us, and I hope in the course of time to get some of them done."

One of the strangest repercussions of his fame after the *Female* volume was an article in *Confidential* magazine titled "The Sex Book Kinsey Didn't Sign," which claimed that he had collaborated on Ross Lockridge's best-selling novel, *Raintree County*. The story asserted there had been a close personal relationship between the two men, that they had common interests and that Kinsey had been greatly disturbed over the novelist's suicide. More explicitly, the article identified Kinsey as the professor hero of the book, and consequently identified him with what this character said and thought in the novel.

I knew Lockridge, since he lived across the street from me before he went East to teach and write his novel, in seven years of tremendous and shattering toil. I remember seeing him after he came home, rich and famous, raking autumn leaves apathetically in his front yard, a strangely bent and broken man just before his tragic death.

Kinsey, however, could not remember ever having met Lockridge, and knew nothing about him when the writer was producing his book. He had a speaking acquaintance with the novelist's family, but little more than that. No one who had read the book and knew Kinsey would ever have confused Prok for five seconds with the flamboyant figure of "the Perfessor" in the novel. But the pure fabrication of the magazine story spread about the country and was reprinted widely, and I suppose there are those who still believe Kinsey was the hero of *Raintree County*.

Every day's mail, it seemed, brought something else a little odd. Early in 1954 Kinsey got one of the very few critical letters from the young he ever received. It came from four University of Florida coeds, who signed themselves "The Vicious Virgins" and wrote in their charmingly illiterate way:

A frustrated college girls came across one of your reports in a recent magizine. We don't agree with your idea's of before marriage relations with the opposite sex. Just because we have gone through our lives without the sex realtions and our church, school, and home have taught us that it should wait for marriage . . . Does this prove that we will enter marriage with a bias idea of sex relations with our husbands? We can't imagine running around trying out everyone for size, much like a new dress or a pair of socks. Do you recommend that we do that? That's the impression that we got from your report.

How do you figure experience before marriage will aid in marital happiness? Why will one experience *before* marriage benifit us more in gaining satisfaction, that a *year* with our husband.

Another thing that we would like to have cleared up is your definition of petting? Do you recommend that to us? We still think that verginity is the highest vertue of womanhood. And want to save it for marriage. Tell us if we are wrong?

Kinsey told the "Dear Vicious Virgins":

I suggest that you go to our book and look up specifically the chapters on pre-marital intercourse and petting. You will find that we have never advised what any sort of behavior should or should not be, and that we have recorded factual data there which does not add up to the statement that you have gleaned, evidently from newspaper or magazine articles written by other persons.

By this time Prok was becoming a little accustomed to having his name bandied about in odd places, so I presume he was only amused when a student at Cal Tech sent him the lyrics of a song to be used in a student revue. He was worried about libel, and asked Kinsey's permission. The song was called "There Are Two Sides to Every Question," and the lyric in part ran:

My name is Dr. Kinsey and my books are quite informal
And I tell you things you thought were wrong are
  altogether normal.
But to keep all of my royalties in big round numbered
  checks,
I'm on a worldwide survey now to find another sex.

Permission was granted, which was most unusual. Ordinarily, in such cases, Kinsey replied forthrightly that if there was nothing libelous or otherwise illegal in the applicant's material, then there was no reason to ask permission; if there was, Kinsey promised he would sue.

In June 1954 came the trip to Peru. Kinsey had looked forward to it, anxious to explore the archaeological treasures in erotic art which awaited him there. In his investigations he was delighted to discover the Catholic attitude in South America to be unlike the almost solid wall of opposition he had encountered in the United States. He wrote to his friend Dr. Robert A. Winters:

It is a welcome relief to find that even though the church there has a clear-cut understanding of Catholic doctrine on matters of sex, it also has a considerable appreciation of the realities of human behavior. We found no attempt anywhere down there to fight our investigation of the facts. On the contrary, we found the general opinion in Peru was one of amusement that there should have been so much opposition to a frank examination of the facts in the United States.

After such anticipation, the illness that kept him in bed so much of the time in Peru was a sad aftermath to the Foundation's defection. The painful end of the trip is recorded in a letter to another friend, Dr. Frances Shields:

I did the very foolish thing of going to Peru and staying in bed two weeks and in bed most of the time since I came home. It started with a throat infection which I picked up on that weekend visit to Los Angeles and it spread into a general pelvic infection. Slowly but I think surely I am recovering.

But now it seemed that new irritations sprang up on every side. Soon after he returned from Peru, Kinsey went to San Francisco and gave what he supposed was a confidential talk to a closed committee formed by the office of the state attorney general, Emmet Daly. When a copy of the mimeographed minutes of this meeting was sent to him, as it had been sent to the others present, Kinsey was infuriated by what he read. He blamed the stenographer who did the transcribing, who he said was "completely uneducated in regard to technical terms and in regard to such ordinary things as spelling and sentence construction and the delimitation of paragraphs. It makes the whole thing appear the product of a person who had a sixth grade education." He cited "sent" reproduced as "set" regularly, and "fellatio" spelled "fellacio," and noted "endless sentences without verbs, representing the product of a failure to comprehend where one sentence ends and the next sentence begins."

Even at this time, the Kinsey warmth was always ready for people who wrote in obvious great distress. A San Francisco man sent him a nearly illiterate letter in which he complained that doctors would not operate on him to change his sex, and declared there were only two possibilities left for him, insanity or suicide.

Kinsey replied promptly:

You must not decide that there are only two possibilities in the world. Actually, there are thousands of possibilities and any plant or animal, whether human or some lower species, can never expect to get along in the world until they are ready to face realities and make the most of what is possible. You are asking the whole world to change in accordance with your desires. You have made practically no attempt to fit yourself into the realities of the world. Until you do you are going to be in continuous trouble. This is written to you out of the goodness of my heart, for I wish that life could be made more comfortable for you. I know of no way of that being done until you do face reality.

One of the realities Kinsey had to face was the continuing attack on his work, which seemed never to end. Long after the bitter warfare of 1953, it continued. One that particularly enraged Kinsey, not only because of its character but because it was carried in a syndicated column across the country, began in December 1955 and extended into the next year. The vehicle this time was the column called "Modern Marriage," written by Paul Popenoe, a West Coast marriage counselor, who had been among those who heard the early exposition of Kinsey's work at the Penn State conference but had never been a supporter. His syndicated work was written in the breezy, folksy, wisecracking style of such newspaper advice, which particularly irritated Kinsey. The column that irked him most was published on December 10, 1955. In it Popenoe quoted a correspondent named "Agnes," who wanted to know whether experts agreed that Kinsey had given a correct picture of American manhood.

"Experts agree that he has not," Popenoe wrote confidently in his column. "Or if he has, there is no way of knowing it. Kinsey's Report does not create quite the same impression now that it did when it first appeared. It was hailed as a milestone in the progress of civilization by a lot of eminent men who were not at all qualified to pass judgment on it. When the experts went to work on it—as they always do, with magnifying glass and scalpel—it turned out to be a very peculiar production."

He went on to attack the sample, and asserted that it was "overloaded with college students, and with—I was going to say 'riff raff' but maybe that doesn't sound scientific. I'll use a familiar term from the textbooks, 'marginal men.' " By this, Popenoe meant prisoners, men from "mental institutions" and a state home for the feebleminded, male prostitutes, bootleggers, gamblers, pimps, thieves and holdup men, bums and hoboes.

Having charged that these "marginal men" clouded the sample, Popenoe went on in his careless way to conclude: "Most critics now agree that he has given a fairly good picture of the sexual life of Protestant college students in a very limited part of the nation. . . . As to the rest of the population, nobody knows. Kinsey has done a tremendous piece of work, with many valuable results. However, his publication too often fails to reveal the facts that we really wanted. Don't let him scare you, Agnes."

To this and a subsequent attack on the *Female* volume in a similar vein, Kinsey rebutted:

Why should you be so insistent in criticizing the work that we have done that you have to distort the fact in order to put across your point? You know perfectly well that the women we interviewed and reported upon in our volume were as decent women as those with whom you ordinarily associate. Twice you were part of groups where we got 100 per cent of all the women in the group to contribute histories. This was true at the Marriage Counselors meeting at State College and this was true for three years in succession that Noel Keyes and his successor held classes at the University of California. It was made very plain in our book that the histories of prostitutes and all persons who had prison records were ruled out of the female volume.

You have claimed to be a scientist. As a scientist you should be held responsible in scientific literature for the inaccuracies that you have constantly printed for the last couple of years concerning the nature of our sample. I should be pleased if I didn't have to take time to go to the scientific journals to explain the matter.

It was particularly galling and frustrating for Kinsey to read such attacks in these last months of his life. A man with access to millions of people in a newspaper column could say what he liked, and Kinsey had no recourse except the scientific journals. He did not even know if he would be able to reply with new research in books of his own since the need for money was beginning to be acute in 1955.

He had not given up completely on the Rockefeller Foundation, hoping forlornly that he and Corner, between them, could get more money. Corner agreed to ask on behalf of the Committee, and he discussed with Kinsey on what basis the Foundation could be approached. He appeared to believe that Dr. Morison would not be unwilling, but it would make everything easier if somehow the work for which the grant was made could be given the character of something that would be directly useful to physicians. Perhaps, he suggested, if Kinsey would agree to present the results first in an article in a clinical or clinico-scientific journal, something like the *American Journal of Obstetrics and Gynecology*, or the *Journal of Fertility and Sterility* . . .

What Corner had in mind was the data we had been compiling on abortion, begun at the request of the Planned Parenthood Federation to which Kinsey had given a preliminary report at its abortion conference at Arden House, Columbia University's seminar and conference center, in April 1955. Since he was already committed to presenting a summary of that material, Kinsey thought he might be able to follow Corner's suggestion.

A careful course had to be steered with this abortion data. Dr. Alan Guttmacher, who later became president of Planned Parenthood, was still in Baltimore, where he headed an abortion reform committee which in November 1955 prepared a summarized policy statement on the subject. Guttmacher asked Kinsey to sign it, but Prok was reluctant to do so. It was proper for the committee to recommend policy, he said, but he was against signing anything of that nature. The Institute should commit itself only to factual presentation of data and analyses of their significance.

Besides, Kinsey had reservations about some of the data supporting the committee's resolution. He saw no evidence to support the statement that a "grave influence" was exerted by abortion on the physical and mental health of the nation, and he questioned labeling abortion a disease of society. There were major differences, he pointed out, between the problems of abortion and venereal disease. "In the first place," he argued, "the abortion problem is primarily one of the refusal of physicians to perform abortions. The problem of venereal disease arose from the ignorance of the medical profession as to how to take care of the disease."

According to the committee resolution, attempts to obtain abortion were the result of physical illness or the imperfect adaptation of a woman to her environment. His data, said Kinsey, suggested that economic factors and family planning were the two factors most often involved. "It seems inconsistent for a Planned Parenthood group to suggest that planning of the size of a family represents illness or imperfect inter-adaptation."

There were other points of difference. His histories, Kinsey declared, did not support the committee's assertion that desire for abortion almost always had in it elements of a disordered family, social or economic situation, and if that contradicted the data of clinicians, he assumed their cases did not represent a cross-section of society. Nor could he agree that abortion was a traumatic experience, except in a small number of cases. He had seen traumatic effects following circumcision, he said, and similar effects might follow other kinds of operations the medical profession encouraged. He could not forgive the doctors: "Among the most disturbed persons we have seen are those who are desperately in need of abortions, and find the medical profession refusing to recognize their need."

Kinsey also questioned that a wider knowledge of contraception would reduce the incidence of undesired pregnancies. These pregnancies, he believed, often occurred in situations which were never going to be controlled, even by people who made maximum use of contraceptives. Sex education or higher standards of sexual conduct would not reduce the number of pregnancies either, he asserted. His data showed that the highest abortion rate occurred in the better-educated segment of the population, and he pointed to the Scandinavian countries, where frank and widespread sex education did not prevent an exceedingly high rate of nonmarital pregnancies, leading to the acceptance of a high rate of abortion.

But it was clear that Kinsey considered doctors the real villains in the abortion piece. In the committee's statement, he said, there was only one place where it was suggested that the abortion problem was primarily dependent on unrealistic state laws "and the failure of the medical profession to view the matter in more than a moralistic light."

However wrong Kinsey may have been in some of his views, or however much he may have misjudged the intentions of Dr. Guttmacher and the committee, it was clear that the effort to get Foundation money in support of his abortion data would not work.

Nevertheless, negotiations with the Rockefeller people continued. Dr. Arthur L. Swift, Jr., professor of Church and Community at Union Theological, wrote to Kinsey in September asking him to clear up several questions about the research, and in the course of answering it Kinsey gave the frankest exposition of his relationship with the Foundation he had ever set down on paper:

If the Board of the Rockefeller Foundation wants to seriously raise questions concerning the statistical or other aspects of our research, it would be more efficient and more effective if they would let me meet with them for an hour. In the 15 years since we began dealing with them, no member of the board has ever met me or talked with me with the exception of Dr. Perrin. In the original instance they put responsibility on the NRC's Committee, and then without heeding the recommendations of the NRC's Committee and without asking for first-hand information from us, they began to take direct action on the basis of reports from men who, like Warren Weaver [who had become chief executive of the Foundation], has steadfastly, throughout all these years, refused to meet me.

You ask about the solvency of the Institute at the time of our last Rockefeller appeal. The amount requested from the Rockefeller Foundation would not have taken care of more than one-third of our total expenses. It was hoped that monies received from royalties and the support received from Indiana University (which has totaled one-third of the total cost of the research), would make it possible to carry on for some time. With the loss of the support from the Rockefeller Foundation it has been necessary to draw on the funds received from royalties, and the total research will come to an end in approximately a year if we do not get other support from outside sources. Dr. Gregg and all of our other advisors had always pointed out the desirability of establishing a reserve fund. Certainly it is impossible to keep such highly trained people as we have on our staff if they have no assurance that they will have jobs a year hence. It would be a tragedy to lose such highly trained people if we went through any period of insolvency. Because of the lack of outside support we have had to draw on the reserve fund which we were building from part of the income from royalties.

. . . I find it difficult to understand why a scholar should have to justify the accumulation of a library in the subject in which he is working. This is particularly strange considering that there is no such sex library anywhere in the United States, and probably nowhere in the world short of the Vatican. The extensive bibliography in both of our published books and particularly in the volume on the female is a bibliography only of those titles from which material was actually drawn for correlation with our own data. There are many scholars who consider that this aspect of our volume on the female represents its highest achievement in scholarship. For every title that got into the bibliography we had to search several other volumes to see whether there was other material that similarly might have a bearing on our research. I do not understand any suggestions that the library has been expanded beyond its utility for us. If you will look at the list of projects we have under way, you will see what a diversity of subjects we need to have material on.

You ask how long it would take and how much it would cost to publish our material without further research—"without further research activity." The answer is, of course, that the research has only begun when we gather the data in the field. The collation of the material, the analysis of its meaning, the preparation for publication, is, as we have pointed out in our annual report, the tremendous task that now lies ahead of us. It is for this that we need a budget of approximately $120,000 per year for the next ten years, in addition to the contribution that Indiana University is making.

It is impossible to estimate what royalties from publication may amount to. It is doubtful whether we can count on $10,000 per year in the immediate future. I think publication of additional books will increase this and outside support could then correspondingly be reduced.

With only a few months to live, exhausted and ill, Kinsey was still desperately trying to find ways to finance the Institute in the spring of 1956. By this time Alan Gregg had resigned from the Foundation, effective July 1, but he had already departed for practical purposes, and was vacationing in Big Sur when Kinsey wrote him in April to ask if he had any ideas about raising money. Prok observed that only 10 to 15 percent of the data in the files had been used to publish the first two volumes, and what with additional fieldwork since then, there was enough material to warrant publication of the long series of fifteen to twenty volumes Kinsey had envisioned at the beginning.

The situation was critical, Kinsey said. There was no immediate prospect of enough money for continued fieldwork. Support, if it could be obtained, would make it possible to get the data already at hand analyzed and ready for publication. By this time, too, Kinsey had concluded that it would never be possible to support the research on income from publication. The reserve that royalties had given the Institute was nearly gone, and by holding the staff to a minimum it would be possible to keep going only for another fiscal year, after which the money would run out entirely.

He had asked other foundations for support, Kinsey told Gregg, but found them disinclined to get into sex research, and to Prok this seemed indefensible because, as he saw it, refusal of support amounted essentially to a suppression of information. He was turning now to Gregg, appealing to him for suggestions as to where he could go next.

Gregg's reply was sympathetic, even agonized, but otherwise not helpful. He recalled that he had fallen out with the Foundation's board when it dropped the project, and that, he said, "was an experience for me that I had dreaded, and one which I cannot count among those experiences which gave me the most satisfaction in terms of its steadfastness and detachment. . . . I have occasion to think more than once of Solon's remark when he was asked if he had given the Greeks the best laws he was capable of giving them. He is said to have replied that he had not, but he had given them the best laws they were capable of receiving."

Sadly, Gregg had no ideas to offer. He told Kinsey that from what he knew of the opinions and past record of his successors at the Foundation, he could not encourage Prok to expect sympathetic consideration. Apply to other foundations—that was all he could offer at present. That, and to reaffirm his belief in both Kinsey and the research.

In these closing months of his life, besieged by illness, despairing of getting any money to keep the Institute going and foreseeing its possible demise, Kinsey still maintained the old remarkable courage that enabled him to go on dealing with everyday affairs in his understanding, warm way. I think especially of the voluntary tribute he paid to his old friend Dr. Frances Shields, who had retired and was living in Monterey.

You have been important in the whole history of the research, and have been a source of continued encouragement. In the hall of our new and very modern quarters in our new life science building, we are putting up portraits of a long list of the people who have definitely helped. There is Yerkes, Corner, Hartman, Dickinson, and many others. You are there in a portrait we got through Dickinson's collection; some day we must get a better portrait of you.

Nothing was too trivial, apparently, for his polite attention. A handwriting analyst named Helen King wrote him a letter beginning, "How do you doodle, Dr. Kinsey?" She was doing a book about doodles and asked him to donate one for her pioneer project, to join contributions she had already from General Eisenhower, Walter Winchell, H. V. Kaltenborn and an assortment of governors and senators. Kinsey gave her a one-sentence reply: "I do not doodle. Is there something wrong with me?" Not at all, Miss King assured him; he was in the same company with Mrs. Roosevelt, Grandma Moses, Alfred Lunt, Lynn Fontanne and "many men in the sporting field."

A month before his death, the mail brought a letter from a girl reporter on the Florence, South Carolina, *Morning News*, asking in connection with a story she was writing for information about who determined the sex of a baby, the father or the mother. Possibly there were two schools of thought on the matter, she speculated. Kinsey's reply reflected both his patience and his weariness: "It is not quite correct to talk about there being schools of thought in science. The issue concerns the specific data that are available. On this question of sex determination, the data have been available for the last forty years. You may find the matter explained in any good elementary genetic text."

The year and a half before Prok died was a dark period indeed, as I have indicated, full of anxiety and the struggle to survive, both personally and professionally. Yet in 1955 there occurred one of the great episodes of his life—his trip to Europe. It was an extraordinary journey, a closing chapter in his life that deserves to stand alone.

CHAPTER

XXV

KINSEY ABROAD

Aside from his bug-hunting expeditions in Mexico and Guatemala and two trips to Peru, Kinsey had never been any farther from the continental United States than Cuba before 1955. Cuba was also the nearest he had ever come to taking a vacation. Gebhard and I spent two weeks with him there because he wanted to get the flavor of a different culture and observe it as it related to sex. It was before the proletarian revolution had cleansed Havana of commercial sex, and we made the rounds of the exhibitions and the open houses of prostitution, from the most sordid to the most elaborate, and in the bargain both the homosexual and the heterosexual nightclubs.

We were aided, at least to some extent, by Kinsey's knowledge of Spanish. He was extremely proud of this accomplishment. Others who spoke it said he had an accent but was nevertheless understandable. He himself was completely unaware that he had an accent, and thought he spoke excellent Spanish.

The exhibitions we saw consisted of males and females simulating intercourse in a variety of positions. They were about as nonemotional and nonsexual as it is possible to imagine. To us they seemed to be a series of stilted, formalized tableaux, and certainly taught us nothing about human sexuality except how to exploit it. They also told us something about the American tourist, so hungry for anything sexual that he would accept whatever was offered because it was so difficult to find any such outlet in his own country.

401

In the houses of prostitution, Kinsey demonstrated his ability to relate to anyone. He persuaded the girls to talk freely, and got a great deal of comparative information. One of my regrets is that he never wrote up his reactions to these and other situations. He did, at our insistence, try to do so during and after his European trip, but a great deal of data was lost forever because of his refusal to spend time setting down his own observations. He argued that he was interested in studying human sexual behavior, and wanted only hard data, not "travelers' accounts" and impressions. He was extremely critical of people who wrote such impressions.

That was no excuse, however, for me or the rest of the staff not to have taken on the responsibility of noting down these field observations. My only defense is that Kinsey would certainly have disapproved if we had done so, and he discouraged any idea we might have had of doing it. There would have been a great deal of material to record, because Kinsey was constantly observing, or thinking about what he observed. In Cuba, for example, he consented reluctantly to spend one day at Veradero Beach—one day of relaxation out of the whole two weeks. Even there his conversation, as usual, was largely about the project.

For years he had wanted to go to Europe, but the pressures of the initial research and the preparation of the *Male* and *Female* volumes absolutely precluded it. Meanwhile he got tantalizing glimpses of what awaited him there from various correspondents abroad. Chief of these was a highly articulate skilled amateur observer named R.J., a salesman who lived in Italy but traveled frequently in Europe and North Africa on business. The long correspondence between R.J. and Kinsey, begun at the former's initiative, discloses how Prok managed to observe and record by proxy. But that was not the whole story. R.J. sent us erotic materials of all kinds for the archives, and proved to be one of our most prolific contributors, although he had no professional qualifications.

They had undoubtedly corresponded before, but the first record I find in Kinsey's file is a 1952 letter to R.J. addressed to the British Post Office in Tangier, in which Prok thanks his foreign correspondent for sending him material on the Arab countries. "I am very glad to get it at this time," he writes, "because we are getting some additional information from other people who have had experience in Arabian countries." About those countries Kinsey comments:

The information that one gets from a traveler or from persons who have lived in the country without making an actual survey from a good portion of the population must inevitably reflect their own viewpoints. For instance, we have extended notes from persons who have lived in Arabian countries for long periods of years, and find that the Arabian people are very much restrained and have practically no extra-marital sexual activity and with homosexuality practically unknown. This reflects the restricted experience of such an observer. Other persons have suggested that homosexual activity is more common than any type of non-marital heterosexual activity, and this I am inclined to believe, although I am still uncertain what the averages would be until we can get something approaching a real survey of a good sample. . . .

Certainly the things you report in your last letter are in accord with some things I have from other sources and your discussions of their attitude toward payment for sexual relations is very interesting.

Sometimes R.J. would send him an account of a case he considered unusual, but to Kinsey nothing was very unusual.

Concerning the case which seems to astonish you, [he wrote] I would note that there are some males who are quite capable of four to five and even as many as eight orgasms in a day and regularly average six or more per day. Such persons are able to function as male prostitutes more effectively than those with lesser capacities and I have known a number of male prostitutes, particularly Negro male prostitutes, who have records of this sort.

The information R.J. kept on sending was valuable for comparative purposes. About some of it contained in one letter Kinsey wrote:

It gives me the most detailed information that I have had on Vienna and the first-hand reports that we have had from Russia since the new sex laws went into effect. Both of these things are of very considerable value in our thinking. You are a penetrating observer and your account is excellent in covering the particular sorts of things that are important enough to know.

As the correspondence developed, Kinsey began to see R.J. as an even more valuable source of supply than he had thought at the beginning. Some of his reports were gone over carefully by all of us, and Kinsey asked for more detailed accounts of the exact nature of some of the cases. He inquired if R.J. wanted to undertake making fairly complete histories of some of the people he met, and told him how to do it.

We have had several of our subjects both at home and abroad gather histories of this sort and some of them have been exceedingly useful to us as a check on our own histories. Some of these persons have kept a record which is very systematic and factual and some have written the material out under the various main headings in a more literary style which sometimes shows psychologic and sociologic significance which is, missed in the bare record. . . .

You could also tell us more about the institutionalized homosexual that you find in each of the cities that you visit. I refer particularly to the presence and nature of such places as cafes, restaurants, taverns, turkish baths, street prostitution, organized prostitution in houses or in public baths, and other gathering places which are frequented by homosexuals. I refer to any possible discussion groups or friendly organizations which are limited to homosexual members. I should be particularly interested to know the relationships between the male and female homosexual groups in the area. What are the general public attitudes toward homosexual individuals and toward such institutionalized homosexual groups in these areas? What is the official attitude and how do the police actually enforce the official attitudes? Many of these things you have already reported on for some of the places you have been and a still more complete picture of these things would be very useful to us.

In spite of the difficulties that you sometimes get into with your English, you have a very good literary style, and your observations and powers of analysis are keen and very well balanced. Consequently I am suggesting this sort of thing, which we have had only a very few other persons do for us. We have depended very largely upon our own history taking for the information we have on the above matters.

From R.J.'s reports Kinsey was surprised to see that many of the things his correspondent told him about his European experiences matched the generalizations Kinsey had drawn from the American data. He had no doubt that percentages would vary in different countries, but the general trends R.J. indicated, supported by the reports of other correspondents, seemed to be surprisingly alike in Europe, Japan and other parts of the world.

Kinsey hoped R.J.'s travels would bring him to America, where they would have an opportunity to discuss matters at first hand. He was much impressed with the physiologic data R.J. had given him. This material had led him to conclude that sexual potential in most humans everywhere was about the same, with some indication of a lesser capacity only in certain groups, and perhaps slightly more in Mediterranean and African peoples, as far as greater capacity for frequent activity was concerned. He recognized, however, that this was difficult to interpret because so much of the behavior was a product of these people's lack of inhibition.

By the spring of 1955, as Kinsey noted, R.J.'s reports had become one of the longest and most important records being kept for us by any foreign correspondent, and he commented:

The diaries that we are getting from persons living in other cultures invariably illuminate the attitudes of the particular culture to these matters. They are amazingly different in regard to the way in which people make approaches to each other, as well as in the techniques of the actual contact. A series from Japan, for instance, includes such direct and such ultra-polite formalities as we never get from European or American cultures.

Soon after he wrote this letter Kinsey took the step he had so long contemplated and, with Mac, departed for Europe. The record of his adventures there is contained in the only thing approaching a journal he ever wrote. It needs to be considered with some caution. These are impressions, one must remember, in a sense "travelers' tales," which he hated so in other people, and nothing like the hard data he would have taken if he had been making an actual survey. On the other hand, they are the impressions of a man who was the most highly trained observer of sexual behavior in the world, so they have much more than the usual value. Kinsey was very far from being a simple tourist. It must be remembered, too, that the year was 1955, and the ensuing time has undoubtedly brought some changes. With all these caveats, however, the notes Kinsey took are revealing in many ways.

In the brief European autumn, Kinsey began by touring the Scandinavian countries. His stay was short but he managed to look into a variety of things. The people he talked to were much surprised to learn from him about the depth of American sexual inhibitions, the severity of American sex laws and the difficulties the Institute had encountered in its work.

Somewhat to his own amazement, Kinsey found that he was a celebrity abroad. When he arrived in Copenhagen the press gave him such wide publicity and so warm and favorable a reception was extended to him that it proved disappointingly impossible to go anywhere incognito. Nevertheless, he went out with the vice squad on two different days between 9 P.M. and 2 A.M., visiting thirty or more of the nightclubs or taverns which were known spots for both heterosexual and homosexual contacts. He was immediately offered, too, the help of the chief of police, whom he found to be extraordinarily well educated and tolerant. Since sexual activity for males over eighteen or females over sixteen was not illegal unless it involved the payment of money for specific acts, it was possible for Kinsey, with the help of the police, to talk to the boys and girls who were actually prostituting. They avoided legal difficulties by accepting the money in an indirect fashion. He also talked to a good many of the American soldiers and sailors and Scandinavians who used the night spots for sexual contacts. It would have been difficult, Kinsey said later, to learn more in the limited time he spent in the city, which showed him probably more semiorganized sex than he had ever seen in any other metropolis—thus living up to its reputation, which has recently been greatly enhanced by the repeal of the laws against pornography.

Because of the socialized approach to sex in Denmark, the vice squad men who accompanied Kinsey in Copenhagen could stop a prostitute on the street, introduce her and ask her to tell him something of her story. The police chief told Kinsey it was his job to help these girls, not hurt them—an unheard-of attitude in America. Prok was conscious that the girls were nicely dressed, neat and goodlooking, again a contrast to most of those he had seen in America.

Kinsey was much impressed with the Copenhagen police. Most were college educated, and they were also graduates of a special police school; the chief had even done graduate work. After observing police practice in America, Prok could hardly believe what he saw. He watched a forty-year-old man make obviously sexual overtures to a twenty-year-old boy, an incident to which one of the vice squad men called his attention.

"What do you do about it?" Kinsey inquired.

"Nothing," the officer told him. "They have not broken the law. As long as he is eighteen or over, and unless somebody can prove money is being paid for a specific act, it is nobody's business."

The police nevertheless did try to talk to a boy after such a contact was made, if they knew about it, to ask him whether he had been paid and how he earned his living. Judges were lenient about appearances, Kinsey learned. If a boy was sixteen and looked eighteen, allowance was made for that fact.

In Copenhagen even transvestism was permitted if the individual got special permission from the police. There was little apparent difference between the homosexual bars and nightclubs and other places, and none of the clientele were obviously homosexual. Occasionally, the police told Kinsey, there was a problem with an exhibitionist, but unless he became a nuisance he was only warned. He would be sent to prison, however, if he proved to be a real problem.

Kinsey lectured at the University of Copenhagen and at Aarhus University as well, speaking about American sex laws in particular. He asked the students how many of them would be in prison if their laws were the same as ours, and every student responded. They could scarcely believe such laws existed.

In the lecture room at Aarhus University, there was a shelf on which stood three-dimensional figures of nude males in battle and athletic poses. As he finished his lecture there, Kinsey remarked that it was an experience to have the opportunity to speak in a place where such figures could be displayed.

After one appearance before the student union at the University of Copenhagen, a lively discussion occurred between the students and Kinsey. A Danish friend who was there wrote later that he feared there had been a "linguistically ambiguous expression" used by the discussion leader which might have been misinterpreted. Expressing his gratitude for the meeting, the leader had said in English: "We accept Dr. Kinsey as a human being." Kinsey's Danish friend thought the phrase might have a devaluative meaning in English, and was quick to explain that it was a direct translation of the Danish counterpart, "a warm-hearted man." No Dane in the audience suspected that it could have meant anything else.

There were several sex research projects going on in Denmark, Kinsey discovered, ranging all the way from a man in Aarhus who was making a large-scale study of graffiti on toilet walls to an extensive abortion study at the University of Copenhagen. He paid a visit to Denmark's famous Stürup Institution, a part of the state prison system, set up for the handling of psychiatric criminal cases. This clinic was designed for those who might benefit by intensive psychiatric treatment, and only a select proportion of the criminal population ever got into it. The average Danish prison, Kinsey was told, had only a few hundred inmates in any case; the Danes multiply their prisons rather than increase their size.

Talking to their visitor about penology, the Danish authorities were appalled to learn the size of American prisons, in which more than 5,000 inmates might be held. One who was not surprised was the head of the Danish system, who had visited several American institutions, and remarked that the visit had only confirmed the wisdom of the small prison; none in Denmark held more than a thousand.

The Stürup Institution's patient-inmates numbered not only sex offenders but extreme neurotics, psychotics and a high percentage of the feebleminded. All had been taken from other institutions; there were no original commitments. Dr. Stürup himself took Kinsey to a staff conference and held it in English for his benefit. Kinsey spoke briefly to the staff members, who then discussed their castration program. Two-thirds of them were against it, and said they were not getting the results from it they had anticipated. A follow-up social program had been devised, and a good proportion of the castrates were working on the prison farm. A large number of them, Kinsey understood, were either psychotic or feebleminded, and the psychotherapy they had undergone had apparently done them little good. Sterilization was not the point of the program; reducing sex drive was the aim. Kinsey remained unimpressed by what he saw of this program.

Dr. Stürup held a reception for Kinsey in his home, inviting guests primarily connected with the prison system—psychiatrists and other clinicians. Kinsey found the institutional staff well balanced with psychologists, sociologists and a few psychiatrists, who on the whole seemed strongly antipsychoanalytic. At the party, the head of the prison system asked Kinsey what he thought of Stürup's institution. Prok tactfully replied that he considered one day's observation was not enough to pass judgment.

"Well, I don't like it," the official declared, and when Kinsey asked him what it was he didn't like, he answered succinctly, "The indefinite sentence." That required some explanation. In Denmark, it turned out, a distinction was made between psychopaths sent to prison, where the time was limited by sentence, and psychopathic internment, which was indefinite. In Stürup's institution, inmates could be kept until the staff felt they were ready to be released.

Among the other lectures Kinsey gave in Denmark was one to an association of sociologists and social workers centered around Copenhagen University, but including all the workers in the city. He had been told it was to be a round-table discussion, with about a dozen people, but when he arrived there were more than a hundred so the discussion turned into a lecture by Kinsey on methodology. It was extremely well received, but it was also the only time in Kinsey's European trip that the familiar complaint was raised about the adequacy of his sample. Kinsey noted later in his journal: "They are nowhere near as disturbed as our people. They know that it doesn't make any difference whether it is 37 or 25 per cent, but it is the trend that counts."

While he was in Copenhagen, Kinsey tracked down a scholar who he knew had amassed an immense pile of data and papers on Hans Christian Andersen. No one in Denmark, Kinsey observed, seemed to know who the scholar was, or that he possessed this comprehensive material about Denmark's literary hero. That, Kinsey noted in his journal, was "an excellent illustration of the fact that the world simply must learn that persons with homosexual histories and exclusively homosexual histories have been among the persons who were the most important. I do not share the notion that such persons are the outstanding people, but they certainly have done some of the outstanding things in the world."

In Andersen's case, there had always been hints about his homosexuality, and some knowledgeable scholars had been able to discern it by reading between the lines. But seeing the original manuscripts which the scholar possessed, Kinsey could say unequivocally that they were "straight-out homosexual stories." Of the famed Little Mermaid, Kinsey observed that she was a "mute nymph" who "cannot tell the world how she feels about anything," and similarly, Andersen could not tell the world of his own homosexual love for the people of the world, but the original manuscripts showed his feelings clearly.

The Andersen scholar took Kinsey to many places associated with the beloved writer, including his tomb, which is surrounded nearly every day of the year by children and adults, as tourists know. Few of these visitors, however, realize that there are three bodies in the grave: the attendant in the royal household with whom Andersen was in love; the attendant's wife, who knew about and honored this relationship; and Andersen himself. The attendant's family, who also knew the story, were outraged by this intimacy which continued in death. They took the original markers down and put them in another cemetery some distance away, so that no one would know.

In the course of their conversations the Andersen scholar, who was a member of the medical school faculty, told Kinsey that he had a library of probably a thousand volumes related to the man he had devoted his life to studying. Unfortunately, however, he could not publish in Denmark anything of his own about what he knew because the Danes would have been outraged. He asked Kinsey if it would be possible for him to publish anything in America, and Kinsey assured him he would try to help. The professor said he would like ultimately to deposit his documentary material in the Institute.

Kinsey loved Denmark, as he did all of Scandinavia, and made instant friends there. The people responded quickly to his personality, and he hated to leave them.

Kinsey found that the Danes tended to think of the Swedes as being more liberal than any of the other Scandinavian peoples. Their own attitudes were sometimes paradoxical, he noted. Legally, for example, there was an acceptance of homosexuality, but as Kinsey observed, "I found there was very considerable public opinion against such behavior, and it was the judgment of most of the persons with whom I talked—and I had an opportunity to talk to scores in the short time I was there—that it would do considerable damage to the social or political position of an individual if it was discovered he had a homosexual history, even though no legal action were taken." In Sweden, however, where one of the cabinet ministers had recently been found to have had sexual relations with a teen-age boy, Kinsey was assured that people would be shocked at any suggestion that he be removed from office.

As for premarital intercourse, Kinsey found that Scandinavians taught their young people not that it was wrong to have it, but that it was wrong to have it with someone they did not esteem. He heard this over and over again, from young people, from psychiatrists and doctors. The best estimate he could get from professional groups was that 90 to 95 percent of young men had premarital coitus with the girls they married. In Italy, as he learned later, the exact reverse was true.

In Norway Kinsey got no farther than Oslo. Unexpectedly he found there severe criticism of the nation's great sculptor, Adolf Gustaf Vigeland, whose work is displayed in the city's Vigeland Park and its Vigeland Museum. He learned that the sculptor had signed a contract with the Norwegian government providing that he would be supported for the rest of his life. They furnished him with marble and materials, and even provided other persons to do some of the actual sculpturing. Vigeland himself could do anything he wanted. This contract was signed when he was about thirty years old, and he lived to be seventy. The only condition was that all the artist's work should become the property of the state when he died, and so it is today one of the city's prime tourist attractions, where people come to gaze upon these vital nude figures of men and women in fantastic, sometimes almost grotesque, arrangements, spread through a beautiful park.

Kinsey asked whether the local controversy over Vigeland centered on the fact that his art was nude, or on the political situation created by his contract, or whether it was simply considered not good art today. The Norwegians looked at him in amazement for even thinking the question might concern nudity. The argument was political.

Studying Vigeland's work, Kinsey observed that a high percentage of the figures were male. Investigating further, he learned that the artist's early work had been more nearly divided between male and female, and an examination of his life provided some clues. Vigeland divorced his first wife after two years of marriage, when he was only twenty-one; they had two children. It was twenty years before he married again. Meanwhile he lived with a man who was his valet, art helper and companion, and during that period his work seemed to turn against females. The statues often depicted males wrestling against females, or animals devouring females with apparent male approval. In the Museum Kinsey discovered further that the collection of Vigeland's correspondence contained 140 letters to a single male in a one-year period, and that in the later years of the artist's life one man became the model for all of his sculpture. The inference was clear.

After leaving Norway, Kinsey found himself in England, where he divided his stay between the British Museum and a study of the street and tavern situation, interspersed with conferences with professional groups. The latter included psychiatrists, two lectures to psychiatric groups and staff at the Maudsley Hospital, a meeting with the prison commission, a day spent in one of the English prisons, and a half day with the British Commission working on a revision of the British sex laws.

The British Museum proved a puzzle to Kinsey—"a maze," he called it. He could not get used to the Museum's incredible method of arranging books by date of acquisition, not by author or title, and a cataloging system organized by subject matter but not by author, filed according to the cataloger's decision as to the importance of a particular item. He was equally surprised to find that it was against the rules of the trustees to buy anything that smacked of sex. The job of the curators appeared to be, in part, to persuade private persons to donate such items. They got around the rule against sex by this method, and by the addition of a further rule passed by the trustees that once something was offered to the Museum it could not be refused, nor could anything be thrown away. Kinsey observed of the collection, with some disgust: "There is lots of junk and lots of it without dates or any other data, so that it is impossible to use. When I asked what good it was without any other data, they said they couldn't throw it away because it was against the rules."

From the Institute's standpoint, nevertheless, there were a good many things in the Museum to interest Kinsey, particularly a collection of red figured pottery, some depicting satyrs in erection. "One way of finding anything erotic in the British Museum," Kinsey observed wryly, "is to look for anything upside-down or turned backwards. They are exceedingly reticent about showing anything, although the curators themselves are not reticent in talking about erotic items."

The Museum was once believed to have an excellent collection of Japanese erotic scrolls, but apparently Queen Victoria heard about them and had them destroyed. At the time of Kinsey's visit there had been a recent court ruling that anyone showing obscene material was in fact distributing it, consequently the Museum staff was seriously concerned about its collection.

Kinsey was hopeful that the Museum's difficulty in making erotic acquisitions might enable him to acquire for the Institute library a prized item, the diaries of Aleister Crowley. "We stand a fifty-fifty chance of getting them," Kinsey noted. Crowley was called by Lord Douglas the wickedest man who ever lived, and his sexual history alone was enough to earn him the title he gloried in—"The Beast." Kinsey termed him "the most prominent fraud who ever lived," and recalled that George Sylvester Viereck had once told him in New York that Crowley worked for him as a spy for Germany during the First World War. "But it is difficult to believe," Kinsey observes, "that he ever worked for anybody but himself." Nevertheless, it was precisely this connection, since Crowley was in fact a spy, that resulted in a five-year prison sentence for Viereck. Crowley fled America but was seized in England, where he was faced with a treason trial. He managed to persuade the court that in reality he had been feeding false stories to Germany and was helping British interests all the time.

Crowley kept a diary up to his death, although Kinsey thought it would be difficult to know what was true about him, even in his diary. Two weeks after Kinsey tracked down these papers in England, he found himself in the "temple" that "The Beast" had founded, in Sicily. The temple was a kind of hut divided into two rooms, one the "temple room" and the other a bedroom. There he established the cult of which he was the Great God—the "Great Beast," as he called himself. His curious magnetism drew people from all over the world, who came, gave him their money and became his sexual slaves. Some of these women left their husbands to enter the temple. There were never more than fifteen or twenty people in the cult at any one time, and the total number probably did not exceed forty in the three or four years it flourished.

The Great Beast and his followers were against any kind of religion, in any form, except their own. They held group orgies as a part of their ritual, and included in them the small children the women had brought with them. The disciples were so completely under the domination of Crowley that when they displeased him, he would command them to strip off their clothing and climb over the rugged hillside to a cave where they would live until he deigned to let them come back.

After Crowley's death, the disciples separated into rival black and white magic groups, each one trying to exterminate the other. It was said, without any proof, that the firing of Shepheard's Hotel in Cairo was the work of a "white magic" follower who believed that an important member of the "black magic" group was staying there at the time.

The temple, as Kinsey discovered when he visited it, was presently owned by two brothers who hated each other. They had built a solid wall down the center of the place, and each part of the house had to be rented separately. The walls inside were still painted in British Oriental colors, and were covered with the "most open" (as Kinsey put it) sexual action pictures, which the Crowleyites claimed were good art; Kinsey dismissed them as very crude.

One door in the house had painted on it six scenes of Tibetan temples and the Himalaya Mountains, recalling Crowley's legendary climbing exploits there, which Kinsey doubted had ever occurred. The remainder of the paintings were life-size representations of sexual activity, both homosexual and heterosexual, singly, doubly and in groups, including children. There were also plentiful graffiti, in Crowley's handwriting, all lauding the Great Beast.

Crowley was a drug addict, in the bargain. The doses he took of cocaine and heroin are as unbelievable as his alleged sexual exploits. He fled to North Africa and tried to cut himself off from drugs, according to his diary, but eventually he died of his addiction, although by that time he was seventy-three years old. Kinsey thought Crowley a brilliant writer, and cited his translation from the Arabic of the erotic classic *The Scented Garden* (more often translated as *Perfumed* in other renderings), and a later original work, *White Stains,* as proof.

From his pursuit of the exotic Crowley diaries Kinsey turned to an examination of the famous English prison Wormwood Scrubs. He found this institution like nothing he had known in the United States. For example, the professional staff were the only ones with authority to invite professional visitors. The warden, called the governor, could not do so except by recommendation to the trustees, and then by obtaining their permission. He lacked other powers commonly held by American wardens. Punishment could be meted out only after a trial in the institution, or by an outside court, during which the prisoner was represented by counsel and a record made of the trial. The warden had some latitude, however, in the removal of privileges. Punishment might involve confinement, but never to a special solitary unit, as in America. There were no bars and the cells had doors.

The cell itself was considered the prisoner's private home, where he was allowed to accumulate all kinds of personal property. Cells were either single or triple, and there were, in addition, a few dormitories. Solitary confinement meant simply confinement to the prisoner's room.

Kinsey learned that the prison practiced corporal punishment, but as they told him, "never more than twenty lashes on his bare back." That confirmed something Kinsey had observed in London— the incredible number of advertisements by sadomasochists and the quantity of sadomasochistic houses. Kinsey quoted a few of their ads: "Massage parlor with vigorous massage," "English governess with firm discipline," and similar lures. "There is no doubt about the relationship of sado-masochism and sex in young boys," Kinsey observed in his journal. "This appears in the literature and is confirmed by what I have picked up now."

The physical plan of Wormwood Scrubs was poor, Kinsey concluded, but he thought highly of the clinical staff, which consisted of several psychiatrists, a psychologist and social workers. This staff appeared to be in control, to a considerable extent. The Prison Commission stood at the top of the hierarchy, and the governor could not propose punishment until his recommendation had been approved by the clinical staff, which also had the power to advise release for many reasons other than lack of guilt, and could have a man moved from one job to another. "Assignment, they say, is a matter of therapy and not a need in the institution itself; this may or may not be true," Kinsey noted.

As he toured the prison, he found all the men working at hard labor. He was told they were paid, and were working at specific trades, such as toolmaking, wood turning and foundry work. As he remarked, "They were working in such places as we would never ordinarily allow dangerous criminals to work." He was further astounded to find that the prisoners could take their tools back to their cells. The reason for such permissiveness, he thought, lay in the character of the men themselves, so unlike American prisoners:

I have never seen such meek and subdued persons in any American prison. Their eyes never left their work, and if they did stray and catch the eye of an attendant, they immediately saluted and stood at attention. They always addressed everyone as "sir."

One of the most amazing things was to stand and watch them in their canteen. The line outside the canteen was quite long, yet everybody was absolutely quiet, so different from the horse-play common to American prisons. I asked if they were forbidden to speak, and my guide said no, that this was just a part of the British character. I said that was nonsense. The clinicians would like to have you believe it is their own voluntary way of curbing themselves.

I had a chance to listen in on a group being indoctrinated but apparently my presence bothered the man in charge and he mumbled and stumbled in his speech, and I felt that I had better not stay. Before I left, however, he began with, "You are now criminals, you have been judged criminals, and you will have to bear this for the rest of your lives. You will have to work as hard as you have ever worked, and if you do not learn this, you will have to spend the rest of your days at Dartmoor."

Kinsey thought the prison clinicians kindly, not psychoanalytically oriented, and tolerant of everything sexual. Their work was confined to a select group; only about a third of the prisoners got any therapy. The head of the prison board told Kinsey that there was no therapy at all in the other institutions, or at least very little, and Kinsey's conversations with prisoners who had been in these prisons confirmed this.

The prison work program was considered part of the therapy. Kinsey was told that all men in British prisons were on full-time work for six days a week—a sharp contrast to San Quentin, for example, where he had found that 18 to 22 percent of the men did not have any work to do, and others worked only a few hours for a few days each week.

On the job at Wormwood, if men wanted to go to the toilet, they had to raise a hand, like children in school, and get permission from the supervisor. This was to prevent more than one man from being in the toilet at one time. Kinsey observed that the men were extremely quiet as they worked, and he was told that was because they were paid on a piecework basis, and if they talked they would not make as much money. Kinsey didn't believe it; he attributed it to the strong indoctrination and discipline process when they came into the institution.

As for the sex problem, in which Kinsey was most interested, he was told that masturbation was plentiful—hardly surprising, since that was a universal phenomenon—and the clinicians assured him they did not object. If the governor objected, they said, it would do him no good because he had no authority on the subject. It was their business, the clinicians said.

Kinsey was permitted to sit in on a group therapy meeting in a dormitory. A young psychiatrist had done a good job of getting the prisoners to talk freely, Kinsey noted, partly because he had convinced them that nothing they said would get on their records no matter what it was. The group, who lived together in the dormitory, seemed eager to "spill everything." To start the session and break the ice, the chief psychiatrist asked the men to tell what they were in for. It was, as Kinsey said, "a rather pitiful performance." There was a minister who said he had sinned all his life; he was in for homosexual contact with boys. Kinsey felt that he and the others were telling the truth, because the psychiatrist asked only a few additional questions, indicating that he already knew the story.

Eventually the discussion came around to what the prisoners did to take care of their sexual needs in prison. The clinicians had previously told Kinsey the men had so much work to do that this was not a problem. In the group, however, many said they masturbated—so many that Kinsey was moved to observe, "I have never seen such high rates." Some also admitted to homosexuality.

A good many of these men were no more than eighteen, although there were some around forty. About two-thirds had done time at other English prisons. Kinsey got them to compare institutions, and they said the kind of therapy they had been getting in the group and from the clinicians was something they had never experienced elsewhere.

The primary discussion in the group centered around a meeting the dormitory inmates had held the night before to consider the case of two of the men who were developing a homosexual interest in each other. One was about forty-five, the other not quite twenty. The group concluded that they wanted to beat up the two men, but they were afraid of the older man, who was big and strong. According to the Kinsey scale, this man had been a 2 but now was a 6. He freely admitted in the group that he was interested in the boy. But the others were also inhibited from giving him the beating they apparently wanted to administer because the boy refused to make a statement that he resented the other man's approaches.

Kinsey then talked to the group and gave them what he called "a condensed version" of his beliefs about the adjustment that had to be made in prisons, and the psychological and physiological needs for emotional release. The psychiatrists, he thought, seemed to egg him on, and Kinsey appeared to be happy "about the things we gave the men to think about," as he wrote later, and added: "I have never met a group of clinicians who were more acceptant of these things and who really wanted to get to the bottom of these questions." An obstacle to solving emotional problems was that heterosexual contact was extremely restricted; the prisoners had very few opportunities even for visits from wives or families.

"The most shocking thing about the institutions," Kinsey wrote later, "was that 30 per cent of [the prisoners] were in on sex charges, and of these the highest incidence, 60 per cent, were in for homosexuality." Higher penalties were being given on such charges than for forced rape. Some men had done as much as six years on a homosexual charge. Kinsey concluded: "There isn't any doubt of it from all other quarters that England has become utterly rabid on the homosexual question. So much in contrast to Norway." (Yet it was England, only a decade later, that broke away from its past and revised its laws on homosexuality.)

The Prison Commission, which had been so helpful in arranging Kinsey's visit to Wormwood Scrubs, turned up to hear both of his lectures at Maudsley Hospital. Sir Lionel Fox, then head of the Commission, was so enthusiastic that he declared the lectures must be put into print. He asked Kinsey to come back to England and go through every one of the English prisons and make an assessment of them.

"I have never had such an ovation from any professional group," Kinsey wrote later of these lectures at Maudsley Hospital. "They were not only listening but were absorbed in the lecture." As a result, he was asked to meet with the government commission working on the sex law problem. He did so, discussing such topics as prostitution and the age of consent.

While he was in London, Kinsey had lunch with Oscar Wilde's son, Vyvyan Holland, whom he described as "rather a sober and dullish businessman." Present also at the luncheon was a psychiatrist, "with a psychoanalytic slant of a definite Freudian cast," as Kinsey put it. One can only imagine Holland's reaction when Kinsey baited the psychiatrist by, as he explained, trying "to get him to extend this Freudian theory to rabbits, etc." Kinsey recalled that the psychiatrist was very much surprised, which one could hardly doubt, but he was "apparently appreciative of the new ideas we planted in his head."

Guided by a British friend, Kinsey and his wife toured Piccadilly Circus and Soho on a Saturday night. In those days, before prostitutes were mostly driven off the streets, it was a scene unique in both Europe and America. Kinsey thought he had never seen so much blatant sexual behavior. He estimated perhaps a thousand prostitutes in the area between 8 P.M. and 3 A.M. Although it was against the law to solicit, they were soliciting nonetheless in the most aggressive way, both males and females. A policeman had no right to arrest anyone unless there was a complaint, and Kinsey saw only one arrest.

During his stay in England, unlike most visiting Americans Kinsey was not much impressed by pub life, which of course is hardly surprising considering his own life style. He found the pubs "amazingly small," and the first time he walked into one he saw an American whom he recognized as a homosexual model whose history he had taken in New York. They carefully avoided each other. In general, Kinsey thought, the pubs were "a very dull sort of place."

Kinsey reported that the English prostitutes seemed surprisingly trim and neat by comparison with girls in other countries. It was only when he got away from the center of things that he saw "the old worn-out hags," and in the lowest-level places, the "old, farm stock women" common in every country.

At the London Zoological Gardens, Kinsey spent some time with the curator, who discussed animal sex behavior with him, and the two compared notes. On the whole, Kinsey wrote later about his British tour, "I am quite convinced that we inherited a lot of our [Puritan] attitudes from our English forebears."

After England, Kinsey proceeded to France, where everything went wrong for him as far as his lecturing was concerned. The lecture had been arranged by his French publisher, who had been warned in advance that the purpose was *not* to sell books. Consequently Kinsey was scheduled to speak to the country's oldest professional medical group, and the president of this organization, accompanied by a swarm of reporters, met him at the airport. Kinsey was favorably impressed by the French press: "The reporters were pretty decent and got the story pretty straight."

The head of the medical society was a gracious host who gave Kinsey a small reception at his home before the lecture. But then the trouble began. It was a Monday, which happened to be a holiday, and Tuesday was to be another nonworking day, so that most of the professional people had left Paris to enjoy a long weekend. The man who had done the French translation of the books was to translate the lecture sentence by sentence, and at the airport he had done well enough with the reporters. But at the lecture itself he could not keep up. One of the publisher's editors, who was present, came to the rescue. His English was so good that halfway through he repeated a sentence in English instead of translating. The speech was about concepts of normality and abnormality, including biologic and sociologic concepts.

Kinsey had few kind words to say for the French police, whom he found a sharp contrast to the British bobbies. He was convinced that they showed considerable animosity toward Americans, particularly those arrested on homosexual charges. Kinsey thought the French were hypocrites about homosexuality, exhibiting much public disdain toward it while at the same time they exalted Gide and Cocteau. Everything, Kinsey noted, was done to honor women. He observed that a very high proportion of shops on the streets were for women's wear—the opposite of what he would see later in Rome.

Kinsey recorded Mac's remark at the end of three days in Paris: "I get the feeling that the adoration of the female is a very selfish thing here. It's what the female means for them. She exists for the male, and not as an equal." Women's Liberation could scarcely have put it better.

Making a dutiful visit to the Folies Bergères, Kinsey was bored by it, although he admired the elaborate spectacle and approved its frank and open sexual references. He noted, however, that the scene which amused the audience most had only a suggestion of sex in it.

After his short stay in Paris Kinsey went on to Italy, which he explored for three weeks—"little enough," as he said later, "but it gave me time for first-hand exploration and observation." He found it a complete contrast to everything else he had seen. "It is a man's country," he wrote, "and interestingly enough, I talked to a good many women who said they did not resent it."

Kinsey found sexual attitudes much the same in Italy as in Latin American countries, and as he would later observe them in Spain. Italians did not have intercourse with "decent" girls before marriage, but with many other girls, including prostitutes. Families kept their daughters locked up at night. At the lower levels it was not uncommon, he was told, for a girl to refuse intercourse before marriage, and her fiancé would not think of asking her, but she might prostitute to raise money for her trousseau, to no one's dismay. In Italy, he wrote, "the notion that one has sexual activity is accepted and there is a minimum of interference for males."

In Rome Kinsey saw practically no streetwalking, but he supposed that was because of the number of houses of prostitution. Some houses in Naples, as he discovered, employed as many as 150 girls. Brothels had been pushed back into the smaller houses and off the main streets so the tourists wouldn't see them.

The typical whorehouse in Rome, Kinsey noted, had a waiting room with a bench around the wall for the men to sit on, as well as individual chairs. The bedrooms were in the recesses of the house, or upstairs, and when the girls were not occupied with a man they would come down and exhibit themselves. In the best houses the girls had on rather elaborate clothing; in the average ones they wore very little; and in the poorest they were down to a small triangle.

"I saw as many as seven girls in one house who were unemployed," Kinsey wrote, "with twenty to thirty males sitting around. Usually the madam sat at a table or perhaps on a raised platform at one end of the room, and she would chant from time to time, 'There are two (or three, or seven, as the case might be) girls available.' In one place the madam would remain silent for a time after this announcement, and then yell suddenly, 'Come on, boys, let's go.' Sometimes she added, 'Why don't you go to the Colosseum or the

Janiculum Hills?' " Kinsey estimated that about 80 percent of the men who came into the houses went to bed with a girl.

In contrast to the Cuban houses Kinsey had seen, no one made any physical attempt to keep a man there until he was ready to do business. In fact, the girls hardly talked to the men. Some males apparently visited a string of houses and did not have intercourse in any of them. No attention was paid to men who came to erection and then masturbated mildly. Interestingly, some homosexual males found the brothel areas good cruising places.

Prices were regulated for each house, and in those preinflation days Kinsey found that the cheapest fee was twenty-five cents, on a scale going up to seventy-five cents—about as cheap as he had ever recorded. The men who went upstairs came down, stopped at the desk and paid the madam as they went out. Kinsey estimated the average age of the customers at between twenty and twenty-five, with some in their thirties and occasionally an older man, along with quite a few teen-agers.

After France, where there was always an undercurrent of excitement about the female and sexual activity with her, Kinsey found Italy just the opposite. "I have never seen males who were less interested where females were concerned," he wrote, "even those who went off with the girls." The girls themselves, for the most part, were "rather sloppy, fattish Southern Italians," he wrote, "nowhere near as attractive as the London girls or the 'homey' girls in Scandinavia." The most attractive, apparently, were those who came from Turin or thereabouts, and they were the ones who were mostly nude.

In Naples one night, Kinsey talked to a girl from Turin. It was a rainy evening and the house was nearly empty; the girl complained that she had had only nine men that night and could not live on this kind of trade. Kinsey had already discovered that one of the things distinguishing cheap houses from the better ones was that the former took about five minutes per man, and the better ones about ten minutes. Of the girl from Turin, Kinsey wrote: "I have never seen any sex machine who had less emotion for the Southern Italian male than she did."

While he was in Rome Kinsey talked with Alberto Moravia, the novelist, for several hours. Moravia had plans to make a survey of sex in Italy, in partnership with a London attorney, a project inspired by Kinsey's study. The writer felt that neither he nor anyone else, however, would have much luck getting Italians to give case histories. Kinsey had a different view. "What I think," he wrote later, "is that none of them have the guts to do it, and I think what they will do is to go to a bunch of priests, businessmen and other people and get their impressions." Kinsey encouraged Moravia to carry out his plan, but told him he thought it would be too bad if they did not do it on the basis of case histories.

As to sexual behavior, Kinsey found mouth-genital contact rather uncommon in Italy among the prostitutes. Anal intercourse was even more rare. He observed a good deal of male prostitution and was told frequently that every male had homosexual activity, even married men, as well as preadolescent and adolescent boys, although it was pointed out that one would seldom find an exclusively homosexual male.

It was perfectly apparent to him, Kinsey noted later, that most of the males he saw looking for sex would have accepted it from either males or females; the only difference was that they would be paid for it if they were brought to climax by males, and would pay for it themselves if females accomplished it. Consequently, a man might look for males first, then go out and have sex with a girl, since the girl would cost less than he had been paid by the male, and he would make a slight profit. As a small experimental project Kinsey began collecting histories of southern Italian males, with the help of an Italian researcher.

At the time Kinsey was in Rome, the Colosseum was the center for sexual activity. Its dark passageways, innumerable niches and corners made it an ideal place. There was an altar at one end, with a perpetual candle burning in memory of the martyrs, and on the first night Kinsey was there it happened to be a holy night. He witnessed the weird spectacle of people holding services at the altar while unrestrained sex was going on all around them. Kinsey saw more than thirty couples in every kind of sexual encounter, from petting to intercourse.

Many different kinds of people were cruising the Colosseum— prostitutes, homosexuals and those looking for a variety of sexual contacts. The most notable thing about it, Kinsey thought, was the absence of violence, which could be expected in a similar American scene.

Another part of Rome where there appeared to be much sexual activity was the Spanish Steps, then a homosexual center, although it was traditionally a cruising place for both heterosexual and homosexual contacts. During the Marian Year, the Vatican had insisted that girl prostitutes be removed from the Steps by police because they wore nothing beneath their dresses, and anyone looking up from below could see their genitals. Young homosexuals around the Steps seemed older to Kinsey than the Colosseum inhabitants; they appeared to range between sixteen and twenty, while at the Colosseum there were many as young as thirteen or fourteen. A notorious movie house near the ruins provided a place for older men wanting to make contacts. Inspecting it on a Saturday evening, Kinsey found the house packed, and a constant stream of people going in and out of the rest room, where the assignations were made. Both males and females were using the same facility.

On a balmy night, Kinsey reported, the fields around Rome were filled with copulating couples, both heterosexual and homosexual. The police were making no attempt to restrict this traffic, even though money was involved in perhaps as much as 95 percent of the cases.

In Naples Kinsey had the valuable services of his knowledgeable friend R.J. They purposely chose a rainy night to visit the houses of prostitution, as Kinsey usually did if it was possible, because a slow night meant more opportunity to talk to the girls and the madams. Since it was an extremely quiet evening, they had an exceptional chance to carry on conversations, R.J. acting as interpreter where it was necessary. But then, in order to get out of the house without doing any business, R.J. asked for what he thought would be impossible, a thirteen-year-old girl. The madam did not even seem surprised; she let it be known that girls of almost any age were available, and the investigators had to think of another excuse.

Perhaps the most exotic place for sexual activity that Kinsey found anywhere in Italy was on the Tiber in Rome, where several houseboats operated as restaurants during dining hours but were centers later in the evening for male homosexual prostitution.

It was widely believed by many of the Italian experts Kinsey talked to that southern Italy was the most homosexual place in the world. Prok doubted it. He believed it was surpassed by several countries in the Middle and Far East. However, there was no doubt, he concluded, that the glorification of the male reached an extreme in Italy. Certainly sex seemed to be a primary commodity in Naples, among both males and females.

I don't suppose that we spoke to any person of any age, male or female, in the city who didn't promptly offer to find sexual relations for us. Several girls came out of a house in a back alley and hung on to our hands, begging for money, and when we came to a cross-alley, a woman came out and got rid of the girls, then we had her for two or three blocks. It was the same way with boys, who offered to find anything for us. Any child could tell you where the nearest house of prostitution was, and it was never very far away.

An older male offered to take him to a sexual exhibition in Naples, but this was the only place in Italy where he had such an offer.

Later, when he was in Spain and Portugal, Kinsey found that males tried to hide any appearance of having genitalia. In Italy, however, there was obvious pride in them, and on the average they were large. Italian tailors, he discovered, made a practice of making extra room for them in the pants they cut, so that it came near to being a pocket. Italian men told Kinsey they did not like American-style jockey shorts because they brought the genitalia up into the crotch.

This difference in male attitudes toward the genitals Kinsey had first observed in Cuba, where he saw boys openly touching their sexual parts, in contrast to America, where male children are taught from an early age not to do such a thing. Touching was even more common in southern Italy, where Kinsey saw men in public unzip their pants and reach in and adjust their genitalia, then zip up again. Even well-dressed businessmen did this in the middle of the day in Naples, and no one paid any attention. At times he even saw these same businessmen stroking their penises through their clothing when they had a sudden erection.

Another prime area of sexual activity in Naples was its famous Galleria, where Kinsey found it was possible to observe any number of people out hunting for sex at any hour of the day or night. Young boys masturbated and no one paid any attention, which proved once more, Kinsey wrote, "what a hysterical fear we have acquired of male genitals."

There were both male and female prostitutes in the Galleria. One girl was completely nude to the waist; she had on a gauzy, thin shawl which kept slipping off. Kinsey saw a young, slender boy of twenty or so who was doing a big business with GIs, sailors and older Italian men. There were roving smaller children who would begin by offering to take the visitor to girls, and if that did not work, they would offer boys, their younger or older brothers, and finally themselves. Gangs of young adolescent boys swarmed on American sailors.

The public toilets often were underground, in parks and at railroad stations, and there Kinsey saw men from thirteen to fifty exhibiting and indicating they were ready for sexual contact. Kinsey and his guide saw a boy with an erection who followed them for several blocks until they made it clear that they were not interested.

Sometimes it was difficult to discourage these supplicants. One older male came up two or three times, and after being rebuffed each time, said rather plaintively, "But I have to come to orgasm, and if you are too tired now, I can see you at 2 A.M." Even so, most of the men could not offer sex free; it would have lowered their status. Kinsey surmised this might be a cultural holdover from their Greek and Phoenician backgrounds.

Kinsey thought the Neapolitans very warmhearted. He had not been in the city more than twenty-four hours before the mayor sent his chief aide to see him, giving him an official welcome and offering any facility he desired. When he asked specifically about getting a record of sexual material, the aide said, "Of course."

I should make it clear, I think, that Kinsey was not insensitive to the other aspects of life in Italian cities. His journal speaks often of the poverty in Naples and in other parts of Italy. He was well aware that part of the abundant sexuality directed toward him and any other obvious American was motivated by the desperate need for money. On the other hand, he believed they were very sexual people, in any case, and suspected that they had an extremely high sex outlet, perhaps higher than in any other culture he had seen. Only in the highest-level families was there the strict guarding of women he saw in Spain and the Latin American countries.

In every way Naples seemed more uninhibited than Rome to Kinsey, and he was fascinated with the aspects of sexuality he saw on every hand the longer he stayed. It was noteworthy, he said, that boys in Rome who brought letters up to the hotel rooms were satisfied with a tip, but in Naples they might sit down and make it clear they would be glad to stay longer for other purposes.

Moving over to Sicily, a difficult place to investigate, Kinsey had the help of a Roman friend, Fosco Maraini, whose wife was a native Sicilian and was able to make the necessary contacts. Maraini took him one day to three small fishing villages, as poverty-stricken as any Kinsey had seen. He was shown both the poorest and the better homes, and finally a twenty-one-year-old boy, who didn't look seventeen, escorted them to a fishing boat. When they reached the shore where it was beached, a gang of boys gathered around. One handsome thirteen-year-old looked at their guide, smiled and instantly came to erection, throwing his arms around a boy standing close to him. He followed Kinsey's little party around for several hours, getting as close as he could and always smiling. "It was interesting," Kinsey wrote, "that even in this remote place we were still getting the same picture."

Leaving Palermo, the Kinseys went southward, passing through the town of Catania before reaching Taormina. Of Catania Kinsey observed, "All you have to do is give one look at it and see that it is teeming with sex." The party did not remain there long enough, however, for Kinsey to do any detailed observation.

In Taormina Kinsey found the atmosphere "very Greek," and noted that it was discovered years ago by other Europeans as an ideal spot for obtaining homosexual relations. This discovery was made as early as the 1860s and 1870s by German artists and nobility. One of them, the Baron von Glieden, did a prodigious amount of nude photography there, mostly males, during the eighties and nineties; some of this work was already in the Institute archives, but Kinsey shipped home another quantity while he was there.

It took him less than twenty-four hours to locate the entire collection, through a street vendor. Originally there had been about 10,000 negatives, but the Fascists in the early 1940s decided the pictures were giving Italy a bad reputation and destroyed 7,000 of them. There was, however, a complete set of prints remaining. The man who presently owned the collection, Kinsey found, had been the baron's darkroom man; he was now in his seventies.

Unlike the exuberant Neapolitans, the inhabitants of Sicily seemed a stately, rather reserved group to Kinsey. Sexual approaches appeared almost courtly, and there was a polite reserve about refusals. The town of Taormina was filled with older men who had been photographed as boys by the baron, and they were full of stories about him. Kinsey saw no purveyors of erotica in Sicily, however. As he said, "When sex is so free, you do not have this sort of thing."

Leaving Italy and Sicily, Kinsey ended his tour with stops in Portugal and Spain, where he saw much less to interest him. He found Spaniards a totally different people, physically as well as in other ways. "Their buttocks," he observed, "are a totally different shape and, obviously, genitalia were being held up by inner clothing to prevent anyone's noticing them. They are a rather tight-lipped people; what you see in an El Greco painting is the epitomization of the Spanish male."

Kinsey saw the Spaniards as silent, dull, beaten and church-oppressed. As travelers almost invariably do, he found Barcelona freer and livelier than Madrid, and sex much more evident there. "If I had been there longer and had people to guide me, I could have found all the hypocrisy that goes with the suppression," he wrote. He did not see much streetwalking in Barcelona, but a great deal of pickups in the taverns. There appeared to be no male prostitution in the streets. Most of the sex he found on the waterfront, where American sailors and soldiers were the game, but there were also pimps on the street elsewhere who reminded Kinsey of the same breed in Havana. Kinsey succeeded in investigating one house, which was set up more or less on the Italian pattern. While censorship had curbed the more public sale of pornography, Kinsey found that he was able to buy "a tremendous lot" of sex books in Barcelona.

Kinsey did not get much sexual information in Madrid, and spent most of his time in the Prado. He was a few years too early. Today many of the big hotels, even the most luxurious, have prostitutes openly inhabiting their lobbies and cocktail lounges. And in Barcelona, if he were able to return, he would find the notorious waterfront red light district, the Barrio, famous among sailors for a century, virtually a ghost district, its girls driven to the cafés in the new high-rise apartment buildings, and to those on the side streets, where the blackened window separates their haunts from the clear-windowed gathering places which a respectable woman may enter if she is accompanied by a man.

In Portugal Kinsey noted that once more the people had a different physical structure—long-waisted, with rounded, low buttocks. He lamented that he did not get much material about sex in this "priest-ridden country." When he asked a taxi driver about homosexuality, the man replied that there was none. "Men are men in Portugal," he said. Kinsey noted, "A grand piece of nonsense."

Back home again, with satisfying memories, there was nothing remaining but to write his thank-you notes and dictate the journal from which these observations have been drawn. He expressed particular gratitude to R.J. for his help.

You probably need no reassurance that the help you gave us was of prime importance in those days that we were together, and that sort of help which I got practically everywhere was the thing that made the trip so profitable. I had not anticipated that I could learn so much more about sex at this stage of our research as I did in those seven weeks in Europe.

I esteem your quick thinking and excellent capacity for handling things socially. You have, as has been evident in the long reports you have been giving us, a rare capacity to analyze the factors that are involved in a situation, and to see the significance of what has happened.

Two weeks later, writing again to R.J., Kinsey was still full of the trip.

Let me tell you again how much I enjoyed, personally, the time with you. You may always feel that you added to my education, both as to the behavior of an experienced person like yourself and its effectiveness in a city like Naples. I am very anxious to get back to Naples for a longer stay. This is matched by my interest in getting back to Copenhagen where I shall hope to stay long enough to utilize the suggestions and contacts you have already offered.

And again, three months later: "The three highest spots of my trip last fall were Copenhagen, Naples with you, and Taormina with an equally skilled observer."

To Fosco Maraini, his gratitude was warm and his nostalgia the same.

Your intelligent understanding of some of the anthropological problems that lay back of our study and your personal acquaintance with the situation in

Sicily were very valuable. Of all the places where we were in Europe this last year, Southern Italy and Scandinavia are the two areas I want to go back to. Both of them are remarkably freer in their acceptance of sex than anything in our Anglo-American culture but Italy is as far from Scandinavia as the two poles.

There was a final estimate of the trip in a letter to Hugo Gernsback, the editor of *International Sexology* magazine:

Seven weeks in Europe gave me more new information on sex than I thought possible to acquire in that time. Of course, there wasn't time enough to do everything and I did not begin to get to the places that were important. I had to choose the opportunities that seemed most valuable from the standpoint of the problems we are immediately studying.

It had been an eye-opening experience for Kinsey, and he longed to go back and examine this new world of sexuality which had opened before him. The last letter he wrote to R.J., only a few weeks before his death, ended wistfully: "There is no chance of my getting to Europe this year, but when health and particularly the publishing program allow, certainly I should like to get back there again."

I can only regret that Kinsey did not live to spend more time in Europe, and in Japan, his unfulfilled hope. Then we might have had more than the surface impressions he brought back in 1955, perceptive though they may be, and at least a start might have been made toward understanding the sexual behavior of the human male and female in other cultures, where no full-scale investigations have yet been made that begin to compare with Kinsey's in America.

Europe was Kinsey's swan song. He came home to die.

CHAPTER

XXVI

LAST DAYS

TOWARD THE END, Kinsey appeared to be unusually conscious of death. Shortly after the noted psychoanalyst Karen Horney died, Tripp was having dinner with Kinsey in New York and asked him during their conversation if he had known that Dr. Horney had died the week before.

Kinsey showed concern and surprise. "She *did?*" he exclaimed, with great interest. "Oh, I didn't know." Clearly he was momentarily affected by the death of a woman whom he had never met, and for whose work he had scant respect. One surmises that the possibility of his own death must have been on his mind; it is the only way I can account for so untypical a reaction.

He was not worried about himself, however. What concerned him was the future of the Institute, even though he did not believe in making any plans for it. Early in 1956 he said to Tripp, "You know, I'm worried about the Institute, and I don't mean just the money to keep it going. If I should die, there's something to be said for and something against every choice that could be made of a man to succeed me." Worried or not, he never made a will or any other provision.

Talking to him a little later, with this possibility in mind, Tripp observed, "Of course now that you're famous, somebody certainly will want to write your biography."

431

"Nonsense!" Kinsey said firmly. "The progress of science depends upon knowledge. It has nothing to do with personalities."

He would, I am sure, have hated this book, not for anything it says about him but because he would have thought me wrong to take valuable time from scientific pursuits and waste it on the story of his life, which he would have considered irrelevant.

Somehow Kinsey seemed unable to think of life going on without him, in terms of what other people might do. In June 1956, when it was obvious that he was seriously ill, I tried to talk to him about the Institute's future, but he refused absolutely to discuss it. "When I'm dead, I'm dead," he said flatly. "I have no influence nor any effect whatever on what happens when I'm gone."

While he was alive, however, and in spite of what he had said to Tripp, he *was* deeply concerned about finding the money to keep the Institute in existence. It had become a continuing nightmare for him after the withdrawal of the Rockefeller support, and as he neared the end he was almost desperate about it.

The Institute, of course, had always been in need of money, increasingly so as the mass of data accumulated, waiting to be analyzed. The Rockefeller money, although it kept us alive, had never been enough, and as it proved, Kinsey was a total failure at fund raising. Friends of the Institute had arranged for him to meet rich people who might help us, but he was utterly unable to relate to them in any positive way—this man who had persuaded thousands of people to tell him about their sex lives. When it came to persuading people to give up their money, he was paralyzed. Every experience in fund raising was an agonizing one for him, because he hated to be turned down or to appear self-seeking.

He was well enough aware of the need. He dreamed of getting the research endowed, so that we would not have to be dependent on yearly grants, but that meant getting an extremely large gift from a very rich man. We talked about possibilities, ranging from the more obvious ones to the idea of approaching a rich homosexual, since the research had thrown a sympathetic light on homosexuality, or perhaps a millionaire who was having serious marital or sexual problems, or even a common or garden variety philanthropist who might have a penchant for giving money to projects not in the usual pattern. But whenever he had a chance to talk to a possible benefactor, Kinsey, ordinarily one of the great persuaders of his time, simply froze up and could not ask for money.

This inability had its roots, no doubt, in his difficulty in relating to upper-upper-level people—a problem, I must admit, that I shared with him. We found it more difficult to take their histories than others. It was their arrogance, whether concealed or visible, their complete egocentrism that raised the barriers between us.

There was another reason, too, for Kinsey's difficulty. He lived in a world as self-absorbed and exclusive as that of the rich, and this sometimes made communication almost impossible. Except for his peripheral interests such as gardening and music, Kinsey's world was bounded by the limits of the project. He neither knew nor cared, nor had time to think about, what was going on in other spheres of human affairs, unless they were events of such magnitude that they could not be ignored.

I remember talking to him late one night after he had had dinner with Morris Ernst, his lawyer in New York. Describing the evening, he remarked that a famous actress had sat next to him. It was not hard for him to remember her name, but he had no idea who she was until I told him. Yet he came to know a good many notables in the theater before he died, and took their histories as well.

With people at the top Kinsey felt that he was not in control, as he was with everyone else, and I think that was the underlying reason for his problem. His correspondence shows the record of shattered possibilities, and of how in his meetings with the rich the result always appeared to be more histories instead of more money. I find him writing, for example, to a coffee company executive who had made contacts for him on a trip to Havana, where he had spent four days with several of the recommended people, any one of whom could have easily endowed the Institute. Kinsey wrote to the executive that he found the trip "highly profitable" but, as it turned out, not in a fund-raising sense. Some guests in the homes of his hosts had volunteered to give him their histories, and Kinsey went on happily to ask the executive if he could help to arrange for the taking of these and other histories the next time Kinsey could get to Havana.

Again, in another letter, he has gone to Philadelphia, and through friends has met and had lunch with Mrs. Bevan A. Pennypacker, whose fortune and philanthropy were alike well known. In his letter thanking her, he talks briefly about the support he is getting, the prospects for the future, and asserts that he will follow up some of the leads she has given him. But then he returns to his true interest and concludes by saying that on his next trip he hopes "it will be possible in the course of that trip to get your own history and the histories of some of the other friends in the groups to whom you may be willing to introduce us."

The worst of his experiences in fund raising, and it was truly shattering, was a visit to Huntington Hartford, the A & P heir, in New York. The meeting had been arranged by Tripp, who knew Hartford well. Tripp understood how great was the Institute's need for money —it was more than a year after the Foundation ceased its grants— but he also knew that Hartford's taste in philanthropy was not directed toward such deadly serious scientific enterprises as Kinsey's. Nevertheless, he concluded that bringing the men together would be worthwhile.

Kinsey made the trip to New York in May 1956. He was already ill and, as it proved, had only three months to live, but he was willing to go through a kind of performance he hated for the sake of the Institute. Tripp decided (mistakenly, he believes now) that it would be better for the two to meet without him. He did not know that Hartford, who appeared to be impressed with Kinsey's international reputation, had done the one thing most calculated to unnerve Kinsey. He had arranged a formal dinner party at home, with his wife.

During the dinner, ill at ease with an elegance so far outside his world, Kinsey found himself unable even to bring up the subject of support for the Institute. As for Hartford, he was equally uneasy because he recognized the worth of Kinsey's project but at the same time he was worried about the implications of giving money to it. To the public it would seem that he was "backing sex," and wouldn't people think that this was an indirect commentary on his own sex life?

The dinner, consequently, was a disaster. Marjorie, Hartford's wife at that time, sensed the difficulty and she did her best to act as an intermediary between the two men, who were failing to communicate with each other. "But, honey, what he means is . . ." she kept saying to her husband, trying to argue Kinsey's case. He would explain carefully, in detail, some aspect of what he was doing or wanted to do, for which he would need further funds, but this scientific talk was well beyond Hartford's range of interests, and his attention span became shorter as the evening went on. His growing impatience was obvious. In the end, he declared himself convinced that if the public knew about Kinsey's problem it would be sympathetic and would help, and since it was well known that Kinsey was a "superb publicist . . ."

In brief, the public would help, but not Hartford, and the superb publicist, who was anything but that, knew he had failed again. In the circumstances, it was a particularly crushing defeat. Not only had he failed to get any money, but he had got from Hartford the kind of unsympathetic, uncomprehending reaction that he never experienced in the course of his own work, and it was a shock to him. Kinsey was very tired, and as the evening drew to its dismal close its cost to him was apparent in his drawn face.

This was the last blow in a series of misfortunes that had followed him. Mrs. Kinsey said later that she thought he never recovered from his New York experiences that May. He came home sick and exhausted, and the end was not far off.

We were acutely conscious by this time that he might go at any moment. He had fallen while he was working in his garden, and although he suffered only a slight bruise, it was enough to trigger the embolism which led to his death. As I said early in the book, Prok literally and knowingly worked himself to death. In June, after several small heart attacks, an examination showed that his heart was about 50 percent enlarged. His doctor told him he could still work from two to four hours a day, and if he did he might last another four years. Kinsey disdained that idea. He agreed to reduce his working day to eight hours but no more, regardless of the consequences. That was the way he wanted it. Once his doctor came up to the Institute to plead with him personally to cut down. Kinsey rewarded him by taking him on a two-hour tour of the Institute.

To understand what a concession Prok was making in promising to reduce his workday to eight hours, one has only to remember that for years that day had begun in the early morning, at seven or eight o'clock. Having begun, he pushed on straight through, eating lunch at his desk usually, and pausing just long enough to have dinner, and then going on again until midnight or later.

Albert Ellis tells of visiting the Institute in August 1951 with another psychologist, Ruth Doorbar, at Kinsey's invitation, with an appointment scheduled at 8:30 A.M. Arriving promptly, they found Kinsey already working. He gave them a complete tour of the Institute, explained the record keeping, showed off the treasures of the library and archives, introduced them to staff members, took them to lunch, renewed the tour after lunch, and later took them home to dinner. Ellis recalls that he did not stop for a moment, constantly talking and explaining things, listening intently to whatever his guests had to say and obviously enjoying the whole thing, although he had gone over the same territory many times before.

About 9:30 that night, after giving his guests a recorded concert, Kinsey kissed his wife good-bye, told her not to wait up for him and took his guests back to the office for more conversation. Finally, at 11:30, he made polite motions indicating that he had other work to do, and promised his visitors he would see them again briefly in the morning before they departed. They left him then, while he went back to the work they had presumably interrupted at 8:30 that morning.

It was this kind of pushing, year after year, that ultimately taxed his heart beyond recall, but I must say that for a surprising number of years he seemed to thrive on it. For a long time he tried to avoid doctors, even refusing to have his blood pressure taken.

There was, of course, a compulsiveness about his working. It stemmed from the Judaeo-Christian work ethic which had been a basic part of his early conditioning. His family were religious people and hard-working. They could not imagine any other way of living, and while Kinsey grew away from the strict religious training of his youth, he could never cast off the primary thing they had taught him —that it was immoral not to work. One of his major personal problems, from a psychological point of view, was how to relate to idlers. Men who lived off other men in a homosexual situation, or men who lived off women, were alike anathema to him, yet he realized that such people were part of the population and needed to be understood.

He never took a vacation in his life; even his trips out of the country, to Cuba, Peru, Mexico and Europe, were primarily working expeditions. Reluctantly he permitted his staff the usual two weeks, but it was not easy to resist his influence even in this, and I found myself falling into the same vacationless pattern. The minor recreations he permitted himself, such as going to a Broadway show, found him "working" nonetheless while he sat in the darkened theater— thinking about the sexual implications in the lines, or the sexual lives of the actors.

The obsession with his work, I think, helped him to resist giving in to the minor ills that send most people to bed. Once in New York, when he was scheduled to give a lecture the next day, he woke up in the night with a devastating toothache. I went out, found an all-night drugstore and brought back something to relieve the pain. Next day, although he was still suffering, he gave the lecture as scheduled; to have canceled might have meant losing some histories.

Often he woke up at night with cramps in the calves of his legs, and if I was traveling with him I would massage them in an attempt to relieve the severe pain, which he bore stoically. He refused to see a doctor about this condition, so we never knew what caused it. It was characteristic of him that he would not be babied; he was too busy to go to doctors. Fortunately he liked exercise, especially working in his garden, and I believe this prolonged his life, because he made no other effort to take care of himself.

Gardening and walking, however, were purposeful exercise, as far as he was concerned. He regarded games as a waste of time, whether indoors or out, and hated them all. The only game he ever made an attempt to learn was chess, which we used to play occasionally in the first two or three years we spent together, sitting down over the board at the end of the infrequent days which ended early enough. Sadly, these encounters were a failure. I am an extremely competitive games player, and while Kinsey did not really care one way or the other, nevertheless he did not enjoy losing every time.

Toward the end, probably as the result of so many thousands of hours sitting in a chair interviewing, Kinsey had begun to get a little paunchy. He dieted unobtrusively, never making a point of it, but his stocky body continued to show the extra pounds. There had been other signs that his physical machine was deteriorating. Reluctantly he had to start wearing glasses again. Then we began to notice that this rugged man, whose energy had once been our admiration and despair, was truly slowing down. He was conscious of it, too, and tried to conceal it from us in a variety of artful ways. I remember walking up a hill with him in San Francisco, once an easy exercise for him, and realizing that I had forged ahead, leaving him panting a little behind.

An ordinary man might have said, "Wait a minute, Pomeroy, until I catch up. You're going too fast." Not Prok. Instead he called out, "Just a minute, Pomeroy, I want to look at this marvelous window display," and with his easy facility for speaking, he lectured for a few minutes about whatever was in the window until he caught his breath again.

To Kinsey his body was the enemy, preventing him from doing everything he wanted to do, and toward the end, when he had finally come under a doctor's care, he personalized the stubborn organ that was "setting back the research countless thousands of hours," as he might have told it. He often began statements, "My heart won't let me do this. . . ."

Old friends and colleagues tried to persuade him to slow down, but he would have none of it. Professor Theodore W. Torrey, chairman of the Zoology Department, recalls a conversation with Kinsey only two weeks before he died. He was briefly out of the hospital again and vainly trying to work at the Institute as long as he could every day. "I urged him," Torrey writes, "to think of his responsibility to himself, his family, and to his colleagues and to enter into rest and relaxation for whatever period was required to restore his health. As he walked toward my office door he turned and said, 'I'll think about it, but if I can't work, I'd rather die.' "

It was the last time Torrey saw him.

As early as May of that year he had been in trouble, but it was not until June that he was finally taken to the hospital with the first of the attacks. Near the end of the month he wrote to Harriet Pilpel:

I have been more or less continuously in bed, in the hospital and at home, for the last three weeks. It is this heart again, and it impresses me with the importance of getting our business done systematically, while I can still keep at it. I am in wonderful calm condition today and consequently begin to hope that we have brought that organ down to regularity again.

These three weeks have convinced me that if I undertake to do very much of the fund-raising myself, it will be practically the end of research output for me. On the other hand, I cannot see anything like $20,000–

$30,000 per year for a fund raiser. . . . It is a sink or swim proposition which I should hesitate to undertake at this point.

Meanwhile, the staff has been most excellent in carrying on without me here, and we are very much encouraged in the progress made in preparation of the material for the next book or two.

He wrote this kind of optimistic note to all those who anxiously inquired, almost up to the day he died. He knew he was very ill; the doctors had made that much clear. But somehow he could not conceive that it would all end this way, before the research could be completed. There was so much to do. "In spite of a pessimistic doctor," he wrote to a friend in Tulsa in July, "I shall prove to them as I have in the past thirty years, that you can do more with a physical handicap than they sometimes think."

In a similar vein, at the same time, he was writing to Gernsback:

Apparently too many hours of work and not enough sleep per day, combined with some of the tensions that developed in connection with the problems on my last trip to New York, and subsequently to Detroit and Chicago, stirred up the latent heart difficulties which I have had ever since early childhood. You will admit I have done pretty well in spite of them through the years, and I intend to do better than the doctors think in the next ten years. This time it took four or five weeks to start any definite mend, but the last week has been one of steady improvement. By working part days and making sure to get sufficient sleep, I think I can turn out work again.

Two weeks later he wrote a last letter to his old friend Frances Shields:

I went to the hospital with my heart misbehaving on June 1, and should have gone sometime before that. There is an enlargement of the heart, constant fibrillation, an apical beat of about 140 at the time I went to the hospital and a pulse of anywhere between 40 and 80, and other such foolishment. Failure to compensate induced the problem of water retention. My Indianapolis man was very pessimistic but the young local man who is following me now that I am home is gradually learning to make allowances for individual variation, and learning that I cannot so easily be put down. They have taken sixteen pounds off of me in the last few weeks, which meant undesirable water retention.

I tell you this much detail simply to let you know why I have not written and to explain why at this point there can be no plans for any next trip to the Pacific Coast. During the past four or five days I have been better than I have at any time during the last three months, and I think things may be settling down to a permanent improvement. I get back to the laboratory for part of the day and I am quite hopeful.

We on the staff knew that Kinsey was very ill, but we absorbed some of his optimism and somehow could not believe he was at the point of death. Occasionally we discussed what would happen if he died but we came to no conclusions, nor could we, since Kinsey himself refused to face this eventuality. Certainly there was no diminution of his lively interest in anything that had to do with his research. Shortly before he had to go to the hospital, he was still carrying on a fairly heavy correspondence in the old manner.

I find him writing to R.J., for instance, in one of his favorite roles, theater critic:

I am interested in your reaction to *Tea and Sympathy*. It still gets mixed reactions in this country but it is notable because it is the only play dealing with this subject that has been able to stay on the stage for any length of time. A great many people think it is some extenuation of the boy who is charged with homosexual activity, when in actuality the play is not intended to imply that the boy actually had any such activity and it is primarily a condemnation of the individuals who criticize the homosexual without realizing their own basic capacities in that direction.

The letters became shorter and shorter and stopped altogether in mid-August. The inevitable result of all those years of driving labor, of short nights and long days, of dedication to the point of exhaustion, could no longer be avoided. Martin wrote in his diary on August 25: "Prok died at 8 A.M. He had been in the Bloomington Hospital since the preceding Wednesday or Thursday. I, and family, were traveling, saw no papers, arrived the evening before at a late hour, learning of his illness and death the next morning." Eleanor Roehr, Kinsey's secretary, gave Martin the news, as she did to most of the other staff members.

The funeral was a memorial service. Torrey spoke the eulogy and it was, in general, a melancholy day for everyone. I thought it particularly touching that Kinsey's old friend Bob Laidlaw had come all the way from New York to attend, in spite of the fact that his physical disabilities had put him on crutches and traveling was difficult for him. He was an extremely busy man, in the bargain, yet he took the time and made an unusual effort to come. Since it was late August and many University people were still away on their summer vacations, there were not as many friends present as might have been ordinarily.

Of the thousands of tributes that poured in, I think paradoxically Kinsey might have been pleased most with the one paid him editorially by *The New York Times*, which he had never believed was his friend. He would have quarreled with a part of it, I am sure, but it was an apt summary:

The untimely death of Dr. Alfred C. Kinsey takes from the American scene an important and valuable, as well as controversial, figure. Whatever may have been the reaction to his findings—and to the unscrupulous use of some of them—the fact remains that he was first, last and always a scientist.

In the long run it is probable that the value of his contribution to contemporary thought will lie much less in what he found out than in the method he used and his way of applying it. Any sort of scientific approach to the problems of sex is difficult because the field is so deeply overlaid with such things as moral precept, taboo, individual and group training and long established behavior patterns. Some of these may be good in themselves, but they are no help to the scientific and empirical method of getting at the truth.

Dr. Kinsey cut through this overlay with detachment and precision. His work was conscientious and comprehensive. Naturally it will receive a serious setback with his death. Let us earnestly hope that the scientific spirit that inspired it will not be similarly impaired.

Prok would surely not have agreed with the *Times'* estimate of his contribution to contemporary thought. His survivors at the Institute were especially concerned with the implications of the last paragraph. The powerful figure who had dominated our lives was gone. What next?

PART FIVE

AFTER KINSEY

CHAPTER

XXVII

SURVIVAL AND RENAISSANCE

W E LOOKED at each other and said, in effect, "What do we do now?" There was no doubt about what *Kinsey* wanted to do, what he would have done had he lived. By utilizing data already accumulated and adding still more case histories, he had hoped to produce nearly a dozen books dealing with a wide diversity of topics. In 1950 he had plotted out the whole program carefully in a lengthy summary of what had been accomplished to date and the program he envisioned for the future. It was intended for the Rockefeller Foundation, as a presentation in the appeal for funds, and we all signed it.

Nine books were proposed in the program, as follows:

1. The two books we had already done, which for purposes of the program he was outlining Kinsey lumped together as one. What was needed further, he noted, were more histories from lower social levels, rural groups, devoutly religious people, Negroes and other racial groups. When this additional material was recorded, he meant to revise the *Male* and *Female* volumes. As he pointed out, they did not represent more than 10 percent of the data available. The other 90 percent were to be raw material for further studies.

2. A book on sex laws and sex offenders, to be based on the histories of about 2,000 persons convicted of sex offenses, gathered from inmates of penal institutions in a dozen states from New York

to California, and from the communities in which the inmates lived after they were released. Kinsey saw the value of this as a basis of comparison with people who had never been involved with the law. It was to be a unique study, including the personal histories of various kinds of law enforcement officers who had to do with sex offenders; a comparative study of the sex laws of the states; a comparative study of the sex laws of European countries; and an examination of the historical origins of American sex law and its antecedents in English common law, ecclesiastical law and in Jewish, Hittite, Roman and other codes. There was also a detailed analysis of the legal processes involved in handling sex offenders, and an evaluation of the legal significances of court decisions on sex cases.

3. A study of the development of sexual attitudes and overt behavior in children. This was to be a survey of the attitudes determining the overt sexual behavior of adults as it is developed in the early years of childhood. Here Kinsey meant to use the interviews he had gathered from between 75 and 100 children under seven years of age, most of them between two and four, as well as the reports of parents and other observers of overt sexual activities among children, and the memories of older persons who had recorded the sources of their sex education, their early activity and their early sexual attitudes.

4. Institutional sexual adjustments. In this book Kinsey meant to publish his conclusions about what sexual adjustments were made by men and women in prisons, mental institutions, extended-stay hospitals, boarding schools, the Armed Forces and similar institutions. He had found this problem of much concern to administrators wherever he went, and he believed strongly that it would not be solved until the facts were known and the general public understood what was involved. For this study he would begin with the histories he had obtained from several thousand people who had been inmates or members of the institution he had in mind, but he was aware that thousands of additional cases would be needed for any final estimate.

5. A study of the heterosexual-homosexual balance. In this pioneering work Kinsey intended to explore the factors which contribute to the development of either heterosexual or homosexual patterns of behavior, or patterns which combine both types of activity. It would attempt to distinguish inherent, biological responses from those representing learned behavior. We had already discovered

that learning is much involved in both homosexual and heterosexual patterns. For this work all the histories we had taken would be available, including the more than 4,000 with records of homosexual experience. We had made an intensive examination of several hundred of the latter cases.

6. Sexual factors in marital adjustment. This study would be designed to discover the relative significances of sexual and other factors in marital adjustment, which Kinsey thought would be especially valuable to marriage counselors, psychologists, psychiatrists, social workers, clergymen and other personal advisers. We had, in 1950, more than 9,000 histories of marriages in our files, and we added to them subsequently. In them we had made a particular attempt to get information on the nature of marital adjustments.

7. Physiological studies of sexual arousal and sexual orgasm. Anticipating Masters and Johnson, Kinsey meant to provide in this volume an understanding of the anatomy, especially the neuroanatomy and physiology basic to sexual response, and so provide a sounder basis for the study of the psychological factors affecting sexual behavior. Such analysis, he thought, would also provide basic data for the clinical handling of sex problems, and could affect our understanding of variation in sexual behavior and the nature of female orgasm, with its considerable significance in marital adjustment. This was exactly what Masters and Johnson did so superbly in their first volume. Kinsey intended to use our observed data, about which I have written, as well as several thousands of the histories carrying this specific information. Recognizing the need for more help in the study, Kinsey proposed to add a physiologist, a neurologist and a specialist in sexual behavior among lower mammals to the staff.

8. Prostitution. Here Kinsey intended a study of male and female prostitutes considered as *persons,* in contrast to previous works which had been wholly concerned with the moral and social significance of prostitution. In 1950 we had histories of about 600 female and 600 male prostitutes in our files. We had, besides, a considerable acquaintance with the physical setup and management of organized prostitution and the lives of individual prostitutes.

9. A study of the erotic element in art. As I have made evident at various points, this was a project close to Kinsey's heart. He believed that a study of the extent to which an artist's production

depended on his erotic background would provide some measure of the significance of the erotic element in our total culture. The sex histories of several hundred artists would provide the starting point for this study. Each of these artists had gone to particular lengths to explain the motivations of his own artistic output, and had helped bring together reproductions of his work. Each, too, had served as a juror on a panel judging the erotic content of the work of other living artists and those of past generations. Kinsey meant to include in this book a comparative study of European and Oriental art, providing the opportunity to compare the effects of totally different cultural attitudes on sex.

This was the legacy Kinsey had left us. It was a magnificent conception, a plan that would have taken two decades to carry out. Obviously his hopes exceeded reasonable expectation, since each volume would have required several years of preparation if all were to meet Prok's standards of comprehensiveness and scholarship.

For the moment, however, we could give no thought to Kinsey's plan. The immediate problem was how to reorganize the Institute and obtain financial support. It was clear that the answer lay mostly between Gebhard and me. Martin was not in a position to assume an administrative role, nor did he have any ambition to do so. In any case, his lack of an advanced degree would have precluded his taking on any position of control in the academic structure of the University.

Paul and I discussed the situation and decided that we should run the Institute together as codirectors, taking advantage of our different abilities and talents. We had already set about reorganizing on these lines when the University intervened with a plan of its own. It had decided to make Gebhard executive director, and designated me as director of field research. In addition, we added Professor Torrey to the board of trustees to maintain the tie with the Department of Zoology, and Mrs. Cornelia Christenson, who had been with us several years, was also made a trustee. A counterpart of Kinsey's salary was to be placed in the Zoology Department budget for us, with Torrey's approval, to bring in outside research consultants. The net effect, obviously, was to make Paul the successor to Kinsey as director.

At the time I supposed, although I never knew for certain, that this decision was made because Gebhard was more of a scholar than I, and because he was still teaching in the University, while I was not. In any case, there was no struggle for power between Paul and me for control of the Institute, although there were those who thought so. Gebhard, in fact, was as unhappy about the University's decision as I was. For myself, I was not angry but quite naturally hurt at what appeared to be a rejection. The new arrangement did not affect our relationship; we remained close friends (as we are today) and consulted each other frequently. No unilateral decisions were made.

As the new arrangement developed, Martin was increasingly unhappy with his role in the Institute. He felt, with some reason, that he was simply not consulted during the weeks and months after Kinsey's death. All the discussions were between Paul and me. It was not a deliberate slight on our part, but occurred simply because we had been sharing the major part of the work with Kinsey. Martin was conscious that he had no graduate degree, and was convinced that this was why he could not play a major role in the reorganization. He felt himself bypassed, and naturally resented it. Moreover, he was extremely interested in earning a higher degree, and although we encouraged him toward this goal, we felt that the bulk of his time should be devoted to Institute matters. Martin rightly calculated that on a one-course-per-semester schedule he would receive his doctorate in his dotage. The desire to obtain an advanced degree speedily, plus his mounting dissatisfaction, led him to resign in 1960 and enroll as a graduate student in Johns Hopkins. This proved a wise move. Ultimately he earned his Ph.D. and has continued a research career.

In this transitional period, morale was low for a time and there was a general feeling of disorganization. Still, important events were taking place. The lengthy negotiations with the United States Customs over the confiscation of erotica addressed to us finally came before the Federal District Court, a litigation in which we were joined by Indiana University, as a friend of the court. The ruling was in our favor and empowered us to import for research purposes any erotic materials. This ruling was, and still is, considered most important in the history of the relationship between science and the law.

On the heels of this ruling came the financial rescue which not only ensured our survival, but made continued research possible. In spite of the political hazards involved, the National Institute for Mental Health gave us the first of what eventually proved to be a series of grants. We were in business again, and one of the first evidences of it was the publication of our third book, *Pregnancy, Birth and Abortion*, produced in 1958 by our new publishers, Harper-Hoeber. This volume was prepared and written with extraordinary attention paid to sampling, methodology and data interpretation, so as to demonstrate our scientific competence despite the loss of Kinsey, and to quell the criticism that the Institute was interested only in popular, moneymaking books—although there was nothing "popular," in the conventional sense of the word, about the first two volumes. The third book did not begin to achieve the public acceptance of the earlier works, but it was very well received in scientific circles. In the bargain, it proved to us that we could survive as a productive research organization.

As work continued, there were inevitable changes in viewpoint and policy. These were speeded and fomented, in part, by the addition to the staff of John Gagnon, a sociologist, in 1959. One change was the temporary abandonment of new interviewing and an emphasis on analyzing and publishing the data already accumulated in such large quantity. High priority was given to data retrieval, meaning the transferring of the 18,000 histories to punchcards and/or computer tapes; while still preserving anonymity, this would make the data available to outside scholars and more widely available to Institute members. Another Institute project was to determine which subjects had died since they were interviewed, and whether there was a relationship between sexual patterns and the cause of death.

Meanwhile, I was marking time at the Institute. The only diversions were episodes in the field, which recalled the adventurous early days of my years with the Institute. Two of them I remember particularly, and I think of them now with regret that Prok could not have been with me. He would have enjoyed these excursions.

About 1958 I met a man who, with his wife, owned a resort in the Catskills, a big old-fashioned farmhouse which was run exclusively for transvestites, who came there on weekends. Once a year there was a special convention or celebration, to which transvestites from all over the country were invited—from Canada to California, Maine to Virginia. Another professional sex researcher and I were invited to come as observers, and we spent from Friday to Sunday at the resort.

Seventy-three people had gathered for the event, including nine wives and six or seven transsexuals. Their ages ranged from twenty to seventy, their social level from those with an eighth-grade education to people with advanced degrees. There were those who dressed in women's clothes only on rare occasions, and others who did it all the time. As in nudist camps, where all the conversation is about nudism, the transvestites talked only of dressing and how they looked. There was no radio or television, no newspapers, and although there was a great deal going on in the world at the moment, no one was interested. On Saturday night there was a floor show, with entertainment by the guests—some talented, others the rankest of amateurs.

The transvestites presented striking contrasts. I remember one man, a rich contractor, a big chap about six feet four and weighing 275 pounds, who looked grotesque. But to him the opportunity to dress was so important that he did not care what others might think. On the other hand, there were some who looked like beautiful girls. I filmed the whole affair for the archives of the Institute.

One morning my fellow researcher and I had a group session with the wives. One of them had not known what the affair was to be; she didn't know her husband was a transvestite until she arrived at the hotel. Horrified by the discovery, she started to hitchhike home, but was persuaded to come back. Others, however, not only knew about their husbands, but loved the arrangement. In their daily lives these women would talk about clothes with their husbands and even shop with them when they were dressed. But even these women objected if their husbands dressed in feminine nightclothes or played their role in bed. They wanted a man in bed, and liked the dressing only when it was done for the street.

In taking down these histories, we began to see a pattern emerging. When a man first disclosed to his wife that he was a transvestite —"coming out of the closet," as the phrase goes in those circles—he was likely to be compulsive about behavior, rushing home from work and wanting to dress all the time. If there were children, it was often difficult to get them out of the way. But if the wives could survive this behavior for anywhere from six months to two years, the men would gradually be content with dressing no more than once or twice a week.

Taking histories of transvestites was not always easy for us as interviewers. We would find opposite us a male dressed as a female, and in order to establish rapport, we would identify him in our minds as a female, addressing him as we would a woman. Looking at "her," then, we would have to ask, "How large is your penis in erection?" Or we would be talking to a large powerful woman in man's clothing and ask "him," "How often do you menstruate?"

The second episode I recall from the post-Kinsey days involved a conference of the National Council of Churches, held at Green Lake, Wisconsin, on the grounds of the American Baptist Assembly, an enormous estate once the home of Victor Lawson, founder of the Chicago *Daily News*. It was a place capable of entertaining 2,000 visitors at a time.

The object of the conference was to reassess the position of the Protestant church in America toward sex. A total of 520 ministers representing twenty-six denominations were in attendance, along with a dozen consultants, including eminent psychiatrists, doctors, marriage counselors and psychologists specializing in sex research.

There were plenary sessions every morning, at which one of the consultants gave a paper. In the afternoon the delegates split up into thirty or so different groups to discuss the morning's paper, with a consultant on hand to guide them. The discussion was centered on past, present and future practices in churches concerning the subject at hand.

In my group the atmosphere was extremely tense at the first meeting. The ministers quoted a good deal from the Gospel; the consultants, including myself, were not finding it easy to communicate with them. The delegates were not all clergymen, in fact. One, a doctor from Nebraska, could not even look at me directly when he talked in the group, and during a coffee break, when the conversation was about oral-genital contact, he turned abruptly and walked away.

That incident occurred on a Wednesday. By the end of the week, he began to be far more relaxed and objective, as the others were, and on Friday he came out flatly for having the churches recognize oral-genital contact as a permissible form of human sexual behavior.

It was typical of the experience all the groups were having—tension at first, then a gradual relaxation into a free and enthusiastic exchange. Near the end, one minister remarked, "You know, we keep talking about 'them,' but how about 'us'? I will admit that I've had homosexual experiences in my lifetime, and I'll bet a lot of you have. Raise your hands if you have." Five out of the twenty delegates in the group raised their hands.

Returning to Bloomington from Green Lake, I could only think how much Kinsey would have enjoyed the conference, and back at work in the Institute I was confronted once more with my growing unhappiness there. For one thing, there was no hope of advancement. More important to me, I began developing a small private practice during the evening, and it convinced me that I would have a much more rewarding future as a consulting psychotherapist and marriage counselor. The question was where to begin.

I considered San Francisco briefly, but friends gave me discouraging reports about the difficulties of starting a practice there. When Bob Laidlaw heard what I contemplated, he urged me strongly to come to New York, assuring me I would have no difficulty whatever in starting. He was right. I left the Institute in November 1963, and in less than eight months I had a full practice.

In every way it was the best move I could have made. The years with Kinsey had been the greatest experience of my life and our work together had been of inestimable value to me. But after his death terminated our close relationship of thirteen years, it seemed that some of my devotion to the project had gone with him. I had been inspired and driven by him, carried along by his tremendous enthusiasm and dedication, but in the aftermath of his death I felt that a major phase of my life had come to an end. My last two years at the Institute had been largely unproductive, and I knew it was time to go. Still, the decision to make such a radical change of occupation at the age of fifty was not an easy one. Once made, however, I could see that it was right.

Before leaving I was able to help produce the fourth Institute volume, *Sex Offenders: An Analysis of Types*, which appeared in 1965, a year after my departure. This enormous and definitive volume was published by Harper & Row. It met with good reviews and subsequently became more readily available in a paperback edition.

The Institute has continued to grow and, like other growing things, to change in orientation and in staff. Rather than employing the former monolithic approach of having the entire staff devote itself to one project at a time, the Institute now serves as a coordinating umbrella organization containing a number of researchers pursuing sex research studies alone or in conjunction with other staff members. Due to this diversification, the original interview schedule of questions that Kinsey designed has been abandoned and a new set devised especially for each new project. In addition to interviewing, some mail-out and hand-out questionnaires have been employed in certain studies. Another innovation is the occasional use of professional interviewers from polling and survey organizations, hired temporarily by the Institute and given some additional training. Such "contracting out" of interviewing was inaugurated by Gagnon and by Dr. William Simon, who joined the staff in 1965, in two studies of which they were project directors. While the quality of the interviewing is below that of the Institute staff, it is nonetheless adequate and does serve to free the senior staff for planning, analysis and writing.

There has been a shift away from the almost purely descriptive approach employed in the Institute's earlier work. Now there is increasing concern with the social and psychological elements associated with sexuality and with the context which gives the meaning to sexual behavior. For example, the Institute is no longer particularly interested in how a person masturbates nor in the frequency with which he does so, but rather in what that masturbation signifies. Is it an act of loneliness and frustration? Does it represent a retreat from sexual relationships with others? Is it accompanied by a sense of failure and guilt? Or is it a happy sensual appreciation of one's body and an affirmation of life and sexuality? These are questions which, in our more advanced state of scientific knowledge, the Institute believes merit priority.

The changes have brought with them an increase in productivity. From 1967 to 1971, Institute members published no less than six books and approximately fifty journal articles and book chapters. This is substantially more than had been published in the preceding twenty-eight years. The range of the books has been wide: Gagnon and Simon's book on *Sexual Deviance*; Gebhard's book, in collaboration with J. Raboch and H. Giese, *Die Sexualitat der Frau*, also available in English; *The Personality of a Child Molester: An Analysis of Dreams*, edited by Alan Bell and C. Hall; *Deviance: The Interactionist Perspective*, edited by Martin Weinberg and E. Rubington; and most recently, *Homosexuality: An Annotated Bibliography*, edited by Weinberg and Bell; Cornelia Christenson's *Kinsey, A Biography*; and *Homosexuals and the Military*, by Weinberg and Colin J. Williams.

The staff today is larger than it was in the Kinsey era, when it totaled nearly twenty at its maximum. Now it fluctuates between thirty and forty, and during periods when graduate students are trained and employed as recruiters or interviewers, the total number of Institute personnel approaches sixty. This growth has had some unfortunate results. For one thing, there can no longer be the close communication and camaraderie possible in smaller groups. Then, too, increasing space needs have caused the Institute to expand into separate buildings. At present the main offices, library and archives are in one building, most of the research offices are in another, two rooms are utilized in a third structure, and storage facilities are in a fourth. This is a far cry from the old days in Biology Hall, when any staff member could have communicated with any other by stepping across the corridor.

Typical of contemporary life, there has also been a considerable turnover in staff. The days of permanent commitment to a university or research organization appear to be gone. Nevertheless, the Institute has continued to attract able researchers. In 1966 Dr. Alan Bell, a former Episcopalian priest, with a Ph.D. in counseling psychology, joined the staff, becoming a senior psychologist at the Institute the following year. He is also an associate professor in the Department of Counseling and Guidance at Indiana University. Bell served as field director of the Institute's study of a homosexual community in Chicago, and is currently directing a large study of homosexuality in the San Francisco area, besides acting as vice-president of the Sex Information and Education Council of the United States.

Albert Klassen joined the Institute in 1967 and is currently directing a survey of the nation's attitudes toward various types of sexual behavior. James Elias was an Institute member from 1967 to 1970, and during that time undertook a study of high school students and the effects of sex education. In 1968, Gagnon and Simon resigned. Gagnon went to the State University of New York at Stony Brook, where he joined the faculty and completed his Ph.D. Simon went to the Institute for Juvenile Research in Chicago.

More recent staff members are Martin Weinberg, senior sociologist, and associate professor of sociology in the University; and Dr. Colin Williams, research sociologist and assistant professor of sociology. Weinberg, whose principal interest is the sociology of deviance, together with Williams is concluding several studies on homosexuality.

Meanwhile, the continuing grants from the National Institute of Mental Health, supplemented by increased support from the University, have made all this growth possible. The annual budget, which stood at about $80,000 in the fifties, when Kinsey was dependent on the Rockefeller Foundation, has climbed recently until it now varies between one-quarter and one-third of a million dollars.

While Kinsey's publishing program has been abandoned, in large part, and the 18,000 case histories he compiled are still far from being fully analyzed, the Institute does not lack for projects. These are among the recent ones:

A study of college students, using a national random sample of nearly 1,200 males and females, who were interviewed as to their sexual behavior and attitudes.

A comparative study in which the adult alumni of a private secondary school with a rather good sex education program were compared as to their sexual and marital lives with similar individuals whose education did not include a sex education course.

A study of 485 predominantly homosexual white males, concerning their social and psychological adjustment.

A study of 405 male and female high school students, comparing the knowledge, attitudes and experience of those with and those without formal sex education in the school.

A study of about a thousand males and females who were wholly or chiefly homosexual. Aspects of adjustment, attitudes and behavior were covered, and a comparison made with a control group of about 600 individuals. This study was made in the San Francisco area.

A national survey of public attitudes toward varying forms of sexual behavior. This survey will be based on a random sample of 3,000 adult males and females.

A cross-cultural study, involving about 1,500 questionnaire returns, comparing the adjustment of homosexual males in the United States with those in Amsterdam and Copenhagen.

Besides these projects, and several smaller ones, the Institute carries on other activities. One is teaching. After the marriage course that Kinsey began came to an end in 1940, there were no more formal courses dealing with sexuality given by Institute members until the 1960s. Then a seminar for psychiatric residents at the medical school was begun. Subsequently the Institute developed an annual seminar for graduate students and an intensive ten-day to two-week summer program designed for physicians, psychiatrists, educators, social workers and other professionals concerned with sexual matters.

Another function of the Institute today comes under the head of "services." In addition to being called upon to lecture or participate in panels, staff members are frequently asked to serve as consultants and resource persons. A large and growing amount of requests for data and information floods in from individuals and organizations. Trying to cope with this demand drained too much time from research until funds were obtained to establish and staff an information service.

Still another service function is making the Institute's magnificent library, archives and other resources, except those of a confidential nature, available to qualified people. This concept of the Institute as a repository which scholars, scientists and clinicians might use did not materialize until the 1960s. There were the inevitable problems of excluding unqualified people, and those motivated only by commercial considerations, not to mention the discouraging of aimless browsing, but these problems were brought under control and the Institute has been invaluable to a large number of visitors, some of whom come from foreign countries expressly to work there for varying periods of time.

Opening the library and archives to nonstaff people had an additional worthwhile, though unanticipated, result. When individuals based most of their books or articles on Institute resources, they always stated this in an acknowledgment or a foreword. But since these prefatory pages are seldom read, the Institute was not getting the recognition due it as being important, if not essential, to the publications of many scholars. To remedy this situation, an Institute Monograph Series was established, titled "Studies in Sex and Society," with Basic Books as the publisher. Anyone depending heavily on Institute resources for his publication was asked to publish in this series, providing his work met with Institute approval. It was decided later that if a particularly worthwhile book was associated with the Institute in any fashion, even though most of the work had been done independently, it could also be a part of the Monograph Series. Thus far, four books have been published in the series: Steven Marcus' *The Other Victorians; Art and Pornography,* by Morse Peckham; *Studies in Erotic Art,* edited by Theodore Bowie and Cornelia Christenson; and *Human Sexual Behavior: Variations in the Ethnographic Spectrum,* edited by Donald Marshall and Robert Suggs.

The library and archives stand as an enduring monument to Kinsey's lifetime of devotion to his work. Since this collection is so extraordinary, and so little known to everyone but a relatively few scholars, I think it is worth describing. If it had no other distinction —and it has many—it would be outstanding as the largest collection of erotica in the world, larger than the British Museum's and presumed to be more extensive than the legendary Vatican collection. State and grant money have not been used to build up either the library or the archives. Instead the Institute has spent its own funds, saved from book royalties and fees, and it also depends heavily on donors, as it did when Kinsey was alive. Fortunately, donations of money or materials to the Institute are tax deductible. The donors include individuals, organizations and state and municipal institutions. Prison wardens, for example, send erotic drawings and writings taken from the inmates, and police departments donate confiscated materials.

Under its head librarian, Rebecca Dixon, the library now contains roughly 25,000 volumes, plus uncounted reprints and brochures. Anything that is relevant to human sexuality in any way merits consideration for possible inclusion. In addition to virtually all scientific works on human sex research, numerous specialized fields are strongly represented, including physiology, abortion, sex law, prostitution, psychology, marriage counseling and many other related topics. Nonscientific published materials, such as popular books and articles, are included. The Institute has a large collection of fiction, poetry, art books, girlie magazines, nudist magazines and the publications of various sexual (and antisexual) organizations. Included is the largest collection of erotic literature assembled in any one place. A considerable number of Institute books are the only copies extant, as far as anyone knows. One reason is that sexual literature is particularly subject to destruction, either intentionally or through wear, and it is seldom protected in a library.

Among the portions of the library that make it unique is its collection of material on sadomasochism, both literature and history—everything from pulp magazines to classic books. Another subcollection of exceptional interest is a gathering of erotic fiction since 1900, including galley proofs of *From Here to Eternity*, in a first version which the publishers would not print until the author, James Jones, made some deletions. There is also an edition of *Ulysses* illustrated by Matisse; a first edition of *Lady Chatterley*, with erotic watercolor illustrations in the corners; and an eleven-volume edition of the erotic classic *My Secret Life*.

A clippings file in the library contains articles from the popular press and newspapers on sex, and a bound collection of clipped material on the *Male* and *Female* books. There are various editions of these books in other languages. Locked-case books contain explicit erotica, besides imported pictures and texts.

The library has a card catalog system referring to books and reprints by author, title and subject. Needless to say, the subject classification requires a great deal of time and labor, and the subject cards are not complete. A formidable job for the staff is the cataloging of all the articles in professional journals. Even with the help of three assistants and some clerical help, the librarian can scarcely keep abreast of the flood. At least she is spared one traditional chore. The library does not loan books—a harsh but wise policy.

The archives, staffed by a head archivist and an assistant, comprise a remarkable diversity of materials. There are roughly 50,000 still photographs, ranging from old-fashioned "cheesecake" to explicit pornography, from 1855 to the present. There are 1,500 films,

7,000 slides, 26,000 prints of erotic art and 1,100 erotic objects. The archives also hold material on humor in erotic art, and folk art.

In the art section of the archives there are drawings, paintings and etchings, some originals by noted artists, others reproductions or photocopies. Besides the work of talented professionals, the collection includes amateur efforts, and one unique section is devoted solely to art produced in prison. The geographical and chronological distribution of the art collection is spotty; some cultures, as Japan's, are strongly represented, while there are no examples at all for other cultures. In part this simply reflects the fact that certain peoples at certain times produced much erotica, while others produced little or none. Another reason, however, is that the Institute has never had, until recently, enough staff to investigate the field of erotic art with any thoroughness. It still lacks an adequate acquisition budget. Like the library, the archives rely heavily on donations. Nevertheless, some of the erotic art objects in the collection, especially the pre-Columbian, are of museum caliber.

Another valuable collection is the film archive, which contains scientific or documentary films of animal and human sexual behavior, a small sample of avant-garde films with sexual content and more than a thousand pornographic "stag" films, some of which date back half a century.

Among the items which make the library unique is the small collection of audio material—105 recordings, including folk songs, interviews and seventy-four tapes. There are also such exotic items as sadomasochistic sounds, sounds of lovemaking, and more ordinary items such as a sex education film, 102 doctoral dissertations on microfilm, and twenty-one vertical file drawers full of ephemera—catalogs of sex materials, advertisements for them and ads for motion pictures.

One section of the archives consists of biographical materials, letters, diaries, memoirs, records of sexual activity and similar personal items. These are kept under maximum security, and identifiable items are available only to the senior staff.

The size and scope of the library and archives is a tribute to Kinsey's vision and was in large part made possible by his policy of putting all book royalties, lecture fees and other income into the

Institute fund. It was this money which built the core of all the collections.

One could say that the library is a monument to the past in more than one way. It represents empirical research, the kind of inquiry on which Kinsey based his work. Staff members today are involved in their own research studies, instead of being part of a "family," as we were in Kinsey's time. They are exploring behavior in depth rather than making the kind of gross study we were engaged in. They are describing rather than surveying.

In the old days, no one could have come to work for Kinsey without giving his history first. It was a condition of employment, which a few employees in the lower echelons resented. Today's staff would resent and resist on principle any such thing. They would provide information about their sex lives if it was part of the job, but would not give a history as a condition of employment. The change is apparent, too, in the students the staff members teach. More and more, these graduate students wonder why anyone even raises questions about sexual behavior. It seems old-fashioned to them, although it would not be difficult to demonstrate that it does concern most of the population.

The members don't talk about their own sex lives freely, as was the case in Kinsey's day, when members spoke openly about their own sexuality to other members of the senior staff. Another major difference is that staff members do not often travel together, as we did constantly, producing a kind of cohesion that does not exist now.

Perhaps the greatest difference, however, is that the nature of the research itself has changed. The approach is sociological, and a whole new generation of researchers has been trained in a different way. Mass surveys are no longer considered worthwhile; the accepted form is hypothesis testing. No one thinks of going into a piece of research in the spirit Kinsey did, saying, "Let's find out what's happening." Now the researcher begins with a hypothesis, a framework, a model, and then he tests it. Thus Kinsey's grand design is gone. Even if there were any inclination to carry it out, it would not be possible in the framework of hypothesis testing—and contemporary research lives on such grants.

Speaking only for myself, I believe that, in a field such as sex research, one cannot question in the prevailing mode until more is known about the subject through the kind of research Kinsey did. In brief, it is my opinion that methodology is running ahead of science.

Looking back on the history of the Institute with an objectivity that only distance can provide, it is clear that Kinsey built well. As a student of change in sexual behavior and attitude, he might not be surprised at the changes in research goals and methods, but whether he would approve is another matter. As just one example, I feel certain he would be appalled, to use one of his favorite words, at the manner in which the questionnaire, which he abhorred, has so far replaced the face-to-face interview. Nor would he countenance the abandonment of scientific empirical research, in which he devoutly believed, for modern sociological methodology. On the other hand, I am sure he could find only pleasure in the continued growth and productivity of the organization he founded, and to which he quite literally gave his life.

CHAPTER

XXVIII

WHAT IT ALL MEANT

THERE HAS BEEN nothing quite like Kinsey's books since he published them. Everyone who does any extended writing on the subject is compelled to quote from them, and it is now apparent to virtually everyone, as Kinsey well understood, that sex behavior does lend itself to research. He believed in more careful thinking, and in specific objectives. These two things, he was convinced, were the necessities for further research.

It could be argued that if he had lived he might not have been able to continue in the old way for an unlimited time. He was having differences with the staff before he died, on matters of priorities and definitions. Kinsey clung dogmatically to the thesis that the instrument he was using—the interview in the framework he had constructed—was the chosen instrument and he had no intention of abandoning it, or even modifying it significantly. The staff believed there were dead ends that could be cut off. Martin quietly carried out some projects of his own without staff permission or approval. They gave him great satisfaction, and in the end he turned out to be correct in what he had planned. By and large, however, there were no major conflicts, and none leading to anxiety or bitterness. Kinsey was so strong that the rest of us had no choice but to respect his wishes.

It was difficult for him to acknowledge it, but he did make mistakes, in which we all shared. One was to break the age groups in the wrong places. According to United States Census practice these divisions occur as follows: 14 and under, 15 to 19, 20 to 24, 25 to 29, and so on. At the Institute we divided the groups into 15 or under, 16 to 20, 21 to 25, 26 to 30, and so on. Thus our five-year age breakdowns could not compare directly with the United States Census age divisions. Further, in recording sexual behavior by age groups, we used an individual's sexual history even if it did not extend through an entire five-year period. For example, if a 25-year-old man who was married at 24 was having marital intercourse at the rate of five times a week, we would include him in married males in the 21-to-25 bracket.

The truth was that Kinsey simply did not have all the mathematical advice he required at the beginning, and as the research went on the resulting defects were built in and could not be changed. But Kinsey insisted that his methodological errors were actually minute, and if corrected would not have changed his final results by more than a fraction. As subsequent testings proved, he was right.

Two important errors remained, nonetheless. One was the fortuitous gathering of homosexual histories so that the sample was not representative of the whole spectrum of homosexuality. The other was the overweighting of prison samples.

Tripp believes that one of Kinsey's major contributions to sex research was that a significant part of the legal profession took his work seriously. A good many judges read his books, which influenced their handling of cases involving sex. On the other hand, as I have documented, he antagonized some of the psychoanalysts and psychologists. They felt threatened by what he had done and tried to dispose of him by questioning the statistics on which the research was based. Yet by now most of them are compelled to admit that Kinsey's work is the standard in the field.

The research also had another far-reaching effect in getting through to laymen and challenging the conventional morality. Many of them got over their initial shock, and in this sense Kinsey's work paved the way for the present sexual evolution, often mistakenly called a revolution. His two volumes on behavior were, as I have noted, rewritten by many people for the popular press, including books, magazines and newspapers. Few other books in America have ever had their ideas so widely disseminated. Thus the results of his work were known all over the world.

Kinsey's concept of total outlet has been criticized by some people, who say it is not possible to take orgasms from masturbation and add them to orgasms from intercourse. I believe that in some places and in some instances it *is* possible, and that the concept of total outlet is a valid measure. True, it does have its drawbacks, but it is of some importance. The development of differences between social levels, particularly in the *Male* volume, have been used constantly, and also have validity, as have the religious differences we found, and particularly the emphasis on the degree of religious devotion rather than the denomination.

Of less significance is the effect of age at adolescence or age at puberty on subsequent sexual behavior. More important are the effects of aging, and the different aging patterns in males and females, which I feel have value in clinical areas.

We felt that the last five chapters in the *Female* volume—dealing with anatomy, physiology, neuroanatomy, psychology and endocrinology—were lost in that book. There was simply too much material, and those five chapters could have been made into a book by themselves; they might better have been published that way. As it was, we hoped the information would gradually come to light as people got to know the material better.

The comparison of males and females in the *Female* book constitutes still another of Kinsey's contributions. We even made some small additions to Freudian psychoanalysis, in the few places where we were able to supply data which would help in looking at some of its various phases, such as the developmental periods of masturbatory, homosexual and heterosexual activity. Here, as in other places, we sometimes had no data, and there were areas where none could be gathered.

All these are general observations, however. If someone were to ask me to assess Kinsey's lifework, I think I could narrow it down to eight major contributions.

1. *The fact of the research itself.* Like Everest, it was there and we conquered it. For the first time, a large body of sex information was gathered, so monumental and so comprehensive that it has not

even been approached. Working on such a tremendous scale, talking to 18,000 people about their sex lives, getting it all down on paper and analyzing it—that was a major accomplishment. No research in human behavior on so broad a scale had previously been attempted. Along with this, one has to consider the peculiarly American trait of counting noses. If this project had been undertaken in Europe or Asia it might never have attracted any attention or even succeeded, but in America we like to count things. As a result, the research was done and it accomplished the primary objective of making such investigation acceptable.

2. *The establishment of base lines.* As a consequence of this broad assault on what people do sexually, we established certain base lines. They were not always exactly what we said they were, as I have noted. The magic 37 percent of males who had one or more homosexual experiences was, no doubt, overestimated. Probably 33 percent would have been closer to the mark. But whether it was 33 or 37 is not important. The important thing is that few people would have believed, before our Report, that a third of American males had had at least one homosexual experience.

The same thing could be said for the figures on premarital intercourse, with the added importance these statistics gave to educational levels. They showed that 98 percent of males who had not gone beyond the eighth grade had had premarital intercourse; the figure for those who had not gone beyond high school was 85 percent, while about two-thirds of those who had gone to college had such activity. Among females, the distinctions were not as sharp, but the general trend prevailed—that those with less formal education had more premarital intercourse than those with more.

As for male extramarital intercourse, we recorded more than 50 percent, but I am sure we got a good deal of cover-up with this figure which there was no possible way to check. This applies also to the female figures in this category, where the count was 25 percent. In the male figures the error may have been as much as 8 percent. Even though these estimates were not absolutely accurate, however, they were not that far off. In opinion sampling, generally, there is a permissible, or expected, error ranging from 2 to 4 percent. People often compared our sampling unfavorably with opinion polling in elections, but they were not the same. In the famous Dewey-Truman miscalculation, the pollsters were wrong by only 2 percent. Kinsey was well aware of the fallacy of making such comparisons, and he railed against those who made them, but there was nothing any of us could do about it but writhe and damn the critics.

When I was teaching a class in abnormal psychology at Indiana, I looked in the index of the textbook and found that the largest number of references to an individual were to Freud. The next largest number were to Kinsey. This seems to me further proof that we produced a highly significant quantity of base line data, which even some of our severest critics used.

3. *Individual variations.* When we talk about variation among individuals, we mean something like the difference between 1 to 4, or 6 to 20. The smallest person in our society, for example, might be twenty-five inches high, and the tallest eight feet, or a variation of 1 to 10. Again, penis size may vary from the smallest, one inch, to the longest, ten inches. This is the normal kind of range. But in sex behavior, because there are so many variables involved, the range can be from 1 to 10,000. People have difficulty understanding this fact. For example, roughly 10 percent of women never have orgasm, but it is possible for a woman to have 50 to 75 orgasms in twenty minutes. The range is tremendous.

When those of us doing the research became accustomed to the idea of this range, we were exceedingly frustrated as we realized how few people could accept it. One of Kinsey's important contributions was to awaken people to this fact, which was something quite outside their lives. Until then they had been aware only of the range as it existed in their own lives and those of people they might know.

4. *The 0–6 scale.* This scale for measuring homosexual behavior was of prime value in breaking away from the confines of classifying homosexual and heterosexual behavior as two separate, compartmentalized types. The scale could tell the whole sexual story of an individual by applying the appropriate number. Although the scale has not caught on to the degree we thought it would, I think it will become more and more important with time. That was Kinsey's belief, too.

One obstacle to more widespread acceptance of it has been the false notion that it applies only to overt behavior. In reality it is based on such behavior *plus* psychological response, and the number on the scale represents a compromise between them. Suppose a man is married, having intercourse with his wife three or four times a week, and having infrequent homosexual intercourse as well—possibly once a month. Using only this data we would classify him as a 2. But if we added the number of times he masturbated to the accompaniment of male fantasies, and his other inclinations toward men which were not overt, he might be psychologically a 4. It would, in fact, be quite possible to have no overt homosexual behavior and still be a psychological 4. But taking into account both overt and nonovert behavior, he comes out a 3. It might be objected that this is like adding apples and oranges, but we found that usually the overt patterns and the psychological patterns were just about the same. The answer is either to compromise and say 3, or else use two scales. I believe this has been a false criticism, and that eventually the scale will be an important, better form of communication in discussing human sexual behavior.

5. *The concept of total outlet.* If one takes into consideration only one particular outlet, say, marital intercourse, and tries to deduce from that the extent and nature of an individual's sexual interest or drive, one might miss a very vital element and produce a false picture. Many people do exactly that, however, because we are so addicted to the notion of intercourse as the sole measurement. Let us take, for example, a man in his forties who has intercourse about twice a week with his wife. That would be an average picture of sexuality for a man his age. But upon further examination, one finds that he masturbates several times a week, has wet dreams and does some extramarital petting to orgasm, so that in sum he may have as many as ten outlets a week. Another man may have none of these, and his marital outlets may be his only ones. Thus it is necessary to get all the data before one can arrive at a satisfactory estimate of a man's sex life.

This can also be extended to homosexual behavior. A 6 homosexual, for example, may masturbate ten times a week, but have homosexual relations only three times, with perhaps other outlets such as wet dreams.

Another aspect is the percentage of total outlet, which can be derived only if one knows what the total outlet is. For instance, a man having marital intercourse once a week as his total outlet is quite different from another having it once a week whose single act of intercourse represents only 10 percent of his total outlet.

6. *The difference in sexual behavior at different social levels.* The single simplest way we found to measure the difference in social levels was by completed education. I cannot prove it, but I believe that if one took the sex history of a sixteen-year-old boy, it would be possible to tell whether he was going to go on to college, other things being equal. Let us say he had had intercourse with anywhere from three to ten girls, never took off his clothes when he had intercourse, was interested more in the act itself than in establishing any genuine relationship with the girl, did not approve of mouth-genital contact, showed an already waning masturbatory activity and had infrequent wet dreams which were never much a part of his sex life. This boy, it could be predicted, would not be going to college, because his sexual pattern stamps him as lower level, and few boys in that category go on.

Take another boy. He masturbates actively, but he has little or no intercourse, does a good deal of petting, perhaps has a little mouth-genital contact, likes to take off his clothes when he does have sex and probably sleeps in the nude, reacts strongly to all kinds of erotic stimuli and is more or less sexually hopped up a good part of the time. This boy will probably go on to college. He is exhibiting an upper-level pattern of behavior.

There are exceptions, naturally. An interesting one is the college student who has been able to go on because of the GI Bill of Rights, or some other kind of tuition help. To go to college he has had to change his pattern, and when he is there he often sticks out like the proverbial sore thumb. We saw this happen time and time again.

It would be feasible to carry out a study based on this thesis, using the statistics we gathered, but unfortunately it has never been done.

I believe the establishing of social-level behavior was one of the major contributions Kinsey made. The concept has been somewhat altered more recently by the higher percentage of people going to college, and by some acceptance of masturbation seeping down to the lower level and more acceptance of intercourse on the upper level. I might add, too, that we did not get nearly as clear a picture of these differences in females as we did in males, not only because females do not communicate as much about their sex lives, but also because males, being more dominant, have more effect on female behavior than the reverse.

Kinsey and those of us on the staff became convinced that these social-level differences were pervasive and of very long standing, going back to colonial times in this country and to a time several centuries ago in Europe. For example, Aretino, a defrocked priest who lived in the sixteenth century, tells a story about a mother who was teaching her sixteen-year-old daughter how to be a whore. In explaining the ways of the world to her, and describing what people of different kinds want sexually, she outlined exactly the same differences in behavior that we recorded. Recent studies in Finland, Sweden, Germany and Denmark have confirmed these differences.

7. *The effects of aging, as far as sex is concerned.* We noted that in the male there is an early upsurge of sexual activity, but that it begins to decline from the teens onward. While this may seem obvious, it was known only superficially when our research began. In studying the female histories, we were surprised to find that the curve was different, reaching a peak in the twenties, then going on a plateau and beginning to taper off only in the mid-fifties, considerably after and not related to menopause. In both sexes, the duration of the response was astonishing. Sexual activity was recorded up to age eighty and above, a finding amply confirmed by several subsequent studies, particularly those of Masters and Johnson.

8. *The Institute for Sex Research itself.* Perhaps, in the end, it will be a contribution larger than anything Kinsey published. It is the only institute of its kind in the world, and as I have indicated, its resources make it a repository without equal anywhere. More and more people are learning of this tremendous treasure of books, pictures, films, diaries, calendars, magazines, ephemera of every description, and superb art objects.

These, I think, were Kinsey's major contributions, and they would be enough to ensure him a reasonable expectation of immortality as a scientist.

Still others might be added. Nowlis, for example, believes that Kinsey demonstrated that old concepts such as nymphomania had to be viewed in a new and different light, and that the idea of interviewing in difficult areas was a contribution in itself. Kinsey's success, he thinks, showed the possibilities of communicating with people about whatever proved to be necessary to help them, without adopting a diagnostic approach.

Still another contribution Kinsey made, in Nowlis' opinion, was to break through the hypocrisy about sex in the public image. "Kinsey," he says, "pulled up the shade and revealed what was there."

Morris Ernst, looking back on his work as Kinsey's lawyer and as one who wrote a good deal about the research and its effect, believes Kinsey made a large contribution in the field of censorship and obscenity by providing a different, and documented, point of view about social behavior.

Beyond all this there is something else, which I believe was best expressed by a fellow scientist, J. B. S. Haldane, in the *Hindu Weekly Review* shortly after Kinsey's death.

Very many people have blamed him for publishing facts which are shameful, facts which should perhaps be investigated by criminologists and medical men, but which if they are divulged to the public will only lead to the popularization of immoral practices. I understand that some Indian writers have been particularly severe in their condemnations, both of Kinsey himself, and of the American people of whom he has studied large samples.

I do not take this view myself. Perhaps an analogy may help. A number of ancient Hindu temples and a few modern ones are decorated with sculptures showing human beings, some engaged in acts which are normally done in private and others in acts which are considered by many to be immoral even in private. Science is one way of looking at the world, religion is another. Both contemplate the whole world. The men who ordered these sculptures to be made, and those who made them, believed, I think, that they were glorifying a god by portraying the richness and variety of the world. They may not have approved morally of what they portrayed any more than they approved morally of Ravana. But Ravana is part of the glory of God. Without him there could have been no Ramayana. The aim of religions is ultimately to lead men beyond desires for any finite things; but religious art, and the sacred books of religions which forbid religious art, are nevertheless concerned with finite things.

The scientific attitude is not very different. We scientists believe that it is our duty to describe the world as it is. Some of us think that God made it; others do not; but this makes little difference to our description. We also try to find what is behind appearances. Our religious acquaintances say that we have not looked very far. We can reply that our accounts are more consistent than theirs. We certainly cannot neglect sexual behavior either in our account of the world or our explanation of it.

Perhaps Kinsey's most striking result was his complete confirmation of those who believed in the extreme diversity of human beings. He studied a number of healthy and fertile marriages between people of the same age, and found enormous variation in the frequency of sexual activity. It was as if some people ate thirty times as much or slept thirty times as long as others.

In the past, some people have blamed those whose sexual activity exceeded their own. Others have stated that moderation in this respect was harmful. Both were clearly wrong.

Prok could not have put it better, or perhaps as well, himself. But I remember him not only for his formidable contributions, in which I played a part, and the lasting significance of his work, for which I think all of us who labored with him can be justly proud. It is clear by this time, I am sure, that my memories coalesce into admiration for the man himself. He had his faults, as everyone does, and I have not spared him in these pages. But the prickly nature of his dogmatic and aggressive nature is far overshadowed by the warmth and glow of his personality, as it is with so many authentic geniuses, of which he was surely one. His very faults made it possible for him to get his grand design in motion and sustain it through the long struggle I have recounted.

This essentially simple Midwestern professor, living in a highly restricted academic society at the beginning, in time became the international celebrity who could talk to anyone in the world about sexual behavior, from the lowliest prisoner to the great men and women of the world. He remained, thank God, incurably naïve. To see him bringing in a tray of sweet liqueurs before dinner was a wry and happy reminder that Alfred Charles Kinsey, the genius, the world figure, was a simple and unsophisticated man, in the true sense of that word. His curiosity about the world and his endless desire to learn more about it could well serve as an example to those of us who, in this age of anxiety and despair, imagine there is nothing more to learn, or to dream.

INDEX